COLLECTED WORKS OF
CHARLES BAUDOUIN

Volume 2

STUDIES IN PSYCHOANALYSIS

STUDIES IN PSYCHOANALYSIS

An account of twenty-seven concrete cases preceded by a theoretical exposition

CHARLES BAUDOUIN

Translated from the French by
EDEN AND CEDAR PAUL

Routledge
Taylor & Francis Group
LONDON AND NEW YORK

First published in 1922

This edition first published in 2015
by Routledge
27 Church Road, Hove BN3 2FA

and by Routledge
711 Third Avenue, New York, NY 10017

Routledge is an imprint of the Taylor & Francis Group, an informa business

British Library Cataloguing in Publication Data
A catalogue record for this book is available from the British Library

ISBN: 978-1-138-82541-3 (Set)
eISBN: 978-1-315-73901-4 (Set)
ISBN: 978-1-138-82641-0 (Volume 2)
eISBN: 978-1-315-73906-9 (Volume 2)

Publisher's Note
The publisher has gone to great lengths to ensure the quality of this reprint but points out that some imperfections in the original copies may be apparent.

Disclaimer
The publisher has made every effort to trace copyright holders and would welcome correspondence from those they have been unable to trace.

STUDIES IN PSYCHOANALYSIS

AN ACCOUNT OF TWENTY-SEVEN CONCRETE CASES PRECEDED BY A THEORETICAL EXPOSITION. COMPRISING LECTURES DELIVERED IN GENEVA AT THE JEAN JACQUES ROUSSEAU INSTITUTE AND AT THE FACULTY OF LETTERS IN THE UNIVERSITY

BY

CHARLES BAUDOUIN

Author of *Suggestion and Autosuggestion, etc., etc.*

TRANSLATED FROM THE FRENCH BY

EDEN AND CEDAR PAUL

LONDON: GEORGE ALLEN & UNWIN LTD.

RUSKIN HOUSE, 40 MUSEUM STREET, W.C. 1

First published in 1922

Printed in Great Britain by
UNWIN BROTHERS, LIMITED, THE GRESHAM PRESS, LONDON AND WOKING

TO

PIERRE BOVET & EDOUARD CLAPARÈDE

OF GENEVA UNIVERSITY

AS A TOKEN OF ADMIRATION, FRIENDSHIP,

AND GRATITUDE

To explore the unconscious, to dig into the subsoil of the mind by specially designed methods, such will be the main task of psychology during the twentieth century. I am confident that this will lead to great discoveries, no less important, perhaps, than those made during the nineteenth century in the realms of physical science and natural history.—HENRI BERGSON, 1901.

By stressing the dynamic aspect of subconscious phenomena, psychoanalysis becomes a vivifying ferment for psychology. Experimental psychology, while devoting itself to elucidating the machinery of mental processes, has almost entirely forgotten the study of the causes that set this machinery in motion. Psychoanalysis aims at discovering and describing these hidden springs. The work of Sigmund Freud, through the novelty of the ideas it suggests, and through its fertilising influence, has become one of the most important events in the whole history of the science of the mind.—EDOUARD CLAPARÈDE, 1920.

TRANSLATORS' PREFACE

PSYCHOANALYSIS is tersely defined by Edward Jones as " the study of unconscious mentation " (*Papers on Psychoanalysis*, p. 2). Crichton Miller writes (*The New Psychology and the Teacher*, p. 135) : " The aim of psychoanalysis . . . is to reveal to the individual, from his own experience, the unconscious motive that is at work in producing his neuroses." Charles Baudouin, we think, would accept both the definition and the statement of aim ; but he would certainly stress the view that psychoanalysis has to deal with the normal more than with the pathological, that it is to be looked upon as a method of re-education rather than as a curative method. He takes, of course, the same view of autosuggestion. His desire is to coordinate the essentials of intuitionism (the Bergsonian doctrine considered apart from all metaphysics), the teachings of the New Nancy School, and the theories of psychoanalysis, as contributions to educational science, psychology, and philosophy. The present volume, therefore, consists of studies in psychoanalysis from this outlook, though incidentally we find in it valuable therapeutic applications of the study of subconscious mentation.

We begin this preface by defining psychoanalysis, because it is a term which has hardly found its way into the most modern dictionaries, and because it is one used by many persons who have no more than the vaguest idea of its meaning. Before going on to a brief account of the analytic method, we wish to say a few words concerning the unconscious—or, as Baudouin prefers to call it, the subconscious. Even to-day there are many facile critics ready to say that you cannot study unconscious mentation because you cannot study a contradiction in terms or a non-existent entity. Nevertheless the subconscious is just as " real " as any other intangible entity we have to postulate for the intelligible presentation of experience. Bertrand Russell shows in *The Analysis of Mind* that the concept "consciousness" is itself less simple and obvious than most people are apt to imagine. Certainly to those who read Baudouin's book with an open mind it will soon become apparent that the inferential datum, subconscious, is no less real than the immediate datum, consciousness. Let us put the matter in the more concrete phrases of "behaviourist" psychology. A great deal of human behaviour remains incomprehensible so long as we try to explain it as the outcome of the consciousness of which the doer is aware. Yet it becomes perfectly comprehensible when we realise that it is the outcome of something closely akin to consciousness, but of which the doer is unaware. This something-akin-to-consciousness-of-which-the-doer-is-unaware - and - which - determines - behaviour, determines also thoughts and feelings, including the thoughts and feelings both of health and of disease. For short, we call it the subconscious or the unconscious.

Whilst the individual unconscious is anathema to many, the "collective unconscious" of the school. of Jung is itself anathema to analysts of the school of Freud, who regard the later developments of Jung's teaching as the aberrations of a mystic. Even Baudouin, who uses the term, is careful in most instances to enclose it in inverted commas. Objectors have unquestionable warrant for maintaining that there is no such thing as a collective unconscious, any more than strictly speaking there is a "collective consciousness," or any more than there can be a "mass of suffering." We are individuals, and each one of us thinks and suffers alone. But we are likewise gregarious beings, and this fact may plausibly be considered to endow the "collective unconscious" with a conceptual reality, though at a more abstract remove than the individual unconscious. Thus, just as the term "collective consciousness" is used, with no mystical significance whatever, to denote a consciousness which is supposed to be practically identical in a very large number of minds, so the term "collective unconscious" is applied to unconscious mentation of the same character. But the idea of the "collective unconscious" does not play any considerable part in Baudouin's studies. He is mainly concerned with the investigation of the individual unconscious. Two-thirds of his book consist of an account of twenty-seven concrete cases examined by the analytic method.

Baudouin's procedure for the study of subconscious mentation does not differ from that of the Freudian school of psychoanalysts. But he leaves his readers to infer the details. Moreover, in this country at any rate, such hazy ideas still prevail as to the nature of the analytic method that a brief exposition of its details seems appropriate.

With Baudouin, as with Freud, the interpretation of dreams provides the most important clue to the working of the unconscious. Of great importance, too, is the analysis and interpretation of day-dreams (cf. Varendonck, *The Psychology of Day-Dreams*). In Baudouin's terminology, the common element in dreams and day-dreams is to be found in the " outcropping of the subconscious " (see *Suggestion and Autosuggestion*, Part II, Chapters Two and Three). Reminiscences, especially reminiscences of childhood, have also to be dealt with; these reminiscences often seem trivial, but the significant point is apt to be this—that among the myriads of trivial experiences, certain trivialities are remembered. Of great, perhaps of equal significance, is the " remembrance " of pseudo-reminiscences, the existence of " memories " which seem real to the subject's consciousness until their veridical reality is dispelled by the work of psychoanalysis.

Dreams, of course, are to a great extent symbolic, and in this connection Freud remarks (*Introductory Lectures on Psychoanalysis*, p. 157) that it is a pernicious error to " think that the translating of the symbols is the ideal method of interpretation and that you would like to discard that of free association." The analysis has to be pursued by asking the subject for associations to the main items in the dream, the day-dream, or the reminiscence (see Glossary, association, etc.). Every dream, perhaps every day-dream and every reminiscence, has, or may have, a latent content as well as a manifest content. The latent content is what the analyst has to discover if he is to " interpret " the dream, and thus to make the subject aware of the trends of his own unconscious. To quote Freud once more (op. cit., p. 143): " You will make use of the two complementary methods: you will call up the dreamer's associations till you have penetrated from the substitute to the thought proper for which it stands ; and you will supply the meaning of the symbols from your own knowledge."

One point of the utmost importance in the technique is the condition of the subject when the analyst is demanding associations. Freud writes (op. cit., p. 88) : "When I ask a man to say what comes to his mind about any given element in a dream, I require him to give himself up to the process of free association which follows when he keeps in mind the original idea. This necessitates a peculiar attitude of the attention, something quite different from reflection, indeed, precluding it." The reader should note that this is only another way of describing what Baudouin terms "contention," i.e., "the psychological equivalent of attention, minus effort." It is also akin to "spontaneous attention" (interest) as contrasted with "reflective attention." But, *qua* contention, it is, according to Baudouin, preeminently the state of mind requisite for the "outcropping of the subconscious" (see Glossary).

When Freud says that the analyst will supply the meaning of dream symbols from his own knowledge, he is far from implying that the interpretation of the symbols is an arbitrary affair. Just as in the use of the microscope the power to interpret the visual images is attained only by long experience, and by collating the microscopist's personal experience with that of others, so here. Consider, moreover, the use of language. In this matter we are all familiar with the symbolism that is obvious and deliberate, the symbolism known as metaphor. But every student of linguistic science knows further that language is full of hidden symbolisms, is packed with symbols whose significance has been forgotten. There is no hard and fast line between such symbolism and the symbolism of dreams, the symbolism whose meaning is veiled from consciousness until revealed by psychoanalysis. Now one of the most notable of Baudouin's contributions to analytical science, and a matter upon which he differs from the Freudian school, is his careful study of condensation (see Glossary) in its bearing upon representation by symbols. The Freudians regard symbolisation (in dreams) as the means whereby the workings of the unconscious are veiled from the conscious mind. But Baudouin writes (p. 27): "Condensation . . . is the first stage in the creation of the symbol. I look upon symbolisation as a general law of the imagination, and not as being necessarily the outcome of the masking of forbidden representations."

The teaching epitomised in the foregoing quotation serves, like much that Baudouin writes, to bridge the gulf between the Freudian enthusiasts and those who dissent from Freudian theories and interpretations. Mary Arnold-Forster, in *Studies in Dreams*, writes (p. 112): "My experience convinces me that it is not true to state that all dreams are symbolic, any more than we can accept as of universal truth the Freudian theory that they are all symbols of repressed desire." Nevertheless, it is doubtful if there are any dreams free from condensation, as Baudouin defines it. Passing to the second criticism, we think Baudouin would agree that not all dreams are "Freudian dreams." Probably everyone has such dreams *inter alia*. But it is the "Freudian dreams" that serve as grist for the psychoanalytic mill—and psychoanalysts are no more free than lesser mortals from the tendency to count the hits and ignore the misses. Hence their belief that *all* dreams are "Freudian dreams." Baudouin, however, nowhere commits himself to such an assertion. We believe he would accept the main conclusions of Mary Arnold-Forster, whose fascinating volume should be read by all interested in dream life and in the possibilities of regulating dreams by autosuggestion. Her theories and methods square with Baudouin's own teaching anent the control of the subconscious.

This brief account of the psychoanalytic method has not been given to enable amateurs to begin the practice of psychoanalysis upon their friends and relations, nor even to enable them to undertake the first steps in the exceedingly difficult art of autopsychoanalysis. It has been given to make it easy for the beginner to read Baudouin's book, because he will have grasped certain essentials of technique at the very outset. Though it was not primarily written for the beginner, we regard *Studies in Psychoanalysis* as perhaps the best work for the beginner hitherto published. We consider it better for this purpose than Freud's *Introductory Lectures on Psychoanalysis*, which has recently been made available in English. The study of Freud should come after that of Baudouin, not before. Having read these two volumes, the reader may usefully turn to Jung's *Collected Papers on Analytical Psychology*, and to his *Psychology of the Unconscious*, as authoritative expositions of the teachings of the Zurich School. His mind thus enlarged, the student will return with delight to the clarity of what is destined to become known as the Geneva School, and will read the *Studies* again and again. For, heartily as we may share Freud's "dislike for simplification at the expense of truth" (op. cit., p. 238), there is much justice in Baudouin's complaint (infra, p. 22) that: "The realm of the 'unconscious' is necessarily obscure; but the psychoanalysts would seem at times to have taken a positive delight in peopling it with shadows."

To the graduate in analytical literature we would not impertinently offer any hints as to how to read this book. But to novices in the field, and in especial to those who open the *Studies in Psychoanalysis* solely because they have known and valued the author's *Suggestion and Autosuggestion*, we venture to say: Do not, at a first reading, trouble much about the Theoretical Part. This is written mainly for experts, is of import to them, and will interest them greatly even when they differ from the author. But, if you are a beginner, when you have finished the General Survey, go straight to the Case Histories. Read them in the light of what has been said above about method and with the aid of the Glossary. Thereby you will be able to enjoy a course of Psychoanalysis without Tears, and will then find yourself in a position to master the Theoretical Part with the smallest modicum of difficulty. Such, it will be noted, has been the author's own path of approach. He has worked by the inductive method. In the Case Records he is feeling his way and gaining his experience from day to day. The Theoretical Part represents his conclusions at the date of writing.

The beginner will enjoy, and even the expert who is not a hard-shelled adherent of one of the rival schools will value, the concreteness of treatment, and the gradual initiation into psychoanalytical ideas by the inductive method. The practice of many psychoanalyst writers has rather been to attempt a bludgeoning of the acolyte. (We do not talk of their patients, but of the readers of their books !) They take cock-shies at us with the Oedipus complex, saying : " You wanted to kill your father in order to take his place with your mother —that's the kind of beast *you* are ! " They rub our noses in it ! But Charles Baudouin gently leads us on to discover our less amiable peculiarities for ourselves. He suggests, perhaps, but he does not insist. He attempts no more than to make us realise that "everything happens as if" so and so were the case. In fact Baudouin treats us as the gentle psychoanalyst treats patients, and not as the rough psychoanalyst treats readers. He thus avoids prematurely applying to certain fundamental complexes the somewhat brutal handling which has made many persons needlessly hostile to psychoanalysis.

We now come to the feature of Baudouin's book which will most effectively disturb the complexes of many psychoanalysts. We refer to what the author terms the " mixed method," the coupling of psychoanalysis with suggestion. " Psychoanalysis," writes Baudouin (p. 31), " is incompatible with certain forms of suggestion ; but it is perfectly compatible with others. I regard the intolerance which some analysts display towards suggestion as no less deplorable than the sceptical attitude of practitioners of suggestion towards analysis." It is in the latter respect that Baudouin takes a different road from Coué, to whom suggestion unaided seems an all-sufficient therapeutic method. The deliberately conjoined use of suggestion and psychoanalysis is Baudouin's contribution as a pioneer in the field of therapy. But an attentive reader of the *Studies* will soon realise that the author's dominant interest in psychoanalysis lies in the application of the method to the realm of art. This will be the topic of Baudouin's forthcoming volume *Psychoanalysis and Æsthetics*. The hostility of certain analysts towards suggestion leads sometimes to a " censorship " of the very word. A noted German psychoanalyst, whose " orthodoxy " no one would dispute, congratulates himself on the disappearance of morbid troubles when, in addition to analytical treatment, a continuous process of " incitation " (Aneiferung) is employed by the physician. This pundit was reading a paper to a psychoanalytical circle, and he would not sully his hearers' ears with the obscene word "suggestion"! Freud himself is less fastidious. Baudouin quotes (infra, p. 111) a liberal utterance concerning suggestive therapeutics; and on p. 380 of the *Introductory Lectures* we read that in the later stages of the analysis the neurotic patient's internal conflict is "by means of the analyst's suggestions lifted to the surface, to the higher mental levels, and is there worked out as a normal mental conflict." Again, on p. 381, he speaks of "changes in the ego ensuing as a consequence of the analyst's suggestions." Nevertheless, from the seven pages which, in his *Introductory Lectures,* Freud devotes to the topic of suggestion, we can only gather that his natural devotion to psychoanalysis has led him to ignore the latest developments of suggestive therapy. He was certainly unaware, at the date of these lectures (delivered in 1915 and 1917), of the theory and practice of autosuggestion as expounded in *Suggestion and Autosuggestion,* or he would not lay the stress he does on "the problem of the nature and source of one's suggestive authority." The point cannot be argued here. The *Studies* will have to fight its own battle with the Freudians. Suffice it to quote Baudouin's pragmatic conclusion (p. 31): "The method to which experience has led me, the method whose results are recorded in this book, is founded upon *an unceasing collaboration between autosuggestion and psychoanalysis.* Many, I know, regard this as a heresy. Whether it be heretical or not, I am confident that immense advantage can be derived from such collaboration." Readers must not, however, expect to find in the present work more than passing references to autosuggestion. Upon that topic the author has delivered his message in the earlier volume. But the translators may venture to make a point which Baudouin has omitted to make for himself. Attentive students of Chapter Twelve, "The Search for a Guide," will come to realise that autosuggestion must owe a large part of its power and its extraordinary vogue to the fact that it enables those who practise it to find *within themselves* the guide of whom they are in search, and enables them in many instances to free themselves from fixations without recourse to the aid of the psychoanalyst.

Jung, says Crichton Miller (op. cit., p. 203), "wants to build for the future." Freud, impatient of large and vague generalisations, and sedulous to perfect and keep immaculate a rather narrow technique, speaks regretfully of the days when Jung "was a mere psychoanalyst and did not aspire to be a prophet." Baudouin, less ambitious than Jung, but more ambitious than Freud, strives to collate the new psychology with the old, but also reaches out towards the future. He writes (p. 28): "The intelligence ensures our adaptation to the real; the imagination ensures the adaptation of the real to ourselves." Neither task can be adequately achieved without perfecting our knowledge of the subconscious. In a somewhat different sense from that in which the phrase is used by Freud (op. cit., p. 163) most readers of the *Studies* will feel of psychoanalysis that "if you give it your little finger it will soon have your whole hand." Immense is the fascination of a research that is destined to produce as great a change in man's life as was caused by the discovery of articulate speech, a greater change than was caused by the invention of writing or printing. "The study of abnormal psychology—including its variant produced by artifice—has thrown more light on the workings of the normal mind than all the centuries of academic study of the latter." Thus writes Morton Prince in his foreword to Arnold-Forster's work on dreams. May we not hope that man, the tool-using animal, is on the eve of learning how to use the most stupendous of all tools—his own mind?

EDEN AND CEDAR PAUL.

LONDON, *July*, 1922.

TABLE OF CONTENTS

PAGE

TRANSLATORS' PREFACE 7

CHAPTER

I. GENERAL SURVEY 21

1. The two Categories of Psychoanalysis . . 21
2. Guiding Principles of the present Work . . 27

PART ONE: THEORETICAL EXPOSITION

II. SKETCH OF AN AFFECTIVE THEORY OF THE ASSOCIATION OF IDEAS 37

1. From Associationism to Psychoanalysis . . 37
2. The Laws of affective Association . . . 42
3. Dreaming and Action 56

III. DYNAMICS OF THE AFFECTIVE LIFE, AND THE EVOLUTION OF INSTINCTS 65

1. The Function of the Dream.—Dreaming and Play 65
2. The Idea of an Evolution of Instinct . . 75
3. The Genealogy of Tendencies 84

IV. MIXED METHOD: PSYCHOANALYSIS AND SUGGESTION . 101

1. Contrast 101
2. Conciliation 105

PART TWO: CASE HISTORIES

CHAPTER PAGE

V. CHILDREN 119

1. Linette: Dreams of forbidden Pleasures. Fixation upon the Mother 120
2. Mireille: Fixation upon the Mother. Refusal of the feminine Role 135
3. Robert: A Schoolboy's Feelings about School. Introversion (Analysis of a School Essay) 141
4. Jean: Protest against the Father (Analysis of a School Essay) 145

VI. THE CRISIS OF ADOLESCENCE 148

1. Raoul: Budding Virility. The feeling of Constraint 149
2. Kitty: A young Girl's Passion for a Woman 152
3. Gerard: Vacillating Sublimation. A State of Conflict 159

VII. ATTITUDE TOWARDS THE PARENTS 168

1. Miriam: A religious and social Calling inspired by the Cult of the Father. A State of Conflict 169
2. Marcel: Dread of the Father. Timidity and undue Scrupulosity 176
3. Otto: Repressed Virility. Awkwardness and Constraint. A philosophic Trend . . . 183

VIII. THE INSTINCT OF SELF-PRESERVATION AND THE INSTINCT FOR MOTHERHOOD 199

1. Autopsychoanalysis. Dreams during an Attack of pulmonary Tuberculosis 201
2. Yvonne: Fears concerning Childbirth . . . 209
3. Renée: Refusal of Femininity and of Motherhood 211
4. Martha: Longing for Motherhood. Menstrual Irregularity 216

CHAPTER PAGE

IX. TYPICAL NERVOUS DISORDERS 217

1. Alexander: Anxiety States 218
2. Roger: Psychasthenia. Impotence 234
3. Germaine: Spasm of the Eyelid. Fussy Activity 247

X. MENTAL DISORDERS 254

1. Bertha: Introversion. Delusions of Persecution. Neuralgia 255
2. Ruth: A fixed Idea. Impressions of Rape . 262
3. George: Mental Aberrations in an Epileptic 265

XI. SUBLIMATIONS 272

1. Alfred: Stammering. Maladaptation to social Life. A Taste for Music 273
2. Ida: Sexual Shock at Puberty. Maniacal Disturbances. Æsthetic Sublimation 276
3. Adam: Sublimation in Danger 279
4. Jeanne: Non-Acceptance of Marriage. Thwarted Maternal Instinct. Vacillating Sublimation . 282
5. Queenie: Fixation upon the Father. Æsthetic and religious Sublimation 294

XII. THE SEARCH FOR A GUIDE 301

1. Rynaldo: Change of Analyst. From Hostility to Sympathy 302
2. Stella: Sublimation of the Idea of the Guide 319

GLOSSARY 327
BIBLIOGRAPHY 335
INDEX 341

CHAPTER ONE

GENERAL SURVEY

1. The two Categories of Psychoanalysis

ALMOST the only book by means of which readers of the French tongue can gain a knowledge of the principles of psychoanalysis is Régis and Hesnard's faithful exposition of Freudian theory.[1] This work should be read by all students of psychoanalytical theory. In the present study, I write from an entirely different point of view. My primary aim has been to expound psychoanalysis as concretely as possible, by the record of a number of cases analysed by myself. As far as concerns the theory upon which the practice is based, this cannot be purely and simply Freudian, for I have also assimilated the ideas of other psychologists, such as Adler, Jung, and Flournoy; and, furthermore, my theoretical outlook has necessarily been modified by the data, however slender, of my own experience. Thus I make no claim to do over again the theoretical work which has been so ably done by Régis and Hesnard; my book is not a study of the authorities. I approach the problem from the other side, where it is concrete and individual.

These considerations will explain one of the difficulties of compiling the volume; they will account for what may be regarded as its defects. My aim has been to produce a record of my own work which might interest experts, not to write a popular treatise for beginners. On the other hand, I was writing for French readers, most of whom are in fact beginners in this subject. Consequently it was incumbent on me to deal with general principles, many of which are trite matters for the expert. Have I been clear enough to be comprehensible to the general reader; have I been concise

[1] Régis and Hesnard, *La psychoanalyse des névroses et des psychoses*, 1914.

enough to escape being tedious to the expert? I do not know. But I am not without hope that the way in which I have had to write my book will prove to have been an advantage after all. I believe that a theoretical discussion of the general principles of psychoanalysis is eminently desirable, even though such an examination may be considered superfluous by certain psychoanalysts, extremists of their school.

There is good reason for surprise that a thought trend so notable both in quality and in quantity should still be little known in France. Freud's most important work, *Traumdeutung* [1] has never been translated into French. There is a great contrast, in this respect, between France and the English-speaking lands. *Traumdeutung* was translated into English in 1913, and psychoanalysis has now become a household word in Britain and the United States. Works on philosophy, various aspects of science, and even popular science, have been written by persons who have made the new outlook their own.[2] To return to France, the neglect of psychoanalysis in this country is readily explicable—quite apart from the war. Nor are all the reasons wholly discreditable to French thought.

A regrettable indifference, routinism and parochialism, have doubtless played their part. But the psychoanalysts are not free from blame. The realm of the "unconscious" is necessarily obscure; but they would seem at times to have taken a positive delight in peopling it with shadows. They have been neologist to excess; some of their theories are fantastically bold; not a few of the exponents are fanatics. These characteristics of the new doctrine were naturally repugnant to the French mind, which loves clarity and good sense and is humorously sceptical. Psychoanalysts have

[1] See complete bibliography at end of volume.

[2] A few instances may be given. Philosophy: W. H. R. Rivers, Mind and Medicine, 2nd ed., 1920; Bertrand Russell, The Analysis of Mind, 1921. Psychology: A. G. Tansley, The New Psychology and its Relation to Life, new edition, 1922 (this work is directly inspired by psychoanalysis); Anonymous (The Plebs League), An Outline of Psychology, 1922 (this exposition of psychology for working-class students is likewise permeated with psychoanalytical theory); Millais Culpin, Spiritualism and the New Psychology. Sociology: W. M. Gallichan, The Psychology of Marriage, 1917 (it is significant that on p. 64 the author describes C. G. Jung as "one of the greatest psychologists of our day"); Eden and Cedar Paul, Creative Revolution, 1920 (these writers lay especial stress on "the new lights Freudianism sheds upon the problems of revolutionary communism"). The list might be greatly extended.

occasionally done their best to justify Nietzsche's aphorism: "The German spirit is a form of indigestion." They would appear, too, to have found it pleasing to break down all the bridges connecting their "new science" with the psychology of yesterday. Like Christopher Columbus they have discovered a new world, have thereupon renounced allegiance to the old, and have even been inclined to deny the existence of the old.

We ought not to break down these bridges, but rather to strengthen them. Where could such work be more successfully carried on than at Geneva, the meeting-place of two cultures? We have to thank the late Théodore Flournoy for having guided our footsteps in this direction, for having sought out the points of contact between the psychology of William James and the psychology of Sigmund Freud, and between their respective terminologies. Flournoy's *Une mystique moderne* is a model of that scientific tolerance which is less common than people are apt to suppose. The Genevese group of psychoanalysts is guided in the same spirit by Edouard Claparède; this spirit likewise animates Pierre Bovet's remarkable study *L'instinct combatif*. I wish to take this opportunity of expressing my indebtedness to all these colleagues.

Such originality as the present work possesses will, then, be due to a search for points of contact between psychoanalysis and ordinary psychology. These points of contact must be found if the science of the subconscious is to be made assimilable. Claparède holds that it does not suffice to translate psychoanalysts' writings into French. He considers that as far as may be, we ought also to translate their thought, their terminology, their very theories, into forms more familiar to French minds and to non-Freudian psychologists. Unquestionably, an unmodified exposition of the psychoanalysis of the schools is apt to produce on unfamiliar ears the effect produced on Pascal by the Spanish Latin of certain Jesuit fathers. "Can these fellows really be Christians?" he asks. I am not certain to what degree a "translation" of this kind is possible. But I am sure that a discussion of the relationships between psychoanalysis and ordinary psychology is essential, and I believe that it will throw light on many points that are still obscure.

In the field of theory, I have endeavoured to show the ties between the psychology which has now become classical, that of Ribot, James, Bergson, and Claparède, to say nothing of the almost forgotten Jouffroy. At the same time, I have borne in mind Descartes' methodological rule: "Divide the subject into as many subdivisions as you can, for this will help you to solve the difficulties." It seems to me that in the totality of ideas which pass by the general name of psychoanalysis, at least one great distinction ought to be made.

(*a*) Psychoanalysis starts by laying the foundations of *an affective theory of the association of ideas*, a theory which discerns in affectivity, *often subconscious*, the cause of the ostensibly incoherent creations of the imagination. It is upon this that the new method of studying the subconscious has been based.

(*b*) This affectivity which is discerned behind the imagination, is in its turn linked by psychoanalysis with instinct. To the psychoanalysts, all the higher sentiments appear to be products of the evolution of a crude instinct. Thus we arrive at *a biological theory of affectivity*, which is likewise an evolutionary theory of instinct.

It follows that there are two categories, sufficiently distinct, though not hitherto sufficiently distinguished:

(*a*) imagination explained by affectivity;

(*b*) affectivity explained by instinct.

The former theory, which is supported by an abundance of facts that anyone can observe for himself, is all the better for being separated from the latter theory; for this, though in broad outlines it appears acceptable, is complicated in matters of detail by a number of hypothetical and contradictory formulas. We must leave to to-morrow the perfectionment of this biological theory. By confusing the issues, by trying to compact the two theories into one, we run the risk of giving a hypothetical aspect even to data that are based upon an extremely solid foundation.

Larguier des Bancels, in his recent work *Introduction à la psychologie*, writes (Avant-propos, pp. 13–14): "The American school draws a distinction between functional psychology and structural psychology. Structural psychology analyses the phenomena; it endeavours to discover their mechanism; in a word, it describes them. Functional psychology is concerned with the purport of these same phenomena, and seeks to elucidate their biologic role. Here we have two perspectives. They are equally legitimate but the observer cannot occupy two viewpoints at the same time. Aristotle's psychology is functional psychology. Locke remains the master of structural psychology. The doctrine of the faculties is a return to Aristotle. The associationism of the nineteenth century carries on the tradition of Locke and his eighteenth-century successors."

The first category of psychoanalysis (the affective theory of association) is a structural psychology ; the second category is a functional psychology. We have here " two perspectives. They are equally legitimate, but the observer cannot occupy two viewpoints at the same time." They are related to one another just as anatomy and physiology are related to one another. Now it is certain that the dynamic and functional point of view which has been the favourite outlook in psychology since James, is the only one enabling us to formulate an integral science of the phenomena of existence. We have no more right to blame Freud than we have to blame William James for having wished to construct a dynamic psychology. Nevertheless we are entitled to add that the second point of view (functional) must be a sequel to the first (structural). When people begin to give functional explanations in default of a sufficient descriptive foundation, they must never forget that they are formulating mere hypotheses. These may of course be extremely useful in research as guiding ideas ; but they are dangerous, for many people are inclined to make of them a slippery descent into an unscientific finalism. A dynamic explanation is the goal we must seek to attain ; but all dynamic explanations will be provisional so long as our static descriptions remain inadequate. In like manner, when we have to trace a continuous curve representing experimental data, we must not endeavour to do so until we have directly determined a sufficient number of isolated points through which the curve has to pass. It is the business of functional psychology to trace the curve ; but it is the business of structural psychology to ascertain the points through which the curve must pass.

This distinction between the two categories corresponds to the distinction which Bovet has drawn between psychoanalysis as a *method* and psychoanalysis as a *doctrine,* for whereas the method is essentially based on the former theory, the doctrine is built on the latter.

"Psychoanalysis," writes Bovet, "is, above all, a method for the study of the subconscious. To initiate ourselves into psychoanalysis is to form an idea of this method and to attempt the manipulation of this instrument.

"Frequently, however, experts in psychoanalysis, identifying the method with the results, present it to us as a body of doctrines bearing upon the nature of the subconscious ego, and offer it to us as a new psychology. In this they resemble a Pisan of the seventeenth century who should have given the name of 'telescopy' to Galileo's opinions concerning the satellites of Jupiter and concerning the solar system in general.

"It is well to point out that the wide differences which separate the various schools of psychoanalysts (those of Freud, Adler, and Jung, respectively) do not impair in any way the value of the instrument which they all alike use as a means of study. The differences relate to the interpretation of the facts which psychoanalysis has revealed. Let us suppose that two astronomers, independently studying the planet Mars, detect the phenomenon which is known as the gemination of the canals of that luminary. Perhaps one astronomer will tell us that the gemination is due to some peculiarity in the refraction of light, whereas the other will ascribe it to a seasonal variation in the distribution of the waters of the planet. But the existence of such disputes does not justify us in contending that telescopes are useless. Rather should they urge us to perfect our utilisation of telescopes, or to supplement their employment by other methods which will enable us to reduce the uncertainties attendant on the interpretation of the phenomena we are observing." [1]

I shall perhaps, when I come to the concrete exposition of cases, be charged with having failed to abide by my own distinction. I am aware that it is extremely difficult to avoid adopting the current methods of exposition. Conversely, in practice it is sometimes difficult to disentangle the fact from the interpretation. Simply by recording a fact, we interpet it; and language is a web of interpretations. When, therefore, the reader comes across a functional inter-

[1] Pierre Bovet, La psychanalyse et l'éducation, pp. 4–5, 1920.

pretation which seems to him to lack adequate verification, let him prefix the words: "Everything happens as if . . ." This prefix will not conflict with the essence of my thought.

2. Guiding Principles of the present Work

Thanks to this distinction, I have at least been able to avoid the perpetual mingling of comprehensive functional hypotheses with the description of the affective laws of the association of images (Chapter Two). I therefore regard the *symbolism* of dreams as a natural result of the working of the laws of *condensation* and *displacement*, and I do not apriori consider symbolism to be the purposive masking of repressed and "censored" mental processes. This notion of the "censorship" has been strongly criticised, even by psychoanalysts (Rivers, for instance). There are plenty of cases in which it is not necessary to invoke such a hypothesis, whereas condensation is a persistent fact. This condensation, which groups images characterised by a common affect, groups them so as to form a single composite and new image, is the first stage in the creation of the *symbol.* I look upon symbolisation as *a general law of the imagination,* and not as being necessarily the outcome of the masking of forbidden representations. This applies equally to artistic symbols, which have with good reason been compared to the spontaneous symbols of dreams. An author may use a symbol to disguise his thought and thus throw an official censorship off the scent; this is what Montesquieu did in his *Lettres persanes.* On the other hand, an author may use a symbol simply as a means of self-expression; this is the practice of the symbolist poets.

The *condensation* of images lies at the very root of creative imagination. This implies that creative imagination is the direct outcome of an affective state, so that we might say that sensibility itself is the true creator of new images. Condensation is more powerful in strong affective states than in weak ones; it is more powerful likewise in dreams than in waking states. This leads us to ask what may be the common element in affective states and dream states, and we realise that the two types of condition are characterised by a suspension of activity, of spontaneous movement. Both affectivity, and the dream or the reverie which affectivity engenders, are pent-up action.

Thence we pass to the dynamic outlook (Chapter Three), and we ask what can be *the function or functions of the dream* (and of such kindred states as reverie and æsthetic creation). First of all, we look upon the dream as an exercise of the creative imagination. In this respect its usefulness, even from the point of view of action, is evident. The intelligence ensures our adaptation to the real; the imagination ensures the adaptation of the real to ourselves. But when we come to consider the remarkable law of *displacement* (whose working is manifest in dreams), the law in virtue of which an affect is detached from its real object and transferred to another object, we cannot but assimilate the *dream* to *play*, in which the imagination of the child effects like displacements. If we study the conditions of dreaming and of play, their kinship becomes even more apparent. Since Karl Groos wrote on the subject, play has been looked upon as an outlet or exercise for unutilised tendencies. The dream, a manifestation of pent-up action, is in like manner the outcome of unutilised tendencies. In the dream, these tendencies are discharged; they exercise themselves; they enact the possibilities of their future evolution.

For tendencies evolve. They are the psychological manifestation of instinct; and instinct, which was long regarded as immutable, is now looked upon as susceptible of development. In man, above all, instinct is malleable. Naturalists have shown that *suppressions* and *transformations* of instinct occur among animals. Psychologists (William James, for instance) point to the same phenomena in man. Freud's originality lies in this, that he discloses the link between suppression and transformation. Suppression is apparent merely; although the instinct is repressed, it still lives in a modified form. Approaching the matter from the other side, we may say that an instinct which has been transformed is preeminently an instinct which has been restrained.

Thus psychoanalysis culminates in an evolutionary theory of instinct. The transformations of instinct are clues to the affective life; and the higher sentiments are nourished by instinctive forces. Freud has turned his attention to the evolution of the sexual instinct; Adler, to the instinct for power. Jung attempts a synthesis of the two systems, unifying under the term *libido* all instinctive energy. But this unification belongs rather to the realm of philosophy than to that of science. From the psychologist's point of view we are inclined to ask whether the reconciliation of Freud's views with Adler's should not rather be sought upon a deliberately analytical platform; and whether, instead of considering all instincts as manifestations of one single kind of energy, it would not be better if we were more modestly to study the evolution of each instinct by itself. *Psycho-analysis is an evolutionary theory of instinct; it ought to become an evolutionary theory of the instincts.* We need not hesitate to admit that a number of different instincts can participate in the genesis of the same higher sentiment. This purely analytic path, which is not the path of the systematist, is the one which British and French writers upon psychoanalysis appear to be following. Both Rivers and MacCurdy have studied war neuroses as functions of the instinct of self-preservation, and Bovet has written a monograph on the combative instinct. Henceforward we must deliberately work along these lines. Thus we shall free psychoanalytic science from that systematiser's spirit, from that inappropriate metaphysic, which have been its bane, and which have prevented superficial observers (and even some persons of first-class intelligence) from recognising its value as a contribution to positive science.

In the practice of psychoanalytical re-education, it will, moreover, be fruitless as a rule to attempt a choice from among hypothetical interpretations when these belong to the second category (the biological theory of affectivity). Freud, Adler, and others have secured successes by explaining to their patients that the symptoms with which these were affected were due to causes which they themselves (the psychoanalysts) have inferred as the outcome of the analysis. Now each analyst has his own theory, and the causes explained to the patient vary from analyst to analyst. Yet the practical successes of the treatment are indubitable. Does it not follow that we should be mistaken in attributing these successes to remote causes of an extremely hypothetical character, when immediate and far less hypothetical causes are competent to explain them? Or, following Bovet's terminology, may we not say that the curative power of psychoanalysis depends more upon the method than upon the theory which guides it.

At this stage, sceptics will obviously declare that the results are not due to a knowledge either of the affective causes or of the biological causes, but that everything is the outcome of *suggestion*. This objection merely proves that the objector is ignorant of psychoanalysis. All the same, despite its naivety, the psychoanalysts will do well to take the criticism into account. Those who have studied suggestion, and in especial those who are familiar with the work of the New Nancy School,[1] are well aware that the factor of suggestion plays its part in every method of treatment and in all kinds of education. Purely physical therapeutic methods do not escape the working of this law; statistics have demonstrated its importance in connection with the treatment of consumption.[2] But in psychoanalysis, where we have to do with the nervous system and the subconscious (which is preeminently the field of suggestion), and where in addition an intimate affective relationship is apt to be established between teacher and pupil, there can be no question but that the factor of suggestion is powerfully operative. This does not deprive the method of any part of its objective value; but when the psychoanalysts would fain prohibit suggestion, they are asking the impossible. *Seeing, then, that it is inevitable that suggestion should accompany the analysis, would it not be better to guide this suggestion instead of trying to ignore it?*

Here we again reach a point where a great many analysts, intolerant in matters of practice no less than in matters of theory, seem to have wished to break down the bridges behind them. The only psychology, they tell us, is psychoanalysis; and in like manner they insist that psychoanalysis is the only psychotherapeutics. They discard suggestion as an obsolete method, superseded by analysis, and in conflict with the latter. For my part, I believe that this supposition of a conflict between psychoanalysis and suggestion is based upon a number

[1] See the author's other writings, enumerated in the Bibliography.

[2] Louis Rénon, Tuberculose pulmonaire chronique, "Le Monde Médicale," January 15, 1914. See also Baudouin, Suggestion and Autosuggestion, pp. 97–9.

of false hypotheses, and upon misunderstandings which I am endeavouring to clear up. Psychoanalysis is incompatible with certain forms of suggestion; but it is perfectly compatible with others. I regard the intolerance which some analysts display towards suggestion as no less deplorable than the sceptical attitude of practitioners of suggestion towards analysis.

The method to which experience has led me, the method whose results are recorded in this book, is founded upon *an unceasing collaboration between autosuggestion and psychoanalysis* (Chapter Four). Many, I know, regard this as a heresy. Whether it be heretical or not, I am confident that immense advantage can be derived from such collaboration.

Generally speaking, throughout this work *more stress is laid on the normal than on the pathological.* In my view, analysis is a method of education or re-education rather than a curative method.[1] In many cases, the internal conflicts which the analysis has to resolve cannot be looked upon as morbid. Pfister is right in insisting that we must call normal education to our aid. Even where we have to deal with morbid symptoms, we shall help the patient by showing how these have developed through the hypertrophy of conditions that are perfectly normal, so that our therapeutic analysis will take the form, not so much of an amputation which cuts everything away, as of a cauterisation which removes what is superfluous. Psychoanalytical experience merely confirms our view that the difference between the pathological and the normal is only one of degree. But, like every medical method, it has begun by considering the pathological, and its consideration of the normal has been a secondary reconstruction. This *pathological method* is an excellent one; and its application to psychology has brought about the maximum of progress, for, precisely because the pathological is a hypertrophy of the normal, the pathological is as it were the normal seen through a microscope. Hypnotism and suggestion constitute one way of applying this method; psychoanalysis is another. But if psychoanalysis, like suggestion, has naturally followed the route from the pathological to the normal, it is essential to impress upon psychoanalysis (and to do so more vigorously than has yet been attempted)

[1] I take the same view of suggestion.

the inverse movement—the movement which, as far as suggestion is concerned, was initiated at Nancy and carried to its logical conclusion by the New Nancy School. The Salpêtrière School, having discovered suggestion in persons suffering from hysteria, looked upon it as a morbid phenomenon, and was inclined to detect hysteria in everything. The Nancy School, psychological rather than pathological, inverting the order of research, set out from the normal phenomena which had been revealed by the light of pathology, to pass on by degrees to the study of morbid modifications.

The route from the pathological to the normal is one of research; the route from the normal to the pathological is one of exposition and synthesis. The two methods are complementary. Whenever the study of the pathological has thrown light on a normal phenomenon, we must do our utmost to deduce the pathological from the normal, and thus to put things in their places. The psychoanalysts have rarely reversed the engine in this way. Consequently Han Ryner, though as a thinker he is sympathetic towards psychoanalysis, once asked mischievously whether the doctors would not soon be talking of "chronic normality" or "acute health."

In this realm of thought, an error of terminology is current, and the experts are themselves largely to blame for its existence. I refer to the identification of the words "nervous" and "neuropathic." Analysis undoubtedly confirms the supposition that the three terms "nervous," "affective," "imaginative," have kindred connotations. But we must not infer, as some are inclined to do, that moral sensibility and imagination are pathological manifestations. The nervous person is a potential neuropath, just as a biped is a potential cul-de-jatte;[1] but he is not necessarily a neuropath. We have no right to describe aesthetic, philosophical, and religious phenomena as forms of the neuroses and psychoses. Nevertheless certain analysts employ phraseology which conveys this impression. A professor of the University of Geneva, during a philosophical discussion with a psychoanalyst, found it necessary to interject good-humouredly: "But what difference do you make, then, between a metaphysician and a patient suffering from dementia præcox?" Such errors

[1] A person who has lost both legs.

of terminology may entail errors of thought, dangerous errors. Some psychoanalysts seem to regard the whole human mind as an elaborate sexual perversion ; others, as an imaginative compensation for an organic inferiority. Following this line of thought, man might be defined as " a neuropathic animal " ; and it is perfectly true that the human nervous system possesses a delicacy of poise, and consequently a liability to injury, which is unknown among ruminants.

A person of nervous temperament may develop into a neuropath, but he may also develop into a genius. It depends upon which line he is switched on to. This is the significance of the well-known formula : " A neurosis is an unsuccessful work of art ; a work of art is a successful neurosis." We must not, of course, infer that the two things are equivalent. The difference between failure and success may perhaps represent the whole difference between the pathological and the normal, for the normal is essentially a successful adaptation. A runner may become the champion ; it is also possible that he will fall and break his leg. He will not think it funny if you tell him there is no difference.

If we take the normal as our starting-point, we are taking a psychological outlook instead of a medical outlook, and consequently we are building an additional bridge between psychoanalysis and the classical psychology. For the aim of the classical psychology was to describe the mind of the normal man, of a man so normal that he was at times stupid. (We remember some of the truisms of the scholastics, the eclectics, etc.). For a long time psychology had to pay for the fact that its origins were exclusively philosophical ; during this period it was largely restricted to the domain of solemn and futile generalisations. We have to thank Auguste Comte for having run atilt, not as has been declared against psychology in general, but against the psychology of the schools ; and we have further to thank him for the appeal to pathological methods of study, which were destined to furnish such brilliant results a few years later. But we must avoid the opposite extreme, must avoid undue eagerness to study the pathological where classical psychology was unduly inclined to study the normal—though such undue stressing of the pathological is an almost inevitable characteristic of methods that are medical in their origin. By studying the normal aspects where medical psychologists have studied the pathological, we shall be able to integrate the two methods in psychological science. It is very probable that the normal phenomena of which we are in search have already been noted, though not perhaps fully understood, by psychologists; we may find that they have been named, and have been coordinated with a whole system of known facts. We have to act as interpreters between the respective tongues of psychology and pathology. Perhaps, too, we have to act as interpreters between the French of the psychologists and the German of the pathologists.

This much is certain, that we should serve French thought an ill turn if we allowed it to persist in its ignorance of such a movement as psychoanalysis. We may note, indeed, that French writers are beginning to show an interest in the question. So judicious an authority as Pierre Janet, though critical and even harshly critical of many psychoanalytical interpretations, deplores that prejudices against psychoanalysis are prevalent in France,[1] and devotes a long study to this method.[2] H. Piéron, again, has written an appreciative essay on a work by Rivers which is entirely based on psychoanalysis.[3]

An absurd chauvinism is perhaps still responsible for hostility to a "German doctrine," and the joke of the matter is that the founder of this alleged "German doctrine" is an Austrian Jew. In any case, truth has nothing to do with passports and birth certificates. Freud's psychology, like Einstein's physics, is an extant fact. We cannot suppress a fact by refusing to look at it; this is the wisdom of the ostrich. No one can do away with a revolution by imitating Louis XVIII, who spoke of 1814 as the twenty-second year of his reign. Nor can anyone get rid of the fact that Galileo lived and wrote. The pontiffs who excommunicate, succeed only in excommunicating themselves. The movement of human thought goes on outside their church, and quietly leaves them stranded. *E pur si muove!*

[1] Pierre Janet, Les médications psychologiques, 1919, vol. ii. p. 268.

[2] Ibid (Les traitements par la liquidation morale), pp. 204 et seq.—Cf. the same author's Rapport àu Congrès de Londres, 1913.—Pierre Janet was at the outset distrustful of psychoanalysis. To-day he is far more sympathetic.

[3] H. Piéron, Une adaptation biologique du Freudisme aux psychonévroses de guerre (a review of Rivers' Instinct and the Unconscious), "Journal de Psychologie," Paris, 1921, No. 1.

PART ONE

THEORETICAL EXPOSITION

CHAPTER TWO

SKETCH OF AN AFFECTIVE THEORY OF THE ASSOCIATION OF IDEAS

1. From Associationism to Psychoanalysis

WHY and how do ideas and images become associated, so that one calls up another; above all, why does this happen when there is no rational tie, and in the absence of voluntary effort? How can we explain the spontaneous and apparently capricious progress of a mind which "is thinking about nothing," and which, all the same, is thinking about a thousand things? Since the days of Plato and Aristotle these questions have aroused the interest of many philosophers. In modern times they have been the especial concern of the empiricist school of Locke, of the French sensualist school (Condillac), and in particular of the British school of the nineteenth century which is specifically known as the associationist school (Hamilton, John Stuart Mill, etc.). For these philosophers, association was of supreme importance, inasmuch as they looked upon "simple ideas," or images, as atoms, as elementary psychic units; and they considered that the manifold combinations of such units sufficed to explain the whole life of the understanding. The combinations, it will be remembered, took place in accordance with the laws of *contiguity*, *similarity*, and *contrast*. Two images became associated when their objects had been perceived side by side; or when they were like one another; or when they were contrasted. More precise differentiæ were subsequently added to these vague general laws. The *force* of associations was measured (experimental work of Ebbinghaus, Müller and Pilzecker, Jost); the *rapidity* of associations was measured (Münsterberg, Scripture); associations were classified in accordance with the characteristics of the associated terms and their varying mutual relationships, of form or colour, co-ordination or subordination, etc. (classifications of Wundt, Münsterberg, Claparède). With the passage of the years, however, the vast hopes of the associationists were disappointed, and the basic defect of their theory was gradually revealed. The mistake was that the associationists had tried to explain the interaction of the images by the inherent characters of these images, without appealing to any external force; much as if an observer, ignoring the presence of a magnet and its properties, should endeavour to understand why iron filings in a magnetic field group themselves along the lines of force while considering these filings as mere independent particles. Such an observer might make interesting observations on the positions of the particles, and he would be able to formulate certain laws; but to arrive at an explanatory and synthetic principle would be beyond his power. Underlying the associationists' doctrine and invalidating it, is an implicit postulate that the representative life is self-explicable, that the fantasies of the imagination can be made comprehensible by a study of the nature of the images. People came to realise that this doctrine was inadequate and arbitrary, and to suspect where the "magnet" was to be found—in the affective life.

This appeal to the affective life became more and more necessary in proportion as psychologists renounced the eclectic theory of independent "faculties"; but it is interesting to note that in the writings of Jouffroy, one of the eclectics, we find foreshadowings of the modern affective theories. In his *Cours d'esthétique,* he supplements the theory of association (17th Lesson, p. 121) by a remarkable theory of the symbol (18th and 19th Lessons, pp. 131, 139). Thanks to association, says Jouffroy, every sensation, every idea, is enabled to evoke and to signify states of mind which transcend it, thus becoming a symbol. Jouffroy opines that this property is one of the foundations of artistic expression. He goes so far as to say: "Everything that we perceive is symbolical, for everything that we perceive arouses in us the idea of something else that we do not perceive" (p. 133).

This theory of the symbol, in which Jouffroy shows that he has an inkling of the muffled affective resonances of a perception or an image, was for a long time ignored. Everyone is familiar with it to-day, when psychoanalysis has made symbolism fashionable. G. Dwelshauvers writes: "Associationism did not make its way into France before the days of Taine and Ribot; but Jouffroy was familiar with the principles of the associationist school, and the associationist theory suggested to him another theory, far more comprehensive and more profound. We may call it symbolism."[1]

"Far more comprehensive and more profound" is perhaps hyperbolical. We must resist the temptation to fill out the term employed by Jouffroy with all the ideas which the word now arouses in our minds, ideas that were not present in his when he used it. But as a foreshadowing, the utterance is significant.

When we come to Ribot, the affective factor is explicitly invoked. A fundamental matter, and one whose importance was fully realised by this author, is what we shall call *affective association*, or *condensation*. He describes it in the following terms: "Representations which have been accompanied by the same affective state, tend henceforward to be associated; their affective similarity forms a link between the separate representations. This is not the same as association by contiguity, which is a repetition of the experience; nor is it the same as association by similarity in the intellectual sense.[2] The states of consciousness are linked, not because they have previously occurred together, nor because we perceive similarities between them, but because they have a common affective tone. Joy, sadness, love, hatred, surprise, boredom, pride, fatigue, etc., can each become a centre of attraction grouping representations or events which are devoid of any intellectual interconnection, but which have the same emotional tinge—joyful, melancholy, erotic, etc. This form of association is common in dreams and in reverie, that is to say, in a state of mind when imagination works in perfect freedom."[3]

This passage is so important, and the author states his views so simply, that it was worth quoting in full. We shall

[1] G. Dwelshauvers, La psychologie française contemporaine, 1920, p. 33.

[2] That is to say *objective similarity* (shape, colour, etc.), the only similarity with which the associationists are concerned when formulating the "law of similarity."

[3] Ribot, Essai sur l'imagination créatrice, 1900, p. 31.

see shortly some picturesque examples of this *condensation.* Enough for the moment to indicate its importance. In another work Ribot writes: "Substantially, this form corresponds to what official psychology denotes by the vague term 'the influence of the feeling on the intelligence.'"[1]

This influence is not an occasional matter; it is persistent. We cannot fully understand the intellectual life as a whole unless we take into account the subjacent realm of feeling. Rignano goes so far as to maintain, as regards various forms of insanity, that these disorders of the intelligence are fundamentally disorders of feeling. He adds that attention can be reduced to affective phenomena.[2] If feeling thus helps us to understand the working of the intelligence, it is all the more necessary to have recourse to a study of feeling when we wish to understand that more primitive and spontaneous form of intelligence which is known as imagination.[3]

In addition to describing condensation, Ribot gives an excellent account of what he terms the *transference* of a feeling. Transference may, in a sense, be regarded as the inverse of condensation. Here a feeling, instead of grouping round itself a number of separate images, is itself dispersed over a number of associated images. Ribot writes (*Logique des sentiments*, p. 4): "Transference may result from similarity. When an intellectual state has been accompanied by a strong feeling, a similar state tends to arouse the same feeling. It may result from contiguity. When intellectual states have coexisted, the feeling linked with the primary state tends, if strong enough, to be transferred to the others. The lover tends to transfer the feeling which is at first associated with the person of his mistress, to her clothing, her furniture, her house. In an absolute monarchy, reverence for the person of the king is transferred to the throne, to the insignia of power, to everything which is more or less closely connected with the monarch."

Anyone, however, who attempts to unravel phenomena of such a character—condensation or transference, for example—is likely to be led astray unless he knows that in many cases this interplay of feelings and images goes on unawares.

[1] Ribot, Logique des sentiments, 1905, p. 22.
[2] Rignano, Psychologie du raisonnement, 1920.
[3] Baudouin, The Affective Basis of Intelligence, 1920.

Everything happens as if such links were effected, but as if they were effected in the subconscious (or "unconscious"). Ribot, therefore, is perfectly right when to the "affective factor" he adds the "unconscious factor," which is fundamentally a form of latent affectivity. Thus "at first we have an unconscious working equivalent to a series of judgments of value, and proceeding by analogy. Subsequently, and mainly, we have an imaginative construction, consisting of associations radiating in various directions, but unified by the unconscious selective process of a dominant desire."[1]

At the same date, both Flournoy and Claparède were drawing attention to these facts. Claparède describes the *evocation* of an idea through the instrumentality of a feeling: "Feeling here plays the part of an ordinary psychic element in conformity with the laws of association. When two intellectual states have been accompanied by the same affective state, they tend to become associated. The affective state which cements them may either remain conscious or may disappear from consciousness. Flournoy has given a lucid explanation of the phenomena of coloured hearing by invoking an affective association of this character."[2]

In 1903, Claparède was already aware of the importance, in this relationship, of the early works of Freud: "The leading characteristic of affective association is its tenacity. We note this in certain pathological cases. A psychic element which has become linked with an emotion is averse to forming fresh associative ties. For instance, we hear of a patient who was unwilling to wash the hand which his sovereign had touched. Here the affect associated with the hand was inhibiting any new relationships into which the hand might have entered. Breuer and Freud[3] explain in this way the tics or habit-spasms, the contractures, and the other morbid symptoms, from which hysterical patients suffer."[4]

Claparède also borrows from Ribot the theory of *transference,* and borrows Ribot's examples. With Ribot, he distinguishes between *transference by contiguity* (e.g., the venting

[1] Ribot, Logique des sentiments, p. 4.
[2] Claparède, L'association des idées, 1903, p. 348
[3] Freud, Paralysies hystériques, p. 41.
[4] Claparède, op. cit., p. 346.

of wrath upon inanimate objects belonging to an enemy), and *transference by similarity* (e.g., a mother drawn towards a young man who resembles her dead son). At this date, Claparède was already identifying the term *transference* with the term *Verschiebung* (displacement). In Freud's writings this idea of *displacement*, which was destined ere long to play a great part in psychoanalysis, was more complex than the "transference" referred to by Ribot. According to Freud, the feeling is not merely related to a new object, but is partly or wholly detached from its former object. We shall see that this substitution is of supreme importance in dreams, and that it is one of the phenomena which are prone to mislead us in their interpretation.

To-day, the inadequacy of associationism is generally recognised. Throughout his philosophical writings, Bergson inveighs against this atomic formulation of mental phenomena. Let me quote a specific passage: "We do not contest the truth of the 'law of similarity,' but . . . any two ideas, any two images chosen haphazard, however discrepant they may be, will always be found to have some element of similarity, for it will always be possible to find a common genus to which they can be assigned." [1]

Brunschvicg, likewise, stresses the consideration that everything can be associated with everything else. In the interplay of the images he distinguishes, in addition to a function of juxtaposition, a function of fusion.[2] We are now in a position to presume that affectivity plays its part in this fusion. Ribot, in the passage previously quoted, actually spoke of states which "are linked" under the influence of the affective factor. We have seen that Claparède says that a feeling "cements" two images.

2. The Laws of affective Association

No one who undertakes an impartial study of the psychoanalytical conception of the imagination, or of the psychoanalytical view of association in general, can fail to notice how closely akin this conception is to that of Ribot. I point out the fact, not in order to detract from Freud's title to

[1] Bergson, L'énergie spirituelle, 1920, p. 153.

[2] Brunschvicg, Introduction à la vie de l'esprit, 3rd edition, 1920, pp. 12–17.

originality, but in order to show that Freud's ideas are less subversive than is commonly supposed. Indeed, many of Freud's writings are contemporary with those of Ribot, and some antecede those of the French psychologist. As far as our present outlook is concerned, Freud's originality is to be found in his study of imagination and association in dreams. This field was peculiarly well adapted for the discovery of the affective laws, which operate with exceptional vigour in the world of dreams. The laws run parallel with those formulated by Ribot, but they are more comprehensive. Condensation, displacement, and the role of the subconscious, form the foundations of the psychoanalytical theory of dreams.

Let us first consider CONDENSATION, the *Verdichtung* of Freud. Ribot, in the passage previously quoted, states that this form is "common in dreams"; and he points out that, through condensation, the images, not content with being juxtaposed, "are linked." The psychoanalytical view is that this intimate linking may be regarded as normal in dreams, a combination so close that keen scrutiny is requisite before the combined elements can be distinguished. Our dreams resemble the "composite photographs" obtained by partial exposures of the same photographic plate to the image of a number of different persons of the same family, in order to bring out "family traits." In the case we are now considering, the family trait is a likeness of feeling or emotion which serves as a link between separate memories. Thus it is that in a dream the landscape we have never seen, but which nevertheless we seem to recognise, is an amalgam of a number of landscapes which we actually have seen. Peculiarly applicable to these dream landscapes is Amiel's saying: "A landscape is a state of mind." In like manner, in a dream, several persons may fuse into one, because of a common impression they have made on us, or because they all have the same significance for us. This is why we often feel that we have dreamed of a person or a thing "which all the same was not precisely that person or that thing." It explains, again, the amusing phrases of Marinette (six years old), relating a dream which she had after I had told her the story of Hercules: "I had a dream about the lion man. He wasn't father, but he was a man who was father. There wasn't any lion, but all the same it seemed as if there was a lion." Here we have an obvious and simple condensation of father and Hercules. As a typical instance of condensation I may refer to the dream of the youth Raoul, one of the subjects whose cases are discussed in the second part of this book. He dreamed of a post-chaise which was a condensation of the family motor car and the school omnibus, or, in a more general sense, a condensation of the family environment and the school environment; whilst the driver was a condensation of the head master and the dreamer's father. The affective state around which this condensation had crystallised was a feeling of constraint and of protest against authority (p. 150). In the first dream of the subject Alexander (p. 221) we have an obvious condensation of his home with his friend's house, of his mother with his friend's wife, of his father with his friend.

Condensation is far more conspicuous in dreams than in the waking state. Freud goes so far as to say that condensation "has no analogies in the fully conscious state."[1] Broadly this may be true as regards vigorous condensations, to which Freud apparently wishes to restrict the term *Verdichtung*—condensations in which the subject cannot distinguish the combined elements. But there are no hard and fast lines. Various grades of condensation exist. Thus we have *composite images* (*Mischbildungen*) analogous to the centaur of fable, in which the components (man and horse in the case of the centaur), though fused into a whole, can readily be distinguished. By stages, we pass to looser condensations, and finally we reach the simple *evocation* (affective association) of Claparède. I hold, however, that fairly vigorous condensations are met with in the waking state. The name is peculiarly appropriate for those compound memories in which the subject believes that his reminiscence is one of a single experience, whereas it is in reality a reminiscence of two or three distinct experiences, which occurred perhaps at widely separated dates, but were all accompanied by the same feeling tone. This is especially common in our memories of childhood. In the subject Kitty, we note the same thing in recent memories. She fuses into one reminiscence a gift which she had on her fifteenth birthday and one

[1] Freud, Die Traumdeutung, p. 462

which she had on her sixteenth birthday (p. 153).[1] Vigorous condensations occur in works of art, in pictures or poems, and are preeminently manifestations of creative imagination. Speaking generally we may say that, *other things being equal, condensation is more vigorous:* (1) *in a strong affective state than in a weak affective state;* (2) *in dreams than in the waking state.*

The *duration* of the condensation must be considered as well as its degree. Some condensations are almost instantaneous, and this is especially frequent in dreams. Some, on the other hand, are persistent. These latter, of course, are the condensations which have been "cemented" by a powerful emotion or feeling, and in this connection the emotions or feelings of early childhood are of supreme importance. Condensations of such a character, enriched in the course of life by many kinds of emotions and new images, are all the more intricate because their essential elements are usually buried in the subconscious. One of the main functions of psychoanalysis is to "extricate" them, to disentangle them.

We may naturally enquire how so important a phenomenon as condensation could have escaped the notice of the associationists. One reason is, the part the subconscious plays in the matter. Another reason is, the peculiar conditions under which condensation takes place. The two states which favour the occurrence of condensation, namely dreaming and strong emotion, are states over which there is little control and in which observation is difficult. Nevertheless, ought not the associationists at least to have recognised the significance of the lesser degrees of condensation common in the waking state; and ought they not to have been careful to distinguish this phenomenon from simple association by similarity? In this case, too, the reason of the omission is obvious, and has important implications. The reason is that *the elements associated or condensed through the medium of a common affect, are usually associated or condensed in accordance with the ordinary laws of association* (*contiguity or similarity*).

To use Freud's terminology, we have here an "overdetermination" (*Ueberdeterminierung*). This means that the

[1] This condensation was favoured by a strong association by similarity which was superadded to the affective factor.

appearance of each element is the effect of a conjunction of causes any one of which seems competent to produce the effect. Freud speaks of over-determination chiefly in the case of images resulting from a multiple condensation, and when each feature of the image is the climax of a "chain of thoughts." But enough attention has not been given to the fact that another form of over-determination is that in which condensation and simple association are simultaneously at work. We may express the matter thus:

1. *Among various images susceptible of association by contiguity or by similarity, those which have a common feeling tone will most readily become associated;*

2. *Among various images susceptible of association in virtue of their common feeling tone, those which are also susceptible of association by contiguity or by similarity will most readily become associated.*

This I believe to be the real reason why the associationists have overlooked the point. The images or ideas linked by a common affect were already linked, it seemed, by the ordinary laws of association. Content with the explanation of the association by similarity or by contiguity, the associationists did not realise that there was any need to look farther afield.

Let me give examples from dreams of my own which will serve to elucidate this type of over-determination.

In a dream I see a drawing of Christ's head, with a crown of thorns that resembles a staircase, which is called "automatism." When the picture is turned, it represents the head of Louis XVI and also the death-mask of Pascal.

Here we have a medium degree of condensation, for the different images of Christ, Pascal, and Louis XVI, which make up the composition, are still distinguishable. All three of them died in their prime, and all were persons of mark (a god, a genius or a saint, and a king). The death-mask of Pascal was one which I had drawn when I was sixteen, and had hung on the wall of my room. Analysis of the dream shows me that it concerns an "ego" which no longer exists. It concerns the ardent idealism of youth; above all it concerns the religious faith of childhood, and childhood reaches its critical term at sixteen. The condensation of the three images is obvious, but it is also clear that there are simple associations between them. The link between Christ and Pascal is closer than the other links, for this death-mask which I had drawn in former days was framed in some of Pascal's thoughts, and one of these was: "Christ's passion will endure till the end of the world; we must not sleep as long as it lasts." The number 16 forms the link between Louis XVI and the drawing of Pascal, which I had made when sixteen years old.

The crown of thorns, which is a staircase, and which is called automatism, is the outcome of a more vigorous condensation. The analysis discloses in it a number of elements. The affect which unites them is the sense of oppression by the "automatism of life." But this automatism is itself a compound. First of all, it is the mechanism of nature, of which when I was sixteen science had given me the idea and the feeling; and this realisation of mechanism in nature had initiated my loss of the old faith. Secondly, the automatism is the distressing monotony of daily life. (The staircase was called up by a real staircase of three hundred steps, like the days of the year; and in addition by Laforgue's verse, "What a dreadfully daily thing life is!")[1] Thirdly, the automatism is *L'automatisme psychologique* by Pierre Janet, which had been one of the first books to turn my attention towards psychology; and at the time of my dream I was engaged in psychological study and was suffering from overwork. There were additional elements in this condensation besides the three I have named. But here likewise it is easy to detect the ordinary associations between these elements. In this respect the name of Janet's book is typical. The book had been brought into the matter both by its title (simple association) and by its significance in my life (condensation). Another association, quite superficial, linked the book to the staircase of three hundred steps. This staircase was known by the expressive name of Tire-Jarret [the calf-puller], and in recording another dream in which the staircase had appeared to me I had, by a slip of the pen, written the name Tire-Janet. Superficial associations like this have been freely noted in dreams by other authors before the days of Freud. Not only do they exist, but they exist as between images which may also be linked by some deep feeling. This

[1] "Ah que la vie est quotidienne!"

is why Freud declares that an indifferent trait common to the beings who, in a dream, combine to form a composite personality (*Mischperson*) masks the existence, between these same beings, of a significant trait, common to them, but repressed. More generally,[1] he declares that behind every superficial association (of shape, colour, assonance, etc.) there is hidden a deep association between the same elements. As the outcome of repression, he contends, there has been a displacement of the deep association towards the superficial association.[2] I do not think that the supposition of repression and displacement is always necessary in these cases; but the coexistence of the superficial tie and the deep (affective) tie is of frequent occurrence. Associationism takes note only of the superficial tie. An associationist would have detected the superficial ties in the foregoing dream, but he would never have suspected that the dream gave expression to regrets for the regal and divine life of youth, and to protests against the mechanisation of real life, against the overwork and the monotony of the daily round.

Here is another example, also taken from a dream of my own. At first sight the associations seem purely superficial, this time of an auditory character.

I awake remembering some fragments of a dream in which I have been guided somewhere by a person who was like "Monsieur Laederach." In real life this gentleman had played a part in a lawsuit in which I had had to defend my ideas upon suggestion, which, it seemed, had been regarded as revolutionary. An obsolete law against magic had been invoked by the prosecution! The affair had turned out all right in the end, but had been very troublesome to begin with. In the half-consciousness of waking I attempt to analyse my dream, but first of all, beneath the name Laederach I hear, as if in harmonics, the words "Leider-ach, Umfrid, Unrat, Henrath." Are these merely superficial associations? The strange thing is that the closest auditory association is between the first and the last words of the series, between Laederach and Henrath. It seems to me as if Unrat had been called up by Henrath, and Umfrid by Unrat. At the moment of waking, I follow the sequence *in the reverse order*. When I have found Henrath, it seems to me (I was not sure at the time, but I

[1] Freud, Die Traumdeutung, p. 239. [2] Ibid., p. 418.

was able to verify the supposition afterwards) that this had been the name of a man who, when I was quite young, had acted as my guide in a foreign town, and who had cheated me extensively. The happenings in this town constituted my first experiences of serious action on my own initiative; indeed they represented one of the crises of my life, my first vigorous attempt to shake off the dominance of environment, my first affirmation of my own ideas—an affirmation whose outcome was that I was cast off by some of the persons most dear to me. (I then perceive that the guide, Laederach, of my dream had been condensed with Henrath both as regards personality and name.) But my dream has contained a word-play on the name of Henrath, for the last syllable of this name, Rat, means in German "adviser," a term which can well be used to denote a guide. I disparage him by calling him Unrat, for I interpret this as meaning "evil counsellor," before I recall that it really signifies "filth." But "Laederach" is also "evil counsellor," which I express quite simply by breaking up his name into the two German words Leider! Ach! (Alack! Alas!). The deep affective tie marked by the superficial associations begins to become apparent. The word Umfrid, less intimately linked to the others on the surface, gives fuller expression to the deeper ties. Its signification in my mind is "the opposite of peace," just as Unrat signifies "the opposite of good counsel." Umfrid is also the name of a German pastor distinguished during the war for the courage with which he championed pacifist views, a course of action which led to his persecution. Now the ideas which, at the time when I had been acquainted with the guide Henrath, had cost me some of the dearest friendships of youth, had also been social ideas of a pacifist character, and I had bitterly reflected that one who desires peace begins by sowing strife in the minds of those around him. (Here we have a reminiscence from the Gospels: "Think not that I am come to send peace on earth: I came not to send peace, but a sword. For I am come to set a man at variance against his father, and the daughter against her mother.") A similar reflection, less bitter and more ironical, had crossed my mind when I had seen how my ideas concerning suggestion, which were benevolent and were unquestionably pacific, had involved me in a fight. The affect which had linked the four words dominated the entire dream. It was a call for the courage of self-affirmation; for the courage that is needed to emerge from a somewhat pusillanimous quietism; to confront life, in spite of all the filth (Unrat), all the distresses (Leider! Ach!), and all the struggles (Umfrid), which one has to encounter during the active realisation of an idea.

The analysis shows the complexity of such a condensation. Beyond question, this word is an extremely general and imperfect label for a number of phenomena which must be studied more closely. The state which gives rise to a condensation is in most cases something much more than a simple emotion; it is an *affective thought*, one with very definite shades, and each shade (Unrat, Leider-ach, Umfrid) has to secure its own expression in one of the elements of the condensation. In fact, we have a regular network of ideas and images interconnected in multiform ways.

DISPLACEMENT (*Verschiebung*) is in point of form a simpler and more obvious phenomenon than condensation, though in essence it is perhaps more remarkable. We have previously pointed out that it is of the same nature as what Ribot terms transference, but more comprehensive. The displacement with which we are concerned is a displacement of the affect or affective stress, a displacement in virtue of which the feeling or emotion is more or less completely detached from its real object in order to become attached to another object. It might be spoken of as a transference attended by forgetfulness, complete or partial, of the point of departure. Ribot referred to the way in which reverence for the person of the monarch may be transferred to the throne, to the insignia of power. Sometimes the starting-point is entirely forgotten, as when the worship of a relic is not superadded to but substituted for the worship of a saint. Religious ritual and national custom abound in examples of such substitutions. They are by no means uncommon in individual life. Our apparently irrational preference for certain flowers, or for certain colours, frequently depends on the fact that very early in life these flowers or colours became associated in our minds with the personality of someone to whom we were deeply attached, but whom we have now forgotten. Unreasonable fears have, in many cases, a like origin. Displacements of the same character, but transient, occur from moment to moment in dreams. In the child Linette (pp. 120, 121, dreams I, II, and III), we observe certain elementary displacements, some occurring in the waking state and some in dreams. In especial, a little nigger doll filches the feeling which had been attached to a black kitten. Again, a large, white, and straight-limbed doll takes the place of the nigger doll, which is small, black, and seated like a child in a bath. In the latter case we have a displacement which is the sequel of an association by contrast.

It might seem at first sight as if displacement were merely the extreme degree of transference, but I think we should be wrong to define displacement thus. *Displacement may occur without transference.* I wish to emphasise this point, which is often overlooked, for its recognition will enable us presently to effect a more comprehensive synthesis.

Displacement of affective stress may occur within the limits of a condensation. In a dream we may condense, into an integer, objects to which we have reacted in similar fashion, although these reactions may have differed greatly in intensity. We condense the starting on a railway journey with an anticipated change in our mode of life. Or we condense an examination we had to pass in early youth with some trial we are undergoing in our adult life, and perhaps we add to the condensation a real feeling of physical distress from which we are suffering during sleep.[1] Or we may condense a pleasure of the table with an erotic pleasure. All these condensations are achieved because the elements are associated by a common affect. We cannot in their case speak of transference (in Ribot's sense), for transference is the extension of an affective state to images with which it was not previously associated, whereas here the various images are already stamped with the same affect. There is no place for transference; but the field is open for a displacement of affective stress. Such condensations are composed of elements of varying importance; now, in the dream, the most important element may become secondary, and an element of minor importance may assume the leading role. When dreaming of an examination, for example, we may cease to think of the matter which is

[1] During sleep, such a sensation, having no links with an external cause, functions much as if it were an image.

troubling us in our waking life; we believe that we have merely been dreaming of this examination of long anterior date, and we are astonished because it seemed so important to us in our dream.

We are led, therefore, to distinguish two forms of displacement:

1. In a condensation, the secondary element of the condensation may become the principal element;

2. In a transference, the secondary element (that to which the affect is transferred) may become the principal element.

We may therefore define displacement as follows:

Given an integration of representative elements TINGED WITH THE SAME AFFECTIVE SHADE WHETHER BY CONDENSATION OR BY TRANSFERENCE, *displacement is the work which tends to detach the feeling or emotion from its principal object in order to attach it to secondary objects.*

But this distinction between two forms of displacement will enable us, upon another foundation, to effect a new synthesis. It seems to me that even in displacement by transference there is a certain amount of condensation. In a dream in which such a displacement occurs, the new object of the feeling is no longer quite what it was before. Something that belonged to the primary object of the feeling appears to be transferred to the new object; certain elements of the old object have, as it were, passed over in company with the affect. The subject Renée, who is pregnant, has a dream (p. 213, dream III). In this dream, the womb from which her child will come takes the form of the door (*portière*) of a railway compartment (displacement as a sequel of association by similarity): but the door is not an ordinary door; it is very heavy, and she has to carry it (*porter*—perhaps there is a verbal link here between *porter* and *portière*), it is almost too much for her. The door, that is to say, is endowed with some of the traits belonging to the object which it typifies, and it has therefore become the condensation of two objects. We might say that when an affective state is transferred from one object to another, there is then realised, as between these two objects, that tinging by a common affect which mades condensation possible. Consequently, although transference appeared to us substantially the opposite of condensation, we have now to recognise that transference itself involves a certain measure of condensation. Nor need this surprise us when, following Freud, we have learned that the most superficial associations, the associations which transference makes use of, serve as a rule to mask deep, affective associations, which are the germ of condensation.

In practice, henceforward, we shall regard every displacement of stress as belonging to the first category, and as taking place between condensed elements which are of unequal importance.

This displacement of stress is conspicuous in most nightmares. On awaking we feel it was absurd that we had been so terribly frightened by some object which was hardly important enough to arouse alarm. The reason for the alarm was that we had displaced to this harmless object the affective stress properly attaching to some real cause of distress. Our thought had been deformed, much as a word is deformed by stressing a syllable which ought not to be stressed. One of my subjects dreamed of being attacked by a yellow dog. This dream was founded upon the reminiscence of an attack actually made by a dog during childhood, but the peculiar yellow colour of the dream dog was the colour of the waistcoat of a doctor who had recently attended the patient. Condensation had been effected, so that the attack by the dog had been fused with the attack by the doctor (the patient's dread of the medical treatment). But, in the dream, the recent cause of distress was almost hidden in the image of the dog which had been the old cause of trouble. The subject Yvonne (p. 210), who is pregnant, falls asleep obsessed with the fear that the birth of her baby will take place on a Sunday, and that she will not be able to get a doctor. She dreams that the stove-pipe is blocked, that it is Sunday, and that no chimney-sweep is to be had. Sometimes the main object of the emotion, the matter with which the subject is chiefly preoccupied, is entirely effaced, thrust down into the subconscious; what should have been the stressed word or stressed syllable remains unuttered.

Displacement, like condensation, may be fugitive or persistent. We have said that transient displacement is frequent in dreams. The symptoms of neurosis, on the other hand, are the outcome of fixed displacements. For example, the object of an intense desire is associated or condensed with a particular morbid bodily state; the desire is displaced upon the morbid bodily state, which the subject then realises (autosuggestion reinforced by the desire [1]) in a stereotyped form, as a tic (habit-spasm, etc.), a neuralgia, a contracture, or a paralysis. The subject Germaine (p. 247) has a spasm of the eyelid which symbolises, for her, marriage and enfranchisement from maternal authority. The subject Bertha inflicts upon herself a neuralgia which symbolises enfranchisement from her present environment and access to a freer and more intellectual life (p. 256). Slips of memory, " mistakes due to absent-mindedness," etc., may be explained in the same way as the tics or the neuralgias. They are all examples of displacement translated into action.

Reference was made above to persistent and intricate condensations, dating perhaps from early childhood, and buried more or less deeply in the subconscious. Such condensations are almost always accompanied by displacements. The displacements lead to thoughts and actions, which the subject misinterprets, being ignorant of their true origin. The name *complex*, which as generally used in psychoanalytical literature lacks precise definition, may be applied to such subconscious condensations accompanied by displacements. The subject Otto (p. 185) hates singing when the singer is a man ; he is clean-shaven, and he imagines it is for æsthetic reasons that he wants no hair on his face ; bellicose sentiments revolt him, and he believes that this aversion is conditioned by purely philosophical reasons ; he is retiring and awkward in ordinary life : these are all manifestations of a complex of *protest against the father and of refusal of virility*, which is subconscious, but which the analysis brings to the surface and disentangles.

Acquired tendencies are in large measure determined by complexes ; the character is moulded by them ; they masquerade as inborn traits.

We are now in a position to summarise the chief laws of affective association.

1. *Evocation* (Claparède) or *affective association*. Two ideas tinged with the same emotion or feeling tend to call one another up mutually.

2. *Condensation* (in Freud's terminology, *Verdichtung*).

[1] In this autosuggestion, desire plays the role of auxiliary emotion.—See Baudouin, Suggestion and Autosuggestion, p. 114.

This resembles evocation, but the ideas (images) are fused instead of being merely associated. Condensation is an extreme form of affective association. We pass from simple evocation to condensation by insensible gradations (weak condensations, composite images).

3. *Transference* (Ribot). The emotion or the feeling attached to an object (or idea) is extended to the objects (or ideas) associated therewith in accordance with the ordinary laws of association (contiguity, similarity, sometimes contrast).

4. *Displacement* (in Freud's terminology, *Verschiebung*) Given an integration of representative elements tinged with the same affective shade (whether by condensation or by transference), but unequal in importance; displacement is the work which tends to detach the feeling or emotion from its principal object in order to attach it to secondary objects.

5. *Over-determination.*[1] The elements which are associated (condensed) in virtue of their being tinged with a common affect, are usually associated as well in virtue of the objective laws of association (contiguity, similarity, contrast).

We see that these new (affective) laws, far from claiming to replace the old (objective) laws of the associationists, are continually invoking the aid of the old laws. The earlier experimental work upon association by no means loses its value; it gains a new value, and calls for fresh experimental work to round it off. Bleuler has understood how much light these experiments upon association can throw "upon the unconscious and upon diagnosis";[2] and C. G. Jung, working on the same lines, has carried on in Zurich extensive and able researches on association, both in normal persons and in persons suffering from mental disorder. Jung considers that in this way he has secured statistical confirmation of Freud's ideas. Errors in the reproduction of associations already made, marked divergences whether by excess or by defect from the average time of association, serve to reveal complexes (*gefühlsbetonte Komplexe*).[3]

[1] We use this term in a more restricted sense than that in which it is used by Freud.

[2] Bleuler, Ueber die Bedeutung von Assoziationsversuchen, p. 6.

[3] C. G. Jung, Psychoanalyse und Assoziationsexperiment, p. 258.—Regarding Jung's experiments upon association time, cf. Régis et Hesnard, op. cit., p. 140.

The foregoing laws apply both to the waking state and to the dream state. Dreams are characterised by a bewildering multiplicity of rapid and rich condensations and of instantaneous displacements.

3. Dreaming and Action

We have said (p. 45) that condensation is more vigorous :

1. In strong affective states than in weak affective states.
2. In dreams than in the waking state.

Can these two propositions be subsumed under one formula ? In other words, have affectivity and dreaming a common element ?

Rignano maintains the paradoxical theory that dreaming is non-affective. We must point out, however, that this author distinguishes between " affect " and " emotion," and that he does not deny the " emotivity " of dreams. If, therefore, we had to accept his view that there are no feelings [*sentiments*] in dreams, we must nevertheless realise that, in dreams, feelings exist in a latent form. These latent feelings would be competent to explain the condensations (just as, in an association by similarity, the consciousness of a similarity of low degree may not be apparent to the mind). However this may be, what Rignano writes about dreams is the weak point in his admirable theory concerning the affectivity of the intellectual life. This theory would gain in strength and unity if it were generalised so as to apply to the representative life as a whole, and especially to the life of dreams.[1] Frank introspection, and psychoanalysis which is an introspection induced by the analyst, are continually giving evidence that the substratum of dreams is strongly affective.[2]

Conversely, affective states in the waking life are imaginative states and tend to induce reverie. Affectivity and imagination run in couples. The poet's liveliest images are dictated by intense emotion. These are familiar facts ; but the analysis of condensations renders our knowledge of them more precise. *Vigorous condensation, the outcome of a strong affect, is the preeminent characteristic of creative imagination.* Affectivity influences association much as heat influences

[1] Baudouin, The affective Basis of Intelligence.

[2] So that Freud defines a dream as an imaginary wish fulfilment.

certain mechanical mixtures, changing the mechanical mixture into a chemical compound. Perhaps we are wrong in using the term creative *imagination* ; it is the *affect* (conscious or subconscious) which is the creator, and which synthetises the images into new unities.

All this, however, was implicit in the psychology of condensation. What we must discover is whether there exists any other likeness between the affective state and the dream state, which may serve as a support to condensation. The main likeness would seem to be that neither of them is active. Doubtless affectivity precedes and guides action ; we may even say that this is its biological function ; but it *discharges* itself into the action and loses itself therein. Hunger is an affective sensation which incites to the act of eating, but disappears in proportion as hunger is satisfied by eating. If the affective state is to be maintained, the primary essential is that it should not be completely discharged in action. "Possession is the death of love," said one of my subjects. Thus we may contrast "affectives" with "actives." Now it is when activity is maintained in such a fashion, i.e. when the discharge of affect into action is incomplete, that it is accompanied by imaginative production, reverie, condensation. Imagination, dreaming (in the sense of reverie), thus manifest themselves as substitutes for unrealised action ; they presuppose a surcharge of affect, a surplus of undischarged affect. During sleep we have analogous conditions ; sleep is characterised by the suspension of motor activity. It is then that we have dreams, which are nothing but pent-up activity.

Freud's concept of *regression* [1] comprises a number of diverse phenomena, such as an imaginative return to scenes of infancy, the translation of abstract thought into images, etc. But, essentially, regression is what we have just been describing : the suspension of motor reactions ; and the phenomenon whereby the mental stream, pent-up as if by a dam, undergoes a reflux into imagination and dreams. The Freudian idea of regression is challengeable for the very reason that it is too comprehensive, embracing phenomena which, though they are linked, are preferably distinguished ; nevertheless, through the Freudian concept of regression our attention has been drawn to the affiliation of the phenomena in

[1] Freud, Die Traumdeutung, pp. 427 et seq.

question. What Freud speaks of as "regression" has traits in common with what Jung terms "introversion," with what Pierre Janet[1] describes as a relaxation of the "function of the real" and as "derivation," and with what Bergson refers to as "inattention to the present life."

We should be wrong to consider regression as necessarily morbid. When we study the matter from the medical side we are sometimes compelled to do so, for we then have to deal with unmistakably morbid regressions, such as the neuroses. This reflection justifies the gradations established by Janet among psychological phenomena. He writes: "If this fixing of gradations is to be genuinely interesting and useful, we must formulate them, not from the outlook of our artistic or moral preferences but from the outlook of life, health, and illness."[2] The purely psychological outlook is different, and Bergson is careful to avoid implying that what he calls "inattention to the present life" is necessarily morbid; for this inattention, this temporary detachment from useful action and practical life is what renders possible the development of the spiritual life. The defect of the term "regression" is that it has disparaging connotations. If we continue to use it, we must detach it from such ideas. Motor activity is doubtless the normal way of reacting to impressions, but we must not therefore infer that the suspension of motor activity is morbid or in any sense "inferior." Were this conclusion true, uncontrolled reflex action would be the standard of normality. But the whole of mental development is founded upon suspensions of motor activity. Inhibition, the activity which does not take the form of immediate action, but is "pent up," determines the passage from reflex action to instinct; it determines the appearance of consciousness, whose specialty seems to be the storing up of possible reactions, the forming of combinations between them, and the choosing from among them, instead of allowing them to discharge invariably and mechanically along the same path (reflex action). Consciousness is an accumulator and a commutator. May it not be that states of vigorous condensation are the same things to an even higher degree, since they give rise to creative imagination? Even from the outlook of action we must not underestimate dreams. The dam whereby for a brief

[1] Janet, Les obsessions et la psychasthénie, vol. i. [2] Ibid., p. 477.

space the mental stream is pent up may serve to give us, as it were, a head of water, so that the accumulated energy may in the end find vent in a more effective discharge.

From the new outlook we have reached through the study of condensation, all the psychology of perception and of dreams needs revision. I cannot now discuss the matter, and I merely point it out. Obviously we have here an extensive and fresh field for investigation.

In a lecture delivered in 1901 Bergson [1] sketched a noteworthy theory of dreams, which he now regards as capable of being rounded off by Freud's theory.[2] Bergson insisted on the part played by the sleeper's sensations in the elaboration of the dream (retinal patches or "phosphenes," noises from without, kinæsthetic sensations); but his original contribution is the way in which he shows how these sensations call up a number of memories, and give body to them, to constitute the dream. A retinal sensation of a green patch with white points may successively or simultaneously become a field with sheep on it or a billiard table with its balls. This has analogies with condensation; but in addition to the combination of images one with another, there is a combination of images with sensations. We might add that this latter combination, just like condensation, is established upon the effective foundation which is supplied from moment to moment by the sensations of the sleeper, and especially by his kinæsthetic sensations. But Bergson shows that man's mode of perception in the waking state does not, in this respect, differ from his mode of perception in dreams.[3] In both cases, perception is a combination of crude sensation and of memory. We know that when we are reading we do not really perceive all the letters; we project our memories to fill out sketchy perceptions; and the actual perception is a result of the amalgam; our perception has in it hallucinatory elements. The difference between (waking) perception and a dream is that in the former the memories which are superadded to the sensation are carefully selected with an eye to utility and possible action, whereas in the dream no such selection takes

[1] Bergson, L'énergie spirituelle, pp. 91 et seq.
[2] Ibid., p. 114, note.
[3] Bergson, Matière et mémoire, passim.

place. Both in perception, then, and in the dream, a process of combination occurs which reminds us of condensation, and which, like condensation, presupposes an affective basis.

But the affectivity which underlies the combination known as "perception" is essentially useful in character. It may be the outcome of the duplex affective state (interest, dread of making a mistake) which, according to Rignano, lies at the basis of attention.[1] On the other hand, the affectivity which underlies the dream is disinterested; and it is precisely this "disinterest" which, according to both Bergson and Claparède, characterises sleep. If the disinterest were complete, we should arrive at Rignano's theory of non-affectivity; but it seems better to insist that the suspension of interest relates essentially to interest in useful action.

The theory of perception and of dreaming will be elucidated by a careful study of hallucination. Condensations occur in hallucinations, just as they occur in dreams; and the condensations of the former can be analysed in the same way as the condensations of the latter; furthermore, a well-marked affective state is dominant in hallucination. Mourgue, in a detailed work on hallucination, attaches considerable importance to the idea of Leuret, of Tours, who speaks of "twilit states"; Leuret declares that "there are no hallucinations, but only hallucinatory states."[2] But the form of hallucination which is of especial interest in connection with the theory of perception and dreaming is what I have called "hallucination by compromise,"[3] in which the subject makes use of real perceptions and modifies them in the sense of his vision, to which they give a body. Here we have the same phenomenon as that noted by Bergson in the case of dreams (the transformation of the green retinal patch into a meadow or a billiard table). Of course the real sensation calls up the image in virtue of an association by similarity, but there can be no doubt that it likewise calls it up in virtue of an affective association which underlies the condensation. When the real object perceived by the poet spontaneously becomes image and symbol, both these processes are also at work. It is

[1] Rignano, Psychologie du raisonnement, p. 49.

[2] Mourgue, Etude critique sur l'évolution des idées rélatives à la nature des hallucinations vraies.

[3] Baudouin, Suggestion et autosuggestion, pp. 34 et seq.; English translation, pp. 47 et seq.

probable that in every hallucination we could detect such a compromise to a certain extent; it occurs in dreams, and it occurs in perception. According as the nature of the affectivity varies in each case, we find a different form of compromise.

Dream states have been contrasted with states of attention. It has been said that attention is a restriction of the field of consciousness, whereas dreaming (and reverie) are an expansion thereof. This is true. But we learn something more when we agree with Bergson that the restriction of the field of consciousness is mainly the outcome of the requirements of useful action. As for Freud, he helps us to specify under what form the expansion of consciousness occurs in dreams and states of imagination; preeminently, this form is a condensation consisting of multiple elements. Experience shows further that dream states and states of imagination are states of "outcropping" of the subconscious.[1] We may also say, states of *symbolism*, in which affectivity, predominantly subconscious, is constantly undergoing translation into images.

If the dream is a suspension of the active faculties, and if logical and rational thought is essentially directed towards action, it need not surprise us to find that when we dream we "think in images" like the great poets. We can also understand why Freud makes thinking in images one of the characteristics of what he terms "regression." In especial, he shows, how even logical relationships appear in dreams as imagery—a simple succession, for example, representing causality.[2] But the symbolism of dreams is mainly the subjective expression of affectivity. Freud seems to reserve the name of "symbol" for the collective symbols that are the outcome of associations which are deeply embedded in the psyche of the race. This is why he says that "the task of the analyst is not rendered easier but more difficult by the existence of symbols in dreams. The technique of interpretation by the free associations of the dreamer is not usually valid for symbolic elements."[3] But the significance of the term symbol speedily became enlarged in psychoanalysis. It

[1] Baudouin, Suggestion et autosuggestion, pp. 106 et seq.; English translation, pp. 128 et seq.

[2] Freud, Die Traumdeutung, pp. 236 et seq.

[3] Ibid., p. 261.

is proper to admit that a *symbol* is the natural outcome of the interaction of the laws of condensation and displacement. In a condensation, the various images condensed through the instrumentality of one affective thought, are symbolic of that thought; in a displacement, the accessory who or which has taken the stress, is symbolic of the principal who or which has forfeited it. In a dream of my own recorded on pp. 46 et seq., the heads of Christ, Pascal, and Louis XVI symbolised a mental state of regret for the days of adolescence; the crown of thorns which was like a staircase symbolised the feeling of oppression produced by the automatism of life. In Yvonne's dream (p. 210), the chimney-sweep symbolised the accoucheur. When we understand the laws of condensation and displacement, the symbolism of dreams and states of imagination is no longer mysterious. Collective symbols do not differ in their nature; they merely presuppose that the condensations and displacements on which they depend are such as occur in a very large number of minds (or, perhaps, that they have been hereditarily transmitted in accordance with Darwin's opinion concerning the inheritance of associations). Furthermore, if it is true (as Freud maintains) that the free associations of the subject are hardly applicable in explanation of these collective symbols, the interpretation of the latter requires extreme discretion, for it is by the associations which occur in our subject that we are enabled to interpret the symbolism of his dreams without interpolating our own fantasies.

I do not propose to give details here concerning the technique of such an interpretation. I consider that this technique is essentially based upon the difference between vigorous condensation and weak condensation. If we ask a subject in the waking state to follow the thread of the associations of ideas which come to him apropos of his dream, we secure what is tantamount to a decondensation of the dream. The elements which had become subconscious owing to a vigorous displacement, likewise reappear in these associations. It now becomes possible to see in what sense the various associations must be understood in order to form a logical whole.

Freud has been greatly struck by displacements of affective stress, and this strange phenomenon of a transposition of values was certainly calculated to rivet the attention. Nevertheless it would be an exaggeration to say that every dream is substantially built up upon such transpositions. We shall do well to remember that condensation, not displacement, is the primary law of dreams; that condensation is invariable in dreams; that displacement itself occurs within condensations; and finally that condensation, quite apart from displacement, is theoretically adequate to produce symbolisation. Freud has himself noted the "plurality of the meanings of the dream";[1] and Pfister writes, "symbols are inexhaustible."[2] This multiplicity is the outcome of condensation. In the case of dreams no less than in the case of poems we should be wrong to represent the symbol as an integer consisting of only two terms. This is true of an allegory, coldly and deliberately constructed by a sterile imagination. But the symbol is essentially manifold; it is a note rich in overtones, and on this depends its power of calling up associations. Through the working of displacement, one or other overtone may be reinforced at the cost of the fundamental tone. But we must never lose sight of the integer; and, in fact, is there in this integer a tone which, objectively regarded, is fundamental? The greater or less importance assigned to this or that element is a judgment of value, and our judgments of value are determined by our outlook. This is why several alternative interpretations of a dream are possible, and why they are not mutually exclusive.

Let me give another example from one of my own dreams. I dream of a mummy who is King Charles X, and who holds a pen in his hand without being able to write. The wall crumbles into dust which falls on the mummy's sleeve, and he shakes his arm to get rid of the dust. I wake in a fright, to find that my head is lying awkwardly on my right arm, which is "dead," and in which I feel "pins and needles." In the half-waking state these pins and needles seem to me identical with the dust which I have just seen falling upon the mummy's sleeve, and I *see* each pinprick as if it were a grain of dust. The sensation which has served as the point

[1] Freud, Die Traumdeutung, pp. 208, 254.

[2] Pfister, Was bietet die Psychanalyse dem Erzieher, p. 84; French translation, p. 147; English translation, p. 126. (In the English version, "symbols" is misprinted "symptoms").

of departure of the dream is obvious, and we are entitled to suppose that the dream symbolises the sensation. On the other hand, this sensation has entered into a compromise with deeply submerged psychic elements. I need not give all the details of the analysis, but it is not difficult to recognise in my dream the same complex as that which underlay the dream of the three heads recorded on pp. 46 et seq. (Obvious is the association between Louis XVI and Charles X; the mummy of my dream was the reminiscence of a real mummy I had seen when I was fifteen years old, and its figure was such as I must have had at that age.) We are therefore justified in assuming that the dream about the mummy symbolised the same complex. Which is more "important," the sensation of pins and needles in the arm, or the complex? Manifestly the answer depends upon our outlook. To a physiologist, the former is more important; to a psychologist, the latter. A fortiori, in the complex itself, in which there are several convergent elements (intellectual, religious, æsthetic, political, and sexual), are we entitled to say confidently that one element or another is more "important"?

To me it seems rather that a dream resembles an orchestra. A number of instruments are playing; sometimes one is dominant, sometimes another. At will, the ear can follow the notes of one instrument or another; the importance assigned to any particular instrument remains purely subjective to the auditor. Hence arises the possibility of various interpretations and of very different theories. Probably the sexual basis of dreams, so sturdily envisaged by Freud, is almost invariable; no less invariable, perhaps, is the basis of organic sensations supervening during slumber. But we must never lose sight of the "plurality of the meanings of the dream"; we must never cease to attend to the orchestra as a whole.

CHAPTER THREE

DYNAMICS OF THE AFFECTIVE LIFE, AND THE EVOLUTION OF INSTINCTS

1. The Function of the Dream[1]—Dreaming and Play

WE have been led to the conclusion that dreams, and indeed imaginative activities in general, are symbolical of the affective life, and especially of subconscious affectivity. This symbolism is equivalent to a disguise. But those are inaccurate exponents who declare apriori that the disguise is purposive, and who say: "The function of the dream is to disguise an affective thought; *with that end in view,* the dream employs different processes, notably *condensation,* which amalgamates several images into an irrecognisable blend, and *displacement,* which substitutes one image for another." Phraseology of this kind is permissible in a summary exposition or in a popular essay, when the writer's sole aim is to give a general and striking account of psychoanalysis. It is, however, unsatisfactory from the scientific point of view. We may point out that Freud begins by expounding the laws of condensation and displacement. Not until after that exposition does he consider the disguise which results from condensation and displacement; and this belongs to what we have called the second category of psychoanalysis. Whatever may be the answer given to the question concerning the function of the dream, the structural description of the two laws will be unaffected.

The celebrated Freudian theory of the *censorship* and of *repression* is one answer to the question as to the function of the dream. We may summarise the theory as follows.

[1] Under "dream states" I include reverie in the waking state, poetic creation, etc., as well as dreams during sleep. These last are typical of all the states in question.

Representations and feelings prohibited by prevailing systems of moral and social ideas, and for that reason felt to be shameful and distressing, are automatically forced down into the "unconscious." In dream states, control and "censorship" are relaxed, and part of the repressed content of the unconscious finds its way back to the surface; but the censorship, however sleepy it may be, is still awake, and the repressed content of the mind can only make its appearance in consciousness by "showing a white paw," by disguising itself. This process of disguise, which renders the distressing ideas irrecognisable, and therefore less distressing, may be considered to function as the "guardian of sleep."[1]

The present writer has no wish to depreciate the theory of the "censorship," which has been one of the most valuable contributions of Freudian psychology. The theory was suggested by the study of hysteria; it has helped to elucidate many of the obscurer problems both of this disease and of normal psychology. But the question we have now to consider is whether the theory of the censorship is entitled to take its place as a general explanation of dream states.

Other psychoanalysts have looked at the matter in a different way. Nevertheless, their ideas have been borrowed from Freud, for Freud's outlooks, cursory sometimes but unquestionably those of a man of genius, have sweepingly and vigorously embraced most of the aspects of the problem. In general, therefore, the modifications that have been made in his theory by other investigators consist merely of a modified dosage of the various elements which Freud himself contributed.

Freud, for instance, drew attention to those constituents of the dream which are not merely infantile, but archaic. Writing of symbols (collective symbols), he says: "That which is to-day linked under the form of the symbol has presumably constituted at the outset a conceptual and verbal unity."[2]

He considers that the thoughts of primitive men display striking analogies with our own dreams, and he includes the idea of this resemblance in his polymorphic concept of "regression." C. G. Jung lays considerable stress upon this archaic aspect of dream states. We dream, he says in sub-

[1] Freud, Die Traumdeutung, pp. 432 et seq., and 446 et seq.
[2] Ibid., p. 261.

stance, as our ancestors thought, and as children think to-day. The conceptions which presided over the languages, laws, and religions of primitive men, reappear in us in the form of dreams.[1] The reappearance of the motifs of ancient myths in the dreams and the deliriums of modern man is a fascinating theme of study.[2]

From this it is but a step to the theory of W. H. R. Rivers, who finds fault with the Freudian "censorship" for its "teleological" character. According to Rivers it is needless to suppose that there occurs in the dream an intentional process of disguise, or one directed towards a biological goal. To understand the dream, he says, we have to accept the view that the mental life consists of superposed stages (respectively corresponding, doubtless, to the successive grades of nerve centres). The uppermost stage, the last storey to have been built, is that of voluntary and rational phenomena. Now, as Ribot[3] and Janet among others have shown, the most recently acquired psychic phenomena are the least stable. According to this view, the dream would represent a suspension of the phenomena of the latest stage (the idea is an old one); consequently—and this is the important point—the dream must necessarily be a return to earlier forms of thought. Hence dreaming is not symbolical in order to achieve a disguise. It is symbolical merely because it is a "regression" to archaic and infantile modes of thought, to modes of thought which are essentially symbolic.[4] This point of view seems to have been generally accepted by British and American psycho-analysts.[5]

The problem of the function of the dream as a means of disguise will become clearer if we subdivide it. The disguise is effected in accordance with the working of the laws of *condensation* and *displacement*; furthermore, condensation and displacement contribute unequally. Condensation simply confuses the issues; the real disguise is the outcome of displacement. If the only phenomena we had had to consider had been those of condensation, it is highly probable that

[1] C. G. Jung, Wandlungen und Symbole der Libido, pp. 7–37; Psychology of the Unconscious, pp. 3–41.

[2] C. Schneiter, Archaische Elemente in den Wahnideen eines Paranoiden.

[3] Cf. Ribot, Les maladies de la personnalité, introduction and conclusion.

[4] Rivers, Freud's Concept of the Censorship.

[5] S. E. Jelliffe and Zenia X. Psychoanalysis and Compulsion Neurosis.

the question of a purposive disguise would never have been raised. On the other hand, the importance which Freud gives to this question arises from the way in which, as previously noted, he has been especially struck by the phenomenon of displacement—for displacement is disconcerting, and is very apt to arouse the impression that it must be the work of a mischievous imp. It behoves us, therefore, to study condensation and displacement separately in this connection.

We have considered *condensation* as the fundamental law of dreams; in general, also, as the acute form of affective association. In the latter respect, the phenomenon is no stranger than simple association by contiguity or similarity. Doubtless, such phenomena could be expressed in the terms of a theory as to their purpose, a functional theory; but it is another question whether we as yet possess the elements upon which an adequate theory of this character could be founded. If, however, we remember that condensation lies at the very base of creative imagination, and that the latter is to some extent a primary condition of all progress, we shall catch a glimpse of the direction in which we may fruitfully look in order to discover the function of condensation. Whereas association by contiguity and association by similarity (objective associations) inform us regarding the fixed elements of external reality and favour our adaptation to that reality, condensation (affective association) enables us to conceive new combinations in conformity with our affective needs and preparatory to actions which will modify external reality so as to adapt it to these needs. We certainly have no longer any right to ignore the "regressive" (archaic and infantile) elements of dream states; but we must be no less careful not to forget that dreams are manifestations of creative imagination. Now creative imagination is what inspires every new action and every discovery. A condensation summarises our affective experience just as a concept summarises our objective experience. Both are essential as concerns our action upon things. In the dream, action is suspended, but it is suspended in order that we may prepare the better for action in the future. The Iliad incites Alexander to conquer the world.

In a word, condensation is the essence of creative imagination, and the function of the latter is easily understood.

The intelligence, we repeat, ensures our adaptation to the real; the imagination ensures the adaptation of the real to ourselves. Of course intelligence may sometimes construct systems of abstractions which lack solid foundation, and imagination may wander into the realm of pure fantasy; in such cases these functions have turned aside from their goal, as any function may turn aside; they are *at play.*

But play is itself an adaptive function. It has been luminously described as such by Karl Groos.[1] Claparède[2] and the modern educational reformers base on the recognition of this the stress they lay upon the role of play in education. If, with such an idea in our minds, we turn to consider the law of *displacement,* we can hardly fail to see that this latter has a similar function.

Claparède has outlined a "play theory" of dreams, comparing them to play as this is understood by Karl Groos. This play would be precisely what we have noted above, an exercise of creative imagination. The notion harmonises with Claparède's general theory of sleep; for Claparède regards sleep as an active process, as an *instinct,* as something with positive functions. He writes: "To some degree, from the biological outlook, dreaming would have a function analogous to that which Groos ascribes to play; its role would be the exercise of certain activities (creative imagination, etc.) which are useful to the species, but which have not always a chance of activity in the individual life."[3]

Claparède further points out that Flournoy noted the same "play character" in the productions of mediums—phenomena which are doubtless akin to dreams.[4] The play theory of the dream has been further elaborated by one of the psychoanalysts of the Jung school, Maeder, who looks upon dreams as a preparation for life. Freud's criticism of this idea[5] does not settle the question for it is based upon a preconceived theory. Freud complains that the elements to which Maeder appeals do not properly belong to the dream

1 Groos, Die Spiele der Tiere, 1896: Die Spiele der Menschen, 1899.

2 Claparède, La psychologie de l'enfant, pp. 430–61; Experimental Pedagogy, pp. 121–38.

3 Claparède, Théorie biologique du sommeil, p. 325.

4 Flournoy, Nouvelles observations sur un cas de somnambulisme, p. 248

5 Freud, Die Traumdeutung, p. 451.

because they are not unconscious; but the question at issue is precisely whether the dream is necessarily the expression of elements thrust down into the unconscious, and disguised. Moreover, whereas the problem remains difficult so long as we contemplate the dream integrally, it is greatly simplified when we confine our attention to the law of displacement.

We cannot fail to be struck by the similarity between displacement in dreams and displacement in play. This perpetual substitution of objects indifferent in themselves for the real objects of interest, this way of representing persons and things by substitutes whose analogy with what they represent is sometimes exceedingly remote, is not this the method of the child at play? For such a child, a stick between the legs becomes a horse; a carpet is the sea; a bundle of rags is a doll. In most cases, the displacement is transitory and not very profound. But the child may at times forget the point of departure, may treat the substitute as if it really were what it represents, may beat a playmate like a real enemy (and perhaps be very sorry for it afterwards). Or a child may mercilessly pull off a butterfly's wings, and when chidden may quietly answer: "But I've only moved it from the air-force into an infantry regiment!"

Need we add that symbolical realisations of desire find their place in play as in dream? A child at play endows itself with attributes which it "dreams" of acquiring.

We shall be told this merely proves that dreams are manifestations of an infantile mode of thought. So be it! We can do no more than apply a corrective to Freud's thesis by emphasising one of Freud's own ideas. What else can one do with this titan of forerunners? It is true that dreams are manifestations of an infantile mode of thought; but *for that very reason* dreams must in certain respects resemble play, and one of the functions of the dream must be closely interconnected with the function of play.

If the dream resembles play in its content, it resembles play likewise in its conditions. Play has long been regarded as a manifestation of surplus energy. Since the publication of Groos's books we have come to realise that the surplus here in question is that of an instinctive tendency which has not yet found (or which in some cases has lost) its true goal; and which is therefore dissipated upon various objects. For such a tendency, play is an outlet and an exercise. In this way, playing with dolls is an outlet and an exercise for the embryonic maternal instinct; chess, and various competitive sports, are outlets for the combative instinct.[1] In our second example, and speaking generally as far as concerns the games of grown-ups, it is more appropriate to speak of an unemployed instinct than of an embryonic instinct. The sports of adults are outlets for unemployed instincts.

Similar considerations apply to dreams. We have recognised the existence in dreams of "pent-up action," that is to say, a tendency which has encountered some obstacle to its free expansion. The dream is an outlet for the tendency (we shall see by and by to what extent the dream may also serve to exercise embryonic tendencies). The difference is that in play the outlet takes the form of subsidiary action; whereas in the dream, action remains imaginary. But in play, imagination participates quite as much as action; and, conversely, a dream may become definitely active and may culminate in somnambulism. Numberless gradations exist. These are plays of imagination. Art, which some theorists compare with play and others with dreaming, is in truth a synthesis of the two.

We thus return by a devious route to Freud's formula that *the dream is the fulfilment of a wish.* Most people are inclined to object that the dream is a manifestation of other emotions besides wishes, including fears. Freud definitely declares that the dream is a *disguised* wish fulfilment. Let us put the matter more cautiously by saying that the dream is a symbolical wish fulfilment, understanding by the term "symbolical" the joint action of the laws of condensation and displacement. This does not imply that a censorship aiming at disguise is necessarily at work. Nevertheless it is certain that, assuming the existence of these laws, the censorship insists upon their being put into operation. In practice, no doubt, there is an element of "disguise" in most dreams.

However there is no need to invoke the idea of disguise to enable us to infer that a dream in which the dreamer feels afraid, a nightmare for example, is at bottom likewise the

[1] Bovet, L'instinct combatif.

expression of a wish. "The dream is the expression of a wish" and "the dream is the expression of the affective life" are substantially identical affirmations. The only difference is that the first formula represents a higher degree of abstraction. Spinoza[1] already looked upon the "wish" as the essence of all the "passions" (that is to say of all the affective states) and modern psychology, following Ribot,[2] has recognised that the *tendency* (of which the *wish* is the primordial manifestation) lies at the very root of the affective life.

Freud admits that in the dream, underlying the conscious wish we may detect in it, there is an unconscious wish whose intensity has been displaced on to the object of the superficial conscious wish. But he adds that the unconscious wishes of which he speaks are "fixed" routes open "once for all" to reactions.[3] Does not this amount to saying that "unconscious wishes" are almost identical with the "tendencies" of the classical psychology? Now it is quite certain that a specific wish can always be regarded as a manifestation of a tendency. Freud would add that the tendencies disclosed in dreams have been *repressed.* This can only be asserted without qualification if we follow Freud in his identification of "repressed" with "censored for moral or social reasons." But the contention becomes strictly logical if we understand by repressed tendency, *thwarted* tendency. The obstacle to free expression may be internal or external: a conflict of tendencies; moral grounds; the absence of the normal object of the tendency; disillusionment; or, furthermore, the physiological impossibility of action (the last category includes the state of sleep itself). It is probable enough that, among these forms of repression, Freudian repression (by censorship) is peculiarly important. But I am sure that we strain the facts, or at least commit ourselves to a needless hypothesis, if we reduce all repression to this form.

The Freudian concept of repression is complex. To begin with, it sometimes implies the repression of an isolated experience, and sometimes that of a tendency. It is certain, however, that the two phenomena are not identical. The

[1] Spinoza, Ethics.
[2] Ribot, La psychologie des sentiments.
[3] Freud, Die Traumdeutung, p. 434, with note on this page.

repression of an experience is a systematic forgetting of the past; that of a tendency constitutes an inhibition for the future. Yet the two phenomena are intimately linked; for a tendency is repressed when a number of experiences relative to this tendency (a number of sexual experiences, for instance) have been systematically repressed. But is this the only way in which repression of a tendency can occur? May there not be repression of a tendency which, from the nature of the case, has never been exercised? Besides, consciousness does not instantly comprehend a tendency as such; it comprehends the isolated experiences which nothing but a complicated process of reflection can subsequently link up to form a single tendency. This means that the moral and social censorship is not competent to bring about the repression of a tendency except in those cases in which the tendency is a sequel of the repression of isolated experiences.

But the concept of repression may be analysed into distinct elements from another point of view. For Freud, a tendency is repressed when it is:

(*a*) thwarted, and
(*b*) thrust down into the "unconscious"[1]
(*c*) by the working of the moral and social censorship.

These three conditions are not perforce invariably linked. As we have just pointed out, a tendency can be thwarted (*a*), by other means than that of the censorship (*c*). It may be thwarted by some external obstacle, through lack of stimulus. This often happens with the tendencies of children (quarrelling, the instinct of the chase, manipulating things) when these tendencies have not been manifested at a suitable moment, etc. Yet in such cases the tendency is thrust down into the subconscious (*b*). On the other hand, a tendency can be thwarted without being for that reason thrust down into the subconscious. Take the very simple instance of hunger which cannot be satisfied, and which becomes all the more insistent. A tendency that is thwarted but not thrust down into the subconscious can induce dreams—dreams in which there seems to be no occasion for disguise. Those who

[1] Baudouin prefers to speak of the "subconscious" rather than the "unconscious"—the term employed by Freud and Bergson. For Baudouin's reasons for this preference, see Suggestion and Autosuggestion, pp. 275–6.—TRANSLATORS' NOTE.

have had to make the best of the very strict diet imposed during convalescence from typhoid, will doubtless remember that, as soon as the appetite began to reassert itself, they dreamed of Gargantuan feasts. Freud himself refers to the occurrence of such straightforward dreams in children, who in the dream frankly satisfy a thwarted wish. Again, the thwarted wish can induce symbolical dreams, without being either thrust down into the "unconscious" or condemned by the censorship. This symbolism has no warrant upon the theory of purposive disguise, since we have to do with a conscious wish. To explain it, Freud is compelled to look below the conscious wish, in search of a deeper wish which is unconscious and "repressed." It would obviously be simpler to regard symbolism in this case as due to the working of laws (condensation, displacement) which always function more or less in dreams, and which do not have the disguising of thought as their essential purpose. We are all the more justified in such a supposition since we believe that we have discovered other functions for these processes.

It seems to me that among the three elements (*a*, *b*, and *c*) which combine to make up the Freudian repression of a tendency, the first (the fact that a tendency is *thwarted* or *imperfectly satisfied*) is sufficient to induce dreams, and even symbolical dreams. Nothing is more likely than that in most cases the two other factors (the forcing down into the subconscious, and censorship) are also at work. Freud, though his theory is not perfectly sound, may well be right in practice. But it is important to distinguish between the various elements of "repression."

The symbol is the natural form of the affective imagination. When the writer of *The Song of Songs* symbolically lauds all the parts of the body of his beloved, he does not disguise the reality of his vision; he does not repress, but gives expression to, what is in his mind. He expresses it symbolically because the symbol is the natural language of strong feeling, of an overpowering tendency. Wherever there is a surcharge of wish, feeling, and emotion, there the dream and the symbol make their appearance. The "surcharge" is the particular variety of repression necessary and sufficient to induce them.

While accepting, therefore, in the main, the Freudian

formula of the dream, we replace the term "wish" by the term "tendency," and the term "repressed" by the term "unsatisfied." *The dream manifests the (symbolical) realisation of an unsatisfied tendency.*[1] It should be added that what is true of the dream is true of "dream states" in general.

Thus the dream has been referred to the tendency, of which it represents the surcharge. But the tendency in its turn is a manifestation of instinct.

2. The Idea of an Evolution of Instinct

For a long time, instinct was dogmatically regarded as immutable. It was, however, a logical development to supplement the theory of the evolution of species by the theory of the evolution of instincts. If one species grows out of another, and if each species has instincts peculiar to itself, the inference is inevitable that instincts undergo transformation. That which theory led us to expect, has been verified by experience, and this affords important additional confirmation of the theory of evolution.

Spalding[2] led the way by showing that certain instincts make their appearance at a definite stage in life. If, during this stage, the instinct is thwarted and is not allowed to manifest itself, it will subsequently fail to appear. The reader will perhaps remember Spalding's experiments on chicks. A chick separated from the hen for the first days of its life does not acquire the instinct of following the hen, and is incapable of acquiring it later. These experiments are in part the foundation of William James' theory of instinct. James formulates what he terms the *law of transitoriness*,[3] to the effect that "many instincts ripen at a certain age and then fade away." Thorndike[4] has generalised this law yet further by contending that every instinct thwarted by circumstances disappears. Better known are examples of instincts which are *transformed* in order to adapt them to new circumstances. Since horses have been introduced into America,

[1] Piéron (*op. cit.*) associates repression ("suppression," according to Rivers) with the general biological phenomenon of inhibition.

[2] Spalding, "Macmillan's Magazine," 1873, vol. xxvii, p. 282–93. Quoted by Romanes, Mental Evolution in Animals, pp. 161–5.

[3] James, The Principles of Psychology, vol. ii., p. 398.

[4] Thorndike, The Elements of Psychology, p. 188.

the American oriole has taken to pulling hairs out of horses' tails to build nests with. Some of Forel's experiments have revealed remarkable inhibitions and transformations of instinct in ants.[1]

What concerns psychology is to discover analogous phenomena in man, and we owe to William James the opening of research in this direction. James showed, not merely that man possesses instincts, but that man has more instincts than any other animal. The old contrast between "intelligence" allotted to man and "instinct" allotted to lower animals, had blinded us, so that the importance of instinct in our own species was hidden from our eyes. As Drever shows,[2] the same prejudice led investigators, even when studying instinct in man, to regard it rather as a physiological than as a psychological phenomenon, to look at it from without instead of from within. Towards intelligence, we incline to take precisely the opposite attitude, a purely psychological one; and not until quite late did psychologists begin to study the physiological conditions of intelligence—being led to this by way of pathology. A study of the psychology of instinct is still more recent.

James drew up a nomenclature of human instincts, and applied to most of them the *law of transitoriness,* whose bearing on the problems of education he was prompt to recognise. If a child does not learn to ride, fish, and shoot at an age when these instincts normally appear, it will be difficult for these sports to be learned later in life, even in the most favourable circumstances. Similarly, there is a special age for the development of the taste for drawing, of that for manual training, of that of collecting. The new pedagogy, the educational method mainly based upon the development of a child's natural interests, owes a great part of its success to this principle, for the child's spontaneous interest reveals an instinctive need.[3]

While recognising that instincts can be suppressed, we have also recognised that they can be *transformed.* It was important to detect the latter phenomenon in man as well

[1] Forel, Les fourmis de la Suisse, 1874.—The observations are summarised by Romain Rolland in The Forerunners, pp. 175–84.
[2] Drever, Instinct in Man, 1917, pp. 88 et seq.
[3] James, Talks to Teachers, 1899.

as in animals. Above all it was important to discover a tie between the suppression of instincts and their transformation. Such a tie was discovered by Freud. Bovet writes: "Two men, one fifteen years later than the other, have achieved a complete change in the current psychological views of instinct. . . . James gives the name of instinct to certain very precise reactions in animals. . . . Freud, when he speaks of the sexual instinct, envisages a group of phenomena which are similar to those of which James speaks, but far more intricate. His theories carry matters considerably further, but they do not conflict with the theories of James."[1]

Freud has studied various transformations of the sexual instinct.[2] He was first led to regard this instinct as made up of a number of secondary tendencies (auto-erotism, homosexuality, algolagnia or sado-masochism, inspectionism and exhibitionism, etc.) These exist to some extent even in normal persons, grouped around the main tendency, sexuality properly so called. When the main tendency is repressed, the instinct is derivatively applied to one or more of the secondary components, and a *perversion* ensues. We are far too apt to regard perversions as physiological and congenital. Psycho-analysis usually shows that they are psychological and acquired; in these cases, the analysis cures them.[3] But in many instances the perverse tendency is repressed in its turn; it may become entirely unconscious, and show itself only in dreams. Then the instinct seeks new derivatives. *Neurosis* is one of these. Freud looks upon every neurosis as derivative, as the outcome of the refusal of a specific perversion; hence the formula "a neurosis is the negative of a perversion." But derivation may also occur in a moral, intellectual, æsthetic, or religious direction. This is what Freud speaks of as *sublimation*—a successful and beneficent derivation. I do not agree with Freud in all the details of his theory, but the occurrence of derivation is a fact.

The more remote the object upon which the derivation is effected from the object towards which the instinct was primarily directed, the more questionable the interpretation may seem. A clearer formulation is therefore requisite for the

[1] Bovet, L'instinct combatif, p. 107.
[2] Freud, Drei Abhandlungen zur Sexualtheorie, 1905.
[3] For a typical example, see Freud, Ueber die Psychogenese eines Falles von weiblicher Homosexualität, 1920.

principle of the method in accordance with which we deduce the existence of such transformations. I incline to formulate this principle as follows.

When we were speaking of a single affect common to all the elements of a condensation, and functioning as the cause of that condensation, the phrase was schematical. Two different objects cannot arouse one and the same affective state; they can merely arouse analogous affective states. It is the likeness of the affects which gives rise to the condensation. We find that condensations are effected as concerns *objects whose affective colourations seem entirely unrelated* (for example a crude sexual desire and a purely æsthetic sentiment). Such a condensation becomes comprehensible if we assume that the two affective states have, unknown to the subject, a common biological parentage. In the case just mentioned, where we are concerned with a crudely instinctive tendency and with a higher tendency, it is only on the evolutionary plane that we can conceive the two states to have a common biological parentage. The hypothesis of such a common parentage is verified:

1. When the history of the subject proves that the development of the second tendency is a sequel to the total or partial suppression of the first;

2. When the same condensation and the same historical development occur in a great many subjects (this item of evidence is even more convincing than number one).

The principle is often implicit in the reasoning of psychoanalysts, but it is advantageous to consider it explicitly. By its light we are repeatedly able to verify many of the views advanced by Freud concerning transformations of the sexual instinct in the human psyche.

We see, then, that the essential phenomena of the suppression and transformation of instinct (whose recognition has led to the overthrow of the time-worn dogma that instinct is immutable) are witnessed in man as well as in the lower animals; and we see that in man the transformations of instinct are remarkably numerous and plastic. Moreover, we have detected a tie between the two phenomena. The suppression of an instinct is apparent merely; and suppression is the preeminent cause of transformation. A transformed instinct is, before all, a thwarted instinct.

We are now in a position to understand the services which the study of instinct, long disdained by psychology, is called upon to render to that science. Instinct has a psychological aspect; and we are continually encountering instinct in the affective life, of which it is a permanent element. The psychological importance of instinct depends upon the phenomena of the transformation of instinct. Owing to these transformations, instinct is often at work in matters with which at first sight it seems to have no concern.

The psychological phenomenon whose affiliation to instinct was first grasped was *emotion.* William James writes:[1] "Every object that excites an instinct excites an emotion as well." When he comes to deal with such phenomena as fear, etc., he is in doubt whether they should be classed among emotions or among instincts. The peripheral theory of the emotions,[2] supported by James, is closely connected with this identification of emotion and instinct. Inasmuch as a system of motor reactions underlies instinct, it is reasonable to enquire whether the motor reactions are not the self-sufficing cause of the emotion.

From this outlook, emotion has been regarded as the "psychological aspect" or "affective aspect" of instinct. Such is the formula employed by McDougall. According to McDougall, the emotion of *fear* is the psychological translation of the instinct of flight.[3] This view has been criticised by Thorndike, who would prefer to restrict the term "pure instincts" to denote "specific responses to specific situations,"[4] without any bearing upon possible emotional accompaniments. Thorndike's position is hardly tenable, and Drever[5] has categorically reasserted the thesis of James and McDougall. Larguier des Bancels will not consent to regard emotion as the psychological aspect of instinct; he says that emotion is "instinct which has gone wrong."[6] He gives the following example: "We obey an instinct when we get out of the way of a carriage on hearing the sound of its approach. We are

[1] James, The Principles of Psychology, vol. ii. p. 442.
[2] Cf. Baudouin, Suggestion et autosuggestion, pp. 47–51; English translation, pp. 61–66.
[3] McDougall, An Introduction to Social Psychology, p. 49.
[4] Thorndike, Educational Psychology.
[5] Drever, Instinct in Man, pp. 150 et seq.
[6] Larguier des Bancels, op. cit., p. 240

a prey to emotion when we stand in its way with feet rooted to the ground, or when we dance about in front of it." In like manner he says, a man who is guided by the "combative instinct" makes ready to deliver a blow, remaining cool and self-possessed; whereas anger makes him lose his head. This distinction, like Thorndike's, is difficult to maintain; it serves mainly to draw attention to the disorders of instinct, Nevertheless, although the formula "emotion is instinct. gone wrong" is unquestionably an exaggeration, it is suggestive, for it emphasises the fact that *the affective aspect of the phenomenon develops at the cost of the active aspect.* We have had occasion to note this before. A certain amount of emotion is the normal accompaniment of instinct; but the emotion develops at the expense of the instinct properly so called. For good or for ill, and whether or not the emotion be instinct gone wrong, violent emotion is a transformation, an evolution, of instinct. The evolution presupposes that part of the instinct has been diverted from its primary function. Here we are in line with the observations of Romanes, who notes that the emotional manifestations accompanying instinct grow more intense as we rise in the animal scale, and that they attain their maximum in man.[1]

But the psychological evolution of instinct does not end with emotion. This is not the only psychological aspect of instinct; we may call it the acute psychological aspect. The enduring psychological aspect of instinct is what in Ribot's psychology is termed *tendency*. Emotion is manifested when a tendency has a violent encounter with its object. In default of this shock, a tendency does not manifest itself by emotions, but through other forms of the affective life (feelings, passions); for the tendency, as we have pointed out above, underlies the whole of the affective life. It follows, then, that the affective life as a whole is based upon instinct. The classical distinction between *primitive tendencies* and *derived tendencies* (or acquired tendencies) thus becomes perfectly clear. Primitive tendencies are the expression of instinct pure and simple; derived tendencies are the outcome of the transformations that instinct undergoes in the individual, especially when instinct has been thwarted. These tendencies may represent a derivation of instinct towards new ends,

[1] Romanes, Animal Intelligence, pp. 155, 270, etc.

moral, æsthetic, or spiritual; bearing this in mind, we can easily understand why James Ward assimilates instinct to *talent*, regarding talent as an instinct in process of formation.[1] The *interest* manifested for any particular object is the pre-eminent sign of a tendency, whether primitive or derived. In either case we have to do with a force that is instinctive in its origin; and the new pedagogy has good reason for assigning a biological role to interest, and for considering that educationists should pay particular attention to this matter. Finally, when James tells us that man has more instincts than any other animal, we must understand here by the term "instinct," numerous *tendencies*, increasingly psychological in character, which can undergo development in man, but which result from the evolution of a much smaller number of crude *instincts*.

From the theoretical outlook, the number of these crude instincts may perhaps be very much restricted, for it is doubtful apriori whether every primitive instinct is capable of the same evolution. The idea that *the affective life, including the higher feelings, represents an evolution of instincts*, must be accepted as a general proposition. It is a natural deduction from the theory of evolution, and people will become familiarised with it just as they have become familiarised with the idea of the evolution of species. Hardly anyone is now unwilling to admit that man is descended from animal ancestors; why, then, should anyone take offence at the idea that our highest feelings arise out of instincts. But although the general notion of this evolution must be accepted, we are not yet in a position to work the idea out in detail.

We spoke of a possible genesis of feelings from a restricted number of instincts. Freud, in this connection, attaches especial importance to the sexual instinct, and that is what has made many people find the theory repugnant. As we shall see shortly, other instincts besides the sexual can and do play their part. Freud does not deny it. Moreover, as Pfister well says, it is as absurd to be angry with Freud for his outlook as it would have been to blame Christopher Columbus for having discovered America only, without discovering Australia and the North and South Poles. Not merely was the line taken by Freud the boldest one, and also

[1] Ward, Psychological Principles, 1918, p. 449.

the one which it was the most urgent to take, but in addition it is easy on theoretical grounds to demonstrate that the sexual instinct must have had exceptional importance in the genesis of our feelings. Here are three propositions the truth of which it is very difficult to deny.

1. The feelings represent an evolution of crude instincts. (This is the conclusion to which we have just been led.)

2. The instincts which evolve are preeminently instincts that have been repressed or thwarted. (This was proved above.)

3. The sexual instinct is one of the two or three of the most potent among the instincts, and it is also one of those upon which the greatest number of repressions are imposed in social and civilised life. (The facts are obvious.)

Anyone who accepts these three propositions will have to accept, as a perhaps unexpected but necessary corollary when they are juxtaposed, the contention that the evolution of the thwarted sexual instinct has a preponderating importance in the genesis of our feelings.[1] I do not think that Freud's main idea goes far beyond the terms of this proposition.

Obviously there is no reason for neglecting the part played by the other instincts. In the case of several of them we shall find that there are certain transformations easy to follow, similar transformations to those which Freud has described in the case of the sexual instinct.

Speaking generally, we can distinguish two kinds of transformation :

1. Sometimes the thwarted instinct seeks derivatives in actions different from those towards which it was primarily directed, but it remains essentially active. (Example, the combative instinct finds its derivative in sport.)

2. Sometimes the instinct is satisfied with "regression" (Freud), "introversion" (Jung), "objectivation" (Bovet), in the affective and imaginative world. (Example, the combative instinct finds its derivative in epic imagination.)

The distinction corresponds to that between play and dreaming ; moreover, as in the cases of play and dreaming, intermediate forms, mixed derivatives, are met with.

[1] The same affirmation may be found in the writings of an author who is by no means an adherent of psychoanalysis. Cf. Paulhan, Les transformations sociales des sentiments, 1920, p. 151.

In either case the derivative is formed as the sequel of the displacement of affective stress upon an object different from that towards which the tendency was primarily directed. But whereas in dreaming and in play the displacement was momentary, here it is persistent, and the tendency has definitively secured a new object. Moreover, the analysis of displacement in dreams has thrown an unexpected light upon the process of derivation. *Derivation is the projection upon a dynamic plane of that which is displacement upon a static plane.*

Unquestionably derivation is always heralded by displacements which have vacillated a little before undergoing fixation. Here we approach a new aspect (which has been foreshadowed) of the function of play in dreams. Dreaming appeared to us at first, in adults at any rate, to be an outlet for an unemployed instinct; whereas the play of children seemed to us to be, in addition, the exercise of an embryonic instinct. But a derivative which is in course of development is, strictly speaking, an embryonic tendency, an evolving instinct.

In certain cases, the displacement that occurs in a dream appears quite plainly to be an embryonic tendency, playing, vacillating, exercising itself. It is in such cases that we are entitled to speak of dreams that point out the way. The subject will eventually follow a path which has appeared to him in a dream.

We shall find instances of such dreams in several of our subjects. Gerard, an adolescent, exhibits a vacillating sublimation; this vacillation finds expression in dream V; the tendency towards Catholicism which manifests itself in the dream will eventually, in this subject, become a real tendency, a wish to be converted. Roger has, towards the close of the analysis (from dream XIX onwards), several dreams which point out the way, and in which a budding sublimation is sketched. But the most typical case is perhaps that of Jeanne, who vacillates between æsthetic sublimation and moral-social sublimation, and who plays upon these two possibilities (in dreams IX and X). It is thus that a child will play at different trades or professions before feeling that its choice of a life occupation has been made. Such dreams are entitled to be termed dreams that point out the way, inasmuch as the tendencies and the conflicts of tendency which come to light in the dreams are as a rule more or less subconscious, and the analysis of these dreams helps the subject to become aware of his own trends. I may adduce the example of a young man who during childhood had little predilection for combative exploits but who was nevertheless continually dreaming that he was a soldier. When he was nineteen, this tendency entered his waking consciousness, and he adopted a military career, for which he had long been preparing in his dreams just as others prepare for such a career in play.

In view of these facts it is easy to realise that the dream-play which is termed " art " has the same function for humanity at large that dreaming and play have for the individual. Art is not merely an outlet for unemployed tendencies ; it is also a play, an exercise, in which these tendencies seek new objects, in which they imagine the diverse possibilities of their future evolution. *Might we not define the higher art as a dream which points out the way to mankind in search of its goal ?*

3. The Genealogy of Tendencies

When there repeatedly occurs a condensation of images tinged with affects which to consciousness seem to have no connection with one another, there are, as we have learned, grounds for supposing that these affective states are really akin. Imagination is based on affectivity, affectivity on instinct. Just as the condensation of different images commonly results from their being tinged with kindred affects, so the *condensation of different affective states* is the outcome (if we may use the term) of the common instinctive " parentage " of the affects. These two principles correspond to the two successive categories of psychoanalysis. *In the dream, a condensation of images is the only immediate datum from which we can start.* Sometimes this condensation is explained by a kinship of the first degree, an affective kinship between the images. Sometimes we must go deeper for an explanation ; there is diversity not only between the images but also between the concomitant affective states, and the uniting element must be sought in the instinctive parentage of the affective states. This latter form of kinship is not usually within the realm of consciousness.

But here again, schematically considered, there are two alternatives. The affective states may represent different stages of evolution (a crude tendency and a higher tendency), and it is only under the evolutionary form that we can conceive their kinship. Of this nature is the case considered above, when we took as an example the condensation of a sexual tendency with an æsthetic tendency. If there is kinship between these two tendencies, it is because some of the latter represent an evolution of some of the elements of the former. In the alternative case, the two affective states which undergo condensation do not obviously belong to different stages of evolution. For instance, we may be concerned with two sentiments developed by civilisation, such as the filial sentiment and the conjugal sentiment; or with two crude tendencies, such as the combative and the sexual respectively. Again, when we have to do with developed sentiments, the solution of the difference may take place on the affective plane. In certain subjects there is a definite likeness, a likeness of which the subject is *aware*, between the conjugal sentiment and the filial sentiment. "You are my sister and my mother as well as my beloved," says Don Carlos in Verhaeren's play *Philippe II*. Are we then to be satisfied with the affective likeness, and are we to say that in such subjects one sentiment serves as symbol of the other—and if so, which is the symbol? Are we to look for a biological foundation, to say that one of the tendencies has developed out of the other, and that filial affection contains the germs of conjugal affection? If we have to do with two crude instincts, are they derived one from the other, and how; are they derived from a common source; is their biological tie used by the dream only as a pretext, so that one serves as symbol of the other—and, once more, which is the symbol?

This way of stating the problem gives us some idea of its intricacy. Certain feelings, certain instincts, form condensations which are encountered unmistakably in a great number of persons. It is manifest that the feelings are akin, that the instincts are akin. But what is the nature of the kinship? It is here that the question becomes involved. We shall see a little more clearly if we bear the following principles in mind:

1. In every "symbolisation," as previously pointed out, we must be extremely circumspect in deciding which of the terms symbolises the other, and which is the essential element.

Our judgment as to what is symbol and what symbolised is a very subjective affair. We shall often find it more prudent to be satisfied with noting that there is a relationship between the different terms, and to refrain from specifying precisely what the relationship is.

2. This relationship, in all cases, and even when it exhibits itself as an affective likeness of which the subject is aware, can in the last analysis be reduced to a biological kinship (instinctive parentage), and can always be looked upon as a function of evolution. But the relationship does not per se tell us anything as to the nature of this evolution.

3. The nature of the evolution can only be decided by historical considerations. Thus alone can we determine whether we have to do with an evolution of tendencies acquired by the individual, or with an evolution of instincts proper to the species.

Psychoanalysis leads us to the following conception. The affective-instinctive forces, in short the tendencies, which work in the depths of our being, are interrelated in ways analogous to those which the theory of evolution has elucidated as existing between species. They are blood-relations; they grow out of one another. Below, there are certain crude instincts; above, we have the burgeoning of the higher feelings. But this statement is a mere skeleton. We must clothe it with flesh; we must show how the tendencies are akin, distinguishing between near relationships and distant; we must in a word, draw up the genealogical tree of our tendencies.

To put the matter more clearly, let us follow up the comparison with the origin of species. The reader will remember that the biological theory of evolution both generally and as regards details is logically grounded upon the data furnished by three sciences: comparative anatomy; paleontology; and embryology. Comparative anatomy detects the remarkable homologies between the organs of different species; finding, for instance, an arm in the skeleton of a bird's wing. Paleontology discloses the order of appearance of the various species in geological history, and thus elucidates kinship by descent. Embryology shows that the individual development of the higher beings from germ-cell to adult is an epitome of the development of species revealed by paleontology.

Psychoanalysis to-day, in its study of tendencies, is in much the same position as comparative anatomy in relation to the study of species; psychoanalysis is able to detect remarkable kinships between tendencies. In addition, in certain cases, psychoanalysis is able to secure data analogous to those furnished by embryology, as when it elucidates the history and the transformations of a subject's tendencies. Finally, with Jung and his school, psychoanalysis undertakes stupendous excavations in the paleontological strata of primitive thought and the "collective unconscious"; it aspires to exhume the fabulous monsters which are supposed to enjoy a revived existence to-day in the infantile states of the human mind.[1] But this "psychic paleontology" and "psychic embryology" are still in the faltering stage of early childhood, and we have often to be content with the "comparative anatomy" of tendencies. The last, even, exhibits many gaps. This is why great caution is needed when we are constructing a genealogical tree of tendencies. In the conceptual sphere, the idea of their evolution is forced upon us; as a fact, we can verify such an evolution in many instances, and we owe the possibility of this verification to psychoanalysis; but there is a great deal more work to be done before all the details of the genealogy can be known to us.

Manifestly, then, in this domain there is plenty of scope for conflicting interpretations. We must not therefore refrain from interpretations; they are essential to the exposition and linking of the phenomena. But we must never forget that these interpretations contain large hypothetical elements. If psychoanalysts would always bear this fact in mind, they would not furnish us with the spectacle described by Claparède: "They sometimes confound hypotheses with facts, ignore the need for systematic doubt, and mistake a theory for a creed. Hence they suffer from intestine dissensions. They are split up into petty, warring chapels, hermetically sealed to the profane; and they enter their respective chapels with a mystic air of self-satisfied superiority, as if they were the hierophants of some esoteric doctrine.—Such are the foibles of mankind. . . ."[2]

[1] An interesting monograph upon this topic is Aurel Kolnai's recently published work, Psychoanalysis and Sociology. But, for the reasons given in the text, this author's conclusions must be accepted with reserve.

[2] Claparède, Introduction to Freud's La psychanalyse, p. 21.

We have already noted the exceptional importance attached by Freud to transformations of the sexual instinct, regarded as the product of numerous components capable of independent variation and of unequal degrees of modification. According to this view, an evolution of the sexual instinct underlies many of the higher manifestations of the mind. Energy that was primarily sexual is thus looked upon as taking the form of a stream which divides into a number of branches, subsequently perhaps coalescing and separating once more. If one branch is dammed, the obstructed portion of the stream flows into lateral channels, and may there give rise to new derivatives which are sometimes of great moral and social value. To give expression to this idea of the conservation of a stream of energy, quantitative in character, Freud uses the term *libido*.[1] Its meaning is not very strictly defined, and its significance has been rendered all the more obscure inasmuch as various disciples have employed it in divergent senses. As Freud himself uses the word, "libido" would seem to be a designedly plastic term to denote an essentially mobile reality. Even though it be true that libido does not always signify precisely the same thing, we must not bear a grudge against Freud for this, seeing that the libido is a real entity in process of evolution. Jung shows that the concept has undergone expansion in proportion as Freud has grasped the existence of more numerous relationships between the sexual elements and other elements.[2] If a simple definition of libido is possible, it will run as follows: *Libido is sexual energy considered from the outlook of its faculty for undergoing transformation and evolution.* In this sense we may say that the "libido" participates in this or that higher sentiment, just as we may say that Plato's skeleton retains a vestige of the simian tail. We are concerned here with a developmental relationship and not with identity, and this is why Freud can propound the paradoxical formula of a "sexuality independent of the reproductive instinct."[3] Nevertheless, as Claparède[4] points out, there remain certain

[1] Freud, Drei Abhandlungen zur Sexualtheorie.
[2] Jung. Wandlungen und Symbole der Libido, p. 124; The Psychology of the Unconscious, pp. 143–4.
[3] Freud, La psychanalyse, p. 56; see also Introductory Lectures on Psychoanalysis, p. 276.
[4] Cf. the discussion in Freud, La psychanalyse, p. 70.

obscurities in the concept of libido. But this much is certain, that it is unjust to charge Freud with finding libido in everything, and with reducing the whole human mind to an evolution of the sexual. In a letter to Claparède (1921) he writes categorically concerning this matter:

"I have repeated and asserted as plainly as possible apropos of transference neuroses (*Uebertragungsneurosen*), that I have drawn a distinction between the *Sexualtriebe* [1] and the *Ichtriebe*; [2] and that for me libido denotes only the energy of the former, of the *Sexualtriebe.* It is Jung and not I who makes the libido equivalent to the instinctive urge of *all* the mental faculties, and who combats the idea of the sexual nature of the libido. . . . . As far as I myself am concerned I fully recognise the existence of the group of the *Ichtriebe,* and of everything which the mental life owes to these instincts. But this latter point is ignored by the general public; it is purposely hidden from the general public. The same sort of thing often happens when my theory of dreams is being expounded. I have never contended that every dream expresses the realisation of a *sexual* wish, and I have frequently affirmed the contrary. But all to no avail, for people go on saying the same thing over and over again." [3]

We shall shortly have to consider Jung's ideas, but we must deal first of all with Adler's theory. It is grafted upon Freud's reserves in favour of the *Ichtriebe.* Adler, who is said to have been Freud's first disciple, applies his master's principles to the instinct of self-preservation, or rather to the instinct of the *expansion* of the personality (an instinct analogous to what Nietzsche termed the will-to-power). But his application of them is so drastic that he attributes to this instinct for power many of the results attributed by Freud to the sexual instinct; consequently the same phenomenon could be interpreted quite differently by Freud and by Adler. In imaginative creations Adler discerns *compensation* [4] for a real inferiority; the development of a mental tendency may manifest itself as the fixation of such a compensation for a feeling of organic inferiority. (This recalls the case of a

[1] Sexual instincts. [2] Ego instincts.

[3] Quoted in Freud, La psychanalyse,, p. 70.

[4] Adler, Ueber den nervösen Charakter, 1919, pp. 24 et seq.; The Neurotic Constitution, pp. 18 et seq.

stammerer who dreams of becoming an orator, and who, if he be a Demosthenes, may actually become an orator.) In addition a neurosis is a means of dominating the entourage.[1] A boy who is being coddled for a sore throat may develop symptoms of asthma in order to keep everyone at his service.[2] Or, again, a mother may pamper her children in the unconscious determination to tyrannise over them.

Adler goes further, and whenever he encounters sexuality he regards it as a symbol of power. The sexual allusions of neuropaths are purely symbolic (*sind nur ein Gleichnis.*)[3] The sexual attitude of these patients is the outcome of their feeling of weakness, and of their dread of normal sexual relations, in which they run the risk of encountering "a partner more powerful than themselves." They therefore simulate a perversion; or they shun sexuality altogether; or, conversely, they become "Don Juans" or "light women" for fear of a "unique partner" who would be likely to subjugate them. A woman, again, may manifest her will-to-power by falling in love with a man who is weakly or an invalid, and owing to repression her true motive will assume the mark of compassion.[4] In consequence of the will-to-power, a neuropathic woman may wish to play a virile role, and may repudiate motherhood, or the sexual life in its entirety (a case in which Freud would have spoken of homosexuality). The menopause is characterised by an increase in neurotic symptoms because it tends to arouse a feeling of inferiority.[5]

Adler, like Freud, is a sagacious and at times a pitiless psychologist. He is in line with a number of caustic students of human nature such as La Rochefoucauld and Nietzsche, who delight in detecting "egoism" and the "will-to-power" behind every human feeling. But in Adler's case this view does not lead to pessimism, any more than in Freud's, for psychoanalysts do not look upon sexuality or egoism as prisons from which there is no escape. Freud tells us that sexuality can undergo sublimation. So can the will-to-power. We must recognise the parallelism between Adler and Freud in spite of the differences between them. Freud contrasts the

[1] Adler, Ueber den nervösen, Charakter, 1919, p. 35; English version, p. 13.
[2] Ibid., p. 130; English version, p. 138.
[3] Ibid., p. 135; English version, p. 144.
[4] Ibid., p. 113; English version, p. 119.
[5] Ibid., p. 75; English version, p. 76.

"pleasure principle" with the "reality principle." The neuropath is out of harmony with the real because his only guide is the "pleasure principle." In like manner, for Adler, the principle of "power" is essentially normal; but where the neuropath goes astray is that he becomes obsessed by this as his only principle, that he makes of it his "guiding fiction," forgetting the real. What is true of the power principle for the individual, is true likewise for the group, and Adler writes these vigorous words at the beginning of the second edition of his book *The Neurotic Constitution*: "In the interval between the two editions of this work, the world war and its sequels have intervened; there has been the most terrible of collective neuroses into which our neuropathic civilisation has hurled itself in virtue of its will-to-power and its policy of self-assertion. . . . This reveals itself as the elemental outcome of the lust for dominion which has been everywhere let loose, stifling or artificially misusing the undying sentiment for human solidarity."

The quotation is enough to show how much faith in humanity there can be in men who are nevertheless dominated by pitiless realism. For Freud, as for Adler, the principle of neurosis is essentially an egoistic principle. The former speaks of the pleasure principle, and the latter of the power principle.[1] In both cases there is maladaptation to the real, which is also the social. In both cases, the task of psychoanalysis is to reestablish the adaptation, and in so doing it does altruistic work. It is an *education in confraternity* (*Erziehung zur Gemeinschaft*).[2]

The foregoing considerations will facilitate the reader's understanding of the attempt made by the Zurich School of psychoanalysts, and notably by Jung, to effect a synthesis of the respective theories of Freud and Adler; and also to understand why it is that in this synthesis, which stresses the traits common to the two Viennese psychologists, the emphasis has generally been laid upon the idealistic aspect of psychoanalysis, upon its role of labourer on behalf of altruism.

But great as is the interest of the common features of

[1] It is amusing to note that the names of these two men of science are symbolical of their respective theories, for "Freude" signifies "joy" or "pleasure," and "Adler" signifies "eagle." (This is a tip for those who like mnemonics!)

[2] Op. cit., Preface.

the two doctrines, the differences between Freud and Adler are no less interesting. These differences, and, above all, the fact that Adler sees a symbol where Freud sees a reality (and conversely), confirm the difficult primary theory which we formulated above. A judgment of value, we said, markedly subjective in character, decides the important point, decides what is the " symbol " and what is the thing " symbolised." A symbol can be interpreted in various ways, even though an objective relationship exists between the elements of which it is composed.

Jung's proposed synthesis is founded mainly upon two principles :

(1) the expansion of the concept of the " libido " ;
(2) the distinction between the " introvert " and the " extrovert."

1. The expansion of the concept of the libido was pointed out in Freud's letter to Claparède. Jung, showing that Freud has progressively expanded the significance of the term "libido," considers that this expansion ought to be carried yet further. He applies the concept so as to include every tendency, not excepting those which Freud speaks of as the group of " ego instincts."[1] The term libido as employed by Jung is likewise somewhat obscure, but we can use the same definition that we used to explain the Freudian significance of the term if we substitute the word " instinctive " for the word " sexual." Then, *libido is instinctive energy considered from the outlook of its faculty for undergoing transformation and evolution.* This conception implies the fundamental unity of all the instinctive energies, thus recalling, in the mental sphere, the general notion of *energy* in the physical sphere. It is, however, easy to see that such a use of the term libido veils a hypothesis, which is almost a metaphysical hypothesis. But the expansion of the concept has certainly the merit of enabling Jung to harmonise Adler's terminology with Freud's.

2. This " libido," this mental energy (which has been compared to the " vital impetus " [élan vital] of Bergson),

[1] Jung, Wandlungen und Symbole der Libido, Part II, Chapter II; Psychology of the Unconscious, Part. II, Chapter II.

is both centripetal and centrifugal, tends both towards the ego and towards the outer world. Here we have two compensatory functions. According as one or other predominates, the subject is an *introvert* or an *extrovert*. The introvert will be mainly a thinker, the extrovert will be mainly a man or woman of feeling or of action. The "Ichtriebe" dominate the introvert, whereas the "Sexualtriebe" dominate the extrovert; thus to the introvert Adler's principle mainly applies, and to the extrovert Freud's principle mainly applies.[1]

Jung's conclusion is broadly tolerant: "Up to a certain point, the sexual theory is perfectly correct, but it is one-sided. We should consequently be equally wrong were we to reject it outright or to accept it as universally valid."

For Jung, the psychoanalytic method "is based upon the theory of the two types" (of introvert and extrovert). The neuroses and the psychoses correspond to an exaggeration of one function or the other (extroversion in hysteria, introversion in neurasthenia and in dementia præcox). To cure these patients we must develop in them the function which they lack. This can be done, for the lack is apparent merely; the missing function is repressed into the subconscious.

Jung's synthesis is a praiseworthy effort to unify psychoanalysis, to subsume under one head theories which might seem conflicting. We owe much to Jung for his specialist studies, and above all for his application of the Freudian method to the psychoses, but we find it necessary to criticise his attempted synthesis. This theory is so generalised that its outlines grow hazy. The distinction between the two types is nothing more than a convenient formula which we must not be unduly ready to accept as corresponding to an absolute reality. As for Jung's concept of the "libido," this is even more impalpable than Freud's; it has become protean. Such extremely general notions are by no means futile, but we have to ask ourselves whether they possess the qualities requisite for scientific terminology. Here we touch the root of the matter. *Jung's synthesis is philosophical rather than scientific.* Broad syntheses are excellent when we wish

[1] This distinction forms the basis of Jung's book, Psychologischen Typen, 1921.—Jung has also expounded the idea briefly in French, Contribution à l'étude des types psychologiques.

to summarise the present state of knowledge, but they are not favourable to the process of research.

From the scientific point of view the question arises whether it would not be better to harmonise the respective theories of Adler and Freud upon a platform purposively analytical. The constructions of Freud and of Adler are already vast syntheses open to criticism for their tendency towards systematic generalisations—and this tendency itself explains their conflict. Is it the best corrective to subsume these two theories in a synthesis yet more titanic? Perhaps it is, for the philosopher. But would not the psychologist be well advised to try the opposite method?

Psychoanalysis has already a superabundance of ambitious generalisations. We must remember that this branch of science has hitherto been mainly developed in the Teutonic lands, and that the German spirit has ever been more inclined towards metaphysics than psychology, towards synthesis than analysis. Consequently, by the irony of fate, at each step forward *psycho-analysis* has to an increasing extent run the danger of becoming *metaphysico-synthesis*. I do not know that this need be regretted. Owing to the nature of the object of study there was a risk at first that psychoanalysis would lead to a collection of disconnected facts; and the synthetic spirit was requisite before the science could become the imposing force it now is. But given the requisite synthetic foundation and now that the vast design has been traced, we shall find it advantageous to work upon a smaller scale. Freud, a disciple of Charcot and Bernheim, expected great things of France—just as formerly Nietzsche, the forerunner of psychoanalysis, had expected great things of her. "Freud had imagined," writes Claparède, "that the French mind, noted for its versatility, would be readier than the German mind to understand the finer shades of the mental life and the hidden implications of the subconscious; he expected to receive, across the frontier, if not the approval, at least the attention which his compatriots refused with scant courtesy. . . . Yet, strange to say, the French have been the very last to interest themselves in his work."[1]

At length, however, the hour has come, and we are entitled to expect that the French spirit will guide psychoanalysis.

[1] Claparède, Introduction to Freud's La psychanalyse, p. 6.

in the genuinely " analytical " direction desiderated above, Such a movement is already manifest, not only in French Switzerland, but also in Britain. It is time that the movement should become fully conscious of its own trend.

Psychoanalysis is an evolutionary theory of *instinct* ; it ought to become an evolutionary theory of *the instincts.* Implicit in this formula is the difference between the two outlooks. Instead of generalising the term " libido " to denote so comprehensive an object as " instinctive energy," we shall prefer to speak of a " libido " peculiar to each instinct. Better still, perhaps, we shall prefer to abandon the concept altogether ; or at least to surrender it to philosophy, where it may have a useful part to play (only, in that case, we may have a preference in France for the term " élan vital "—vital impetus). We shall carefully consider the suggestion of Claparède, who wishes to replace the term libido by the term *interest.* It is not simply a question of words. " Libido " is tendency looked upon as energy. " Interest " is a positive psychological fact, one which we are entitled to look upon as the *sign* of the tendency. There is no danger that the conception of interest will lead us astray in metaphysical and mystical directions. Furthermore the advocates of " libido " conceive of it as a uniform energy, as being in the singular number ; whereas in speech and thought we are accustomed to deal with " interests " in the plural, and not with " interest per se." We have an " interest " for hunting, dancing, study ; each tendency has its appropriate " interest." *Interest is defined as a function of the object of the tendency ; whereas libido demands to be defined per se.* Our view is that interest undergoes displacement, that it is transferred to new objects, that it evolves. We may say that a child concentrates interest on play ; a youth or a girl on study or amusement ; an adult on business, ambition, ideas. Thus the term " interest " is both supple and precise ; it fulfils our desideratum ; it is a psychological and analytical notion. Whether we adopt the word or not, we can in any case accept Claparède's outlook : " Psychoanalysis has contributed great and splendid truths to psychology. It would be a pity if the advance of the science were still to be hampered by an abstruse theory of the libido. Hoping to avoid this shoal, I have endeavoured to give the theory the form which seems to me the only legitimate one in the present state of our biological and psychological knowledge. No other form is legitimate, because no other form is intelligible."[1]

Once more recalling Descartes' famous rule, let us "divide" our topic. We certainly shall not forget that instincts, like species, are akin; and that instincts, like species, attach to a primitive unity. But what should we think of a man of science who, being a theist, was satisfied to explain every natural phenomenon simply by the words, "this comes from God"; or of an evolutionist who was satisfied to explain the origin of every living being by the formula, "this is a development from the primitive unicellular organism"? The "libido" sometimes gives us the impression of being an explanation of this kind. "This is the outcome of the libido." What interests science is to know *how* it "is the outcome."

We must therefore study each instinct separately, doing our utmost to trace its possible metamorphoses in the human psyche, and without denying that the higher manifestations of this psyche may be the outcome of several instincts. Not only shall we decline to have forced upon us an alternative between an "explanation by the sexual instinct" or an "explanation by the instinct for power"; we shall be prepared to take into account, not merely both these instincts, but, if need be, a number of others as well.

This analytical study has begun. Several British psychoanalysts, and in especial Rivers and MacCurdy,[2] have applied Freudian methods to the diagnosis and treatment of war neuroses. Their description runs on parallel lines with that of Freud; but in their view, in what they term war neuroses, the *instinct of self-preservation* takes the place given by Freud to the sexual instinct in the "peace neuroses." In war, it is this instinct of self-preservation which mainly tends to be repressed by the censorship, here taking the form of the conventions of military life. War neurosis may manifest

[1] Claparède, Supplementary note to Freud's La psychanalyse, p. 72.

[2] Rivers, Instinct and the Unconscious, 1920; The Repression of War Experiences, 1918.—MacCurdy, War Neuroses, 1918.—Cf. also Culpin, Psychoneuroses of War and Peace, 1920. This author inclines more towards Adler's outlook than towards Freud's.—Consult also Ernest Jones, War Shock and Freud's Theory of the Neuroses, in Papers on Psychoanalysis, 1918; also Eder, War Shock, 1917.

itself as "anxiety neurosis;" and this, in war patients as in peace patients, is the indication of an acute *conflict* between what has been repressed and the consciousness.[1]

An interesting perspective opens out to investigators in this field. We may expect that there will shortly be issued a series of monographs upon the different instincts. Pierre Bovet has led the way in his study of the combative instinct.[2] He studies the apparent suppressions of this instinct, which arise, either because the instinct has not been exercised during the stage of development when it normally appears, or because it has been thwarted later in life. The author goes on to show the transformations that result from these apparent suppressions. The instinct finds derivatives in sport, secures expression in the study of history, or is sublimated in moral strife.[3] Condensations are effected among the images corresponding to the various stages of the evolution of the instinct, leading to the use of fighting metaphors by the derivative or sublimated instinct, which thereby betrays its origin. Loyola, having been a soldier, becomes a soldier of God, and founds the Society of Jesus upon the model of an army. The Salvation Army is a still more typical instance.[4]

The remarks made incidentally by certain authors apropos of one instinct or another could serve as the starting point for such monographs. For instance, Larguier des Bancels, having enumerated the primitive instincts, goes on to say: "The various tendencies we have just been reviewing have a much wider influence than is obvious at first sight. We must not forget that they underlie a great number of complex feelings. Disdain, contempt, and aloofness, are the wrappings for repulsion and disgust. We may say the same thing of hatred."[5]

Is contempt merely the "wrapping" of disgust? Could we not more appropriately speak of an "evolution" of disgust. The same author, discussing the complementary instincts of curiosity and fear, writes: "The prestige of mystery, by which so many adults are still influenced, is compounded of fear and curiosity."[6]

[1] Lépine, in his Troubles mentaux de guerre, also lays stress upon the kinship between the "anxiety states" of war neuroses and states of conflict.

[2] Bovet, L'instinct combatif, 1917.

[3] Ibid., p. 119 et seq.

[4] Ibid., p. 157.

[5] Larguier des Bancels, op. cit. p. 213.

[6] Ibid., p. 220.

Both curiosity and fear, just like the sexual instinct according to Freud, and like the combative instinct according to Bovet, would thus appear to be liable to undergo a religious sublimation. It would be interesting to trace the history of their avatars.

It would be no less interesting to trace the avatars of the maternal instinct. When thwarted or repressed, this instinct may induce specific dreams (as in the subject Martha); or it may find derivatives in art or in charitable activities, especially where these concern children (as in the subject Jeanne).

We catch glimpses, also, of the wealth of knowledge that might be secured by studying the instinct of imitation. This instinct is thwarted in certain introverts. They develop an individualistic attitude, but they are fond of choosing distinguished models upon whom their imitative instinct is concentrated (Schopenhauer, in the case of the subject Otto). Apparently the imitative instinct may undergo sublimation, and *The Imitation of Christ* is a mystical type of this sublimation. The phenomena of the search for a guide, those of "affective transference" on to the analyst, those of responsiveness to suggestive treatment—phenomena hitherto studied by psychoanalysts as functions of the sexual instinct—might have further light thrown on them by being studied also as functions of the imitative instinct.

However, this monographic outlook must not make us lose sight of the synthesis towards which we must tend. Wherever we detect ties between different instincts, we must take careful note of the fact. MacCurdy, for example (in conformity with Dumas [1] and most of the trustworthy observers of war neuroses during the late war), declares that the war neurosis, or the neurosis of self-preservation, is not a special disease. It is, he says, the outcome of the same predispositions as those which could have induced an ordinary neurosis, a sexual neurosis. Many patients suffering from war neurosis have displayed symptoms of claustrophobia, timidity, fear of the sexual [2] (the introvert type; in MacCurdy's terminology, the seclusive tendency). In like manner Bovet shows that there are remarkable ties between the combative instinct

[1] Dumas, Troubles mentaux et nerveux de guerre, 1919.
[2] MacCurdy, op. cit., p. 34.

and the sexual instinct; and that in all species the combative instinct is closely connected with the instinct of courtship. It is certain, also, that instincts have a strong tendency to undergo extroversion or introversion in groups. Repression of the combative instinct goes hand in hand with repression of the sexual instinct and of the social instinct. But all these syntheses, and others yet more general, must only be undertaken as the crown of our researches.

This theory of mental evolution, long since foreshadowed in philosophy, but to which psychoanalysis has given body, is not a discouraging view. The possibility of *transforming instinct* gives new lights to educators, who have hitherto been in doubt whether to ignore instinct or to repress it. Hence Drever and Bovet offer their respective books *Instinct in Man* and *L'instinct combatif* as contributions to the psychology of education. Even the disciples of a spiritualist philosophy have no more occasion to take offence at this theory of mental evolution than at the theory of organic evolution. Such a dynamic outlook would merely make it necessary for the adherents of a spiritualist philosophy to state likewise in dynamic terms its fundamental problem, that of matter and form. Maeder is well aware of this when he writes: "I therefore distinguish clearly, side by side with the *energetic* factor (which is the essence of Jung's concept of libido,) a factor coordinated therewith, the factor of *direction* (orientation). From the static point of view we rightly distinguish between *content* and *form*. Here we have to distinguish between the stream (the energy) and the direction."[1]

Those only who know very little about psychoanalysis can take offence at its generalisations. What does it matter if a higher feeling owes its origin to a crude instinct? Origin is not identity; it is not even *causality* in the philosophic sense. Have we not good reason to congratulate ourselves on having advanced so far along the road?

Everyone knows the poem *Booz endormi*:

> While Boaz was sleeping, Ruth, a Moabite,
> Lay stretched at his feet, her bosom bare.

[1] Maeder, Guérison et évolution dans la vie de l'âme, 1918, p. 67

From this seduction there was to be born a race which Boaz sees in a dream:

> Such was his dream that Boaz saw an oak
> Which, issuing from his belly, stretched up into the sky;
> A race was climbing it like a long chain:
> A king was singing beneath, above a god was dying.[1]

Here we have the poem of sublimation. The manuscript shows that Hugo had first written "issuing from his loins;" then, feeling the need for frankness, he had decided (like Freud) in favour of the cruder word. The tree which is growing thus bears the poet-king David; and, higher up, Christ. I find the idea that all poetry, all glory, all holiness, have this lowly origin, no more offensive than I find Darwin's idea of the "descent of man."

[1] Victor Hugo, Légende des siècles.

CHAPTER FOUR

MIXED METHOD: PSYCHOANALYSIS AND SUGGESTION

1. Contrast

SUGGESTION is in bad repute among psychoanalysts. Nevertheless, psychoanalysis took its rise out of theories of suggestion and hypnosis.

Freud was a pupil of Charcot at the Salpêtrière; he witnessed also some of Bernheim's work at Nancy. He translated writings both by Charcot and by Bernheim into German. His studies concerning hysteria, which were the starting point of his own researches, were greatly influenced by Charcot and by the initial work of Pierre Janet upon psychological automatism. At the date when he was collaborating with Breuer, the hypnotic method was regarded as the preeminent means for the study of the subconscious; it was in subjects in the hypnotic state, and through hypnotic methods of investigation, that Breuer discovered the central fact that certain neurotic symptoms have a psychological significance. It was from this discovery that psychoanalysis was to issue. Freud relates the matter as follows:

"The morbid symptoms disappeared when, under hypnosis, the patient recalled, with physical signs indicative of emotion, how these symptoms had first been induced. During that summer there had been a spell of excessively hot weather, and the patient had suffered greatly from thirst because, without knowing why, she had suddenly become unable to drink. She would take a glass of water into her hand, but as soon as it touched her lips she would thrust it away again like a patient with hydrophobia. During these few seconds there was evidently a lapse of consciousness. She ate nothing but fruit, in order to relieve her thirst. This had been going on for about six weeks when one day, under hypnosis, she complained of her English governess, whom she did not like. She went on to say, with all the signs of intense disgust, that she had been in her governess' room, and that the latter's pet dog, a horrid little beast, had drunk out of a glass. From politeness, she had said nothing at the time. Having finished this recital, she showed signs of intense anger, though she had hitherto been perfectly calm. Then she asked for some water, drank a large quantity, and awoke from the hypnosis with the glass at her lips. Her trouble was permanently cured."[1]

Freud has never made any secret of what he owes to Charcot, Janet, and Bernheim, or of what he owes to his collaboration with Breuer. He writes modestly: "The credit, if credit there be, for having introduced psychoanalysis to the world does not belong to me."[2] Furthermore, as we shall see in a moment, Freud has never shown as regards suggestion the intolerance which is somewhat fashionable in this respect among psychoanalysts. In this matter, as in others, his doctrine is less absolute and more catholic than it is usually represented as being.

But the fact that psychoanalysis took its rise out of suggestion is precisely one of the reasons why many psychoanalysts have a prejudice against suggestion. They are influenced rather by an ill-defined feeling than by a clear idea, but they like to look upon psychoanalysis as the development of suggestion and as its climax. They consider that psychotherapeutics has made a new departure, and that suggestion is obsolete. Let us consider this notion.

There are more definite reasons to fortify the prejudice just described. The prejudice is the outcome of a theory held by the Salpêtrière School, according to which suggestion is intimately associated with hypnosis, and according to which hypnosis itself is a morbid state.

This view, rejuvenated by the data of psychoanalysis, has been succinctly formulated by Ferenczi.[3]

According to this author, hypnosis is the analogue of neurosis. It might be called an artificial neurosis, definable

[1] Freud, La psychanalyse, p. 27. [2] Ibid., p. 23.
[3] Ferenczi, Introjektion und Uebertragung, 1910.

in the terms which Freud has proposed for the definition of neurosis. On the other hand, Ferenczi is at one with the New Nancy School (see below, p. 106) when he considers that in the phenomena of suggestion the subject is the main factor, or in other words that every suggestion implies an autosuggestion. But the existence of autosuggestion does not seem to him to invalidate his thesis. Autosuggestion, a phenomenon initiated within the subject's own nervous system, can, in truth, be more legitimately compared with neurosis than if it were a phenomenon due to the influence of the operator upon the subject.

"The action of the suggester may well be compared with the cause that initiates a psychoneurosis."

If, against this theory, we raise the objection that the majority of persons are susceptible to suggestion or capable of being hypnotised, Ferenczi rejoins: "According to the experience of psychoanalysts, the fact that a very high percentage of normal persons can be hypnotised is an argument in favour of the view that most persons are liable to become affected with a psychoneurosis, rather than an argument against the theory that hypnosis and neurosis are essentially identical."

The author is categorical in his assertion of this identity: "The hypnotiser cannot really arouse any other manifestations than those which neurosis spontaneously induces."

As for suggestibility, this should be regarded as a manifestation of infantile regression. Hypnotic influence has as its basis a parental complex, one of attachment to the father or to the mother. This, sexually tinged, is subconsciously transferred by the subject on to the hypnotiser. Hypnotic processes can be classed in two categories. Hypnosis may be induced either by fear or by love, either by severity or by kindness. We are entitled to characterise the respective forms by contrasting them as "paternal hypnosis" and "maternal hypnosis." Ferenczi goes on to say: "Thus suggestion and hypnosis may be regarded as nothing more than the intentional production of conditions in which the tendency to blind faith and unrestricted obedience becomes effective. This tendency exists in everyone, as a vestige of the infantile-erotic feelings of love and fear for the parents, but ordinarily it is repressed by the censorship. Through suggestion and hypnosis, it may unconsciously be transferred on to the personality of the hypnotiser or suggester."

Such is Ferenczi's thesis, and, even if we were to accept it, it would not be a decisive objection to hypnosis and suggestion. Charcot and many others looked upon these phenomena as pathological, terming them hysterical; but were not thereby deterred from turning hypnotism and suggestion to account therapeutically. Because a substance is poisonous, we must not therefore infer that it can have no curative value. Still, if it be poisonous, we should think twice before using it. Charcot has been widely blamed as a cultivator of hysteria. Unquestionably, Ferenczi's thesis leaves on our minds an impression by no means favourable to suggestion.

We reach the main objection, and I hasten to admit that it requires serious consideration. It has been clearly expounded, in a comment upon one of his cases, by Odier, who shows that in this instance, where psychoanalysis effected a cure, "hypnosis was inefficacious and harmful."[1] The same, or a similar, objection has been made by other psychoanalysts.

It is founded upon two essential phenomena disclosed by psychoanalysis in the study of the dynamics of neurosis. These phenomena are *repression* and *derivation*.

The repression of experiences and tendencies into the subconscious has been shown to be one of the determinants of neurosis. Whether we have to do with an experience to which the reaction has been inadequate, or with a tendency which has been systematically thwarted, the energy thus repressed seeks derivatives; as we have seen, an aim for such derivations is provided by imaginative displacements. The symptoms of neurosis are derivatives of this kind; like dreams, they are a symbolical translation of what has been repressed. Psychoanalysis sets the patient free by revealing the play of repression and derivation, by bringing into consciousness that which was subconscious.

Now what does suggestion do? It denies the symptom. It orders the symptom to become non-existent. Under the menace of *vade retro*, the demon may not improbably disappear. But suggestion, acting in this fashion, has acted just like repression.

[1] Odier, A propos d'un cas de contracture hystérique, 1914, p. 191.

It has been an artificial repression, and if repression was the original determinant of the neurosis it is easy to see that there may be kinship between suggestion and neurosis. What has become of the repressed symptom? Psychoanalytical experience leads us to suppose that it does not really cease to exist, but merely undergoes transformation; that the energy which animated it finds a derivative. Thus the demons leave the body of the demoniac simply in order to enter the herd of swine. The symptom, indeed, does not leave the subject's body, but merely undergoes a change of place and form; driven out of one habitat, it reappears in another; it has doubtless become unrecognisable, but psychoanalysis is competent to penetrate the disguise. According to this view, suggestion can deal only with symptoms; it can merely cut off the shoots without touching the root of the evil, and the morbid sap will find its way into other shoots. Psychoanalysis alone can effect a radical cure.

2. Conciliation

Are these two methods irreconcilable? Pfister, a psychoanalyst whose views are broad and tolerant, does not think so, and he aptly reminds us that Freud does not think so: "Freud has never maintained that psychoanalysis can, unaided, invariably effect a cure. He has never opposed a combination of his own method with other methods, provided that nothing is done to interfere with the course of the analysis. In slight cases, he has even favoured a purely suggestive treatment. But premature suggestion paves the way for disillusionment and makes our educational task more difficult. . . ." Passing on to the more specifically educational point of view, Pfister writes: "Speaking generally, we shall not resort to a far-reaching analysis unless the further development of the individual is seriously hampered. Freud himself shares this view. If suggestion, or a good education in accordance with sound pedagogical principles, suffices to relieve the symptoms, let us follow the simpler course."[1]

These are wise words. Wise, too, are the words of Pierre Janet. Speaking of the decadence of hypnotism and suggestion

[1] Pfister, La psychanalyse au service des éducateurs, 1921, pp. 164, 184; German original, 1917, pp. 94, 105; English translation, pp. 140, 156.

that followed upon their first vogue, Janet refuses to see anything beyond a temporary eclipse. He does not regard very seriously these fluctuations of which the history of science offers so many instances.[1]

The criticisms of the psychoanalysts are, moreover, well-grounded in many cases, as far as concerns suggestion as it was understood by the early schools, and as it is still understood by most persons. But when we turn to consider suggestion as it is understood by the New Nancy School (1910–1920), a school of which few psychoanalysts know anything, the problem assumes a new aspect. This is not the place for a recapitulation of what I have written elsewhere concerning the present position of the theory of suggestion.[2] I merely wish to examine the objections enumerated above in the light of the theory that has been elaborated at Nancy.

From Bernheim and Liébault to Coué,[3] from the first Nancy School to the second, the theory and the practice of suggestion exhibit a remarkable evolution. Those who believe suggestion to be obsolete, those who contrast new methods with it, fail to take this evolution into account. The present theory of *autosuggestion* has issued from the theories of *suggestion* and *hypnotism* held in the year 1880, just as *psychoanalysis* has issued from those theories; but whereas psychoanalysis is mainly derived from the ideas of the Salpêtrière School, autosuggestion is in the line of descent from the first Nancy School.

We have here two parallel and independent evolutions, and they would gain by becoming better acquainted. There are some very interesting points about this historical parallelism. At the same date, 1885–6, Freud was working under Charcot, and Coué was watching the experiments of Liébault. It would, of course, be absurd to institute a close comparison between men so different as Coué and Freud. Coué is what Liébault was, a simple country doctor; he is a man of action and an apostle; his sole aim is to restore health and happiness to thousands, and he leaves it to others to discover the philosophy that guides his brilliantly successful practice.

[1] Janet, Les médications psychologiques, 1919, vol. i. p. 187.
[2] Baudouin, Suggestion et autosuggestion, 1920.
[3] Coué, La maîtrise de soi-même par l'autosuggestion consciente, 1921.

Freud, on the other hand, little concerned about social issues, is the constructor of a whole system of ideas. Nevertheless the two movements can be compared, and have been compared. They have this in common, that they have given an unprecedented extension to the laws of the subconscious, regarded as laws of the normal working of the mind; and that upon these laws they have founded curative and educative practical methods which are far more ambitious than were those of the earlier psychotherapeutists. Strange as the comparison may seem, because of these ambitions both the schools have been compared (by some in derision, and by some in homage) to mystical schools like that of Christian Science. There are close similarities between some of the conclusions to which the respective theories have led. For example, the psychoanalytical theory that mental slips and quasi-mechanical movements betray the wishes of the subconscious, harmonises with the theory of those who hold that suggestion (autosuggestion) exercises, through the instrumentality of our subconscious movements, some degree of control over the happenings of our lives. The practitioners of autosuggestion, like the psychoanalysts, have almost completely abandoned the use of hypnosis, not because they consider it dangerous, but because, in most instances, a simpler method is available. In both cases a parallel progress has been the cause of the abandonment of hypnotism. Thanks to a growing knowledge of the laws of the subconscious and of the imagination, it has become possible to set agoing in the waking state mechanisms which previously could only be set agoing with the aid of hypnosis; this being achieved in the waking state, either by the exhumation of lost or misunderstood memories, or else by inducing a mutinous nervous system to make its submission to the intelligence. Finally, both methods are essentially educative, even though both are chiefly employed for curative purposes. If the master exercises a certain authority, he does so only for a brief season, and his persistent aim is to set the pupil free. Autosuggestion can even be applied in the absence of any director, and simply as the outcome of reading a manual, for in the case of autosuggestion it is preeminently true that there is no absolute need for the affective dependence of the subject upon an operator.

Autosuggestion was in the air in 1910, for we have seen that Ferenczi, working from the psychoanalytical side, was led to regard every suggestion as an autosuggestion. Nevertheless he continued to look upon autosuggestion as a symptom of neurosis. Is there any justification for this view?

One thing which Ferenczi says is perfectly true. The fact that suggestion is operative in a very large percentage of subjects, perhaps in all or nearly all (as Coué asserts, and as I agree), does not, per se, prove that suggestion is normal, or that it has no kinship with neurosis. A phenomenon which occurs in everyone is not necessarily "normal," in the sense of "healthy," if its universal occurrence be *induced*. Everyone can be influenced by suggestion? Everyone can influence himself by suggestion? No doubt, but we can poison everyone, and everyone can poison himself. Here is a simple and obvious objection, but it is one to which suggesters have rarely paid adequate attention.

If we are entitled to consider suggestion, theoretically identifiable with autosuggestion, as a normal phenomenon, this is not merely because it is of constant occurrence, but because it occurs *spontaneously*. When we produce this phenomenon to order, we do not really produce it, we reproduce it. The theory of suggestion which I have expounded in *Suggestion and Autosuggestion*, is based on the distinction between spontaneous suggestion and reflective suggestion. Educative or therapeutic suggestion merely brings into play the psychological laws which are normally and continually in operation; it serves merely to guide their working towards a definite end. Is not this simply a part of the progressive conquest achieved by mankind over tendencies and impulses, which have been coordinated into deliberate actions?

The fact remains that in the practice of suggestion there is requisite a peculiar state of the attention, known as contention or concentration, and that this state has some kinship with hypnosis. But contention or concentration can arise spontaneously in us all, whenever our attention is immobilised, or lulled by monotonous sensations. It cannot be regarded as pathological; and the fact that we employ it deliberately at a given moment, does not make it pathological. If the question of morbidity may perhaps arise in connection with states of profound hypnosis (which are beside the question here, since they have nothing to do with the practical methods we are now considering), it certainly does not arise as far as concerns the states of concentration which are the necessary and sufficient precondition of suggestion.

Furthermore, suggestion as practised at Nancy has never shown itself to be a culture medium for neuroses. That is the important point. Perhaps suggestion may bring into play certain mechanisms which are also at work in neurosis. If this be true, there must be the same sort of relationship between suggestion and neurosis as between art and neurosis, and we might say of suggestion, substituting one term for the other, what we said of art: "A suggestion is a successful neurosis; a neurosis is an unsuccessful suggestion." But in this case, likewise, we must bear in mind that there is a great difference between success and failure. In a word, if we had to accept such a theory, we could say in psychoanalytic terminology that suggestion is a form of sublimation.

Suggestion, we shall be told, might be regarded as a form of sublimation, were it not that it is a *repression* followed by a disastrous *derivation.* Here we reach the last and most important objection. The rejoinder is supplied by one of the laws of subconscious activity, a law which is quite as important as the laws of repression and derivation. I have formulated it as the *law of subconscious teleology*, and it is confirmed every day by the practice of autosuggestion. The law runs as follows: "*Suggestion acts by subconscious teleology; when the end has been suggested, the subconscious finds means for its realisation.*"[1] Posthypnotic suggestion, in which the subject (unaware that the act he performs has been suggested to him) finds excellent reasons for what he is doing, was one of the first manifestations of this law to be noted. Here we are in touch with the phenomenon known to psychoanalysts as *rationalisation*, but the law of subconscious teleology has much wider scope. We know that suggestion can effect the cure of functional and even of organic disease—for the cure of organic disease, foreseen by earlier investigators, is categorically asserted by the New Nancy School. But even where functional diseases are concerned, such cures presuppose an intricate physiological working which takes

[1] Baudouin, op. cit., p. 97; English translation, p. 117.

place in the absence of any detailed suggestions. The end has been suggested, but the subject may be entirely ignorant of physiology and may remain quite unaware of what is going on within him. *This law is of primary importance. A knowledge of it has led Coué to substitute to an increasing extent* POSITIVE *and* GENERAL *suggestions for* NEGATIVE *and* PARTICULAR *suggestions.*

We use positive suggestions; that is to say, we aim at affirming the desirable state, rather than at denying the undesirable state. As I have said elsewhere: "*Veni Creator* is, in all respects, a far more potent exorcism than *Vade retro Satana*. We get rid of evil by filling its place with good."[1] We use general suggestions; that is to say, we direct our thoughts towards the general state of good health, towards self-confidence, etc., rather than inclining to dwell much on specific symptoms.

Experience shows that these positive and general suggestions are extremely effective. Thanks to the law of subconscious teleology, it is needless to particularise by name each one of the devils to be exorcised.

When such suggestions cure nervous troubles, have we any right to talk of repression? I do not think so. If we recall the comparison of repression to a dam, and of derivation to a side branch into which the pent-up stream now flows, such a suggestion does not concern itself with the evil derivative, with the sluggish backwater which is the morbid symptom; the suggestion does not build a new dam in the morbid channel, which might make the waters flow in a yet more disastrous direction. The suggestion works by opening a new derivative, rational and beneficent; by opening a new channel along which the stream then flows spontaneously.

If, however, we find it necessary to formulate a detailed and negative suggestion (I am assuming that we think only of symptoms of nervous origin, since we are not for the moment concerned with the other applications of suggestion), there can be no doubt that the psychoanalysts' objection is valid, and that repression is at work. But we must not therefore unconditionally condemn such a form of suggestion, for it can always be supplemented by positive and general suggestions. To return to our simile, it is as if we were simultaneously

[1] Op. cit., p. 153; English translation, p. 180.

damming up the undesirable backwater and opening a new and satisfactory channel. While this work is in progress, certain fluctuations may occur ; we may find that a rebellious symptom undergoes a displacement whereby the patient's condition is improved. This is what happened to the neuralgia from which the subject Bertha was suffering. Under treatment by suggestion, it was displaced and became less severe. Subsequently a complete cure was effected, as soon as psychoanalysis had revealed the real cause of the malady.

When we recall, as we have just recalled, that psychoanalysis was at first practised upon subjects in the hypnotic state, that it developed out of hypnotic methods, we cannot fail to recognise that neither suggestion, nor hypnosis itself, need perforce lead to repression ; we realise on the contrary, that suggestion, in hypnotised subjects, can set free, can relieve ; we realise that, in hypnosis and through hypnosis, suggestion is competent to exhume what has been repressed.

Suggestion in the waking state can play the same part. It was used by Freud after he had given up the hypnotic method, and before he had adopted the extant method of association and of the analysis of dreams. Let us quote Freud.

" The problem was that the patient had to be taught something which the physician did not know and which the patient had ceased to be aware of. How was this to be achieved ? I then remembered having seen a remarkable and instructive experiment performed by Bernheim at Nancy. Bernheim had shown us that the persons in whom he had induced hypnotic somnambulism, and whom he had made perform various acts, although they appeared to have forgotten what they had witnessed and what they had done under hypnotism, had not really forgotten ; he showed that it was possible to revive these memories in the waking state. If, after such patients have been reawakened, we question them about what has happened, they declare at first that they know nothing of the matter ; but if we persist, if we return to the charge, if we assure them that they can remember, the lost memories return in their entirety.

" I pursued this plan with my own patients. When they said that they knew nothing more, I assured them that they did know, that they had merely to go on talking ; and I even declared that the memory which surged up at the moment when I placed my hand on the patient's forehead would be the right memory. In this way I was able, without employing hypnotism, to teach my patients all that was requisite to restore the relationship between the forgotten pathogenic scenes, and the symptoms that were the residue of these. In the long run, however, the process proved tedious and exhausting, so that it was unsuitable as the basis of a definitive technique." [1]

It does not follow that this method, or some similar method, will prove unsuitable as an auxiliary technique. In many cases, a subject has nothing whatever to say regarding some memory or association; or the subject has merely the vague sense that there is a reminiscence which cannot be clearly recalled. In such instances, I have sometimes taken out my watch and, showing it to the subject before laying it on the table, I have declared that the missing memory would become perfectly clear in five minutes. We would then go on talking of other things, the subject not consciously watching the passage of time; but after the lapse of five minutes, neither more nor less, our conversation would be interrupted by the explanation: "Ah, now I remember!"

Above all, suggestion can aid the clarifying process of the analysis if the operator assures the subject, once for all, that the latter's reminiscences will be revived with increasing facility, and that dreams will in future be remembered without any difficulty. A direct suggestion may even be given that the subject will be *less and less inclined to repress* what is now hidden in the subconscious. Furthermore, the operator can make use of suggestion to minimise the distress which sometimes attends the work of analysis—just as, by suggestion, anæsthesia can be induced for the performance of a surgical operation.

But suggestion is not only useful during the conduct of the analysis; it is likewise helpful, and preeminently so, in the guidance of the subject. Inasmuch as suggestion is at times competent, unaided, to bring about beneficial derivations of the nervous force that has been hemmed up in the blind alley of a symptom, a fortiori it is competent to assist psychoanalysis in this task.

[1] Freud, La psychanalyse, pp. 35–6.

We see, then, that a collaboration, an enduring collaboration, of the two methods is possible. My personal experience has confirmed theory in this matter. I find that a great deal of time and trouble is saved by the use of suggestion in conjunction with psychoanalysis.

When discussing the thesis expounded by Ferenczi, I purposely left unconsidered the question of the *transference* which was supposed to underlie suggestibility. This transference,[1] in virtue of which the subject subconsciously brings into relation with the operator all kinds of infantile and sexual feelings, is not peculiar to suggestion. Indeed, its occurrence first became apparent during the practice of psychoanalysis, and it has been made a ground for objecting to that practice. The rejoinder of the psychoanalysts, and especially of Ferenczi, is to demonstrate that the transference in question is not a direct consequence of the psychoanalysis, and that it occurs in other circumstances, as for instance in suggestion.

Psychoanalytical interpretation must unquestionably be invoked to throw light upon the intricate and hitherto obscure phenomena of the affective relationship which arises, during suggestion and in other ways, between subject and director. Psychoanalysis will elucidate this feeling, as it elucidates other human feelings, by discovering in it, too, "sexual" and "infantile" elements; it will not therefore condemn the feeling. No psychoanalyst would, indeed, dream of condemning it, since psychoanalytical treatment would itself be involved in the condemnation.

"Transference on to the analyst" in psychoanalytical consultations is regarded by psychoanalysts as a preeminent variety of such transferences. All the previously repressed "affects," being suddenly set free by the analysis, are supposed to seek forthwith an object to which they can secure fixation; and the first object they encounter is, we are told, the personality of the analyst. These "affects" are regarded as being more or less definitely sexual in origin.

According to Pierre Janet, there is "a large measure of truth" in this thesis of sexual transference. "We must recognise," he writes, "that in a certain number of cases the patient's words and gestures are absolutely identical with those

[1] Freud, Zur Dynamik der Uebertragung.

of persons in love. Probably there is an analogy between their feelings and those inspired by sexual love."[1]

Nor have I any thought of denying the occurrence of "transference." In the present volume, I record a fairly typical instance (Rynaldo). But in this matter, as in others, I should prefer to avoid an apriori formulation of the problem simply as a function of the sexual instinct. I am inclined rather to ask to what extent the *imitative* instinct may be at work here; to what extent *fear* is operative in arousing the sense that there is need for a protector; and so on. In my opinion, "transference" is an even more complicated affair than has been supposed; and I am doubtful whether it is as stereotyped as most psychoanalysts declare. If we invite the subject to expect its appearance in a certain form, and if we ourselves expect it to appear in this form, the odds are that, thanks to the working of suggestion, the expected will happen. Let the reader recall the law of the "three states" (lethargy, catalepsy, and somnambulism) through which all Charcot's hypnotised subjects passed. The law was true at the Salpêtrière. It was not true at Nancy, because here the collective suggestion that determined the appearance of these three states had not been made. No doubt the three states of lethargy, catalepsy, and somnambulism occurred at Nancy; but at Nancy their appearance in a definite order, as the outcome of an invariable method of procedure, was no longer an absolute law of hypnotism. Is it anything to our discredit if we should find it necessary to make the avowal that at Geneva our subjects are less inclined to show a passion for (or against) the analyst than they show at Vienna or Zurich?

It would seem that "transference," which is an undeniable fact, takes the form, erotic or other, that is imposed on it by suggestion. The most important suggestion, in this connection, is the analyst's conviction of the form the transference will take, for involuntarily he suggests this form to the subject. Suggestions of such a character are some of the numerous spontaneous suggestions which are inevitably made in the course of the analysis; they ought to be guided, to be transformed into purposive and well-defined suggestions. We can "cultivate" a morbid transference, just as it has been

[1] Janet, Les médications psychologiques, vol. iii., p. 403.

possible to "cultivate hysteria." It is equally possible to avoid doing anything of the kind. I consider that suggestion will often enable us, by a direct route, to open to the subject's interest, to his "libido," healthy and broad outlooks towards mankind and the world. If we do this successfully, the crisis of "fixation upon the analyst" is likely to pass unnoticed.

"Transference" is the fundamental condition underlying "influence" or "moral guidance." It thus serves as an additional link between psychoanalysis and suggestion, both of which are based upon this "influence" and this "guidance." Indeed, at one time suggestion was identified with them, until, by degrees, people came to recognise in suggestion a phenomenon peculiar to itself, namely, ideoreflex power or autosuggestion. This does not involve the denial that an affective relationship, a "transference," remains a potent factor of suggestion. Where affective relationship exists, suggestion finds the ground well prepared. This amounts to saying that psychoanalytical practice is an excellent field for suggestion, and that suggestions will inevitably be made in the course of psychoanalysis; it amounts to saying that however much the analyst may wish to ignore suggestion, he cannot help himself in this matter, and that he would act much more wisely were he to recognise that he is making suggestions, and to attempt to guide them. By adopting transference, by admitting with good reason that a relationship of deep sympathy arises between subject and analyst, psychoanalysts have adopted suggestion willy-nilly. Those who proceed to renounce suggestion are like the child who wanted to go to the Midnight Mass if only it could be celebrated in the daytime!

The trouble is that people used to consider the hypnotiser's or suggester's influence as a more or less occult power attaching to his personality, whereas according to the psychoanalysts the secret of the influence resides in the affective disposition of the subject. The old theory is still a popular conviction, but the psychoanalytical view certainly takes us nearer to the heart of the matter. We must, however, bear in mind that the affective disposition of the subject and the personal influence of the director are merely the obverse and the reverse of the same phenomenon, and that personal influence is a reality. It, too, must be taken into consideration before we can lay the foundations of a complete psychology of " transference." In so far as the psychoanalyst exercises such an influence, it is the outcome of a mingling of numerous qualities, which we cannot always expect to find assembled in the same individual: such qualities as the quasi-artistic talent for intuitively divining the subconscious, a severely critical sense, firmness and decision, confidence and self-command, sympathy, moral value—all the qualities which characterise a great spiritual director.[1]

[1] Confession has been termed an " anticipation of psychoanalysis." A Roman Catholic writer (Cochet, Psychoanalyse et mysticisme, p. 562), though strongly critical of psychoanalysis, writes: " Without transference, no cure. As soon as transference has occurred, the doctor's task of moral regeneration resembles that with which Catholic confessors are familiar. It is of great value in a Protestant land, where so many young men suffer from hidden troubles and unavowed torments."

PART TWO

CASE HISTORIES

CHAPTER FIVE

CHILDREN

THE psychoanalysis of children, especially of young children, cannot in most cases be systematically made, for, in them, questioning to discover associations is often difficult. It is better to take the associations as they come, and for this the observer must either live with the child or must get his information from those who do so.

It was by means of such chance observations that I was enabled to analyse the dreams of the two little girls, Linette and Mireille. Though of different ages, they showed the same conflict: a very strong attachment to the mother (partly due to the father's absence), and a marked difficulty in detaching a share of interest from the mother in order to apply it to life in general. Life always seemed something forbidden and dangerous. The foreshadowings of sexuality were accompanied by intense distress, manifesting itself in nightmares.

In the next two cases, those of Robert and Jean, I give analyses of school essays. These can be analysed just like a dream or a poem, especially when the writer is imaginative. Above all, the method is valuable when the teacher has left some freedom in the choice of subject, for then the imagination has free play, or, to put the matter more accurately, it is then entirely controlled by the child's subconscious. Pfister has shown how psychoanalysis can be turned to account at school, but the technique of such analyses still remains to be determined. I think that school essays furnish abundant material, and here we have an additional reason for preferring those in which the choice of topic has been left to the child's imagination free from outward constraint. The analysis will sometimes apprise teachers of humiliating but valuable truths concerning the child's intimate reactions to its education.

Robert is not sparing in the disclosure of such truths. As for Jean, he reveals a protest against paternal authority.

In default of psychoanalysis, it is difficult for adults to realise how intense and even tragical are the conflicts that may disturb the child mind, even at the early age of four. These conflicts are the germs of those which may subsequently develop into neuroses, or may give rise to all kinds of crises. If we make ourselves acquainted with them, we may hope to guard against such evil consequences.

Of course when we are dealing with children, and above all when we are dealing with young children, there can be no question of explaining the conflict to the subject, as we should explain it to an adult. Still less can there be any question of making the child's upper consciousness fully aware of the inadmissible desires which are manifest in the subconscious. But the educator, when he has discovered anything of the kind, must note the fact, and must take measures accordingly.

1. Linette

DREAMS OF FORBIDDEN PLEASURES. FIXATION UPON THE MOTHER.

(from 3 years and 9 months to 7 years.)

First we have a series of dreams and incidents occurring when the child was just four. They show clearly the working of some of the elementary mechanisms of the dream and of affectivity. One of the advantages of studying children is that these mechanisms are displayed in all their simplicity

Linette has a passion for her black kitten, and nurses it all day like a doll. She used to suffer much from nightmares. Thanks to treatment by suggestion, these have become less frequent. But they still occur from time to time, and Linette reveals them by talking in her sleep. Here is her commonest nightmare.

> I. Kitty is running up Mont Salève; it will be lost; it is drowning.—This last form of the nightmare, that of the drowning, is the one which causes the greatest distress.

The family goes on a journey, and the kitten is left behind. Linette is continually asking for it, and, notwithstanding the pleasure of new scenes, she would like to go home to be with her kitty once more. But, while she is away, a girl makes her a present of a tiny doll, smaller than her little finger—a nigger boy with sparkling eyes, seated like a child in a bath. Linette is so overwhelmed with delight that she is hardly able to stammer a word of thanks. Though she has brought a large doll with her, she now thinks of nothing but the little nigger. She no longer talks of her kitten. One night she wakes up crying out:

II. "My little nigger is drowned!"

Here we have her usual nightmare, with the substitution of the nigger boy for the kitten. The doll represented a small, black creature with sparkling eyes, one made to be cuddled. There was enough resemblance to facilitate a close association between the nigger doll and the kitten. Transference was complete. Even more manifest was the transference when, having returned home, Linette rushed off to find the kitten, and suddenly lost all interest in the little nigger. He had been her inseparable companion for a week, but now he was left lying for days in the bottom of the basket in which she had brought him home. He had merely been an understudy, a substitute. Nevertheless she had a fond memory of him and wanted to write a letter of thanks to the donor.

We are entitled to say that there had been a temporary displacement of affective stress from the kitten to the nigger doll. There is no need to invoke any sort of moral repression in order to explain this displacement. If there was anything analogous to a repressed feeling, it simply lay in this, that the natural object of the feeling was absent. The case was on all fours with that of a feeling which undergoes derivation when its first object has been lost. There was no displacement peculiar to the dream state; displacement had occurred in the waking life, and the dream life had followed the lead of the waking life.

About ten days after coming home, Linette had a dream which was not a nightmare. She related it after waking.

III. A young lady had given her a doll; but Linette had dropped the doll and it had broken. She was ever so sorry. A little farther on she had met the young lady who had given her the tiny nigger boy.

I asked some simple questions, being careful that they should not be leading questions.

> Baudouin. What was the doll like in your dream?
> Linette. Like my little nigger, only it was big and it wasn't black.
> B. What colour was it?
> L. White.
> B. Was it sitting down like your little nigger?
> L. No, it was standing up, quite straight, like my Jenny.

Here we have a quaint sort of resemblance! One is reminded of the schoolboy's answer that "cheval" was derived from "equus" by changing "e" into "che" and "quus" into "val." Linette goes one better. Her dream doll is like the nigger—save only that the dream doll is white, big, and upright, instead of being black, little, and seated. It should be noted that "Jenny" is the only one of her many dolls which is made all in one piece, so that it can neither cross its legs nor sit down. The little nigger is seated tailor fashion, which is rather fascinating.

Linette's answers showed that in her dream there had been a systematisation of contrast. The doll and the nigger *resemble one another by contrast.* The image of the nigger is systematically negated. Nevertheless the girl, the donor, who has likewise been temporarily effaced, reappears at the end of the dream. All the other details, the leading details, show themselves by contraries. We note, moreover, that the dream, thus retouched, is no longer a nightmare, although Linette had been "ever so sorry." The feeling of distress is still there, but attenuated. Everything happens as if the feeling had undergone *attenuation by displacement* upon unrecognisable images. In like manner a hot liquid is cooled by pouring it from one vessel to another. Thus the simple instance of this child's dream gives us a vivid picture of what is probably one of the functions of the displacement. The latter is, as it were, a means of cooling the soup, which was scalding hot, and now becomes drinkable. Thanks to the displacement, what would have been a nightmare becomes a dream which, though still disagreeable, no longer induces terror, or screams, or waking with a start.

The matter may be reconstituted as follows. The customary nightmare, that of the kitten, was imminent, for the nigger doll no longer occupied the leading place in the child's mind. By a first displacement, which availed itself of an antecedent mechanism (dream II), the nigger was substituted for the kitten; but the nigger was still too recognisable an image, and a second displacement led to the substitution of the white doll.

At this period suggestions were being made to Linette every evening during natural sleep, the most important suggestion being that she would sleep quietly without any nightmare. Displacement was the means used by the suggestion to overcome the nightmare.

Linette told her dream about the doll in the most natural way possible. Here is another dream which she told her mother as a great secret, almost in a whisper, and with obvious embarrassment. Subsequently, when I asked her to tell me the dream and to give me some more details, she hid shamefacedly behind the door, and would not tell me a word. Here is what she told her mother.

> IV. She had a pain in her back. She was quite alone at the clinic and was being treated.

A "pansexualist" would regard the shame and embarrassment which accompanied the telling of this dream as obvious indications of a sexual dream. This would be jumping to conclusions. Linette shows exactly the same kind of embarrassment whenever allusion is made in her presence to one of her more serious offences or to the subsequent scoldings. This embarrassment makes her do what children are apt to do in such cases. She promptly represses the disagreeable reminiscence, and changes the subject. There is unquestionably shame, but simply moral shame. Now certain data enable me to give a similar interpretation to the shame attendant upon the recital of Linette's dream.

Two or three days before the dream, her mother had had a pain in the back. Finding Linette rather troublesome, the mother had said: "You are tiring me. If you are not a good girl I shall have to go to the hospital for my back; I shall have to send you away to a lodging and you'll be all alone." Linette was afraid that this would happen, and in the dream her fear found expression. There is a condensation of Linette left alone and her sick mother; Linette's "lodging" and her mother's "hospital" are condensed into something betwixt and between, which is called the "clinic." Through this condensation, in which she invests herself with her mother's illness, Linette perhaps gives expression to the feeling that in doing her mother harm she is punishing herself. Certainly the condensation is enough to make her upper consciousness unaware of the real issues; but nevertheless she has a confused feeling that there is something she ought to be ashamed of.

During the journey on which she had been given the nigger doll, Linette had had a great disappointment. It was at Montreux. She had been watching the preparations for the national festival, which was to be held on the shore of the lake. She had been greatly impressed by the sight of the men who climbed ladders to hang up garlands and coloured glass globes. Eagerly she was looking forward to the festival, the fireworks, and the music. But heavy rain at the critical moment frustrated her hopes. A few months later she was with her mother on the shore of the lake, this time at Geneva. She had been playing with a stranger, a little boy. The children's mothers had found it necessary to intervene more than once to keep the peace. A game, begun in high good humour, had ended in a quarrel, and Linette was out of temper when she came home.

The two disappointments were condensed in the following dream (4 years and 4 months).

> V. We were on the shore of the lake, where I met the little boy the other day. There were some white things like fireworks in the sky. Some men were going up ladders. I didn't like it, Mother, because you wouldn't take me to hear the music.

We can recognise the attempt to satisfy in a dream a wish that has not been satisfied in real life; this is why in the dream, she sees things "like fireworks." But the wish is incompletely fulfilled; maternal authority stands in the way of the enjoyment of some of the coveted pleasures (the music), and the feeling of disappointment persists.

Here is another dream, built upon the same plan, embodying

an attempt to realise a forbidden wish, and entailing a disappointment.

VI. Linette breaks her English doll while she is washing it.

Her mother has, in fact, often forbidden her to wash her English doll. In a dream she disobeys; she satisfies her wish; but the hidden thought that things will turn out ill persists, and the doll is broken.

We have thus been able to interpret every one of these dreams by bringing it into relationship with certain wishes, fears, feelings, definite happenings. In each specific instance we have been careful to avoid having recourse to more recondite explanations, to avoid invoking explanations which were not requisite to explain the specific instance under review. Here we have a methodological principle which we should always follow.

This, however, does not mean that, when we have a series of dreams, it would be wrong to enquire whether they do not manifest one or more general trends, over and above temporary feelings.

Linette's dreams are less independent than might appear at first sight. Attention has already been drawn to the resemblance between V and VI. Here Linette is in search of pleasures forbidden by her mother, and the search is unsuccessful. Affairs turn out ill. But more than this; in the last dream (VI), the *doll* which Linette *breaks* while she is *washing* it recapitulates a *motif* we have encountered earlier in the series: the broken doll—the doll which was only a substitute for the nigger (III); the drowned nigger (II); and the drowned kitten (I). This suggests the idea that in the earlier dreams there was something masked, something more than the simple fear of losing the kitten she was so fond of. Would this fear have been sufficient to cause a nightmare? The juxtaposition of the various dreams suggests that the cat, the nigger, and the white doll, may be playing the same role as the English doll in dream VI; now the English doll represents *a pleasure forbidden by the mother.* There are several data to confirm the notion that the kitten was linked with analogous ideas. First of all Linette was continually messing the kitten about, and her mother had had to tell her sometimes to let the poor little beast alone. Next, Linette said one day:

> VII (4 years and 11 months). "I wish I was a kitten!
> "Why?"
> "Because kittens are allowed to eat between meals. But I should like still more to be a mother cat, because they make kittens."

"Kittens are allowed to eat between meals." Here the longing finds expression. The kitten represents the pleasures children are forbidden to enjoy; for Linette, one of these pleasures is that of being a mother in her turn, when she will be able to make up for having had to submit to maternal authority. (We should note that when she is caressing her dolls, or fondling her kitten, which is a living doll, Linette is obviously playing at being a mother.) But in the dreams that have been recorded, the search for forbidden pleasures has invariably culminated in a check or a disaster. We must realise that this search involves something more than childish disobedience. The forbidden pleasures include life itself; the life of grown-ups with all its mysteries; the life forbidden to children, the mysteries of which they may not talk and which arouse a vague sense of fear. The significance of the allusion to the mother cat which "makes kittens" is unmistakable.

We shall get a stage farther on if we consider the circumstances in which the dream of the kitten had occurred for the first time. Linette's mother was separated from the father. The girl had known little of her father, and that little had not been agreeable. When Linette was 3 years and 9 months old her mother had moved house; they quitted a room where Linette and her mother had lived alone together in close intimacy since leaving the father. For Linette, this house-moving was a departure into the unknown, a step towards the mysterious and forbidden reality of life. It was just at this time that Linette was given the kitten. A further new element in her life was that she now had a bedroom of her own. The kitten naturally became associated in her mind with the new house and the new life. To Linette this new life was something on a larger scale than the old life had been, for her mother was no longer the only figure on her horizon.

Now, however, came the usual conflict between the *progressive* tendency, leading out towards life, towards the unknown and the forbidden, and the *regressive* tendency fixed upon the mother. The absence of the father, and the very close intimacy with the mother (since mother and child had rarely been separated for even as long as a few hours), had contributed to make Linette's fixation upon the mother very strong.

On waking after the first night in the new dwelling, Linette had some dreams to tell.

VIII. She had been dreaming "all night." The moon was shining brightly and they were in the old house. She was looking at the moon. Mother was there. Then they both went to bed, and in the morning they got up.

She had dreamed, too, that she had lost all her things during the move.

She had also dreamed that her kitten had run away.

The dreams give definite expression to the regressive tendency. Linette goes back to the " old house " so that mother can be there and the two can sleep together all night. The kitten, which symbolises the progressive tendency, " runs away." The loss of the kitten is annoying, but the image of the old house is pleasurable. There is a conflict between the two tendencies. Linette is quite upset by the move; she hardly knows where she is; she " loses all her things."

We are now led to suspect that the same conflict is betrayed by the dreams previously quoted, all of which were subsequent to number VIII. If, in these dreams, the wish for the forbidden pleasure, the wish to escape from the mother leads to mischief, this is because it is counterchecked by an opposite wish, by the wish to remain tied to her mother. Here, as elsewhere, distress shows itself as the outcome of a conflict.

It is necessary to point out that dreams and fantasies of immersion have often been interpreted as expressions of the regressive tendency and of a flight from life. Some even go so far as to see in these dreams and fantasies the definite image of a subconscious wish to return to the mother's womb, and the collective symbol has been supposed to explain a number of myths and rites.[1] I cannot insist too often that it

[1] Especially the rite of baptism or rebirth. Cf. Morel, L'introversion mystique, 1918, p. 54.

is always hazardous to invoke the symbolism of the " collective unconscious " as a direct interpretation of an individual dream. Still, when an individual analysis leads us to an interpretation which squares with that of the collective symbolism, the fact is interesting. I may note, then, that in Linette's case the dreams of drowning (the drowning of the kitten, or the drowning of the little nigger) seem to me to be expressions of a regressive tendency and of fixation upon the mother.

In certain dreams subsequent to those we have been analysing, these relationships were confirmed.

> IX (5 years and 2 months). Linette dreams that the cat brings the doll into her bed. The cat carries the doll in its mouth.

This shows once more the close and firm association between the doll and the cat.

The next dream is more interesting. In it Linette is substituted for the cat, for in all these dreams she is herself in reality the central figure. Here again, after the lapse of eighteen months, we find the relationship which was shown on the night after the house-moving (VIII), the relationship between the drowning dream and what I shall call the derelict dream (she loses all her things, loses her way). Moreover, in the other dreams the kitten has sometimes been lost and sometimes been drowned.

> X (5 years and 3 months). She dreams every night that she goes for a walk and loses her way. She is in the streets of the town ; there are a great many people. But everyone thinks that she is shopping, and no one takes any notice of her.
>
> She also dreams that she is on the shore of the lake, at the place where a man has been drowned. Mist is rising from the lake. " What does it feel like when one is drowning ? Does one come to pieces ? "
>
> She also dreams that she herself is drowning.

Now that we are aware of this relationship, we shall class other " derelict " dreams in the same group.

> XI (5 years and 3 months). She was quite alone in the town. First of all a bicycle nearly ran over her, and then she really was run over by a motor car.

Is it not pathetic to find in a little girl the initiation of the tragedy which psychoanalysis has so often revealed in adults who have experienced similar conditions in childhood. In Linette's case, as in so many others, the loss of the father and the intense fixation upon the mother are the predominant causes.

At this date the derelict dream undergoes a modification. Linette loses her way and then *some one takes care of her.* The person who takes care of her is usually a girl, and this marks the opening of a period when she had violent and fleeting passions for girls or young women. Less often, the person who takes care of her in the dream is a man.

XII (5 years and 3 months). She dreams that her mother is boarding her out in a market-place. In the market she cannot find what she wants; there are only red and crimson stuffs; there is no lace. There was a wooden staircase at the end of the market, and a young girl in blue made her a cup of chocolate.

The wooden staircase comes from a house where there lives a young woman for whom she had one of her brief passions, but whom she had ceased to care for; the girl in blue is like a lady who paid a visit a few days earlier, and who had at once made a conquest of Linette.

XIII (5 years and 4 months). She has been sent out on to the staircase. On the staircase she meets a girl, whom she asks to take care of her.

She was drowning; the girl waded into the water and fished her out.

Once more we have the relationship between the derelict dream and the drowning dream.

XIV (5 years and 4 months). She was on a road. She was picking grasses. There was a man there who was running after the sun. She had lost her way. A man took care of her, took her to his house, and polished her sabots before bringing her home.

Through the same dream passes the figure of a neighbour's child, a little boy in whom Linette has been much interested for several days. He was badly behaved, used nasty words, and made rude gestures, so that her mother had to send him away.

At the date of these three dreams, Linette's feelings were manifesting an outward impulsion (the progressive tendency). As usually happens in the case of a little girl who has a strong fixation upon the mother, her affections, despite a few vacillations, are mainly concentrated upon persons of her own sex who are considerably older than herself. She does not usually get on very well with children of her own age; moreover, she has few child acquaintances.

Before this blossoming when she was five years old, Linette (notwithstanding such fantasies as VII, the one of the mother cat who makes kittens) found the idea of marriage repugnant as far as she herself was concerned. She got quite annoyed if anyone talked to her about it.

When she was three years and ten months old, she had the following conversation with her mother:

XV. Linette. Will you give me this teapot?
Mother. When you get married.
L. I won't get married.
M. What do you know about getting married?
L. (suddenly overcome with shame buries her head in her arms and then hides head and arms in her mother's lap). I won't tell you.
M. Very well. You needn't get married. You're quite right. Husbands are horrid.
L. Yes, they're as horrid as the teapot.
M. Why is the teapot horrid?
L. Because it burns.

A few pages back we rejected the hypothesis of sexual shame when a simple moral shame seemed an adequate explanation. But in the shame which Linette showed when she spoke of marriage there would seem to have been a sexual element. It is foolish to feel horrified at such a notion. Of course a child does not really know what marriage means. Nevertheless in the subconscious there is a phenomenon which at first we are loth to recognise, but to which psychoanalysis continually brings us back. A confused form of sexuality (it would be better, perhaps, if we had some other name for it) is present in the subconscious long before puberty, and indeed from the very earliest years. What may we suppose to have been the incidents that awakened in Linette's case the sexual shame she exhibited at the age of three years and ten months? They may have been impressions of fear and disgust connected with the memory of her father, with the memory of certain actions and certain words. Whatever the cause, the shame existed, and was attended by a categorical refusal of marriage. This refusal had a strong emotional basis, for the child became quite angry whenever the matter was pressed. The way in which she buried her head in her mother's lap at the moment when she was giving expression to her sense of shame, was another manifestation of the mechanism previously described. On the one hand there was the dread of the progressive tendency, of the tendency towards the unknown and the forbidden; on the other hand, and simultaneously, there was the regressive tendency, the flight towards the mother's womb.

Psychoanalysis shows that in adults the progressive and extrovertive tendency includes within it the sexual tendency; that the fear of life and of extroversion includes within it the fear of sexuality, or the disgust inspired by sexuality. Now all these psychological elements exist *in embryo* in the child; and the embryonic elements have the same mutual relationships as the fully developed elements in the adult.

After the conversation last quoted, Linette had a nightmare. Awaking with a start, she screamed:

> XVI (3 years and 10 months). "There's a toad on my bed!"

A week later, just as she was going to sleep, she twisted the corner of the sheet into a point and said:

> "Look at the little pointed animal which is climbing up after me."
> "What do you call your little animal?"
> "A toad."

In the dreams of adults we know that dreams of sticky beasts and pointed things must usually be interpreted as symbols of the sexual organs. The condensation of the sticky animal and the pointed object into a single image is still more significant. All these things belong to the "collective unconscious." Such examples as the foregoing (for it is not an isolated incident) would seem to force upon us the recognition that, in children, budding sexuality expresses itself by the same images, long before these images can have been the outcome of any personal experience. These considerations lead us to infer that there are genuinely innate associations and condensations. The theory of the inheritance of associations held by the associationist evolutionists, and by Darwin himself, apropos of the acquirement of instincts, would appear to receive from such phenomena a confirmation which the psychological study of instinct per se has failed to furnish.[1] For the psychology of instinct is concerned only with motor mechanisms, and merely assumes the existence of associations of images behind these mechanisms. Psychoanalysis, on the other hand, directly studies such associations.

We shall not here go more deeply into this matter. Suffice it to record without comment a number of Linette's dreams subsequent in date to XVI, and showing images of the same character.

XVII. *a.* One morning, a few minutes after waking, she said: "There is a worm on my counterpane."

b. Waking with a start, she said: "An animal tried to eat me; it was a flat dog without any legs; it crawled."

c. Waking with a start, she cried: "There is a man in my bed!" Then she explained: "There was a man in my bed, and I had to give him some cake."

d. The fairy Carabosse had made her eat slugs and worms; the fairy was sometimes flat and sometimes large.

e. It was at home. They heard the wolf come upstairs and knock at the door. "We shut all the doors tight. But the wolf had with him another animal, grey like pussy, but long and flat. The wolf's animal got in, no one knew how. Outside, the wolf growled and went on talking. The wolf's animal bit my hand, in the place where I pricked myself with a needle in that other dream, and a worm came out of the prick. I cried when the animal bit me."—When the wolf first came, it was small; but when it was at the door, it was big. Sometimes it was little and sometimes it was big.

f. (This dream ended with a scream.) She dreamed of two caterpillars, but there was only one caterpillar. First of all there was a black caterpillar which she had believed to be dead, but which had crawled over her stomach. Then it was a blue caterpillar, larger than the black one. Afterwards it was the black one again.

[1] Cf. the discussion of this theory in Claparède's book, L'association des idées, p. 390.

These dreams, which took place between the ages of four and six, were all attended by feelings of more or less intense distress. They were contemporary with the vigorous progressive and extrovertive impulsion which was previously mentioned (XII to XIV). The idea of marriage, which had been so repugnant, had at length been accepted. When she was five and a half years old, Linette became engaged to a boy of fifteen. This was a new infatuation. Apropos she said:

> Wouldn't it be horrid if my husband were to die before we are married. I know I should kill myself.

She got the following answer:

> Your husband doesn't care much about you.

Linette rejoined:

> You don't know how fond we are of one another.

This passion, like the others, was fleeting. It was succeeded by fresh loves, for members of her own sex this time, and equally transient. Linette's affections are strong but inconstant, and doubtless the fixation upon the mother is the main cause of the inconstancy. Her feeling is trying to break away from the mother, but finds great difficulty in undergoing fixation upon anyone else. She "loses all her things" in this "house-moving." As had happened in her acquaintance with the little boy on the shore of the lake (V), Linette's passions speedily culminate in disappointment. Although the progressive tendency has manifested itself more and more strongly during the last two years, the conflict between the two tendencies persists, and this is the probable explanation of the intermittent reappearance of the distressing dreams.

Linette is still rather unsociable, at any rate as far as other children are concerned. She always gets on better with persons considerably older than herself. This character trait has been accentuated by the fact that she has been brought up at home, without much contact with other children.

A few months at a day-school have only involved her in quarrels and irritation. Her relations with other children have for the most part been unhappy.

When she was nearly seven, Linette learned her first piece of poetry. This is what she chose from among a number of poems:

THE YOUNG MOUSE

A mouse, young and pretty,
Leaves its hole quietly.
It had left its mother.
Its curiosity was sparkling
In its eyes greedy for new sights:
" *Oh, how I long to have*
" *Traversed these hills and valleys!*
" I shall walk in these alleys.
" Had I listened to my parents,
" I should have spent the rest of my days
" In their sequestered nest.
" But at last I have made my way out,
" To roam at will like the winds.
" I can go wherever I please.
" Wasn't it stupid of me
" To pass all my time like that?
" But I'm more than fifteen days old now,
" And they want to keep me caged up
" As if I were still a mouseling.
" *If I jump about at all,*
" *At once comes a rough voice*
" *Crying loudly, 'You're going too fast!'*
" And then this, and then that:
" '*Stay beside me, don't go there.*'
" My mother hasn't much pluck.
" That's quite natural at her age,
" But at mine it's very different."
Just as our little mouse finished this monologue,
It was suddenly pounced upon
By a tom-cat which crunched it up
Without saying with your leave or by your leave.
You, child, reading this story,
Think the matter over again and again:
There's a moral in it!

It is obvious why this tale charmed Linette, for it is a record of the drama which had been played so vividly in her own mental development since the age of four. We have the ill-starred attempt to break away from the mother and to follow the call from without, an attempt swiftly succeeded by retribution. Even the image of the cat, which since the house-moving had symbolised for Linette the progressive tendency and its dangers, appeared in the fable as it had appeared in her own childish dreams. When Linette recited these verses, her eyes sparkled with emotion. Without fully realising it, she recognised herself as heroine of the tale. This was doubtless her first artistic impression ; for what is a work of art if it be not a ready-made symbol, one which thrills us as soon as it impinges, all unawares, upon a drama of our subconscious life ?

2. Mireille

Fixation upon the Mother. Refusal of the Feminine Role.

(7 years and 6 months.)

Mireille, like Linette, was brought up in close companionship with her mother, her father being away. Fixation upon the mother is conspicuous. As often happens in such cases, Mireille likes to play the masculine role ; she has a trapeze in the flat, and uses it a great deal. She hates dolls. She likes to wear knickerbockers, and makes a fuss if she has to put on a frock.

In Mireille, as in Linette, we can note the conflict between the progressive tendency and the regressive. Mireille shrinks from the idea of growing up. She is in the class of the " middle " pupils. One evening her mother had a talk with her as to whether, after the holidays, she was to go into the class of the " big " pupils. Mireille said that *she wanted to stay always among the middle pupils because of the big boys.* She is always rather afraid of big boys. After this talk she had a dream.

> I. All the middle pupils are out for a walk with the mistress. They reach a square. Suddenly a trapdoor opens in the ground, and there is seen a very steep ladder which they have to go down. Most of the children, including Mireille, are afraid to go down. Only Armand and Madeleine begin to go down the rungs.

Armand is rather a saucy lad, and Madeleine is near the head of the class. Commenting on this dream, the mother says that Mireille often expresses a wish that she could stay young all her life, so that she could always be with her mother.

The relationship between the fear of going forward, and fixation upon the mother, is evident. It may surprise the reader that in the dream the bold deed should be symbolised by a descent into the earth. Let us, however, recall Linette's dreams, in which boldness ends in drowning or some other mishap. The boldness is here inseparable from the danger. The dream is the outcome of the conflict between the progressive tendency and the regressive, and the two tendencies coalesce into a single image.

The following is what Mireille calls " a nice dream " :

> II. The whole family was out walking on the bank of the Arve. There were some very funny people who were half alive and half statues. They did not move. Mireille slid down a balustrade to the edge of the river, and suddenly she came down with a bump on to the stones. There she was, down below, with the rest of the family above ; then it was the other way about, she was up above, but she was not frightened. At length she found herself above, alone with her mother, and they picked flowers together.

The mother's comment on this dream is brief but interesting. " Sometimes I go for a walk along the Arve with Mireille. If the whole family is there, Mireille is apt to lag a little behind, looking about, picking flowers, or collecting insects. But if I am out with her alone, she always stays close to me. I fancy she prefers these walks when none of the others are there ; I suppose she is a little jealous."

Evidently the " nice " part of the dream is the last stage, when she is alone with her mother. Before that there has been (as in the case of Linette), a mishap as the sequel of a bold action. As to the significance of the animated statues, some associations would be useful. Still, having made other analyses, we can tentatively discern their significance. A being which was half a statue and half alive could very well symbolise the conflict of the two tendencies, the " statue " representing an unprogressive creature, one which does not grow up, whereas the " animated " component represents the progressive tendency. But whatever we may think of the significance of these " people who are half alive and half statues," the general bearing of the dream is unmistakable.

Now we come to immersion dreams akin to those of Linette's dreams which have the same motif.

> III. Mireille is in a field with two little boys. They are all riding on merry-go-round horses. They have to jump across a stream. The two boys jump first, and reach the other side safely; then she tries to follow, but tumbles into the stream. Now the ground opens, and she slides down a chimney into the kitchen of a lovely house. There are some awfully nice people there, and they give her something to eat. Meanwhile the two little boys have been hunting for her. They come in and tell her about it. Then they all say good-bye.

Here we have a reminiscence of a fairy tale which Mireille had read, and in which the ground opened in this way beneath a little girl. The girl in the story had reached an old woman's house, and had been very well treated there. In the dream, Mireille had only been frightened to begin with. As soon as she reached the bottom of the chimney, the kindness of the people there had put her quite at ease.

> IV. A café close to a wood. Mireille goes into the wood by herself, and suddenly gets bogged. She cries out in a fright. Her mother comes and says: "Never mind, I will wash you." Then Henry [her eldest brother] comes. He gets bogged too, but Mireille is deeper in the bog than Henry. Still, they are not frightened.

Nevertheless, she says that this dream was "rather nasty."

In conjunction with these immersion dreams, let us consider a suffocation dream which she had shortly after the death of one of her schoolmates.

> V. Mireille is lying at full length in her bed. She feels stifled, just as she had felt on the day when she had run about too much. Her mother is there, and feels her arms, her feet and her head. Then the mother says: "She is dead; this time she is really dead." Mireille cannot move.

She says that this dream is "rather nasty, but not so bad."

These three dreams (III. IV. and V) are all built up on the same frame-work—one similar to that which underlay Linette's dreams.

First stage. A progressive action, characterised by life, enjoyment, and boldness "She jumps with two boys"

(III).—" She goes alone into the wood " which is close to a café (IV). (The symbol of the café will recur.)—" As on the day when she had run about too much " (V).

Second stage. The bold act encounters a check, and there is danger of death. " She falls into the stream while jumping across it " (III) ; " she gets bogged " (IV) ; " she feels stifled as she had felt after running about too much ; she is dead " (V). In IV and V, the mother turns up at the critical moment. In III, we may assume that the kindly hosts symbolise the mother. The motif of III would make most psychoanalysts class it among the collective fantasies of " return to the mother's womb." Here, again (if we assimilate the kindly hosts to the mother in the two other dreams), this generalised interpretation seems to square with the individual case. Let us note the fact once more, without attempting a more ambitious commentary.

In the following dream we find once again the " café " and the " wood " of dream IV. There is now a blossoming, not quite free from discomfort, of the progressive tendency. Exit mother, enter Prince Charming.

> VI. They were all together in a café. It was an ugly place. Huge joints of meat were hanging all round the walls as in a butcher's shop. Mireille went out into the garden. All at once a man and a woman tried to catch her. *Her mother had run away without saying a word.* Mireille ran away from them, doubling like a hare. *She was very much surprised that her mother had left her, but at the same time she was glad that she was able to run a little.* She was almost out of breath when an officer came into the garden and said : " Come along, we'll escape together." He ran with her into a wood close by. He took her hand ; she ran beside him ; when there was anything in the way, he lifted her over.

Although distressed at being abandoned, Mireille was at the same time glad because she had escaped from her mother and because she was " able to run a little."

This dream of the officer introduces us to a new series of dreams, in which no analyst can fail to see tentative manifestations of infantile sexuality, and in which, moreover, there reappear some of the symbols we encountered in Linette's dreams (the toad, sticky things, the wolf). In Mireille, these symbols are linked, furthermore, with that of " flesh " (butcher's meat in IV, and ham in VII). The " ham boarding-school " of the dream next to be recorded is obviously akin to the " café butcher's shop " of VI, and this in its turn is linked with the café of IV. There are close ties between all these images, and they elucidate one another.

> VII. It was a funny sort of boarding school where there was never anything to eat except ham. There were huge slices of ham at every meal, nothing else ; no fruit, no vegetables, nothing.

We had better explain that Mireille's imagination has created this boarding-school as a contrast to a vegetarian boarding-school she had recently heard of.

> VII (continued). The bell rang for dinner. Everyone came in ; there were some young men. We sat down, and on everyone's plate was an enormous slice of ham with a tiny piece of bread. I said : " I can't eat." Then a gentleman who was quite close to me said : " Here's some bread-and-butter for you " ; and he gave me a slice of bread. Then I could eat.
>
> We went out for a walk, all schoolfellows together. We came to a field where there was a little toad of the colour of a green ham, greyish pink, which stood upright like a man and was digging. It ran after us and attacked me. It was not very nice, but I didn't mind much.

The mother notes that during a recent walk *in a wood* (a fresh tie with the café near the wood in dreams IV and VI) they had seen a huge toad which had made a strong impression on Mireille. But, sketching an analysis of this dream, she laid especial stress upon the " young men " who joined the rest at dinner : " During the time when we had to live in a boarding-house, it was always the young men whom Mireille was most afraid of. If one of them ventured to look at her or to smile at her, she would burst into tears. Sometimes I had to take her away from table."

> VIII. In class, Mireille was asked to look for a cube in the cupboard. At last she found some white of egg in the form of a cube : a whitish mass, transparent, a little sticky. She took it in her hand. There were some other children ; the white of egg was hidden and they found it. Then it was Mireille's turn to find it once more. But directly she touched

it, the mass began to flow over her, and the more she tried to get rid of it the more she was covered by it. Some other children and some gentlemen came to help her, but the stuff immediately covered them too, and all at once Mireille found herself floating in the air with the others. She had to hold them all up. Suddenly they broke away to get back to the ground, and Mireille was left alone with a gentleman upon a roof. It was nice and nasty at the same time.

The mother, attempting an analysis and supplementing her remark concerning dream VII, said : " If gentlemen come to call on us, she likes to remain unnoticed. One of our visitors, regardless of her feelings, endeavoured to caress her. She showed extreme repugnance, and I suppose that is why she has these dreams in which gentlemen figure."

The refusal of proffered caresses was certainly not due to the pride of a child unwilling to be treated *as a child.* First of all this would not explain the " extreme repugnance ; " and secondly it is not in conformity with Mireille's wish to remain a child, with her dislike of the idea of growing up. Manifestly what she refuses is to be treated as *a woman.* This conception harmonises with Mireille's fondness for the masculine role, which is related to the fixation upon the mother. In one of our adult subjects we shall find a pathological hypertrophy of the *refusal of femininity* linked to a fixation upon the mother.[1]

The following dream is linked to dream VI by the images of " chasing " and of " a wood."

IX. Mireille sometimes dreams of a wolf which chases her in a wood. Sometimes the wolf howls. Sometimes the wolf jumps on her. She runs away, turning round and round as she runs.

The mother records an observation of Mireille's regarding this dream.

" As soon as the wolf has jumped on me, I am not so frightened. It's like going to the dentist. I'm afraid on the way, but it gets better directly he begins."

[1] The case of Renée.—In Renée's case the refusal of femininity was accompanied by a refusal of maternity. In this connection a saying of Mireille's may be recorded : " I don't want to have any children, it gives you such a tummy ache."

I will conclude this series of dreams tinged with latent sexuality by relating one of an "explosion." The "piece of soap" which is the starting point instantly reminds us of the "cube" in dream VIII.

X. "A horrid dream!" She is holding a piece of soap in her hands. Suddenly the piece of soap becomes much bigger and explodes. Then there is a lamp on the table. It is made of *two balls, between which is the handle to hold it by*. Mireille says to herself: "It's going to blow up, and I shall take it." Suddenly the two balls swell up and pinch Mireille's hand; it hurts her a good deal. She turns and looks at the bed. Her mother is lying there with a head that has grown quite small and is all in holes.

In this dream we have a further blossoming of the progressive tendency, and the mother is correspondingly shrunken. But Mireille says that it is "a very sad dream." She is inclined to blame herself: "The explosion came because I touched the soap and the lamp too much." Forbidden fruit! As in Linette's case, we see simultaneous manifestations of the wish for the forbidden fruit and of the fear of it: "It's going to blow up, and I shall take it." The framework is the same as that of dreams III, IV, and V: a bold action followed by disaster, a dangerous attempt to break away from the mother and to push out into life.

3. Robert

A Schoolboy's Feelings about School. Introversion. Analysis of a School Essay.

(aged 12 years.)

Robert exhibits certain traits of a nascent introversion. A studious lad, he is mistrustful and rather shy, thriftily inclined and even miserly. He blushes readily and has fits of timidity, in these respects resembling his elder brother; but in the latter, introversion, timidity, embarrassment which is sometimes ludicrous, and maladaptation to social life, are much more marked, and arouse definite disquietude. In Robert, the traits are in the initial stage. The observer feels that he is of the same type as his brother, and that a push would make him develop in the same direction.

Writing a French essay of which the subject had been given out as "The History of a Five-Franc Piece," Robert relates unawares his own history. He begins as follows:

> After spending a long time in a damp cellar, I was taken out by a bearded man with a long nose and high cheekbones. He looked at me in a way which I did not like; after a time I understood what was happening to me. He was a policeman who had discovered a gang of coiners, who were making five-franc pieces with only 50 per cent. of silver in them instead of 90 per cent.

The analysis of this opening passage is incomplete, but the interpretation of some of the details is plain enough. The bearded man with high cheekbones is a portrait of Robert's father. The "damp cellar" must be classed among the fantasies of a return to the mother's womb. Moreover, in the analysis of the next passage from the essay, it becomes plain that at the end of this episode the "bearded man" takes the boy (the piece of money) in order to send him to school. Thus in the episode of the coiners we may presume that there is a reference to a frequent experience in real life, when paternal severity is contrasted with maternal indulgence. It is interesting to compare Robert's case with that of another of my subjects (Roger, reminiscence VI), where a similar complex is expressed by the image of a "fraudulent bankruptcy." The detail of the "50 per cent. of silver in the coins instead of 90 per cent." points to the tie between Robert's mercenary character, on the one hand, and his introversion and his protest against his father, on the other. The basis of his youthful avarice would seem to be the conjoined wish to rob his father and to escape from his father. Such sentiments are quite common. Let us continue the essay:

> They took me, then, and immediately carried me off to the mint with a multitude of other coins. My sufferings here were indescribable. Sometimes I was being stamped, sometimes I was in the furnace or being handled by all sorts of machines whose use I did not understand. If I remember aright it was when I was in one of these machines that an old man with a stoop nearly got his fingers burned by touching me. We had no time to talk to one another.

The old man with a stoop is a faithful portrait of Robert's schoolmaster during his last year at the primary school. This man was well known for his strictness and his rough ways. It is plain, therefore, that the mint where the coin suffers so much is the school. " All sorts of machines whose use I did not understand " represent the torments the pupils had to suffer in this " mint," where a coin was not even allowed " to talk " to the " multitude of other coins." This is a heart-felt cry ! Robert was diligent, and to outward seeming he was quite pleased with his lot at school. In his essay, however, the real reaction of his inner self finds expression. He naively passes judgment upon the time-honoured educational methods, and makes use of images which educational reformers cannot but find inspiring and delightful. A definite and amusing detail is that of the old man's burning his fingers when torturing the coin. The schoolmaster still had a way of hitting the pupils' fingers with a ruler, although the practice was discountenanced. It is likely enough that, as often happens during this sort of amusement, the master had sometimes hit his own fingers by mistake. Figuratively, at any rate, he had burned his fingers, for the parents of some of the pupils had lodged a complaint, and the school committee had formally forbidden him to use his ruler in such a way. But we may pass to a more genial atmosphere :

> At length, after a few days, I was placed with a dozen of my companions in a comfortable box ; still, we should have liked to have a little more room for our elbows.

This " comfortable box " is the " New School," to which Robert was sent on leaving the primary school. He really likes the place. Instead of the " multitude," his class has now only a dozen members. But he has reached the age when boys begin to feel the need for " elbow room," and when they find any kind of authority somewhat restricting. The feeling of constraint is normal to adolescence, and we shall see that another of our youthful subjects (Raoul) gives expression to it by a similar image.

A little farther on, we come to a sentimental intermezzo :

> Now, owing to a railway collision, I fell with only one of my companions into the grass of an orchard ; at once I struck up a friendship with her, for we were both of us very unhappy. We stayed there several weeks and we began to get tarnished by the rain. But what we found quite amusing was when

> we were able to watch the lizards basking in the sun ; the frogs were hopping gaily, and once one of them hopped on to my companion. One fine spring day, quite early in the morning, I suddenly saw a man who was armed with a great steel blade and seemed quite likely to cut our throats.

The " orchard " is a reminiscence of a real orchard where Robert had been during the holidays, and where he had played with some little girls. It is noteworthy to find here, apropos of an idyll of childhood, the customary images of " lizards " and " frogs." We have already referred to this topic in connection with the " toads " of Linette (XVI) and Mireille (VII). We should also note the feeling of fear (the man with the scythe) which is associated with these first steps towards the unknown in life.

After a while, the coin finds its way into the hands of a grocer :

> The grocer said to his wife : " Add that to your savings."—" Savings ? What for ? "—" You don't know yet. Perhaps we'll go for a jolly motor-boat excursion ; then we shall need the money."
>
> Saved up in this way, I was kept for about a fortnight in a dark and dirty corner ; often, during the night, there were rats prowling all round me.

The motor-boat excursion is the expression of one of Robert's most ardent wishes, to which his parents have not yet seen their way to accede. The dark and dirty corner where the rats prowl is a reminiscence of a story he has read in which some people have been buried alive. It also reminds us of the damp cellar in the first sentence of the essay. As a whole, therefore, this fantasy is of the same type as those which we have come across several times in Linette and Mireille. A progressive wish which remains unfulfilled is succeeded by a regression towards burial (akin to immersion). The same motif undergoes further development and dramatisation in the sequel, when wish passes into action and culminates in disaster :

> The excursion in a splendid motor-boat began. Towards midday, when the grocer was leaning over the edge to admire himself in the water, I suddenly fell head first into the water. By good luck when I found myself at the bottom I was upon a rock and not upon muddy slime. I stayed there a long

> time. There was a long spell of dry weather, and the water got so low that I came to the surface. I found myself lying beside a bone which must, I think, have been that of one of the lake-dwellers. Some men were busily searching amid this lacustrine debris, and the only reason why they did not see me was that I was of almost the same colour as the yellow sand.

Here we have an admirable example of the fantasy, so common in the introvert, of the immersion of some valuable object (the Rhine gold). No detail is lacking. We have the image of Narcissus "leaning over the edge to admire himself in the water;" and we even have an "archaic" element in the form of a lake-dweller's bone. In Robert this five-franc piece which has fallen into the water gives expression once more to the association of avarice with introversion. The drama secures its completion, its denouement, when "a lady" finds the coin and restores it to life.

4. Jean

PROTEST AGAINST THE FATHER.
ANALYSIS OF A SCHOOL ESSAY.

(aged 12 years.)

Jean exhibited to a very high degree the common complex of attachment to the mother and protest against the father. The fact that his parents did not get on very well with one another had made matters worse. Sometimes in his dreams he killed his father. In waking life he was devoted to his mother, and his pet name for her was "ma parfumée."

The pupils were told to write an essay upon a subject of their own choosing. Jean's was entitled "An Execution," and in it he was able to give circumlocutory expression to his complex. The scene was placed in his native city. In the great square there was a parade of the symbols of paternal authority:

> A herald riding a white charger is traversing the streets of the town; he sounds his horn, and all eyes follow the representative of the law.

The herald announces that "the authorities of the town have sentenced to death a certain Henry-Arthur Fourrier [note the hyphenated Christian names—" Jean " likes to write his own name in this way], for " having attempted to assassinate Monseigneur le Duc." This " Monseigneur " may be taken to represent Jean's own father, whom Jean kills in his dreams.

The mother is not forgotten :

> All at once a heartrending voice rose from the crowd, accompanied by sobs : " My son, my little Henry whom I love so dearly, what have you done ? " And the poor woman, driven almost mad, began to scream.

Next comes a detail which has little to do with the subject's conscious mind, and which the master, correcting the essay from a literary point of view, naturally marked with red ink as irrelevant. Nevertheless the detail is of great importance in the plan drafted by the subconscious. Essentially, we have to regard the execution as an act of paternal severity in consequence of some youthful revolt. From this outlook, the introduction of the following incident is easy to understand :

> Henry Fourrier was very well known. Even when he was quite a little boy and when his father had made him go without his dinner because he had been naughty, a neighbour's wife was always ready to give him something to eat.

Once more we have an image showing the mother's indulgence as contrasted with the father's strictness. A few lines later, the allusion to dinner is repeated in a rather original form :

> The execution was fixed for the next day before dinner in order to give an appetite to the spectators.

The hour of the execution approaches, and Jean, though he has a good command of language and rarely uses words amiss, speaks of the man sentenced to death as " the victim." In view of the nature of the crime, this sympathy seems out of place, and the master underlines the phrase ; but from the outlook of the subconscious it is quite in order, for Jean has long since espoused his hero's cause. At length we reach the fatal moment :

> Now everyone was silent, the music too ceased, and Fourrier made his appearance, surrounded by soldiers. His face was

> pale, and he stumbled as he walked. *Behind him came his mother more dead than alive.* The condemned man slowly mounted the scaffold and stood erect, waiting. *The executioner was there too, his face hidden by a mask so that he could not be recognised.*

The head falls into the basket. Is this the end? By no means. An unexpected vengeance is on the way. A troop of horsemen emerges from one of the streets bringing a message from the authorities: "Henry was not the guilty man!" So the authorities had made a mistake! The crowd is infuriated at this news.

> Tears, sobs, oaths, arose from all over the square. The people rushed to the house of the judge who had sentenced Fourrier, but he was not there; they broke down the doors of the house and ravaged the whole place.

An impotent revenge, but revenge none the less; and what a spirit of revolt underlies it.

CHAPTER SIX

THE CRISIS OF ADOLESCENCE

EVERYONE knows that adolescence is heralded by a crisis. We are not so definitely informed concerning the elements of this crisis. Above all, in any particular case, it is difficult to say from objective examination what form it is taking; how it is developing; how far it has developed; or what is the best way of helping the girl or the lad with whom we are concerned in the actual stage of this crisis. It is here that analysis can come to our aid.

The first case, that of Raoul, exhibits the crisis in its simplest form, and as it presents itself in a normal youth. It is characterised by the sudden onset of a feeling of maladaptation to life, by an embarrassment in face of budding virility. We also discern the protest against the authority of father and of schoolmaster which we have already noted in boys two or three years before puberty.

In the case of Kitty we can watch a young girl's passion for a woman. According to Freud, a homosexual tendency, or at least a latent homosexual tendency, appears as a normal phase of adolescent life. Whatever we may think of this idea of a "latent tendency," there can be no doubt that declared passions for persons of the same sex are common at puberty. In young girls, such passions may take an extremely idealised form. Marguérite Evard,[1] and subsequently Casimire Proczek,[2] have both quoted, in this connection, ardent letters from young girls to other young girls, letters which are well worth reading. Kitty's phrases are no less ardent. From these platonic passions there is a gradual transition to unmistakable inversion.

[1] Evard, L'adolescente, 1914, p. 140.

[2] Proczek, Ce que les parents devraient savoir sur leurs filles, 1918, p. 110. —A Young Girl's Diary contains much valuable information concerning this phase of development (cf. Bibliography, Anonymous).

If the platonic homosexual passions of puberty are not so entirely harmless as is usually supposed, it is likewise true that the declared homosexuality of puberty is not necessarily a grave matter. Analysis shows us that most of these cases are connected with infantile happenings and with infantile psychological states.

Auguste Lemaître has recently studied the inversion of adolescents from the psychoanalytical point of view.[1] While struck with the frequency of this precocious inversion, he has secured evidence to show that it is usually the outcome of psychological causes which are amenable to reeducative analysis.

Gerard, the third of our subjects, is a steady young fellow whose trouble is a conflict mainly of the moral order. He vacillates between different ideals. He is in revolt against paternal authority, and yet cannot bring himself to reject it. At the same time he is harassed by sexual temptations. Here we have the factors of a multiple conflict common among adolescents, and one likely to induce a high degree of nervous fatigue.

Analysis can help us to guide the adolescent through such conflicts. We need not necessarily impart all our discoveries to the youth or the maiden concerned. What was said of children in this respect, applies to some extent in the case of adolescents—and sometimes even in the case of adults. We may trouble our subjects unnecessarily by bluntly making them aware of certain tendencies. No one is entitled to declare apriori that all repression is unwholesome. In especial, we should remember that a tendency of which the subject is *not yet* fully aware, and one of which the subject in normal conditions becomes aware only by degrees, is not a repressed tendency. It is inadvisable to hurry development in such matters. Tact is essential here.

1. Raoul

Budding Virility. The Feeling of Constraint.

Raoul is sixteen years of age. He is thoroughly normal, well balanced in all his aptitudes, and in most subjects of

[1] Lemaître, Le symbolisme dans les rêves des adolescents, 1921.

study he is at the head of his class. I shall record only one of his dreams, which is admirably representative of the normal crisis of adolescence

> He is in a first-class compartment with his schoolfellow Louis. Then he finds himself on the railway line running after the train, accompanied by Louis and others. Louis says to him: "What a lark, the suction of the train will help us to catch it." At first Raoul thinks that he will be able to catch up with the train, but soon he is outdistanced. The country is well wooded; there is a house which appears to be an inn; here the train is waiting for them, but it has now become a post-chaise. He gets in, and is disappointed to find how close the quarters seem after the comfortable first-class compartment. The driver of the post-chaise is Monsieur Weiss [the headmaster of Raoul's boarding-school]. With Raoul, there are four schoolboys in the post-chaise. Monsieur Weiss says to them: "Look at these four rolls." The rolls are wall maps; they are very much in the way. The inside of the post-chaise is like that of a motor car in which Raoul usually drives when the family goes away for a holiday; in this motor car they are always crowded up with luggage.

The associations are obvious. Louis is a bit of a dandy, and is fond of showing off. Raoul cannot catch up with the train. In real life he is apt to be outclassed at certain physical exercises, especially running, by schoolfellows who, intellectually speaking, are his inferiors. Always at the head of the class, he finds it rather trying to be aware that his schoolmates excel him as gallants and sportsmen. The train after which he has to run represents the manliness in which he feels himself somewhat deficient. It should be noted that physically he is not very strong.

The headmaster's words remind him that he has really heard Monsieur Weiss say something of the sort to some of the younger pupils who were "packed" into the school omnibus. It annoys him to be "packed" into the post-chaise, and to be still treated as if he were one of the youngsters. He adds that Monsieur Weiss always insists that they should be very careful of their things. The post-chaise, then, is the school, with the constraints it imposes. But it is also the family environment, as we learn from the condensation of the post-chaise with the motor car. This is likewise shown by another associated memory, that of a donkey cart in which the family had gone for a drive through a countryside resembling the one seen in the dream. During this drive they had had to get out in one place and to run after the cart. We see that the headmaster is condensed with the father. He represents authority, an authority against which Raoul is feeling an inclination to rebel.

But the really troublesome things are these rolls they have to carry about all four of them ; each schoolfellow has a roll. The boy is growing up, and is incommoded thereby. What are these rolls ? First of all they are maps of the world. Next they recall four rolled numbers of the review " L'Illustration " which, the night before, Raoul had wanted to put away in his cupboard, and which had taken so much room that he could not get his slippers in. Now " L'Illustration " like the maps, is an epitome of this great world, whose novelty makes its appeal to the adolescent, so that his interest in the new world tends to replace interest in the ordinary routine of the innocent life of boyhood. The same call of the world was symbolised by the train, which contained a reminiscence of an occasion when Raoul had left his native city. Thus the rolls were symbolic of extroversion, of the life of the adult contrasted with the life of the boy. In addition, however, as we learn from numerous analyses, these rolls must be classed among symbols of the sexual organs, among the symbols which are almost always associated with those of the extroverted life of manhood. Thus the rolls would seem to express the various aspects of the budding virility which manifests itself like a foreign body in the physical and mental life of the adolescent—a development which is at first embarrassing.

Subjective embarrassment owing to the appearance of new forces ; objective embarrassment in face of an authority which still restricts the manifestation of these forces ; a sudden failure to achieve adaptation to life, which all at once has outdistanced the lad, so that he is forced to run in the attempt to keep up with it—such would seem to be the characteristics of the crisis which appears sooner or later in the life of all adolescents, however normal. This crisis is invariably distressing, but analysis can alleviate the distress.

2. Kitty

A YOUNG GIRL'S PASSION FOR A WOMAN.

Kitty is sixteen years old. She has a lively imaginative faculty, and feels the need of giving expression to it through writings in prose or in verse. Her temperament is intuitive and highly nervous. She displays nervous symptoms such as are frequent during adolescence : alternate fits of depression and exaltation ; attacks of headache. But the dominant phenomenon in her life is an infatuation for a young Englishwoman whom she knows only by sight. To this lady, Kitty indites the most passionate of her poems ; her only desire is that her love shall be returned. This love makes her very sad, and yet she loves the sadness and diligently cultivates it.

Kitty was four years old when her father died. Since then she has lived in intimate association with her mother, to whom she is greatly attached. She has already had passionate friendships. One of these was for a girl cousin ten years older than herself, with whom she was in close touch when she was herself twelve years old. At thirteen, she idolised the French mistress at school. But none of her former passions has been so overwhelming as that with which she is now inspired for the fair unknown.

This passion has lasted for several months. Eighteen months before the analysis, Kitty had had a dream, and she is convinced that it contained an anticipatory vision of the object of her affection. It was during the night following her fifteenth birthday. We know how to estimate these dreams retrospectively regarded as prophetic, especially when we have to do with so suggestible and imaginative a subject as Kitty. However, as soon as she saw the young Englishwoman, she imagined herself to recognise, feature by feature, the image of her dream, and her passion was the outcome of the shock of this recognition. Here is the dream.

I. She was in a huge forest. An old woman said to her : " Come with me ; I have something to show you." Kitty was frightened, but she went with the old woman, who said to her : " If you look in the glass you will see someone whom you will meet later and whom you will love." Kitty, looking in the glass, at first could see only her own image; then the place of her own image was taken by that of a woman in mourning. [The unknown was in mourning when Kitty met her.]

Having told her dream, Kitty went on talking, and wondered why she had given the unknown the fancy name of Regina. "It's not a name I'm very fond of!" She knows that Regina is the same name as Reine. She has come across this name Reine in a book entitled *Mon oncle et mon curé.* It is the name of a girl in the book "who wants to get married, and with whom at the end somebody falls in love." The name also recalls to her a poem by Louis Duchosal. She quotes some verses of which she is particularly fond :

De la laine de mon amour . .
D'une dame, reine d'un jour.

If we had had any doubt as to the character of Kitty's passion, these associations would suffice to convince us that she is really in love.

Let us now consider the associations with the images in the dream.

"Old woman" calls up the idea of "witch." This already suffices to make us think of one of the symbols of the "collective unconscious," the symbol of the "dread mother." But the words of the old woman : "Come with me; I have something to show you," call up the memory of the same words uttered by Kitty's mother the day before the dream—Kitty's birthday What her mother had to show was a birthday present, two volumes of verse. Louis Duchosal's *Thule,* and Victor Hugo's *Les Contemplations.* She knew both the books, and had expressed a wish to have them for her own.

Such were the immediate associations. A few days later Kitty realised that her memory had been at fault. On her fifteenth birthday she had only been given *Les Contemplations.* The present of *Thule* had been on her sixteenth birthday. There had been a condensation of two kindred memories—a common phenomenon when adults are recalling memories of childhood—but the instance is rather remarkable as concerns memories so recent and so important. We must not fail to note the liberties Kitty's imagination takes with reality, for we shall then understand how easily so imaginative a mind could condense the memory of a dream with the actual sight of a lady in mourning, and become inspired with the conviction that the vision of the dream and the actual vision were identical.

Let us return to our commentary upon the dream. Kitty had looked forward with especial eagerness to her fifteenth birthday. It was a momentous occasion upon which a sort of miracle was to occur, for her naive fancy was that on this day she would " suddenly grow up." The expectation gave rise to a suggestion, to which the impressive dream was a response.

The " glass " recalled to Kitty's mind the cousin to whom she had at one time been so deeply attached. This cousin, when she was going to sing somewhere, used to spend a long time in front of the glass, and Kitty used to say to her, " You'll be late."

The mirror is a common symbol of autoerotism (the myth of Narcissus). We note, in fact, that in the dream the mirror in which Kitty is to see someone whom she will love, shows her at first her own image. The words " You'll be late," addressed to someone who is spending too long a time admiring her own image in the mirror, might be regarded as the expression of an arrest of development at the autoerotic infantile stage which Freud regards as the first stage of the sexual instinct. We must be careful, however, to avoid stressing such ingenious but fanciful interpretations, unless they are explicitly confirmed by the personal associations of the subject.

Cautiously, I endeavoured to explain to Kitty that her infatuation was the outcome of suggestion ; to show her what had been the influence of expecting a miracle on her fifteenth birthday ; to make her aware of the retrospective touching-up of her dream. I also tried to show her that the lady in mourning was akin to her own image, which had been replaced in the mirror by the other ; that this vision was a part of herself ; that consequently she possessed it in herself, and that she was mistaken in her search for it outside herself. Kitty listened to me with interest, but she was so much obsessed by her passion that she could not fail to offer resistance.

Apropos of memories of early childhood, and apropos of a prose poem, *La dame voilée,* written by Kitty at the age of thirteen, I can discuss remoter origins.

Kitty has "always represented to herself the person to whom she is greatly attached as being dressed in black." One day, when she was eight years old, one of her cousins was going to a concert. This cousin was wearing a blue dress. Kitty said to her: "Why aren't you dressed in black? You would look so much prettier?" Now the prototype of this image in black, of this "veiled lady," was Kitty's mother after the father's death. Here Kitty remarks that most of the people she has "idolised" were in mourning. The French mistress to whom she had been devoted when she was thirteen had been "in mourning for her father;" another flame had been "in mourning for her husband;" another, "in mourning for her father."

Furthermore Kitty remembers that when her father died (Kitty being then four years old) her mother had considered her too young to wear mourning. A year later, Kitty had said: "I do wish someone would die in the family, so that we could go into mourning." For her, to wear mourning signifies to be no longer a child Now, to be no longer a child was the miracle to which she was looking forward on her fifteenth birthday. Primarily, therefore, the young woman in black, who then appeared to her in a dream, and whom she subsequently rediscovered in Regina, was the image of herself grown to womanhood. This is why, in the mirror, the image of the woman in mourning took the place of her own image; the woman in mourning had her hair down her back, just like Kitty. As for Regina, she has dark eyes like Kitty's, Kitty being "the only one of the family to have dark eyes." In this image of herself, Kitty externalises the unfulfilled wish of childhood "to be in mourning." Should we add "to be in mourning for her *father*?" Are we on the track of infantile feelings towards her father? This is not unlikely.

In actual fact, however, Kitty's love vacillates between this image of a second self and the image of her mother. Her idols are sometimes "in mourning for their father," and sometimes "in mourning for their husband." But in both cases, and especially as far as Regina is concerned, the maternal traits are more in evidence. The objects of affection are older than Kitty; the cousin is ten years older; the school-mistress is much older; Regina is a married woman with a little boy. Kitty is greatly attached to her mother, and her first love passions are for grown women who are more or less maternal in type.

The passion remains unrequited. Kitty writes to Regina, sends her poems, but has no answer. As far as her upper consciousness is concerned, the love remains as fervent as ever. Below the threshold, however, dissociation is beginning. A month later she told me the following dream.

> II. Regina was dead. It was in a large room. On the table was a coffin draped in black, and there were four candles, for it was late in the evening or at night. In the coffin Regina was lying *dressed in white*, arms crossed on the breast, her hair loose. The husband brought the little boy. Both were crying and Kitty cried too. The husband said: "You must not bear a grudge against her because she did not answer your letter; she was already ill."

Kitty ingenuously informs me that she has dreamed this several times "during the last month." She adds: "I don't think I dreamed it before your first visit." She is afraid that the dream may portend Regina's death. I explain to her that it is only within herself that something is going to come to an end, as the result of our analysis. But there is nothing mournful about this end. She is happy; and, spontaneously, "mourning" has been replaced by "a white dress." Kitty remarks that in the dream she had on the night following her fifteenth birthday (I) the lady in the mirror had worn a white dress. A month earlier, when Kitty first told me of this dream, she said that the lady in the glass wore mourning. I showed her that her imagination was caught red-handed in one of those retrospective distortions which it inflicts upon dreams. Here we have an additional reason why Kitty is no longer impressed by the pseudo-recognition of an image previously seen in a dream. In any case, the substitution of the white dress for the mourning is a good sign. Kitty has begun to escape from being obsessed by the infantile image.

A week later there is a new dream.

> III. A lady tells Kitty that Regina will have to undergo a serious operation.

This "serious operation" is the analysis itself. Consciously, Kitty is hardly changed; as she says, my explanations have more than once made her think things over; but she has not really accepted them. In the subconscious, however, forces are evidently at work.

From this date I no longer saw Kitty, but she begged me not to lose interest in her, and she wrote to me from time to time.

Now came a great surprise: Regina answered one of Kitty's letters. This was not likely to put an end to the infatuation. Kitty was delighted. Regina sent her photograph, and the sight of this photograph sufficed to bring about a spontaneous [1] hypnotic state in Kitty. (I had treated her by suggestion.)

> Sometimes, pretty often but not always, when I look at the photograph I find I cannot turn away my eyes from it. What happens is this. Gradually my mind seems to become clouded, my senses are dulled, I no longer think of anything; I am unable to make the slightest movement; then my eyes grow heavy; then I begin to feel sleepy. At such moments I feel as if I should be able to write a splendid poem, but I cannot hold a pencil; it drops from my fingers, and I lack the power to pick it up. I could stay for hours and hours without moving or speaking. When this sort of trance passes off, I regret its disappearance as a condition of restful tranquillity; I should like it to last for ever.

There is something more remarkable to follow. When she has to do anything disagreeable or difficult, she need merely glance at the photograph, and everything grows easy, even though she does not pass into a state of profound hypnosis.

> Here is a strange instance. A short time ago I had an English composition to write. My mistress had told me to choose my own subject. I was bored; I did not know what to write about; my thoughts were prancing from one subject to another without settling on anything. Suddenly my eyes fell on the photo. Mechanically I took it up, and then, still bored, with the photograph in front of me, I seized my pencil once more. But now, as by a miracle, I found a splendid subject, and I began to write with marvellous ease. I don't know much English yet, but on this occasion *I did*. And

[1] Of course the hypnosis was "induced" by the photograph. But it was "spontaneous" in the sense that it was not deliberately caused by a hypnotiser or intentionally by the subject. Compare the author's distinction between "spontaneous suggestion" and "induced suggestion" in Suggestion and Autosuggestion, p. 28, etc.—TRANSLATORS' NOTE.

would you believe it, when I handed in the composition which I wrote while looking at the photo from time to time, *I found it hard to persuade the English mistress that I had written it without any help.*

Kitty was obviously convinced that Regina was exercising a mysterious influence over her. What really happened, doubtless, was a stimulation, in the hypnotic state, of memory traces that were not sufficiently active to produce an effect in the normal state. In the particular instance we are now considering, they were memory traces of English words or phrases which had been read or heard, but not consciously retained. This indicates the extreme suggestibility of the subject, and only upon the basis of a hypersuggestibility can we understand the genesis of such an infatuation. From the point of view of the analysis the interesting fact is that Regina has become the suggester. Regina has been substituted for me. It is, so to speak a *reversal of transference*; my influence declines somewhat, whilst the obsessive image correspondingly regains power. It is as if the subconscious were making an effort to elude me, to attach itself more strongly to the guiding fiction.

However, fresh disillusionments were in store. Regina was to have spent the winter in Kitty's town, but she decided not to go after all. Then she gave up writing. Kitty's passion grew desperate.

What am I to do? I wanted to attract her in any way I could, but hitherto I have failed. Apparently my poems do not interest her, for she never refers to them (besides, I have given up sending them, for what is the use?) I had counted on them to soften her heart, and I am quite at my wits' end. I have tried everything, all shades of feeling; I have exhausted the most affectionate, the most loving words; I have put all my soul into my letters, and more than my soul. Nothing, not a word.

Months elapsed, and at length calm was restored. The explanations I had given Kitty more than a year earlier, and which she had noted without accepting, were now rediscovered by herself, and were retailed by her to me. Her passion had been sublimated. She understood now what she had previously been unwilling to admit, that Regina was in herself. She no longer wanted to see Regina.

> If I ever meet her, I shall say to her: "For me you are a soul, a god; I do not want to know you personally, for as soon as I know you you will cease to be a god for me."

Simultaneously, the imagery of Kitty's poems, which had hitherto been invariably concerned with feminine and maternal characteristics, is directed towards masculine traits. She has outgrown the stage of homosexual passion. This stage is normal in a girl's crisis of adolescence, but in Kitty it had taken an acute and almost alarming form.

3. Gerard

Vacillating Sublimation. A State of Conflict.

Gerard is eighteen years of age. His case is a conspicuous example of phenomena which are common in adolescents. He suffers from nervous fatigue which paralyses his attempts at intellectual work. The nervous condition is complicated by other elements which need not be considered here. It is, however, easy to recognise the preponderant influence of a state of conflict. The young man's inner life is intensely active; conflicting forces, powerful energies, neutralise one another. Precisely because of the struggle between these contending forces, and because of the consequent fatigue, his effective output is small.

Gerard has lofty moral ambitions. An idealist, strongly religious, extremely individualistic, and animated with a keen sense of individual responsibility, he inclines towards a life that is to be pure and heroically beneficent. He lives chastely, and overcomes even powerful temptation. But he hesitates what path of sublimation to choose, for choice is complicated by the conflict of trends of which he is barely conscious.

Gerard told me of a dream he had had when he was between ten and twelve years old. It is an unconscious self-revelation of this inward disturbance.

> I. He was a dragon. He wore a helmet; he had a mane; he was on horseback. Then he discovered a way of flying. He was walking in the air, much after the manner in which Jesus walked upon the lake.

The dragon is obviously a symbol, not only of virility, but also of sexuality. Apropos of the word dragon he thinks of the mythological dragon, " the animal with the tongue of flame." Likewise, in this connection, he thinks of medieval images: " Leviathan, a huge horned muzzle, devils which issue dancing." In a word, the human beast. " Helmet," evokes " fireman ; " " horse " evokes " pashas with two or three tails ; " and Oriental images which, in other associations, are manifestly erotic. He wishes " to fly "—but Jesus walking on the lake calls up in his mind " the foundering of him who tried to do the like." All his distress is summed up in this phrase. He feels that superhuman forces will be requisite to enable him to reach his ideal.

It is interesting to note that in Gerard's case one of the associations of " flying " was " domination." We are reminded of Adler's ideas concerning compensation and the will-to-power. Physically, Gerard regards himself as a weakling, as incapable of becoming a " dragon." It is extremely natural that he should feel a high degree of spiritualisation to be a possible form of compensation, a means by which he could achieve mental dominance.

Gerard told me of another vision of childhood, one which he had had many times when he was quite young, about six or seven years old. It used to come to him as soon as he closed his eyes before going to sleep.

> II. In the dark there is a host of devils grimacing. Some of them have fiery eyes. These devils' bodies are smooth, green or black. They are beardless and hairless. Some of them are lame. Some have no legs. There are also some legs tiptoeing about.—A red leg.—They all dance by.

A detailed analysis of these visions of the human beast would be superfluous. They are among the plainest of those belonging to the domain of the collective unconscious and to the realm of myth. It is interesting to compare these smooth, hairless bodies, these legless trunks, with the analogous hallucinations of Auguste Lemaître's subject Amédée. This was a lad of fifteen who had hallucinatory visions of a woman of whom he could see only the " head and arms and the upper part of the trunk, and lower down, the crossed legs." She was patting a dog which was hairless and had no legs. Here we have a systematic repression of images that are directly sexual.[1] In Gerard, the vision of the devils completes that of the dragon, apropos of which latter there have already appeared " devils which issue dancing." We should carefully note these images and those with which they are associated —the red leg, the dancing devils, the pashas, and the East. They will help us in later stages of the interpretation. Dancing, in particular, is repugnant to Gerard ; he looks upon it as " a sacrifice upon the altar of the flesh."

Certain other dreams of Gerard's childhood, stereotyped and of frequent occurrence, carry us a stage further.

> III. Gerard was falling down a well, without reaching the bottom.—At other times he was on a railway line between two walls. The train was chasing him. He fell ; he got up again. He was running along the metalled way or along the footpath ; his skin was grazed. He saw in front of him the level crossing where he would be safe. But he fell, panic-stricken, and lay stretched out.

Associated with these images are ideas of suffocation, and childish terrors, especially dread of the dark and of being alone. In connection with the words " lay stretched out," Gerard has a " breathless feeling." He recalls other dreams, suffocation dreams he had when still younger ; perhaps they were dreams unattended by any visual image, dreams in which he was unable to cry out. A tendency to *claustrophobia* is manifest. Must we go so far as to speak of fantasies of a return to the mother's womb ? The subject's associations give no direct indication of anything of the kind ; but in this case as in others, claustrophobia seems to be linked in some way with the maternal complex.

Falling down a well is falling into a forbidden and dangerous abyss. At this stage Gerard has a reminiscence of a well beside which he used to play with other children.

> We sat on the parapet ; we were not allowed to lean over.

With the narrow passage " between two walls " there were the following associations, which were related to the claustrophobia.

[1] For fuller details of Amédée's case, cf. Baudouin, Suggestion et autosuggestion, pp. 38–40 ; English translation, pp. 52–54. Cf. also Lemaître's account, " Archives de Psychologie," July, 1916.

> I have never liked roads between high walls. I've always been afraid of being alone.

But this dread is linked with a state of conflict. He has reminiscences which are promptly organized into a symbol of the conflict.

> The road was running beside *the sea*, and then it led *inland.* The sea was eating away the cliffs. I went to the edge of the cliff, although it was forbidden. The path ran very near the edge of the cliff.

" The sea " and " inland " represent the two terms of the conflict. " The sea " evokes " fear, and at the same time the lure of solitude and the sea." Here we have the side which turns towards solitude and introversion. We have attachment to the mother.[1] " Inland " is the side of life which is virile and extroverted. The path turns away from " the sea " for a time, and leads inland. Gerard fancies that from a cliff he watches the road thus leading " inland." The sight was " a distraction." The road called up reminiscences of bicycling with other boys when " they were going to smoke on the sly." Now we come to images of budding virility and forbidden pleasures. The narrow way leads between the two lives. The anxiety, the customary symptom of a conflict, expresses here the conflict between two fundamental tendencies, the one which keeps along " the sea," and the one which leads " inland."

Free associations to simple words I mention to the subject help us to continue the analysis.

> IV. " Dog."—A dog which laughs and twists its body.
>
> " Twist one's body."—A young schoolfellow who suffered a little from St. Vitus's dance. He laughed like a hysterical patient. Gerard himself. He, too, has nervous movements; he has " a less refined form of degeneration."
>
> " Fire."—Dancing flames. Goblins coming out of the fire; one of Grimm's tales. His ideas are dancing with the flames. This makes him lose the thread of his ideas. Gerard himself once more. His own instability. How easily he is influenced.

[1] The author refers parenthetically to the word-play between *la mer* (the sea) and *la mère* (the mother) as being frequent in imaginative fantasies. The actual word-play is untranslatable, but a similar condensation of images is, of course, common in English. Cf. Swinburne's " Mother and lover of men, the sea," in The Triumph of Time.—TRANSLATORS' NOTE.

We have returned to the dancing devils, and to dancing in general, dancing flames, St. Vitus's dance. What interests us is that Gerard associates these images, whose significance is known to us, with certain physical and moral traits characteristic of his state: first of all with disorderly nervous movements, and subsequently with a mind that is unstable and easily influenced. Dancing nerves and dancing ideas. Thus spontaneously, without suspecting it, he expresses the link between these symptoms and the inward conflict.

This instability, of which he is aware, shows itself above all in moral and religious hesitancy, in vacillations of choice between different forms of sublimation.

V. Here are two dreams of two successive nights. In one of these Gerard attends service in a Catholic church; in the other, in a Protestant church. The Catholic church was in the rue de Tournon, where there is no such church; it was in the place where there actually is a Protestant church, the church of the second dream. In the Catholic church Gerard receives communion, but does so in both kinds. On leaving, he has a talk with a priest concerning liberal Catholicism They stroll together towards the Odéon; they pass beside the Luxembourg.

Gerard has been brought up by his father as a strict Protestant. He remains a Protestant, but is charmed by Catholic symbolism. He finds Protestantism somewhat rationalistic and dry, so that it fails to satisfy all his needs.

The "rue de Tournon" calls up reminiscences of childhood, pianoforte lessons, gymnastic lessons, a trapeze exercise which the gymnastic master used to call "Round the World in Eighty Days" (images of extroversion). Here there are word-plays: Tournon, tourner, is equivalent to the German "turnen," which means gymnastics. There are reminiscences of children's dances, dressing up (*travesti*), wearing masks. In this connection we once more have "symbolism," and once more "dancing."

Subsequently, the Odéon calls up the disguises and the "symbolism" of the theatre; the Luxembourg leads to the Latin Quarter, to Verlaine, and, through other associations, to Gerard's first childish inquisitiveness concerning matters of sex.

In all this we may discern an æsthetic and symbolist trend, by means of which he is enabled to " travesty " and to sublimate the sexual instinct better than he can within the confines of a system of " dry rationalism." Apropos of the " two kinds," he considers that " Protestantism is more dualist than Catholicism." The main significance of this is that Protestantism leaves him more fully aware of his own duality ; does not give him a chance of unifying his religious tendencies with his sexual instinct ; leaves the latter free to pursue an independent existence and to carry on a surreptitious war. Catholic " symbolism," on the other hand, with its warmer and more palpable imagery, supplies stepping-stones, bridges more effectively the hiatus between religion and the sexual instinct.

This dream brought to light a hidden conflict which subsequently developed in the conscious. At the date of the dream, the inclination towards Catholicism merely took the form of a sympathy. A considerable time afterwards the Catholic trend became stronger, giving rise to a crisis, to thoughts of conversion. But doubtless the conflict contained additional elements, for at other times Gerard displayed a socialist trend. He was thus oscillating on either side of the Protestant ideal, now to the right and now to the left. There would seem, above all, to have been a subconscious wish to throw off paternal authority. This conforms both with the Oedipus complex, of which there are several signs in Gerard, and with the intense individualism and the spirit of revolt which are characteristic of his temperament. To safeguard sublimation (which has been modelled by his father's educational influence) and nevertheless to reject his father's authority—such would seem to be the troublesome conflict going on within Gerard's mind.

Taking advantage of this conflict, the lower elements moved forward to the assault. We see this in the following dream which Gerard had a few days later :

VI. One of Gerard's greatest friends, a steady young fellow, an only child, and therefore somewhat spoiled though carefully brought up, had gone to spend the night out with a woman, in Spain. Gerard was greatly distressed, as though he had been personally responsible. His friend had wanted him to come too, but he had refused.

"Spending the night out" called up reminiscences of actual temptations, one evening when Gerard had made a tour of the cafés with some of his friends. "Spain" is "Gil Blas" and a life of escapades. To sum up, everything shows that Gerard is calling his friend into the matter to denote his own double.

The next dream expressly shows that the temptations are reinforced by the vacillations and checks of sublimation.

> VII. Gerard is to preach in a church, at ten o'clock. He is in a garden recalling that of Cluny Museum and Monge Square. He loiters. On taking out his watch he sees that it is eleven o'clock. He has failed to keep an appointment which was a great honour to him. He tries to put the matter out of his mind, this being his usual practice when anything disagreeable has happened. He finds himself back in the garden, having tea with a party of four or five persons.

Cluny, with its museum, brings us to the æsthetic and "symbolist" trend, and to the Latin Quarter. It is in order that he may linger here that Gerard fails to keep the appointment which is such an honour to him. Here we have a new indication of the fact that, when there in a conflict between different forms of sublimation, there is considerable risk that sublimation may completely fail to occur. "Monge Square" reminds him of a tram running off the rails there. He feels that he himself is running off the rails. Having failed to reach the exalted goal, he tries to forget his failure, and lapses into pleasure-seeking. The "persons" at the end of the dream call up pleasure-parties and "dubious company."

Another dream gives unambiguous expression to a sexual lapse.

> VIII. In a hotel. There is a young couple in the next room. The party wall breaks down. Gerard tumbles into the other room.

The associations of "the party wall breaks down": reading Courteline; improprieties. The tumbling into the other room calls up: being caught listening at doors; doing what one should not.

The last dream I shall record shows exceedingly well the state of inhibition resulting from these conflicts.

IX. Gerard was chained by one hand, probably the left. . . . He was entitled to unchain himself or to go for a walk, but he always had to come back to where he was chained. The chain had to be heavy. It was a sort of torture, with a flavour of martyrdom about it. Perhaps Gerard went to see his parents from time to time. He had some books, but his hand hurt, and he found it difficult to hold his books open. He was sitting on some cushions. In an oriental book, he was looking at the picture of a dancing dervish who was dressed in a blue silk robe shot with black, and was wearing red stockings. The close of the dream was definitely sexual.

Gerard is really "chained." This word called up the following reflection :

Life is difficult, we are chained by our surroundings, and we cannot reach our ideal.

The book which he finds it difficult to keep open recalls that he sometimes finds it difficult to read while he is walking ; it is the difficulty of mental work in the state of nervous fatigue from which he is suffering. Something more is at stake than mere work ; what is at stake is the conquest of spiritual force. The word " books " evokes " books I am fond of " ; especially Romain Rolland's *Vie de Beethoven* and Rabindranath Tagore's *Poems*. The first represents for him " force ; " the second " a frenzy of pure love." Being " entitled to unchain himself " calls up the " right to individualism ; " a right which is actually a duty." Here we discern the opposition to his family and to his father's ideal. Going to " see his parents " called up a real desire to see them again. Then he said :

A need for support which is in conflict with individuality To seek support from others is to chain oneself up.

The cushions evoke "rest, which is necessary but treacherous." This " rest " does in fact enable temptation to get the upper hand. The oriental book, the dancing dervish, and the red stockings, are images with which we are familiar (II), and we are not surprised that the dream in which they appear should have an erotic close.

Gerard is chained by his conflicts ; he is exhausted by these internal struggles, and the exhaustion ("needful but treacherous rest ") makes him more than ever a prey to the assaults of the sexual instinct, and thereby his trouble is aggravated. The vacillating sublimation is "a kingdom divided against itself," and confusedly he is afraid that the dominion is about to be overthrown. Previous energies are squandered within this closed precinct, where many fine young fellows are held prisoner, but from which an adequate analysis would set them free.

CHAPTER SEVEN

ATTITUDE TOWARDS THE PARENTS

ONE of the most definite and most general achievements of psychoanalysis is to show that a child's attitude towards its respective parents (more or less marked love or hostility) is related to a definite type of character. I write "related" in order to avoid being too ready to formulate a causal theory. Even when the existence of the relationship in question has been definitely ascertained, and has been repeatedly confirmed by fresh analyses, it remains susceptible of various interpretations.

Let us consider what Freud terms the *Oedipus complex.* This is the condition in which a boy is greatly attached to his mother while more or less hostile to his father. What frequently happens, when the disposition in question is strongly marked, is that the subject exhibits certain character traits which are almost fixed, such as a tendency to shun the world, introversion, timidity, a dread of sexuality and of the virile aspects of life. According to Freud's interpretation, the attachment to the mother is primitive, being a manifestation of "infantile sexuality." The hostility to the father is the outcome of jealousy. The fixation of the "libido" upon the mother gives rise to the subsequent inhibitions. Adler criticises this view.[1] He considers the Oedipus complex to be a manifestation of a child's will-to-power. The boy primarily wishes to take his father's place; hostility to the father is the primordial element; the fantasies in which the boy regards himself as "mother's husband" are merely an expression of this desire; the sexual element is no more than a symbol. The two theses are not irreconcilable.

We are entitled to ask, moreover, whether the psychological type is an outcome of these infantile dispositions, or whether it antecedes and determines them. Adler inclines

[1] Adler, Ueber den nervösen Charakter, 1919, p. 5; The Neurotic Constitution, 1921, p. 8.

to hold the latter view, for he considers that the little boy's "will-to-power" has merely been accentuated by his feeling of weakness; and this feeling of weakness explains the subsequent manifestations (shunning the world, timidity, etc.). The fantasies of return to the womb, the cult of the Virgin Mary, etc., are regarded by Freudians as vestiges of the fixation of feeling upon the mother. Adler, on the other hand, regards them as nothing more than symbols of the longing for security.[1]

A direct study of the history of the early years of life in certain subjects, and the fact that analysis of the infantile causes mitigates the subsequent manifestations, favour the theory that these infantile feelings have a genuinely causal efficacy. But this does not hinder the objects of such feelings from being subsequently regarded as symbols. In any case, dubieties of theory must not make us overlook the solidity of the relations we have been considering. Perhaps the most convenient way out of the difficulty is to say that "everything happens as if" the infantile feelings were the cause of the subsequent developments.

The first case is that of a woman, Miriam, who is strongly attached to her father, and whose whole life is guided by the worship and the imitation of her father. The other two subjects, Marcel and Otto respectively, are men who exhibit the Oedipus complex. In the former, dread of the father has been transformed into general timidity. In the latter, the introversion shows itself physically in a certain awkwardness, and morally in a refusal of virility and a tendency towards philosophical abstraction; the social instincts and the combative instinct have been repressed; individualism is extremely marked.

1. Miriam

A Religious and Social Calling Inspired by the Cult of the Father.

A State of Conflict.

The analysis of this case was incomplete. Moreover, in transcribing it, I shall record only its salient features. These, however, seem to me typical.

[1] Adler, op. cit., p. 139; English translation, p. 148.

Miriam is a woman nearly fifty years of age. Married and a mother, but separated from her family in consequence of the war, she has become a hospital nurse, this representing to her a most important vocation. She is in a state of extreme nervous tension; she is always bustling about like some one who never attains complete self-satisfaction, and has never found a proper balance.

The first dream she told me was not a recent one, for it dated from the time when she adopted her new calling. Overnight she had not yet made up her mind, and as she was thinking matters over she was mentally questioning her dead father, with the feeling that he would approve her choice. The dream seemed to come as an answer, so that it helped her to make up her mind. She communicated it to me in writing.

I. Before adopting my new calling I dreamed of my father. I saw him coming towards me in uniform, but I saw that beneath the clothing there was only a skeleton. The expression of his face was calm and benign. I rushed up to him, wishing to kiss his chest, but he said to me: "No, not there, that has an evil smell; kiss me on the lips." I kissed him ardently. He said: "Don't be afraid. Take the door which is open. I shall be with you, nothing will happen to you, you can be quite easy in your mind. I shall always be with you."

Apropos of this dream, Miriam said that she had had *an extraordinary affection* for her father. She added:

I have always the feeling that father is beside me.

Her father was an army surgeon. She has this reminiscence dating from the age of five.

She was watching her father dressing some wounds, and her wish was to do the same thing when she grew up.

Here are some other memories of childhood:

She would dress up as a boy, an officer, and would play at riding on horseback. She liked to play at being a doctor and to treat corns.

Sometimes, too, she looked forward to becoming a great actress. Her mother had been a great singer, but had given up this career when she married.

We can already discern the starting-point of a conflict between two wishes: first, that for a womanly life, a very active one, artistic and elegant; secondly, that for a manly life, a copy of her father's, subordinated to a strong sense of duty, directed towards the relief of others, and under military discipline. The " extraordinary " affection for the father must have helped to give the second wish the upper hand. From early childhood, Miriam had been very fond of *uniforms,* and especially *military uniforms.* In her present occupation she dresses wounds and wears a uniform. She has thus modelled her life upon the paternal " imago," which is always alive and active within her. (" I shall always be with you."—" I have always the feeling that father is beside me.")

In a second dream, comparatively recent, the preponderant role of the father is again manifest.

> II. I was passing the chapel of my old school. Christ, nailed to the cross, was lying on the ground athwart the threshold. My father was close to the recumbent figure. He said: " You see that it is a corpse. We must raise it. You are a nurse; give me a hand. Perhaps an operation will still help." I drew near, and my father and I together lifted Christ's body from the cross. Then I awoke.

This action of lifting a dead body called up in Miriam the memory of an incident in the hospital when a soldier had to be lifted in the same way. Even without this definite association, it would have been obvious that the dream contained an allusion to her work at the hospital. In this dream, likewise, her father presides over the work. But there is an element which was not expressed in the first dream, namely, the identification of the sufferers with Christ, the subject's fundamentally religious outlook upon her vocation. This tie between an intense and active religious sentiment and the idea of the father can often be noted in women who are strongly attached to the father.

In Miriam this attachment exhibits the characteristic features of the *Electra complex.* In her fantasies (dream I, for example), her fondness finds expression in the images of a sensual love, in which the lower elements are of course repressed. (" Not there, that has an evil smell.") Moreover, when the mother's image passes away, Miriam's fantasies express an extremely intimate union with the father.

Here is a striking instance. While the analysis was in progress, Miriam heard that her mother's death was imminent, and was greatly distressed by the news. After having told me this, she added:

> Last night I took off my nightgown and wore my father's dressing gown. I kept it on all night. It made me feel so much better.

Here we doubtless have an echo of the infantile feeling of love for the father, a jealous love, and one in which she wishes to seek shelter.

Now comes a dream which she has had frequently. This introduces us to a different order of ideas.

> III. I often dream of a ship at sea. I am on the ship. The water is often brown, but nevertheless, the sun is shining brightly.

This same dream, with variations, recurs shortly afterwards.

> IV. Miriam saw herself on the shore of a lake which was dirty and brown. There were a great many people there. She had to cross the lake with a friend.

I have epitomised the dream; it contained allusions to current affairs. But in so far as it coincided with the habitual dream, its general lines were those we have been considering.

"Brown" is a colour which Miriam dislikes. The "lake which is dirty and brown" calls to her mind a canal adjoining the house where she lived with her husband. This "brown water" is as unpleasant to her as mud or fæces. As for "a great many people," in this connection she has the following associations:

> A picnic.—A picnic which Miriam saw on the shore of a lake when she was about eighteen.—Her loathing of this picnic.—A lot of drunken people.—The street through which she had to pass on her way back from her father's house; the street in which there were drunken people.

In another dream there is a change of motif.

V. She had to start on a sea voyage. She saw herself on the sea-shore. The water was blue but there was a heavy swell. She said to herself: "Everyone will be seasick." There must have been a ship somewhere about, but she could not see it.

There was a wealth of associations to this invisible ship:

The Flying Dutchman, which she saw at Frankfort when she was there with her husband in 1889.—They had come late and had left before the end. She remembers one of the scenes with the shadow of a ship. The mirage of a ship which she saw in the Mediterranean.—Mirages she has seen in the African desert. The mirages recall reminiscences: a terrace on which she had tea in the early days of her marriage; her son's beginning to walk.

I should add that the colour "brown"—not repugnant this time, but as if sunlit ("copper-coloured")—appeared in another dream; this leads us to the colour of the Eiffel Tower and to the same year 1889, the year of the Paris Exhibition, the first year of her marriage, the year of beautiful memories and of "amusements." The copper colour in the dream was the colour of a pair of satin slippers.

The elements of dreams III–V are akin and are mutually explanatory. We are concerned with youth, "life," and love; with extroversion, if you will. This is the "voyage" to which the dreams refer.

The "seasickness" and the "dirty brown" call up a repugnant aspect of this life. From various allusions, and by analogy with many other analyses, we can easily recognise the cruder aspect of sexuality. "A great many people" seen on the shore of this dirty water (IV) recalls a "picnic" of which the subject had a "loathing," one she went to when she was eighteen years old (the age of certain initiations); it also recalls images of "drunken people" met when she was leaving "her father's house."

"Nevertheless, the sun is shining brightly." It is the sun of 1889, youth, travelling, the theatre, the first days of married life, and the epoch of her little boy's beginning to walk. But Miriam has a more or less conscious feeling that she was unable to enjoy this life to the full. She expresses this by two very fine symbols, connected with the memory of the play she and her husband went to see in Frankfort. "They had come late and left before the end." This is the first symbol. The second symbol is that of the "mirages" (associated with these the subject has reminiscences of her youth). Here we have the "phantom ship," which was that in which she made her own "voyage."

In a word, Miriam, has not fully accepted a woman's life; and we know the conflict which is the cause of her failure to accept it. Symbolically, she has never been able to quit "her father's house." The fascination of the paternal "imago" has led her to seek a life of a somewhat masculine character, quasi-military, a life under orders, a life of self-denial.

The following dream, which likewise occurred during the period of the analysis, shows that the conflict was still going on at that date:

> VI. An eminence overlooking the sea. . . . Two cliffs between which the tide is ebbing. A casino, music, a fashionable crowd, palm trees. A snake writhing. Miriam starts. A gentleman says to her: "Don't be afraid." But the snake allures her. She says: "The snake typifies cunning." The gentleman answers: "No, it typifies wisdom." She is fascinated. She puts the snake into a basket and gives it to the gentleman. The snake disports itself in a flowery mead. The gentleman says to her: "You must never part from this snake, it is very gentle."

In the sea which is ebbing between two cliffs, and above all in the episode of the snake, purely sexual allusions are obvious. It is remarkable to find once more, in a woman who has never heard of Freud's ideas, this typical fantasy, which has been analysed hundreds of times, and which is as old as the world—or the Garden of Eden. On this tree are grafted all the feelings which have just been evoked by the reminiscences of 1889.

Here are some associations:

> *An eminence overlooking the sea.* A seaside resort where Miriam stayed with her son when he was five or six years old.
>
> *The ebbing tide.* Another seaside resort. This also is connected with her son's childhood. She was there with her husband.
>
> *Snake.* A snake she saw in the Caucasus. She was with her husband and her son. It was a happy time.

The gentleman. This was an intimate friend of her husband. He was the same age as her husband ; he was devoted to their son.

The flowery mead. Her mother.

" The gentleman " is manifestly a substitute for the husband, and the first associations evoke definite memories of the early days of married life. The last association is explained by the fact that this elegant and flowery life is linked with the image of her mother (the singer), just as the life of self-denial is linked with the image of the father. She has never made a definitive choice between these two lives, nor has she been able to harmonise the two. The latent conflict is doubtless largely responsible for her perennial condition of restless agitation.

She dreams of someone who seems to be a substitute for the father, and she remarks that she is on the look out for this person's daughter. She is really searching for herself. Here is another dream.

> VII. Someone gives her a scrap of greyish-blue paper, upon which she can read, as if seen through tracing paper, the words: " Where are you ? Whither are you going ? " The writing is rather like her mother's.

The piece of paper calls up the paper on which she used to write to her husband ; but doubtless the fact that she sees the writing " as if through tracing paper " is in line with the " mirages " of the reminiscences previously recorded. The question " Where are you ? " reminds Miriam that her mother called out these words to her in the garden one day when someone was coming to pay a visit ; this " someone was coming to pay a visit " promptly evokes the coming of her husband. We are still in the same circle of ideas. Nothing could express more aptly than these two questions, the state of a mind which is unsatisfied, which is questioning itself, which is searching.

During the analysis, which was accompanied by autosuggestion, considerable though somewhat fluctuating progress was made towards securing outward and inward calm. The subject was delighted with the results. Unfortunately circumstances made it impossible to pursue the analysis as far as it ought to have been pursued.

2. Marcel

DREAD OF THE FATHER. TIMIDITY AND UNDUE SCRUPULOSITY.

Marcel, a man of thirty-five, a clerk, is timid and scrupulous in disposition. His timidity and scruples are especially manifest in connection with his professional work; it is when he is at the office that they are seen in an acute form.

He is continually wondering whether he has done his work right; he checks an account twenty times over; cannot add up figures under the eye of the head clerk without feeling paralysed with alarm; and he will return again and again to make sure he has locked up the office on leaving. An intense and sudden emotion takes possession of him when he has to announce anyone to the manager, or to tell the latter he is wanted on the telephone. In especial, contact with the manager makes him feel absolutely incapable.

In our first interview I asked Marcel to relate to me any reminiscences of childhood which might occur to him spontaneously. Here were the first memories to arise.

> I (when he was about 8 years old). Marcel had broken a bolt on the front door. His father noticed it when he came home to dinner. He seized the child by the nape of the neck and the legs and threatened to throw him into the cesspool.
>
> II. Whenever his father spoke rather loudly, Marcel was terribly startled. He could not do his school work when his father was there.—Walking one day in the town with his father, he tried to read the name of the street they were in, and made a mistake; he read "Etudes" instead of the real name; his father scolded him severely.

Marcel went on to say that the fear which, in childhood, he had felt for his father, was what he had subsequently felt during his term of military service, and still later in the case of his superiors at the office. Thus spontaneously, knowing nothing of the psychological theories involved, he grasped the nature of the affective transference which dominated his whole life. Originally he had been afraid of his father; later this fear had been transferred to all the persons who wielded over him an authority analogous to paternal authority.

We should carefully note that he was unable to do his school work when his father was present. Moreover, it is extremely significant that the memory of a scolding from his father should be linked with the word "étude." We realise now that, in the transference, office work has been substituted for school work, just as the head clerk has been substituted for the father. We glimpse a relationship between the difficulty of school work in former days when the father was present, and the difficulty of office work nowadays when the head clerk is present; and between the father's anger on account of a broken bolt, and the exaggerated anxiety Marcel feels as to whether he has locked up the office.

I gave the subject a summary explanation of these facts. I enabled him to realise that in his subconscious, whenever a superior was present, he continued to believe himself to be the child whom his father would scold. Then we had a first sitting of autosuggestion.

I saw Marcel a week later. He had noted an improvement from the fourth day after our first interview. When he locks a door now, he says to himself: "I am locking it, I have locked it," and he has no need to verify the fact. When adding up figures in the head clerk's presence he no longer feels stiff with fear.

He told me his earliest memory of childhood.

> III (4 years old). He had taken a basket which he had been forbidden to touch. He fell and cut his forehead.

The father does not appear in this reminiscence, but there is the feeling of disobedience punished, the state of mind of a child who has been told, "God has punished you." Then he went on to relate a dream of a fall when bicycling, and this dream revived a forgotten memory of childhood.

> IV (about 12 years old). He fell from a bicycle.—His father did not like to see him riding a bicycle.

In the subject's mind, the last reflection appeared to be closely linked to the actual memory of the fall. The father had not been there to punish, but he disapproved, and it seemed to the child that the fall had been an indirect punishment. It was not the father; it was (if we may use the terminology of the psychoanalytical school) the "paternal imago" which punished.

We should note also that in this case, as in the case of the basket (III), the indirect punishment was a fall; and that in another reminiscence (I) the father had threatened to throw his son into a cesspool. From our experience of other cases we know that images of falling and of defilement are generally the outcome of a condensation formed around a sentiment of moral lapse and of defilement. This gives us a clue, though we are not yet in a position to follow it up.

The following associations were called up by the image of the bicycle.

> Two things which go very quickly.—A barrel.—Children rolling down a bank.—A swing.

These associations do not, per se, teach us much more than that there is an idea of rapid descent. We know, however, that sensations of rapid descent, and also the sensation of being in a swing, are closely akin to voluptuous (sexual) sensations, and we may expect to see once more the common relationship between such sensations and the feeling of shame. But despite the great probability that this relationship exists in any particular case, it is wiser to say nothing positive about the matter until the hypothesis has been confirmed by the subject's associations.[1]

Marcel went on to tell me the following dream:

> V. He dreamed about his dog. There were some burglars; he wanted to set the dog on them; the animal, which is usually very obedient, refused to budge; thereupon Marcel gave it a beating.

The associations were as follows:

> *To set the dog at them.* To catch, to seize, to bite, "I shall have time to get there, I thought I knew the burglars."
>
> *The dog's disobedience.* "I thought of beating it."
>
> *Burglars.* Burglars caught in the act, taking to flight; people running away and looking over their shoulders.
>
> *To beat.* A gnarled stick.
>
> *A gnarled stick.* "What every man has," the penis.

The last association, perfectly spontaneous, is valuable when coming from a man of mediocre attainments who has

[1] I lay stress on the need for caution in this respect. To doctrinaire psychoanalysts, such caution will doubtless appear superfluous; but I regard it as an essential methodological rule in so delicate a sphere, and in one where investigators have not always been careful to avoid seductive hypotheses and facile generalisations.

no knowledge of psychoanalytical theories, and who has had absolutely no suggestion of the kind from me. Such an association does not of course entitle us to assert, as some are inclined to assert, that the image of a stick is a fixed symbol of the penis; but it certainly shows that there is a definite relationship between the two images.

Again, Marcel told me the following reminiscence. Like that of the broken bolt, it dated from the time when he was about eight years old.

> VI. Some neighbours had a Great Dane. Marcel was on his way back from an errand. When he saw the dog he was frightened and ran away. The dog jumped at him and tore his pinafore.

The symbol of tearing is often akin to that of defilement; this general relationship is in accord with the particular instance. We see, moreover, that the dog calls up the real episode of a fright, which may have had, qua fright, an influence upon the subject's psyche. But there is more than this in the matter. The "burglars" in dream V are shown by the associations to be symbolic of something done on the sly, something blameworthy which people are caught doing. The association of "stick" confirms the notion that we have to do with sexual shame.

The subject went on to tell me of another dream.

> VII. He was being chased by some men. He had a tight feeling in the throat so that he could not make a sound. The anxiety was intense. There were two men. One had come in by the door; the other was hidden under the bed. After talking the matter over, they decided to kill Marcel. The man who had come in by the door was tall, and was rather like Marcel; this was the one who wanted to kill Marcel; he had a coarse, unkempt beard. The other, without speaking, seemed to say: "What's the good of killing him?" This was a short man with a square head and frizzy hair. He reminded Marcel of some one in real life, "a good chap, but inclined to run after the girls."

When asked about "under the bed," Marcel thought of the following things.

> Waiting.—Hiding, and afraid of being seen.—At school they had played at ghosts.—His parents had been superstitious and had talked about ghosts before him.

These ghost stories, like the attack by the dog just recorded, had doubtless contributed to the child's timorousness. Here, likewise, deeper influences are at work. The impression of "hiding and afraid of being seen" is akin to the symbol of the "burglars." Once more we have a blameworthy and shameful action. Moreover, the man hidden under the bed is a symbol of the sexual man. He is indulgent, let us say morally indulgent; whereas the other, standing up face to face and resembling the conscious personality of the subject, is merciless. Here are indications of a conflict, as usual in anxiety states.

The associations to the image of "a tight feeling in the throat" are extremely significant. The subject thinks of a *clasping*, of *hands drawing near.* The "hands," in their turn, promptly call up *large hands, his own,* and, without transition, *masturbation*—a spontaneous association which surprises the subject. This immediately calls up his father's sayings and threats relative to the practice of masturbation, so that at length we have a clear indication of what kind of shameful act is in question. We are brought in touch with a crisis through which so many adolescents have to pass, one whose momentousness is commonly aggravated by brutal threats.

At the word "anxiety," new and important associations appear. Some of them such as *a spasm of anguish* (serrement de cœur), being *clasped* (être serré), confirm the comparison of this anxiety to the impression of *a tight feeling in the throat* (être serré à la gorge)— and all we have just discerned behind this impression. Here are some other associations:

> Feeling of powerlessness.—Feeling (in the dream) of being unable to call his wife.—"If my mother dies, what will happen? This thought makes me sick of life."

Here is an indication of fondness for the mother, a fondness which is often connected with hostility to the father. In Marcel, however, the negative element of the "Oedipus complex" (hostility to the father) would seem to be more important than the positive element (love of the mother). When I enquired about his parents, he gave me additional significant details.

> VIII. He once dreamed that he saw his father dead; "it was all over." (He expressed no regret.)

> At an earlier date, before his marriage, he dreamed that his mother was dead. He has had this dream again, since his marriage. The dream aroused " a terrible *spasm of anguish*," unaccompanied by tears. Moreover, during the dream, he reproached himself; he might have been a better man; he was responsible.

What follows is extremely typical.

> He recalled having had as a child a conscious wish (instantly repressed, of course) that his father might die.
>
> To-day he sometimes feels the wish to die before his mother, so that he may not have to witness her death. This has come especially since he has been married and separated from her.
>
> When he was a child, he had looked upon his father as the adversary. Feeling himself incapable of overcoming this adversary, he had the impression of " retreating before him."

This retreat is preeminently the attitude of timidity. As for the hostility to the father, we regarded this at first as a revolt against brutal authority. Now, however, it appears, though less frankly, to be likewise associated with his fondness for his mother. Obviously, then, jealousy is a constituent factor.

On the other hand the idea of the *mother* is more than once associated with the idea of the *wife*. In the associations of dream VII, the subject has a " feeling of being unable to call his wife," and he promptly goes on to ask himself what will happen " if my mother dies." Then, speaking of dreams in which he pictures his mother as dead, he finds it necessary to locate them as " before marriage " and " after marriage." Marriage is the decisive date at which he was separated from his mother, but the need for the mother remains strong; he is afraid that his mother will die, and the fear is all the more intense because he cannot " call his wife "; he is unable to look to his wife for deliverance from his anguish. He retains the infantile attitude of looking to his mother for help.

We know, moreover, that fondness for the mother (the Oedipus complex) may lead to the repression of sexuality. But the subject tells me, in addition, of a positive cause for repression, and for scruples. He had related an erotic dream.

> IX. The woman in the dream resembled his wife, but was rather red in the face and was fatter than his wife.

Questioning him concerning this dream, I learned that his wife was often ailing. Being himself inspired by strict religious and moral principles, and wishing to lead a very regular conjugal life, he had imposed upon himself, for this reason, a considerable degree of continence. His dream would therefore seem unmistakably to have been an imaginary realisation of a repressed wish; but the scrupulosity of his character made him blame himself for it, and for all similar thoughts. (I reassured him by telling him that it was perfectly normal, and that no one could be held accountable for dreams and involuntary thoughts.) The repression and the scruples doubtless played their part in producing the anxiety dream (VII); another factor was resistance to the possible temptations of masturbation. Anxiety is, in fact, often connected with such repressions and conflicts. The feeling, in the dream, of inability to call his wife, may correspond to the continence imposed upon him by his wife's ailments. But, quite apart from this contingent positive significance, the dream is of great value to us for the light it throws upon the general determinants of the subject's psychic life.

One who sees sex everywhere, a "pansexualist," being aware of the importance of shame that is sexual in its origins, and being informed in this case of the father's threats concerning masturbation, would attribute everything to these factors, and would use them to explain all the imagery in the subject's mind. He would discover sex, and nothing but sex, in the reminiscences of disobedience, insisting that the bolt (I) and the basket (III) were merely symbols of the penis; that the two wheels of the bicycle (VI) represented the testicles; and so on. Although it is likely enough that, in virtue of condensation, the memories of these incidents may contain sexual allusions, I consider that an exclusively sexual explanation would be erroneous. It seems to me indubitable that, on the one hand, the real incidents which form the kernel of the conscious memories, and, on the other hand, the subject's general dread of paternal authority, must also have had their importance as determinants; and I do not think that we are entitled to regard all this as purely "symbolic" of something else. It is unduly venturesome to assert thus categorically that one of the elements of a condensation, one of the least obvious elements, is the only important one.

The subject's characteristics appear to me plain enough: fondness for the mother, protest (a timorous protest) against the father; shame of sexual origin, connected with the father's threats regarding masturbation. The subject's shamefacedness, his dread of making mistakes, and his excessive scrupulosity, were the outcome of these factors.

A cure was effected after seven sittings, once a week at first, and subsequently at longer intervals. Each time, the analysis was followed by autosuggestion. It will be remembered that Marcel noted an improvement as early as the fourth day; during the second week he was aware of "great activity;" in the fourth week a feeling of alarm he had hitherto always had when going down into the cellar had disappeared. During the sixth week the idea of autosuggesting "I shall no longer be able to be timid" spontaneously occurred to him; during the seventh week he became convinced that his timidity had been eradicated. During the ninth week he considered that he was becoming "a trifle aggressive." I kept him under observation for three years.

3. Otto

Repressed Virility. Awkwardness and Constraint. A philosophic Trend.

Otto, a man of forty-three, suffers from a perpetual feeling of awkwardness and constraint. He finds it difficult to express himself. He says that he lacks ease, spontaneity, and readiness. Unaided, however, he has been practising autosuggestion with very good effect. He came to consult me in the hope that psychoanalysis would contribute to his progress.

He was the youngest of a large family. His mother had told him that his coming had not been altogether welcome. Nevertheless, she had always been affectionate, and even indulgent. The father was kindly and well educated; he could read Latin; the farmers of the countryside nicknamed him "the professor." Before learning to write, Otto used to scribble imaginary notes on the margin of books because he had seen his father make notes there. The father was wont to say: "This lad has a future before him."

When he was about twelve, Otto read an essay by Schopenhauer upon duelling, in which the philosopher described an insult as a matter of no moment, and said that to take vengeance by killing the offender seemed disproportionate. Subsequently Schopenhauer became Otto's favourite author, and Otto adopted Schopenhauer's pessimist philosophy. "I read too much Schopenhauer," he said. He also read Helvétius. In poetry, he had a passion for Catulle Mendès.

An intelligent workman, he was self-taught. His mind was formed, without any methodical instruction, by chance reading.

Up to the age of twenty he exhibited a certain tendency towards fetichism for women's clothing. Then he went in for the "simple life," lived wholesomely, avoiding stimulants and excitement of all kinds; the fetichist tendency disappeared. For a long time he was extremely timid; he had no experience of sexual intercourse until he was twenty-two.

Otto gave me the foregoing sketch of his history at our first interview. Then he told me a reminiscence of childhood.

> I. He had been given a hen canary, "one that did not sing." Otto, feeling sorry for the bird, had set it at liberty. Then he had been told that the canary would perish in freedom. Every evening, for a whole week, he suffered from "remorse after he went to bed."

Questioning upon this reminiscence evoked the following responses:

> *Canary*. A canary in his lodging. He says to himself: "Why do people keep birds in cages?" He thinks it a cruel practice. If Schopenhauer influenced him, it was probably because this philosopher's teachings harmonised with his own natural tender-heartedness.
>
> *Hen canary*. A reminiscence from the age of twenty. Some swallows had built their nest in the billiard room of the restaurant. The hen swallow used to sit upon her nestlings, while the father bird spent the night outside the house. Otto's sister, an outspoken girl, said: "He can't sleep with his wife, for there are too many people about." Coming back to the question of being tender-hearted, he says that this compassionate trend disappeared from the time he was twenty until he was twenty-five. During this interlude, he had a craze for shooting, but now, once more, shooting has become distasteful.

One that did not sing. As a child, Otto used to sing. Now he has lost the power. Speaking of instrumental music he says: "In this respect I have retained my spontaneity." But if people begin to sing when he is playing the piano, it "irritates" him. He likes to hear a woman singing, but not a man. Singing sounds to him like "bellowing," unless it is very good. His eldest brother used to sing.

The canary will perish. If the bird should die, it would be all the better off. The pessimist philosophy.

Remorse after going to bed. Insomnia. Anxiety. Otto used to suffer a good deal from sleeplessness; this trouble began when he was two-and-twenty (simultaneously with his first experience of sexual relations), and he did not become free from it until four years ago. He had wanted to lead an ascetic life, being influenced in this respect by Schopenhauer. At first his sexual experiences had only been with professional prostitutes, for he had been too timid to try his luck elsewhere. Only two months ago had he dared to do this for the first time, so that his sexual life now seemed to him more normal. He considered that the change had been brought about by auto-suggestion.

The broad lines thus became manifest at the first sitting: repression of virility, closely linked with the repression of spontaneity, with lack of "ease." Singing, a man's singing, is a symbol both of the virility and of the spontaneity; the disappearance of the faculty for singing which Otto had possessed in childhood is connected with the general repression; it indicates a loss of spontaneity. When explaining that he remains able to play the piano, he says: "In this respect I have retained my spontaneity." His eldest brother, who for him symbolises virility, used to sing; what Otto finds distasteful in singing is the male voice.

We see that the subject is an "introvert." He is attracted by Schopenhauer because he rediscovers his own nature in that philosopher. The combative instinct is repressed as well as the sexual instinct. We observe such tendencies as are common in individuals of this type: a trend towards sympathy with all living beings; one towards pantheist metaphysics; one towards the renunciation of life, an aspiration towards non-entity.

We can likewise catch a glimpse of what seems to be usual in these cases: attachment to the mother, a sort of home-sickness for the mother, the longing to be "incubated" (the mother bird sits upon the nestlings; the father bird is thrust out). It seems possible that the metaphysical aspiration towards non-entity may be linked with fantasies of a return to the womb. The subject is fond of dwelling on the idea that his mother did not welcome him into the world.

The hen canary, which does not sing and which is in a cage, symbolises repressed virility and introversion. The setting of it at liberty corresponds with Otto's first contact with the sexual life and with " the world." The remorse he felt after giving the bird its freedom corresponds with the mental distress ensuing upon his first experiences of this kind.

During the second week of the analysis, Otto had the following dream:

II. He said to his father : " The needles are in one of the drawers of my desk." They were needles for darning socks. Really, there was nothing in the drawer except papers and newspaper cuttings which he intended to send to his brother.

Commentary through associations.

Father. My father was a very good shot.
Needles. An embroidered handkerchief. Needlework.
Brother. The brother is bellicose, and favours the German side. Otto takes the opposite view, and is pacifist. The drawer is full of newspaper cuttings bearing upon discussions Otto has had with his brother, cuttings which Otto was going to send him ; but the war broke out. Otto recalls a dispute which, when a child, he had had with this brother, the eldest of the family. Otto had wanted to keep his long locks ; his brother had scolded him, and wanted to take him to the hairdresser.

He also remembers a country excursion he had made with his brother and some other young folk. He was then twelve or thirteen years old. They had chaffed him, and he had run away all by himself. He had tried to find his way home through the wood and had lost himself.

Darning. Making up a quarrel. The adage which says that you must quarrel before you can make it up.

Socks. Ladies' summer stockings. The old fetichist tendency.

What does all this signify ? The father and the elder brother symbolise virility. The combative instinct (a good shot, a bellicose pro-German) represents virility. Whereas his father is a good shot, Otto hates shooting. The disputes with the brother represent a repudiation of virility. This repudiation has led Otto to cultivate certain feminine characteristics: long hair, for instance; and he quarrels with his brother because the latter has wished him to have his hair cut short and thus make him manly. But what is in question to-day is, a symbolical reconciliation with the "brother," that is to say with virility; what is in question is, a return to the "father." This will be at one and the same time a "making it up" and an acceptance of sexuality. As concerns this matter, Otto explains that he is still affected by an irrational resistance to sexuality, a resistance which entails quarrels with his mistress. He always feels regretful after the sexual act.

The incident of the country excursion likewise draws our attention to the frequent relationship between repressed virility and maladaptation to social life, to camaraderie. This maladaptation tends to increase the desire for solitude, the longing to withdraw into oneself.

Otto sent me three dreams he had recorded in writing.

III. The other evening, when I came home after visiting my mistress, I felt greatly touched in recalling how sweet she had been. . . . That same night I dreamed that, notwithstanding my protests, my father was absolutely determined to come and live with me. My father is eighty years old.

IV. I find myself in A. square in front of the M. restaurant. There were some acrobats with a singing monkey. At the end of the song, by which I was greatly surprised, they took off a sort of hood the monkey had over his head, and lo and behold it was a man.

V. I found myself in a barber's, and I had myself shaved by Monsieur Baudouin, who then attended me to the door, saying: "Come back again for psychoanalysis."

Apropos of III, the subject recalls that when he was coming away from his mistress' house he had wondered to himself: "will she manage to change me?" [To make an extrovert of him.] He had had a cough, and she had made him some lichen tea. To this there were the following associations:

Medicinal herbs.—There is a family tendency to throat troubles.—One of his brothers had been invalided from the army for goitre.

The father represents virility, extroversion. Virility now wishes to come into its own, although the subject still resists. The throat trouble, which recalls the difficulty of singing (I), represents incomplete virility. The subject expects his mistress to exercise a quasi-magical influence over him, to give him a " medicinal herb " which will take him out of himself.

The second dream signifies a protest against one form of virility and extroversion, the crude and coarse form which can never satisfy a man like Otto, who is a person of advanced moral and intellectual development. M. restaurant and A. square are in the centre of the prostitutes' quarter. Apropos of the monkey, the subject thinks of his dislike for singing, which he styles " absurd " in the mouth of a monkey or of a man. He is also reminded that Schopenhauer regards the imitative instinct as a vestige of our simian descent.

> For his own part, he has always been careful not to be imitative. At one time of his life he was accustomed to say to himself every morning: " Don't do what other people do."

This is the individualism of the introvert.

In V, Otto expresses his attitude towards analysis and the analyst. I am " shaving " him and not analysing him. At the outset of an analysis which has not yet been thoroughly accepted, the subject's subconscious is apt to excogitate some such grip in order to depreciate the analyst. On the other hand, apropos of the barber's shop, Otto is reminded that his mistress was at one time a ladies' hairdresser. He still thinks that his determination to shave was (consciously) the outcome of the influence of Schopenhauer's æsthetic ideas. Subconsciously, however, there has been operative the same desire for feminity which had formerly made him wish to retain his long locks. In this connection he recalls an old love affair. His inamorata " wanted an effeminate man," and she cut off his moustache.

We might suppose that in V the subject is assuming a feminine attitude towards the analyst, and that this might indicate the beginnings of " transference on to the analyst." In any case, we must point out that the images relating to the analysis are strangely contiguous to the images relating to love. From love and from the analysis the subject expects what he terms "a cure;" that is to say, the victory which will give him extroversion and "ease."

I had enabled him to recognise in himself the existence of the tendency towards femininity, and it was at this juncture that he brought me three quotations, extremely significant—passages by which he had been greatly struck when he had read them in earlier days.

From Catulle Mendès, *Pour lire au bain*: "What other poet is so feminine as the divine Amarou, whose soul had lived in the body of a hundred women?"

From Han Ryner (one of Otto's favourite authors), *Le manuel individualiste*: "Seneca speaks of Epicurus as a hero disguised as a woman."

From La Bruyère, *Caractères*: "I have known more than one person who, from thirteen to twenty-two, wanted to be a girl, a pretty girl, and then to become a man."

The third of these quotations is peculiarly significant, inasmuch as it was at the age of twenty-two that the subject had his first experience of normal sexual relations.

VI. One evening, when Otto came away from his mistress, he was thinking about his own pecuniary position, which did not allow him to support her on the scale he would have liked.—That night he dreamed that France had gone bankrupt; French money was now worthless; consequently, he had lost 300 marks.—He went for a walk in the woods with a friend. They found an inn there; an orchestra was playing Viennese music, his favourite music.

France is a symbol for his mistress, who is a Frenchwoman. The psychoanalyst is also of French nationality, and there is probably a similar condensation to that which occurred in dream V. It follows that "the bankruptcy of France" may be looked upon as a new way of depreciating me.

The 300 marks have been lent to a friend in Germany, and Otto is afraid that he will never see them again. It is a feeling, rather than a fact that his material situation is not good enough for his mistress; we have to interpret the feeling symbolically; it betokens his imperfect adaptation to love and to life. In addition, France, for him, symbolises "ease." The whole thing bears on his customary preoccupations.

A little further on, fresh problems come into view. Here are the associations of the second part of the dream.

Going for a walk. Otto once lent his mistress a book by Catulle Mendès containing the story of "Theresa's Shift" (Theresa, a convert, goes on a pilgrimage to a place where in earlier days she had thrown away her shift, feeling she could not be bothered with it any longer. She is given a relic to kiss, a relic which is supposed to have fallen from heaven, and she recognises her own shift). Otto recalls a walk with his mistress. They entered a Catholic church. He is fond of the mysticism of Catholic churches.

The woods. In the region where Otto was born there is a forest known as Heilige Hallen. (The name calls up religious ideas.) Schopenhauer mentions this forest as having given him an impression of the sublime.

Inn. The inn in the Place de la Madeleine where the post-chaises used to pull up.

Post-chaise. A picture postcard. Lovers in the days of the old regime. They are in a post-chaise driving through a splendid forest; Cupid is the postillion.

Madeleine. Someone who had sent him an invitation to a religious conference at the Madeleine. He did not go. He has been disgusted by religion because it is in the hands of "exploiters."

Orchestra. The Hofkirche in Dresden. An orchestra "playing some of Bach's fugues."—When Otto was apprenticed, the bell-ringers had taken him up into the belfry. He was frightened, and said to himself: "If they wanted to kill me here, I shouldn't have a chance." He had "a horrid drumming in the ears." All that these fellows had really wanted was a tip.

Viennese music. His brother, who plays the piano very well.

Apropos of the "Viennese music" we may likewise note here that this had turned up previously in the association to dream IV, in connection with the monkey and the acrobats. Otto had said he was fond of Viennese music "in thirds." But he wants "both voices;" he is "not satisfied with the melody by itself." He added that Viennese music seemed to him to be Germano-Slav. A little later he remarked that his mother was of German race, but his father was "a Polish immigrant." Finally he said that he was fond of the Viennese, who were comparatively subtle (rather like the French); he did not care for the North Germans.

We are now enabled to understand what are the two voices to which he refers, and which he wants to have in Viennese music. These two voices are within himself; they represent the mother and the father respectively. We grasp the significance of various terms polarised round these two ideas of the mother and the father. On the side of the "mother," we have Germany and introversion; on the side of the "father" we have the Slav and the Frenchman, the foreigner, extroversion. The terms grouped round either pole are interchangeable, and serve to symbolise one another.

Symbolically, Otto experiences the desire for the "father." —He is not satisfied with the melody by itself, the melody representing the higher pitched voice, a woman's voice. And yet he does not wish to achieve complete extroversion. He needs "both voices;" he wants to fulfil his whole nature, and has no idea of renouncing himself.

All this throws light on the last dream. Originally Otto had religious aspirations; in the terminology of the psychoanalytical school, his repressed instincts underwent a religious sublimation. He was, however, "disgusted" with religion because it seemed to him a form of "exploitation." In the associations to the dream we find two symbols for this idea of exploitation: Theresa's shift; and the bell-ringers who are on the look out for a tip. Besides, both Theresa and Madeleine [Magdalen] are converted sinners; they embody the idea of the sublimation of instinct. But this sublimation culminates in disillusionment. Theresa's experience shows her the fraud underlying what is supposed to be a relic. In like manner, Otto discerns the "exploitation" which he believes to underlie religion. There then occurs in him a phenomenon to which psychoanalysts have not hitherto paid sufficient attention, *the repression of a sublimated instinct.* In this case, it is the repression of the religious sentiment. Schopenhauer then becomes a substitute for religion. A phrase of Schopenhauer's concerning the forest, the "Holy Precincts" [Heilige Hallen], represents a transition from the religious sentiment to the philosophical sentiment.

To-day, however, Schopenhauer in his turn is being subjected to critical examination. Otto has learned the danger of pessimism, and he has an aspiration towards life. Ought he, then, unhesitatingly to throw himself into life, into extroversion? No. "France has gone bankrupt." "Both voices" are essential. Otto cannot renounce sublimation; he cannot repudiate that which philosophy, the inner life, individualism, have brought to him. Hence there is a crisis, which the dream expresses, and attempts to solve.

The image of his mistress is then condensed into a walk towards a church; the post-chaise of which Cupid is the postillion drives through a "splendid forest" like the one which had aroused the admiration of Schopenhauer and Otto. In a word, the images of love fuse with those of religion and of the "sublime." The coarser forms of sexuality (the monkey and the acrobats) have become impossible henceforward. Otto needs a love which can satisfy his spiritual aspirations, one in which "both voices" are present.

The analysis of this dream seems to have marked a decisive stage. Hitherto Otto had been inclined to fear that the "cure" would demand from him a repudiation of the inner life and an acceptance of crude instinct. It was natural, therefore, that he should feel a certain repulsion towards the method and towards the "cure" itself. He has now come to understand that no such demand will be made of him.

Here we have another dream stressing the disgust with which sexuality inspires him.

> VII. I go into a little room, one well known to me, in the house where I was born. Some ladies are seated round a table in this room . . . doing needlework. In their midst is a Frenchwoman. . . . A detail: In the room there is a privy.

Here we again encounter the "Frenchwoman," and also the "needles" of dream II; we already know their significance. The repulsive side is bluntly expressed by the symbol of the "privy." Furthermore, as so often happens, the disgust is linked with fear. Apropos of this dream, Otto recalls the following memories of childhood:

> When he was eleven years old, Otto had stayed out late for a lark. The door of the room he saw in the dream had been locked against him. Not being able to get in, he had been seized with panic.
>
> When he was seven years old, he was in the passage near the same room. . . . One of his sisters had said "bo" to frighten him. He was very timid in those days, and had been scared.

We will continue the analysis by a brief study of some of the works of art which have made a great impression on Otto.

Associations to an engraving by Ludwig Richter, " Little Red Riding Hood in the Forest," leads us to an image of an " old witch." Then comes the figure of his maternal grandmother, of whom he had been very fond just as he was of his mother. He always ran to his mother directly dinner was finished, and everyone made fun of him for this. The reminiscence shows very well how his fondness for his mother made him ridiculous in society, just as we have seen that he was a butt when on a country excursion with other young folk (II). Flight to the mother and flight to solitude are akin.

Next we come to one of Grimm's tales, The Wolf and the Seven Little Kids. This story, one which Otto was fond of reading as a child, is like Red Riding Hood in many respects. The wolf eats the little kids, just as the wolf-grandmother eats the little girl. The " wolf," a cousin of the " witch " and of the " grandmother," appears in Otto's subconscious as a symbol of what has been called the " dread mother," a symbol of the introversion which swallows like an abyss. In the little girl, or the little kids, eaten by the wolf, we have a fantasy of return to the mother's womb. Otto also recalls that the wolf in Grimm's tale had whitened its paw and had eaten a great lump of chalk to " soften its voice." This brings us again into touch with the fantasies anent singing (I). Otto is careful to point out that, in the tale, the goat rips up the wolf and the little kids reappear ; the introversion is not irremediable.

Similar results were secured with another of Grimm's tales, " Snow-Drop," or " Little Snow-White."

All this part of the analysis confirms the existence of a strong " maternal complex," linked to the repression of virility. The complex has the well-known characteristics.

When I had questioned him about these works of art, it spontaneously occurred to Otto to bring me a page from Schopenhauer's writings, a passage by which he had been greatly struck, and which he had read and re-read. He showed me his own French translation of the extract. [The standard English version runs as follows :]

> Because beauty accompanied with grace is the principal object of sculpture, it loves nakedness, and allows clothing only in so far as it does not conceal the form. . . .

I may be allowed, in passing, to insert here a comparison that is very pertinent to the arts we are discussing. It is this: as the beautiful bodily form is seen to the greatest advantage when clothed in the lightest way, or indeed without any clothing at all, and therefore a very handsome man, if he had also taste and the courage to follow it, would go about almost naked, clothed only after the manner of the ancients; so everyone who possesses a beautiful and rich mind will always express himself in the most natural, direct, and simple way, concerned, if it be possible, to communicate his thoughts to others, and thus relieve the loneliness that he must feel in such a world as this. And conversely, poverty of mind, confusion, and perversity of thought, will clothe itself in the most far-fetched expressions and the obscurest forms of speech, in order to wrap up in difficult and pompous phraseology small, trifling, insipid, or commonplace thoughts; like a man who has lost the majesty of beauty, and, trying to make up for the deficiency by means of clothing, seeks to hide the insignificancy or ugliness of his person under barbaric finery, tinsel, feathers, ruffles, cuffs, and mantles. . . .[1]

This man whose beauty is perfect, and who would prefer to go nude, is associated in Otto's mind with a statue of Apollo in the Uffizi Gallery at Florence (he showed me a photograph of it). These two impressions have engendered in him a concrete vision.

"It is," he said, "a vision of what may be called a free and noble ease of manner."

The last words lead us to an aphorism from the old Spanish book translated by Schopenhauer, Baltasar Gracian's *El oraculo manual y arte de prudencia*, a system of rules for the conduct of life. The title of the aphorism in Schopenhauer's version is "Edle freie Unbefangenheit bei Allem," which Otto translates by "Libre et noble désinvolture" [Free and noble ease of manner]. Apropos of this "ease of manner," the Spanish author writes:

"It is the life of talent, the breath of oratory, the soul of action, the ornament of ornaments. All the other graces serve to adorn Nature, but this is grace itself. It shows itself also in thought. Before all, it is a gift of Nature. It owes little to education, for it stands above education.

"It is something more than levity; it is tantamount to daring."

[1] The World as Will and Idea, by Arthur Schopenhauer, translated from the German by R. B. Haldane and J. Kemp, Trübner, London, 1883, vol. i, p. 296. [Book III, § 47.]

In Otto's copy of Schopenhauer's German translation, the last phrase had been underlined.

We perceive the elements out of which his ideal of " ease " has been formed. The existence of this ideal shows that he has never completely surrendered himself to his introversion; that he has always wanted to escape from it. Furthermore, the passage from Schopenhauer's *The World as Will and Idea* is significant in that it shows how this " ease " of thought and expression is associated in Otto's mind with the nudity of the human body. This is the tie we observed at the outset of the analysis.

We must note, however, that this ideal, in which Otto has objectified his desire to get out of himself, is in many respects linked with his introverted state of mind. For, first of all, the ideal is grounded upon the study of Schopenhauer. Next, the statue of the young Apollo has, as Otto himself declared, somewhat effeminate characteristics. Here we encounter once more a latent homosexuality, an inclination towards effeminacy. When asked for associations with the above-quoted passage from Gracian's handbook, Otto produced a phrase from Feuchtersleben's *Zur Diätetik der Seele* (Chapter III) —the book which made so profound an impression upon Carl Spitteler in youth. Here is the phrase:

> " Fantasy is feminine by nature. The feminine life has more staying power than the masculine life; the result may well be . . . greater physical force linked with delicacy and purity."

The following reminiscence was another of Otto's associations in this connection. He spoke of a friend:

> A man extremely orderly, but of a miserly disposition. . . . Nevertheless he was fond of good living, though it upset his digestion—as so often happens with crass materialists.—He had an attack of influenza, was taken to hospital, and at night during the delirium of fever he jumped out of the window. Death was instantaneous.

A few moments later, Otto made the following reflection (in connection with a thought of Schopenhauer's):

> " Hullo," I think, " might one not say that greed for money, regarded as one of the lower forces of matter, ruins the body. We are told that money leads to corruption. Well, just look at the faces of most of our profiteers! "

We know, through other associations, that the idea of money is linked with that of sexuality, of virility.

We may say that in Otto the trend towards effeminacy is even incorporated in his ideal of " ease," where we discern once more, not a repudiation, but an equilibrium (the " two voices "). Here the trend towards effeminacy is spiritualised. The feminine traits which the subject wishes to cultivate in himself are " purity and delicacy." He also aspires towards the peculiar force characteristic of the " feminine temperament." He finds its description, on the one hand in Feuchtersleben, who speaks of " natures woven of ether and moonlight " but capable of astounding everyone by their staying power, and on the other hand in my own book *Suggestion and Autosuggestion* (French original, p. 115 ; English translation, p. 138) :

> " In the foregoing pages, the writer has paid his tribute to the privileged mental position of certain temperaments, women, children, and artists being typical of these. It is possible that . . . devotees of an overstrained 'positivism' will find his remarks a trifle irritating. . . . But it is none the less true that the outcropping which is the essential characteristic of such temperaments must be cultivated by all who desire to avail themselves of the powers of well-controlled autosuggestion."

Thus in the very method of re-education, Otto has been able to discover a justification for his trend, and a way by which it can be guided in a useful direction. In autosuggestion, no less than in the Apollo of the Uffizi Gallery, he finds a synthesis of " femininity " and " ease "—a harmony of the " two voices."

In the passage from Gracian, Otto underlined the phrase concerning " ease of manner."

> It is something more than levity, it is tantamount to ***daring***.

In this connection he tells me that in childhood he was at first rather cheeky, but that he subsequently grew timid. How did this come about ? We are helped to understand the change by an interesting reminiscence.

> During my apprenticeship I was kept under a somewhat Prussian discipline. The first apprentice played the part of

non-com. One day he and I were carrying some pieces of machinery to a big brewery to set them up there. The first apprentice, after having explained to me how he was going to carry out the work, said: "That ought to go all right!" I answered that I was not so sure, for some unexpected difficulty might crop up.

Our little dispute was reported to the employer's son. He told me I was a slacker, and that if I ever said anything of the sort when I was working with him, he would "give me what for."

Henceforward I watched my words carefully, so that my mother said that I had become tongue-tied. Besides, I didn't enjoy myself at all in my life as apprentice.

The master and the first apprentice would appear to have been condensed respectively with Otto's father and his eldest brother. "That ought to go all right" evoked in Otto the idea of the infringement of Belgian neutrality in 1914.

> No doubt our Prussian swashbucklers likewise said to themselves: "That ought to go all right, to invade France through Belgium."

When the invasion failed to achieve its purpose, Otto felt as if he had got even with the first apprentice.

He recalls also that in the master's house there was a canary. He asked whether it was a cock or a hen. The question was considered rather indelicate and this experience made him more and more reserved. He was told that the canary could not sing because it had grown too fat.

We have got back to the first motif. To the repression of virility (in the form of sexuality and the combative instinct) there is superadded the influence of an authority which recalls the paternal authority. No doubt the incidents of his apprenticeship exercised an influence in repressing spontaneity, but this influence would have been much less powerful had not the incidents undergone condensation with deeper and more secret processes.

Apropos of the words "that ought to go all right," Otto further notes that this might be called a formula of ease. It is also a formula of autosuggestion. And this brings us back to the Uffizi Apollo. But here the "virile" side, formerly repressed, is more apparent; it is a formula of the "swashbuckler."

Otto, then, is an introvert with a philosophic trend ; he is strongly attached to the mother. The awkwardness and constraint, the lack of spontaneity, of which he complains, are linked with a general refusal of virility and social life. But this same refusal has contributed to the development of the inner life and of meditation.

The analysis enabled the subject to dissociate the two categories of results ; to rectify the former without repudiating the latter ; to gain a more perfect adaptation to external life without renouncing his internal conquests.

The balance and ease which Otto wished to acquire had been practically attained after the first few sittings He continued the analysis, partly in order to gain perfect mastery, and partly because the study was interesting to him as a man of philosophic temperament.

CHAPTER EIGHT

THE INSTINCT OF SELF-PRESERVATION, AND THE INSTINCT FOR MOTHERHOOD

ALTHOUGH many people speak of Freud as a "pansexualist," he has categorically declared, as we know, that dreams may be the expression of other wishes than those relating to the sexual instinct—even when the term sexual is used with the wide connotations which he gives to it. It might indeed be foreseen that all the instincts would find expression in dreams. Here is a huge domain for explorers.

In the present chapter I assemble four cases, the first of which (autopsychoanalysis) deals with dreams aroused by the instinct of self-preservation; they are concerned with the obsessive idea of death during pulmonary tuberculosis. The other three instances are concerned with the instinct for motherhood. In Yvonne and in Renée the dreams occur when the subject is pregnant. In Martha, they relate only to a wish for motherhood; but this wish is accompanied by a physiological condition (menstrual irregularity) of which the wish is a contributory cause. In all these cases, therefore, the dreams are connected with some definite physiological state; but we are not entitled to regard them as a direct expression of the condition of the bodily organs, as a sort of internal perception. A perception of this kind, especially one aroused by kinæsthetic sensations, may doubtless play a part; but it is certain that, in the causation of dreams, disquietude concerning an organ is more important than the objective condition of that organ. A woman who wants to have a baby may dream of being pregnant just as may a woman who is really pregnant. A consumptive who has been dreaming about his lungs night after night, may cease to have such dreams directly he has been told that examination shows his sputum to be free from tubercle bacilli; yet there has been no sudden change in his physiological state; there has merely been a change in his mental condition.

It is true that the instinct of self-preservation and the instinct for motherhood are not normally "censored" like the sexual instinct. They may be more or less repressed. Above all, impressions relating to them (the fear of death, for example) may be repressed—may be repressed in the strict sense of the term, under the influence of a moral sentiment. This happens in our first case, but the repression has not been vigorous, and the uneasiness is manifest in the waking state. It may happen that the disquietude shown in the dream is one of which the subject is fully conscious. In Yvonne, for instance, we have a dread that the baby will be stillborn, or that the doctor will not arrive in time; in Martha, we have the longing to be a mother; in Renée, the unwillingness to be a mother. Nevertheless, the dreams assume symbolical forms. In especial, the organs concerned, the lungs, etc., are represented by symbols.

In several of his adolescent subjects, Auguste Lemaître has noted symbolical dreams which he found it difficult, without straining the explanation, to account for by the theory of repression.[1] Difficulty vanishes if we admit, as we have been led to admit, that symbolisation is the outcome of the general laws of the imagination; that repression makes use of symbolism and reinforces it, but does not create it.

In the dreams aroused by the instinct of self-preservation or the instinct for motherhood, it is possible that other instincts are simultaneously at work. As concerns some dreams, this is certainly the case. In Renée, the refusal of motherhood is linked with a general psychosexual inclination to refuse femininity, either through latent homosexuality (Freud) or through masculine protest (Adler). Of course, we are always entitled to suspect, in the case of any dream, that unseen instincts are at work. But it would be absurd to insist upon finding them there, and to explain the symbolisation as a manifestation of repressed instincts, when, symbolisation or no symbolisation, these instincts would surely reveal themselves if present.

[1] Lemaître, op. cit., pp. 14, 21.

1. Autopsychoanalysis

Dreams during an Attack of Pulmonary Tuberculosis.

These dreams and fragments of dreams are the transparent symbols of an obsessive disquietude, that of illness and death. In the waking state, this disquietude was partially repressed by a deliberate optimism. The affected organ, the lung, is sometimes denoted by a strange and lucid symbolism. The symbols in question belong to the category of "organic symbols" studied long ago by Scherner.[1] Many of the dreams about to be recorded contain obvious allusions to other preoccupations than the illness. These matters will not be discussed here.

> I. I was out walking alone; I had a book in my hand, I was going to read. The sky was gloomy and overcast. Before me stretched the brown, damp, clayey expanse of the plough-lands, and also in front of me was the dazzling whiteness of a straight road which my path, mounting all the time, was to rejoin higher up. Suddenly from my left, in the ravine, from the direction of the town,—for there was a town,—came the noise of shouting; I remembered that there was a war. Then, close at hand, not more than twenty paces away, I saw a grey-coated man, a shadowy figure, apparently in uniform. I realised that I had been sentenced as a spy, and that I was about to be shot. The man took aim. I saw what was imminent without any sense of fear. I watched the smoke at the muzzle of the rifle; I staggered; I was dead. Then I found myself with a book in my hand, seated in a room, and reading the sequel of the events in which I had just played a leading part. The being who had recently died, and who was myself, appeared in my book in the third person.

Often enough, in fact, I walked in this way holding a book. At the same time it was my custom to scribble notes as I walked. When, inadvertently, I approached any of the forts, I was always regarded with suspicion; was challenged, and asked for my papers. Of course a few words were enough to clear up the difficulty. What annoyed me most on these occasions was the interruption to my work.

In my dream this episode assumes a graver form, for it culminates in my being shot. The soldier who shoots me is

[1] Scherner, Das Leben des Traumes, 1861, pp. 114 et seq., quoted by Freud, The Interpretation of Dreams, 1913, pp. 69–73.

clad in grey, and produces on me the impression that he is a "shadow" a phantom; everything about him calls up the idea of death. The war, symbolised by this soldier, had been the determining cause of the illness.

The shouts of war come from a town lying at the bottom of a ravine. My own home was in the country, in a place overlooking a large town (my native city), situated at the bottom of a valley like the town of my dream. I lived in the country for hygienic reasons, and the "town" represented for me the unwholesome atmosphere in which I had spent my youth, and which had been one of the causes of my illness.

The book in my hand is intimately associated with my work. The war first of all, and subsequently my illness, troubled me mainly as hindrances to the work for which I lived.

The path by which I am ascending in my dream is a difficult one, whilst higher up I catch a glimpse of the "road"—the straight and easy line of action which I should like to reach, but which I fear I shall never reach. The damp weather, which I know to be unfavourable to my health, recalls my illness.

Finally I undergo a sort of resurrection, with the book in my hand. This symbolises the wish and the hope that I shall survive, through the instrumentality of a work which will outlive me.

> II. I was on a terrace which in the rear seemed to communicate with residential flats. It was like an enormous veranda. Beside me, in the shadow, to my left, was my mother, hardly more visible than a phantom. She had some needlework in her hands. It was woolwork; the wool was soft, and of a dull grey colour. I was not frightened; we were talking quite simply. We did not say much; my mother, especially, said very little; hers was an almost mute presence. I was lying flat on my back, my arms stretched wide, the better to breathe; and I thus breathed in the freshness of a starry night, more beautiful and fresher than I had ever known before. It was infinitely good and sweet. I watched in one of the constellations an oval image the shape of certain holy pictures, and I could make out there the face of a man bearded as my father was bearded, inclining forwards as he looked earthward. I fancied that it must be St. Joseph. I think that the man had in his hand a yellow lily (the one known as St. Joseph's lily).

Below, in the bottom of a valley, was the town. Here I could see lights springing up and moving about, as if a torch-light tattoo had been in progress. Now came shouts from the same quarter: "Fire! Fire!" In my dream I understood these words as if the cry had been: "To arms!" Then I realised that the men who were shouting had seen an enemy aeroplane, and that they were about to fire. I think I said to my mother: "Perhaps I shall be hit by a bomb." But neither she nor I stirred. Still lying flat on my back with arms outstretched, I breathed the night. Then I felt a severe blow full in the chest. It was the bomb. I awoke with a start. I could feel my bed, but at the same time I had a sort of hallucination of the sense of touch, for I felt upon my chest the contact and the passage of some cold object. Knowing myself to be awake, I was aware for a moment of physical fear in all its power.

My position, the outstretched arms, and my need for breath, clearly symbolise the illness; so does the death-stroke received full in the *chest.* In addition, I recognise several of the symbols which have been explained in the interpretation of the first dream: the war, the town in the valley from which the shouts come. The cries of war have been replaced by the cry, "Fire!": this suggests that the cry "To arms!" had first presented itself to my imagination, but had been rejected for some reason (perhaps because its meaning was too obvious), and the cry "Fire!" had taken its place. But the substitution had been incomplete, so that when I heard the cry "Fire!" I understood it to mean "To arms!" The same substitution would explain the torchlight tattoo. On the evenings of the French national festival I had often watched the regiments carrying torches as they returned to barracks. Foot-soldiers, naturally associated with war, normally carry arms; just as the cry "To arms!" has been replaced by the cry "Fire!" so the soldiers, in place of carrying arms, carry torches.

My parents are dead. My mother, in this dream, appeared in the grey, phantasmal, and mute form which so often symbolises the idea of death. The soldier of the first dream was also wraithlike. The grey woolwork symbolises the work of the Fates.

When my father died I was a child, and I naively represented the dead as leaning forward out of heaven towards the living, like the St. Joseph of my dream. The St. Joseph's lily grew in the flower-beds of our garden, and my father was particularly fond of this flower. Finally, in the year when my father died, I had a mathematical master who gave me my first notions of astronomy and taught me to admire the stars. The first constellation I learned to recognise was Cassiopeia. I knew that in Catholic astronomy this constellation had been called St. Mary, because of its resemblance to a capital M. The oval image of my dream appeared in the part of the sky where, in childhood, I had seen this constellation. St. Mary is associated with my mother, just as St. Joseph is associated with my father.

This oval image is connected with another memory of childhood, and all these allusions to my parents give expression to my feelings towards them in childhood ; the analysis in this direction would be a lengthy matter. Suffice it to note that the tendency to introversion associated with the maternal complex was at this period accentuated by illness. The tendency and the illness were a retreat (cf. the torchlight tattoo [1]) in face of life. The whole dream is dominated by the idea of death.

The calm and beautiful night, with the stars shining brilliantly, recalls the nights when I had an enthusiasm for astronomy, and above all for the feeling of boundlessness and eternity which astronomy arouses. The same feeling is aroused by death when we contemplate death in a spirit of religious calm, and under the aspect of eternal or universal life rather than under the aspect of destruction.

Thus, by a remarkably rich symbolism, my dream gave expression to something which I would not admit in the waking state ; to the fact that my mind was obsessed by the idea of death. At the close of the dream there even came the animal dread of death, which had hitherto been veiled in contemplative calm ; this latter, also, was a real feeling, but was over-emphasised in order to conceal the equally real fear.

I am inclined to explain the last detail of the dream by supposing that when the sense of sight had fully awakened, the sense of touch was still slumbering.

III. I was standing at a closed window ; I had a feeling of suffocation. I opened the window to get fresh air, but

[1] There is a word-play here which cannot be conveyed in the translation. In French the torchlight tattoo is a " retreat," une retraite aux flambeaux.—TRANSLATORS' NOTE.

> the feeling of suffocation continued. I saw that the shutters were closed; I pushed at them; the left shutter opened with a bang, and was caught back against the wall; the right shutter, as often as I pushed it open, was blown to by the wind. At last I thought that I had got it in its place against the wall, but again it was blown to. Leaning out, I saw that the catch had been wrenched from the wall, and that the wall was crumbling where the catch had been. The wall was built of oolitic limestone, a stone which quickly becomes black at the surface, but which is white when freshly broken, so that any recent fracture is conspicuous; such a recent fracture was obvious where I was looking. When struggling with the wind, I had said these words to fortify myself: "After all, I am three hundred times as strong as destiny." While pronouncing the word "destiny," I knew that I was really speaking of the wind.

The disease is easily recognised in the sense of suffocation. The two shutters, one of which opens while the other is obstinate, immediately make me think of my lungs, for I know that one lung is much more gravely affected than the other. But whereas the most affected lung is the left, it is the right shutter which is stubborn; here we have a symmetrical transference.[1]

Even in the dream, I called the wind by its true name, destiny. The obliteration of the object in the symbol was incomplete, just as in the previous dream the obliteration of the symbol "To arms!" in the new symbol "Fire" had been incomplete.[2] The wind, then, is the part destiny plays in life generally, and in the illness specially.

This wind, a symbol of the disease, synthetises a number of reminiscences and impressions: the wind induces a sense of suffocation; I know it to be injurious to me; etc. In addition, it recalls to my mind a poem by Benoist-Hanappier, under whom I worked at the university of Nancy, and who died (note the relevant detail) of consumption. His death

[1] In the first dream the town where the war was going on, and in the second dream my dead mother, had been on my *left* side, and I had twice noted this detail without attaching any importance to it, and without attempting to explain it.

As far as concerns the shutters, which are symmetrical objects like the lungs, and which open like the lungs for breathing, the symbolism is more transparent; the censorship, therefore, has recourse to a symmetrical transference which did not occur in the two other dreams.

[2] A substitution was effected in the symbols, but not in the intellectual interpretation of the symbols.

made a great impression upon my mind, and it was a few days later that I read the poem. It opens with the verse:

> There was a wind, a high wind,

and it ends with the stanza:

> When I die, when I die,
> I think that a strong, gloomy wind
> Will wail despairingly,
> Echoing the invisible ill,
> When I die, when I die.

The crumbling wall symbolises the damaged lung; when I lean out of the window I discover that this is the cause of the trouble. The oolitic limestone, with its granular structure, is chosen because of its resemblance to the structure of the lungs.

We have still to explain the number "three hundred" in the phrase: "I am three hundred times as strong as destiny." Other dreams lead me to suppose that it is an allusion to the three hundred Spartans who fought under Leonidas. My contest with the disease seemed to me preeminently a struggle of moral energy. This outlook had been confirmed by the results I had secured through autosuggestion in the way of improving sleep and checking cough. My first understanding of the nature of moral energy had come to me, during my classical studies, in striking instances from Greek history. The most impressive of these had been the example of the three hundred Spartans who blocked the road of destiny.

> IV. I was on my way back from a long walk; it was late; the sun had just set. I reached the foot of a steep hill. The road ran straight up the hill like a Roman road; it was worn into runnels; it vanished abruptly at the top of the ascent.
>
> At the bottom of the hill was a signpost, with the legend "Dommartemont, 12 kilometres." I said to myself that I still had a long way to go, and that it would be hard work. But I knew my way home from Dommartemont.
>
> I set out. But I had made only a few steps forward when my heart began to beat violently; flushes of heat rose to my face; I felt that I was going to fall. Then I awoke.

The close of this dream shows that it relates to my illness. The palpitation and the flushes of heat are real symptoms; they play the same part as the sense of suffocation in the previous dream.

A few days earlier I had seen a Roman road. This reminiscence served me as a symbol. The Roman road spontaneously called up the following associations: stupendous tasks, like those performed by the Romans; the labours of Hercules.

Immediately the twelve kilometres of the signpost made me think of the twelve labours of Hercules (analogous to the three hundred Spartans).

Dommartemont is the name of a village in the region where I was born. Thence I know my " way home," that is to say, I know how to find my way back to the life of former days. In addition, by an auditory association, the word calls up Montmartre, the martyrs' hill. The ascent is a heroic one. Evening, the approach of night, symbolises a premature death.

The work of the Romans, the labours of Hercules, the heroism of the martyrs—here are so many metaphors to describe the hugeness of the task and my own weakness in face of it, a weakness which I was only half willing to admit in the waking state.

> V. I was on a country road. Suddenly the wind became so violent that I was blown to the ground. I wanted to make my way back, crawling on hands and knees if needs must, towards the houses from which I had come. The wind was too much for me. My movements were like those of one who is swimming against a stream too strong for him, and the current swept me away.

The road, the wind, the houses to which I was trying to return, are all symbols which can be explained by the preceding dream. My desperate struggle in the dust of the road was strangely reminiscent of the close of Spitteler's poem *Papillons*, which I had been reading attentively not long before the dream.[1] In this poem, the butterfly, after fruitless efforts, falls dying into the dust on the road. In my dream I felt as if I were beating my wings like a butterfly.

> VI. I was in an examination hall and had just finished writing my composition. I had begun to write a fair copy, when behind me I heard the voice of Monsieur B., my old master at the lycée Louis le Grand, asking for the compositions. I made up my mind to give him the rough copy. At this

[1] A French translation of this poem was subsequently (May 1916) published in " Le Carmel " of Geneva, under the title Moine (monk).

moment I heard Monsieur B. saying goodbye to those who were going out. It seemed as if it were a farewell class.

The idea is barely disguised: a premature conclusion; an unfinished piece of work; one has to make the best of a bad job. It must be noted that while I was in Monsieur B.'s class my health broke down, so that my studies were interrupted before the close of the school year.

The next dream, classed as VII, really consists of three successive dreams, which were dreamed in one night as three acts of the same drama. I awoke after each act, and after the first and second acts I had recourse to autosuggestion in order to overcome the painful impression left by the nightmare. The third act signifies a victory, as it were; a happy ending.

> VII. 1. I am holding a strange little marionette. As I look at it, its body becomes hollowed out here and there into holes and cavities, until there is nothing left but a head, where two similar holes soon appear, so that it is now a death's head, while of the body nothing remains beyond a wire skeleton.
>
> 2. I have just bought one of Spitteler's books. I am with some friends. We seem to be coming back from a class. We are talking and larking. Apparently the book falls; anyhow, it is spoiled in some way, and its back becomes pierced with holes, just like those which appeared in the marionette of the previous dream. I am in doubt what to do, and then I make up my mind to change the book. One of my friends says: "You are quite right; unless it is in good condition, no one will be able to read it when you are dead."
>
> 3. In the last dream I am in a room; a butterfly is fluttering in distress against a closed window. I open the window and the insect instantly flies away. I am surprised to see how intelligent it is, how quickly it finds the right road. Its deliverance makes me very happy.

The holes, the cavities, which invade the marionette, or the back of the book hardly need explanation. The marionette and its wire skeleton symbolise our own frailty as parts of the universal mechanism, that mechanism of which the ravages of disease are among the effects.

The book (borrowed from the symbolism of dream I) represents my work. I had seen Spitteler shortly before, and had been much impressed by the vigour of his old age. He seemed to me one who had enjoyed the whole of a great life to perform a great work. A great life followed by a vigorous old age were what I desired for myself, but my illness threatened to rob me of them.

In the terminal dream, a butterfly has taken the place of Spitteler's book. The first of Spitteler's books I read was *Papillons* (V). But whereas in the second act of this three-act dream drama I had merely decided to do something, "to change my book," in act three I triumph. I am surprised at the close that an animal should have so much intelligence. This makes me think of my psychological interest in the unconscious, in the subconscious, in connection with which, suggestion, on the one hand, and psychoanalysis on the other, have revealed to me an intelligent activity of an amazing character. As I have already explained, I consider the triumph to have been mainly achieved by autosuggestion.

VIII. I was in a house to which I have often had to go in the course of my professional duties. Furthermore, it was the house of a man of science who has done excellent work. I hear cries of "Fire!" I go out. People are fighting the flames; they get the better of the conflagration. But whereas the front of the house is practically uninjured, I see that, inside, the left half has been destroyed. The other half has been saved. It contains a large room, where the life of the house can be reconstructed on modest lines.

The "house" is a fresh image associated with my work. The cry "Fire!" is borrowed from the symbolism of dream II. The two halves of the house are the lungs once more. I may add that the appearance of the burned house strongly recalled the crumbling wall in dream III. Although the symbols undergo a certain development, there is a fixity of aspect which assists in their interpretation.

2. Yvonne

Fears concerning Childbirth.

Like the previous instance, this is not the analysis of a "case." It is merely the analysis of the dreams of a woman during the last weeks of pregnancy, dreams which give expression in a rather remarkable fashion to certain disquietudes relating to childbirth.

Yvonne has various dreads. One of them is that her

baby will be born prematurely. In several dreams she gets into a tramcar with a child and lets it drop. Some of the associations suggest that these dreams give expression to the before-mentioned fear. But, in other dreams, other fears are expressed in ways that cannot be mistaken.

One night when Yvonne fell asleep she was obsessed with the dread that her baby would be stillborn. She had just been chasing a large bluebottle fly; it was nearly dead, but it had escaped into a crevice. That night, she had the following dream:

> I. Yvonne had a suppurating wound on the wrist, shaped like a lentil; and several transparent spots, also shaped like lentils, on the arm. She was with her mother, but in her own house. She was going to live somewhere else, in the house of a woman rather like the one who sometimes attends the neighbouring peasant women in their confinements. Pus is squeezed out of the wound several times, but at the bottom of it there is a squashed fly which won't come out. The woman in whose house Yvonne has gone to live says that the hour has not yet come, but that the orifice will enlarge of itself at the right moment.

The allusion to the confinement is so plainly expressed in the dream that comment is superfluous. Is it necessary to stress the description of this orifice, which "will enlarge of itself at the right moment"?

Besides the dread of the stillbirth, we can detect in this dream another uneasiness, one of which the subject is also fully conscious. She cannot make up her mind whether to stay at home for her confinement, or to enter a maternity hospital. She lives in the country, "a long way from everywhere," and she is afraid of being taken unawares.

One Thursday evening, when she fell asleep, her mind was occupied with the problem of what would happen should her baby be born on a Sunday, when nothing would be ready, when all the shops would be closed, and when it might be difficult to get a doctor. That night she had the following dream:

> II. The stove-pipe is choked to overflowing. It is Sunday. No chimney-sweep to be had. She hurries off to find one in a street where there lives someone whose address she had made a note of, in case she could not get a midwife.

This transparent dream was dreamed during the night of Thursday-Friday. It is not unlikely that the subject's disquietude, considerable enough to set the subconscious at work even during sleep, may have acted as a spontaneous suggestion. At any rate, labour pains began on Saturday afternoon, and the child was born the same night—before midnight, however.

3. Renée

Refusal of Femininity and of Motherhood

Renée has long suffered from nervous and sexual troubles. She says that her father was extremely neuropathic, that he had ideas of persecution and believed himself very unfortunate. She herself suffers from sexual impotence (frigidity). Once only has intercourse with her husband (whom she loves) been " normal " ; ever since, she has had to avail herself of masturbation to secure complete gratification, which even then is difficult to obtain. Her sister suffers from a similar impotence (frigidity).

Renée is also subject to obsessions. Sometimes she will fancy herself to be so ugly that she cannot bear to look at herself. She has a fixed idea that she suffers from goitre. She is frequently afflicted by nervous pains, little attacks of nervous irritation, in the cardiac region, round the flanks, and in the chest, attended by a sense of suffocation.

Renée was pregnant. Her state in this respect was the chief cause of her disquietude, and her general nervous condition was most unsatisfactory. Her dominant idea was that she would give anything not to have a baby. She rationalised her repugnance by reasons which, though plausible, were inadequate to explain the intensity of her dislike to the prospect. It was not necessary to dig deeply beneath these reasons before discovering an irrational and quasi-instinctive but intense disgust for motherhood. Here is one of her dreams :

> I. The face of a drowned woman showing above the water, in the twilight. Renée stretched out her hand to pull the body out of the water, but the body disappears.

The associations to the words " drowned woman " have an unmistakable significance.

A swollen body, a fat woman; her breasts quake. . . . This woman laughs; she is repulsive. Beside her is a young girl, slender and fresh-looking. "I've always thought pregnancy disgusting."

This drowned woman is Renée pregnant. She is "drowned" because she feels overwhelmed by the claims of motherhood; she cannot meet them; she says that it is beyond her power to do so, because of her ailments, and because she is not well enough off. But the fundamental thing is her disgust; and when we ask for associations with the "pulling out of the water," we once more get images tinged with disgust.

To pull by the hair.—Lice. Itching. A dirty comb which combs out lice.[1]

Some writers, and Adler in especial,[2] have pointed out that such a refusal of childbearing may be part of a general refusal of femininity and a "masculine protest," a subconscious wish to play a man's part. Renée certainly seems to exemplify this theory, and her repudiation of the coming child would appear to be a particular instance of her general refusal of the woman's part, or of her maladaptation to it.

Here is another dream.

II. Coming away from a party. A leopard lurking in a dark corner. An evening party. Renée was there with all her family: her relatives and her husband. She shows the leopard to her mother and her sister. All three run away into the depths of a wood. As soon as she is safe, she notices that her husband, her brother-in-law, and her father, are not there. She wonders what has happened.

The associations are frankly erotic.

Party. Lots of people.—Men in evening dress.—Women in low dress.—Lascivious glances.—The scene reminds her of a nook in the wood, where a very smart party had been held. . . . Reminiscence of a walk with her husband, during the early days of their marriage.

Dark corner. Lovers.

Leopard. Cries of alarm mingled with laughter.

The depths of a wood. The same walk with her husband.

The significant point, however, is that in this erotic setting, which recalls the walk with her husband, Renée dreams that

[1] Possibly this is an allusion to masturbation. [2] Op. cit., p. 155.

she runs away with two women, her mother and her sister, whereas her husband, and the husbands of both the other women, vanish. Here we have a perfect example of a "homosexual fantasy." We discern a flight from sexuality properly so called, and a fixation of the feeling upon the persons of the mother and the sister.

The next dream introduces the question of the pregnancy, but it is linked to the foregoing dream.

> III. Renée entered a suburban train with her mother and her sister. Her mother had to get into a different compartment, some way off. Before the train started, the mother had lingered with Renée and her sister, and high words had passed between her mother and her sister. The doors were being shut. The mother was standing on the platform when the train started. Renée was afraid her mother would not be able to get in; she was angry with her sister, whom she accused of risking their mother's life. She tried to open the window in order to look out, and the door opened. In her hand she was holding a dress which had to be mended. The dress fell on the platform. In order to pick it up, Renée jumped out of the train while it was in motion; then she ran after the train. She saw that her mother had got into the compartment all right. When she stooped to pick up the dress, it had become a compartment door and was very heavy. She picked it up and had to run carrying it. She managed to throw it into the compartment. Her sister was no longer there. Instead there was a young couple, quarrelling. She thought that the man was wrong and the woman right.

The "suburban train" reminds Renée of returning home with her husband in such a train. In dream III, as in dream II, we notice that the mother and the sister have been substituted for the husband, and we draw the same inference.

We can pass lightly over the points which the dream and the associations appear to suggest, but which would have to be confirmed by a more elaborate analysis. Apparently the mother who lingers with her daughters represents the fixation of the infantile sentiment upon the mother; then there is a vacillation between the mother and the sister; finally the sister disappears to give place to a "couple," whose relations are not perfectly harmonious. Let us confine ourselves to inferences which are more adequately verified, and more pertinent to the question with which we are now concerned.

As in all the subjects who refuse their appropriate sexual role, or who are ill-adapted to perform it, the associations emphasise the repugnant aspect of sexuality. In the next compartment to that in which she sees herself with her husband, there are some young fellows singing lewd songs. The door which is being shut has the following associations:

> The porter. A reminiscence. Renée was quite young. A young man caught hold of her leg on the platform: a porter interfered and everything was all right.

This porter who keeps order and who "shuts the door" might be regarded as an interesting symbol of the "censorship" or repression after a sexual shock. Let this pass. We will follow the train of images.

The "dress" recalls to Renée an old dress, a blue costume. "It suited me very well; I was wearing it the first time I met my husband." Then the dress, fallen on to the platform, calls up a "puddle of dirty water; splashes of mud; soiled shoes." The word "door" has the following associations:

> Cushions, greasy from people's heads. She does not like to rest her own head there. She kisses her husband, and their heads roll on the greasy places.

This brings us back to the dirty hair and the lice in the associations to dream I. The association to the symbol "very heavy door" is: "I have a pain in my stomach." The weight she has to carry is always the burden of pregnancy. Next come associations in which Renée imagines herself stumbling under the weight. She falls and is crushed—just as in the earlier dream she was drowned.

Thus the interest of this dream is the way in which it links up three elements: the fixation of feeling upon the mother and the sister; disgust inspired by sexuality; refusal of maternity.

The homosexual trend is latent and purely psychic; it has never given rise to actual perversion. (Nevertheless, the subject declares that homosexual relationships do not seem repulsive to her.) This trend, even though it remains psychical, doubtless underlies the frigidity in heterosexual intercourse. The family history, the possibility of morbid inheritance from the father, and the fact that her sister's case resembles her own, might lead us to suppose that there is organic predisposition; but psychoanalysis has taught us to guard against over-ready assertions of this kind. In any case we must not overlook the psychological determinants. The subject reveals one of these in the following reminiscence :

> IV. Her father had been cold to her from childhood onwards. He was unkind to her mother. All the same, when she was a young girl she had felt her senses stirred when she was close to him. She had been greatly disgusted by this; "but I could not help thinking that he was a man."

This may indicate that originally there was a fixation of sexual feeling upon the father, followed by a forcible repression, leading to the sense of disgust; ultimately this may have given rise to the refusal of sexuality and of the woman's part.

This last trend is likewise shown in typical reminiscences of childhood.

> V (about 6 years old). An accident. Some little girls sliding down a banister. Renée wants to do the same. At the turn of the stair she is going too fast and loses her balance. Her hands are grasping the banister, her head is over the well of the staircase, and her legs are hanging over the stair.

Here we have a boy's game imitated by girls. This constantly happens at the age which, in Freudian terminology, is termed the age of "infantile homosexuality." But, having reached the "turn in the stair," where it is necessary "to get a new balance," Renée "is going too fast," and undergoes arrest at the stage of "infantile homosexuality." As in the association to IV, we pass immediately to symbols of repugnance. Renée recalls that, in one of the weird notions of childhood, she had spat upon the banister so that one of the others might get her hands messed; falling into her own trap, she had messed her own hands. (There may be an allusion to masturbation here.) This spit recalls her father, grown old, and coughing; and it is attended with the idea of disgust mentioned in connection with IV. But to the first word of this reminiscence V, the word "accident," we have the following associations :

> Tramcar. . . . A vehicle in motion. A fat woman who gets out while the car is moving, and falls down.

We are back at the theme of dream I. This reminiscence, then, confirms the relationships which we have deduced earlier in the analysis. It sketches a psychological profile.

4. Martha

LONGING FOR MOTHERHOOD. MENSTRUAL IRREGULARITY.

I give a fragment from an analysis. Martha, who has some sons, shows evidence at this moment that she wants to have a daughter or regrets not having had one.

> . . . She finds herself in a strange house, although the garden is the garden of their own home. . . . Out of the basement window there issues a little naked girl whom she takes in her arms. Shortly before, she was offered some opera-glasses. She refused them.

The " basement window " is rich in associations. It is a " partially blocked window "—" The sort of thing I don't like."—She likes " big windows." She has no use for anything that wants to hide. She likes a natural and wholesome love, not one which is " hygienised and mechanised."

The opera-glasses she has refused belong to the same order of ideas. They symbolise the " hygienised " and the " mechanised." Martha does not like using opera-glasses even at the theatre. She likes what is natural. " I prefer to use my own eyes."

Her conjugal relations are such that she cannot expect a fresh pregnancy except from an illicit union. It would have to be " hidden " ; her frank nature protests against having to put up with a " basement " window instead of a " big " window. But she wants a daughter none the less, and in the dream her wish secures fulfilment. The little naked girl issues from the basement window.

Martha had not seen this meaning in her dream, but the analysis was quite satisfactory to her. The feelings which the analysis discovered in the dream really were her conscious feelings.

In the same sitting, the first of her analysis, she had spoken of irregular menstruation. The analysis led me to think that this trouble was only a substitute for the desired pregnancy. I put the idea before her, and the same month the trouble disappeared. (Autosuggestion had been simultaneously practised.)

CHAPTER NINE

TYPICAL NERVOUS DISORDERS

ONE of the convictions to which psychoanalysis has led us is that the subconscious complexes which underlie neuroses, and the subconscious complexes which explain normal character traits, are essentially identical. Superadded to what occurs in normal cases, the appearance of a neurosis presupposes certain special conditions, such as that the complex should be more intense than usual. Above all, we must probably assume that accidental causes are generally superadded, such as a psychic predisposition, a moral rebuff, overwork, etc. Before the rise of psychoanalysis, causes of the latter category were regarded as the essential causes of neuroses. Certainly, we must not neglect their study, but we gain a profounder grasp of etiology by analysing the subconscious complexes. The fact that these complexes also exist in persons whose health is normal, is apt to make people doubt whether psychoanalysis really discloses the specific cause of neuroses. A simple comparison will show that this objection is invalid. Before the discovery of the tubercle bacillus, pulmonary tuberculosis, or, as it was then termed, " consumption," could be supposed to arise as an outcome of overwork, a disappointment in love, etc. Similarly with neurasthenia. In the case of tuberculosis, we now regard such causes as accidental causes, which have an effect only through diminishing the resistance of the organism ; the specific cause is the tubercle bacillus. The tubercle bacillus, like the subconscious complex, exists in healthy human beings, but the healthy organism is resistent. In this sense it has been said that we are all more or less tuberculous. In precisely the same sense it may be said that we are all potential neuropaths.

This is why the analysis of the neuropath's persistently infantile attitude towards the parents is of primary importance.

We have seen that different forms of this attitude correspond to different types of character ; they also correspond to different types of nervous disorder. We might even say that the nervous disorders from which any patient suffers are caricatures of that patient's psychological type.

Alexander and Roger both exhibit the complex of attachment to the mother, with its usual accompaniments, the dread of reality and the refusal of sexuality. In Roger, this refusal actually leads to a physiological condition of impotence. In Alexander, the antagonism to the father is complicated by latent homosexuality, by a voluptuous delight in suffering inflicted by the father, and this feeling underlies anxiety states which take the form of vertigo. Germaine, on the other hand, is greatly attached to her father, and is definitely hostile to her mother and her sister. Her morbidly fussy activity depends upon a subconscious wish to outdo her sister. The spasm of the eyelid from which she suffers is over-determined, for underlying it are a desire for marriage and a wish to escape from maternal authority.

Of course we have encountered and shall encounter nervous disorders in many other subjects. But the cases grouped in this chapter seem to me typical. Moreover, they are free, or almost free, from complication with certain other elements (mental troubles, the progressive course of a sublimation, the eager search for a guide) which will practically monopolise our attention in subsequent chapters.

1. Alexander

Anxiety States.

The subject is a schoolmaster, who is also a student of psychology. Although he has not fully grasped the theories of psychoanalysis, he knows something about them. I mention this point because it may have influenced the course of the analysis, and may, through suggestion, have made it conform more closely to the classical type. On the other hand the subject's mental calibre, his habit of self-examination, were conditions favourable to precise observation.

Alexander is thirty-nine years of age. The first detail he gives me is that the death of his mother, which took place when he was nine or ten years old, exercised a great influence over his development. (He is familiar with the theory of the "Oedipus complex.") He was very fond of his mother, and he was her favourite. He was the second child. He did not care much for his eldest brother, who was rather jealous of him. His feeling towards his father was tinged with a certain antipathy, for the father was "rather tyrannical," though he made sacrifices for his sons. Alexander, when quite a little boy, used sometimes to have the grotesque idea of hitting his father or his uncle. The father wanted to become mayor of the village, and his political interests often took him away to town; the mother was very jealous during her husband's absences. The father has married again.

Relations between the father and the paternal grandfather were broken off from the time of the father's remarriage. Alexander, of whom the grandfather was fond, was the only tie. He had a dislike for his uncle, his father's half-brother, younger than the father. He said to me: "I smoke because my uncle doesn't like me to smoke. . . . Whenever he has tried to help me, things have gone amiss. . . . You don't mind my smoking?"

One of the central ideas of his life is that he must not allow any woman to interfere with him in the pursuit of his end. Though he has had opportunities, he has, generally speaking, been careful to avoid falling in love. The adoptive mother of one of his pupils has shown an affection for him to which he has made no response. He had an exalted passion for a young woman, who had been a playmate in childhood, and whose education was entrusted to him. When he had to come to Switzerland in order to finish his studies, he began a declaration. The young woman said: "The matter is not in my hands, but in my father's." Wounded by this reception of his advances, he broke with her and set out for Switzerland.

After a failure in his career, he suffered from a sudden obsession. He was constantly turning over in his mind the phrase: "Something is going to happen to you." Contemplating his thought, he would reply: "This is absurd; I am going off my head." It was at this date that he looked up one of his uncles, who was a doctor. Since then, when he closes his eyes, he sees old women, misshapen and making grimaces; or sometimes wild beasts, or human figures which change into beasts. In these visions, the figures of women, especially old women, predominate. He recalls one feminine torso in particular, an old woman with hollow eyes.

In the period immediately following the above-mentioned failure, he was haunted by ideas of suicide. After his rupture with the young woman (about two months afterwards) a definite anxiety neurosis began. He was then in Zurich, and a feeling of anxiety or sadness took possession of him every evening. He was taciturn, lost his appetite, and was affected with hypnagogic hallucinations. He was troubled by obsessive anxiety states, and notably by a feeling of instability, of vertigo, when he thought about the movement of the earth—this occurring especially while attending natural-history lectures. Alexander was treated by Dr. Frank [a Zurich psychoanalyst], and his condition greatly improved. At the time when he came to Geneva, the acute anxiety states troubled him only by way of occasional relapses lasting a few hours. The obsession concerning the movement of the earth persisted; he was also still troubled by the grimacing figures. When he came to consult me, he had already begun to practice autosuggestion unaided. By this means he had for ten days or more succeeded in ridding himself of these visions, but the other symptoms persisted.

At our first sitting, the existence of the "Oedipus complex" became apparent. The subject is aware that he has this complex—too keenly aware, perhaps, for he is biased by the theory. But he knew nothing about this theory at the date when the manifestations began, and there can be no doubt that he is really affected with the Oedipus complex. Psychoanalysts tell us that images of grimacing old women (the witch, the "dread mother") are familiar symptoms of this complex. Antagonism to the father is another sign. This hostility is generalised or extended towards various persons who might exercise an authority akin to the paternal (the elder brother, the uncle). Alexander expects the analysis to bring about in him a symbolical reconciliation with "the father." He notes that the first doctor whom he went to consult after the neurosis developed was an "uncle." He seems already to have identified me with one of these quasi-paternal figures, with the father against whom he protests.

His uncle had blamed him for smoking, and that is why he smokes; and it is immediately after he has explained this to me that he starts smoking in my presence. Inasmuch as I know that for him, since childhood, "uncle" and "doctor" have been intimately associated, and that I myself therefore embody for him something of both these attributes, I understand the situation. As so often happens in these analyses, his subconscious is led to me by his conscious, as a haltered calf is led to the slaughterhouse—and the subconscious is rebellious.

Here is the first dream of which he brought me the record. He awoke twice in the course of the dream, but it was resumed as soon as he went to sleep again.

I. He was in his native region, perhaps in his native village. Even while the dream was in progress, it was not quite easy to be certain where he was. It seemed to be the place where his best friend and sometime schoolmaster, Pierre, lived, though Pierre really lives on a little island. He arrived towards evening, alone or with one companion. He does not know why he did not visit his friend immediately. There was a conflict in his mind, for he wanted to see Pierre. Next day he learned that Pierre had just died. He was remorseful. He could not go to see his friend's body, for the relatives knew that he might have called the day before. He went out, taking the first road that offered, and found himself at the place where, on the previous evening, he had had the mental conflict. He was now accompanied by a girl, who may have belonged to the locality or may have been a Swiss. The place was a green field in springtime. He does not remember what he said to the girl, but now he saw his friend's wife coming towards him. She was oddly dressed, not in mourning, but wearing a coffee-coloured gown, with a fashionable hat and a crape veil. She ran up to him and threw herself into his arms. Sexual excitement. He had expected reproaches, and was greatly astonished. She gave him some sketchy details concerning Pierre's death. He went back with her towards the house. (At the moment when she had approached him the young girl had disappeared). He entered with the wife. The house was unrecognisable. Terrible disorder. In the dream they lived on the ground floor, whereas really they lived on the first floor. Seized with terror he awoke (this was the second waking). Falling asleep again, he found himself back in the house. His friend's body was headless, and this had been the cause of his alarm. He cried out. In a basket to

> the left was the severed head. The eyes were closed. The face was pale, but not stiff. Terror. Change of scene. Alexander found himself in the laundry. Pierre's wife was there, also her niece, who is the same age as himself. He greeted her. His terror was now forgotten. He had a feeling which he thinks was sexually tinged. The wife was washing clothes; the water was dirty, looking almost like black blood. The clothes grew dirtier while being washed.

Apropos of this dream, Alexander recalls that seven years ago his friend's wife and her niece had come to stay in the village. The wife had been taken ill and took to her bed. He had been for a walk with the niece to the place seen in the dream; it was in the spring. The niece had said that she was not in love with anyone, that she did not "feel like a woman." She seems to be the symbol of an impracticable love, or of love refused. Pierre's wife was the most intimate friend of Alexander's mother. Pierre himself, the old friend, had in Alexander's boyhood been his schoolmaster. Pierre's wife and Pierre are respectively condensed with Alexander's mother and father. The setting of the scene is the outcome of a similar condensation. The district is simultaneously Alexander's native village and the place where Pierre lives; the house is Pierre's, but in the dream he lives on the ground floor like Alexander's parents in reality.[1] Pierre and his wife may be regarded as impersonations of Alexander's father and mother, and the whole dream is a variation upon the Oedipus drama, love of the mother and murder of the father. Notwithstanding his knowledge of the Oedipus complex, Alexander had not, prior to the analysis, realised that this was the meaning of his dream. However, the murder is not direct; it would even seem that the real culprit must have been the mother, that she is a sort of Clytemnestra. But the black blood at the close, the spot which cannot be washed out, must certainly be the blood of crime, like the blood of Agamemnon in the ancient tragedy. By association, the black blood and the dirty water arouse images linked with the idea of the mother.

[1] The "coffee-coloured gown" reminds the subject of the excellent coffee which he has been used to drink at his friend's house, and of the way in which he felt more at home at Pierre's than with his own people.—Pierre has written to Alexander that he regards Alexander as "friend, son, and brother, rolled into one."

A reminiscence of childhood. A confinement. Notwithstanding the superstition which forbids it in this region, the blood-stained water had been allowed to flow into the street. The woman who had just been confined was the mother-in-law of Alexander's sister.

We are certainly reliving the Oedipus drama, but in this case the mother is at fault. The son does not make advances; she makes them, and he is astonished by them. Nevertheless, when Alexander was asked for associations to the words "she threw herself into his arms," he said: "The little child runs to its mother's arms." We seem to see revealed here a complex which the subject condemns, and from which he is now liberating himself.

Alexander, in the dream, was "greatly astonished" by the widow's advances. The associations to this were:

> Injustice. To protect the culprit one loves: the attitude of the mother to the child. Reminiscences of acts of injustice suffered through strictness (acts of paternal injustice).

Asked for associations to the word "disorder," the subject recalls that his father was greatly put out by disorder, by untidiness of any sort. In the dream he takes vengeance for his father's strictures and tantrums. The father was dead, and, though there was "terrible disorder," he could no longer protest.

Here are the associations of the "head in the basket":

> St. John the Baptist's head. The church of St. John in his native village. Here there is a picture showing St. John's head in a charger.—The church has been rebuilt. Between the demolished church and the new church there is a passage, and as a child Alexander was terribly afraid of this place.

Apropos of "terror," he adds that he used to be very timid. He was greatly impressed by stories of the "black man" (image of the father). Questioned about the "rebuilt church," he went on:

> The house in the dream may perhaps have been the house where his mother was born.—The house where Alexander himself was born has been rebuilt; the old house and the new; the two lives, that of the child and that of the grown-up.—How he used to enjoy being at church when he was a little boy.—Later he had a crisis which destroyed his faith. But

> later still he became religious once more, in a wider sense.—His mother had had religious inclinations, but not his father (though the father ultimately grew religious). When Alexander was a child, his father had never gone to church. The father was a man of action; it was while he had been mayor of the village that the building of the new church had been completed.

The subject has told us what these two churches were, that they signified the life of the child and the life of the grown-up. The former is linked to the idea of the mother; the latter, to the idea of the father and of "activity." Alexander has never completely broken away from the life of childhood; the "passage between the churches" alarms him; he has not really traversed it. In other subjects I have encountered like symbols to his "passage" for the expression of a similar crisis;[1] the same remark applies to the symbol of the old house and the new.

Apropos of the same images, Alexander recalls his fear of the cemetery. Before his mother's death he used to like seeing funeral processions and to be shown dead people. But after she died, he could no longer bear such things. In the evening, as soon as the lamp had been lit, he found it impossible to remain alone in the room. He was terror-stricken, and was obsessed by his mother's image; subsequently this image was transformed into an image of the witch, of the "dread mother."

The "crape veil" over the widow's face reminded him of his girl playmate; he pictured her in mourning after her brother's death, although he had never seen her thus. At bottom, presumably, he fancies her in mourning for himself, for he loved her like a sister. The condensation of this girl with the widow suggests a link between the love for his girl playmate and his attachment to his mother. Such a love, readily idealised, is fairly characteristic of a young man affected with the "Oedipus complex." This, doubtless, was the attitude of Dante towards Beatrice; and I have shown that it was probably the attitude of Verhaeren.[2]

Alexander tells me that, except for his old playmate, the women with whom he has been in love have always been older than himself; once only has he been on intimate terms

[1] See pp. 161–2, the case of Gerard and the symbol of the road by the sea.
[2] See my forthcoming study, Psychoanalysis and Æsthetics.

with a woman of his own age; she was a mother. The unconscious search for a woman whose type will harmonise with that of the maternal "imago" is obvious here.

Love for woman qua woman has been repressed. The person who accompanies Alexander in the dream is first of all a mere wraith about which he is not sure; later it seems to be Pierre's niece, a girl who says she cannot love anyone and that she "does not feel like a woman." This wraith disappears as soon as the widow comes upon the stage. The image of the mother has put that of the other woman to flight.

The rupture with the girl playmate is, as usual in such cases, ostensibly brought about by reasons that are quite inadequate. The true but hidden reason is that the beloved would cease to be the sister (she is "in mourning for her brother"), and that the ideal love would pass into the realm of realities.

It is necessary to point out how, once more, sexual reality is linked with "reality" in general, with outward activity. (The father is a "man of action.") A significant fact is that the nervous disorders begin to affect Alexander after a check in his career, and that they become fully developed as a sequel to a sentimental check (the rupture with his old playmate). The two checks are one. They express the same failure of adaptation to "reality."

Alexander reported three dreams occurring in one night. In the first dream he had visions of old women chiding and grimacing; of heavy shoes, the laces of which were iron chains. The subject still felt himself to be a prisoner.

In the second dream Alexander saw one of his little brothers, son of the step-mother. They had to go down a mountain road; night was falling. Alexander said to himself, in the dream:

> II. "If I were alone, I could go down all right; but I have to look after my brother."

Seized with fear, he awoke. Apropos of the last phrase, he thought:

> "If I were alone, if my father had not married again, I should have no difficulty in carrying on my studies; I should have more money."

He thinks also that he was "inclined to be tyrannical" towards his younger brother, whose education he had taken in hand. This implies that he had assumed towards the little brother his father's attitude towards himself. His aim in adopting an educational career was to become an educational reformer in his own part of the world; this would have been a way of getting even with his father, and of making a protest against the education he had received.

Apropos of this dream he also recalls a reminiscence of childhood:

> III. His father strikes him, lifts him, and throws him down.—Later, in the visions of his neurosis, he sometimes found himself looking at a fine view, and fell from a height.

This is associated in the dream with a feeling of fear, and with the vertigo experienced in high places. No doubt we are on the track of the cause of his obsession about the movement of the earth.

A little later, in fact, Alexander went on to tell me that in childhood his conception of God was based upon the image of his own father. He had no idea of God as love, but only of God as tyrant, as Jehovah. He added that for him the "fear that the earth will fall" was vaguely associated with the religious sentiment. In childhood he considered that "God must have done terrible things, for God is terrible." At this period he was affected with a metaphysical curiosity which found satisfaction in myths:

> Rain is God going for a drive in his cloud chariot. God has a watering-pot which he fills at a cistern. When he empties the watering-pot, it rains.

The sense of vertigo induced by the thought that the earth will fall would seem to be the outcome of a similar mythical transposition. God is the dread father. He has lifted the world as Alexander's father lifted the little boy. And God has thrown the world into the void.

As to his disquietudes concerning the little brother (Alexander's inclination to tyrannise over him; the feeling that the little brother is a nuisance, a restriction of his own powers) they are real enough. But the dream masks something more. When he is asked for associations, "little brother" calls up

" little demon " ; and the word " demon " is further associated with " sexual organ." This little demon is a sinister and satanic power. We glimpse here once more the condensation which psychoanalysts have so often detected, that of the " sexual organ " with the " little brother " or the " child." The repressive attitude towards the little brother represents a repression of sexuality. The idea of the " demon " which is a nuisance and which involves a restriction of power leads us to the subject's uneasiness concerning masturbation. But on this point we shall learn more from the third of the three consecutive dreams.

> IV. A deal table. The Kaiser is seated at the table, and with him is General N., who in the dream is chief of the general staff. . . . The Kaiser smiles triumphantly, saying: " The game is in my hands now. Bulgaria, Greece, and Turkey are on my side." But then he begins to weep. Alexander is pleased to see the Kaiser weep, but he says to himself: " Are the Germans still at their spying ? "

" Table " suggests a " counter in a bank "—and the money troubles which passed through his mind a moment ago in connection with the " little brother." The " Kaiser " represents the " tyrannical father." Apropos, Alexander recalls that when he was thirteen or fourteen years old he was at a meal when his father was piesent. All at once he left the table without apparent reason, and, barely conscious of what he was doing, practised masturbation. He has a vague sense that this ridiculous action was in some obscure way a protest against the father. To the words " the game is in my hands " [in the French, " je les tiens "] came the association " I hold it " [je le tiens] ; the " penis " ; " masturbation."

" Spying by the Germans " is the paternal espionage. Furthermore, " espionage " calls up the sound " sp," and the two letters " s " and " p " ; the former suggests the " female organ," the latter suggests the " male organ." The two letters also suggest " two demons."

Among these various associations, those at least concerning the " little brother " and the " demons " do not appear to have been suggested by theories previously known to the subject. Alexander did not recall having heard anything anent Freud's observations on this particular point.

Apropos of " general staff " came the following associations :

> Something absurd. General Ludendorf ; his name ; *ludere* is the Latin for " to play " ; *Dorf* is the German for " village " ; native village. A militarist state. " I am a pacifist ; I have a contempt for officers." A distressing thought that everywhere army officers are more highly esteemed than savants.

Here, as elsewhere, the repression of the combative instinct is linked with sexual repressions and with protest against the father. The Kaiser, the " officer," is the father ; the " savant " is Alexander himself.

This analysis, which has stirred the depths, caused, as sometimes happens in such cases, temporary excitement. " Visions " recurred ; " demons " and animals. In these visions, male figures were more frequently seen than of yore ; they encroached upon the images of the " dread mother." We shall see in a moment that this presaged the transition to homosexual fantasies. A kind of doubling of the consciousness now became manifest ; while part of the consciousness was a prey to the images, the other part was a tranquil observer. This was a new feature, and it reassured the subject. Besides, the crisis only lasted for about twenty-four hours. On subsequent evenings, an autosuggestion sufficed to restore mental calm.

With the following dream we definitely reach a new phase of the analysis. The maternal complex is no longer in the foreground, for its place has been taken by homosexual fantasies.

> V. As in most of the dreams previously recorded, Alexander does not know exactly where he is. Travelling, presumably. An accident. The engine is coming. A young man wishes to cross the rails. He has not the time. Alexander is frightened. He watches the young man, who only just misses being crushed. He sees him from behind, with two oval holes in the seat of his trousers. He says to himself : " I wonder if he has money enough to buy another pair of trousers ? "

" Accident " suggests " moral rebuff." " Engine gives the following associations :

> Terrible. When Alexander was a little boy, he was always afraid of railway engines. Especially of the headlights glowing like two eyes. It was " God looking at me." He wanted to go to confession to the engine.

In further conversation, the holes in the seat of the trousers are associated with "homosexuality"; and once more with the "two eyes of the railway engine." It is just as in dream IV, the supervision exercised by the "tyrannical father," "German espionage." It is also the "dread God." In addition, it is a homosexual fantasy, a continuation of the masturbation reminiscence which was one of the associations to dream IV.

In his objective life, the subject has never been homosexual. He merely has the virtual tendency towards homosexuality which is usual in connection with the Oedipus complex and the repression of sexuality. The tendency displays itself as blameworthy, as "censored." The concluding associations show this.

> *The seat of his trousers.* Something injurious to society.
> *To buy another pair of trousers.* Falsehood. The injustice of society. Society uses money to hide its ugliness.
> *Hole.* Little windows through which one can look at ugliness.

Once only we get back to the maternal complex, in the following association:

> *Crushed.* The sound "cr . . ." Tearing. The hole out of which a child comes.

The word "rails" suggests "things running." The words "he has not the time" call up the arrest which the subject feels to have taken place in his own development (owing to his attachment to the mother, and to infantile feelings), and the need that he should accelerate this development. He feels that the analysis is itself the necessary acceleration of development.

At the close of the analysis of this dream, he recalls another dream, quite short and definitely homosexual.

> VI. A man (apparently rather old). Viewed from behind, naked, leaning well forward. The upper part of the body cannot be seen. But the genital organs are visible (they recall the two oval holes in the seat of the trousers of the man seen in dream V).

Apropos, the subject feels impelled to say that in sexual relationship he is not averse to being "underneath." He goes on to speak of the religious sentiment. As a child he had been fond of picturing the joy and the suffering of a martyr. He had been told that at Easter the Jews killed children and drank their blood. He took a particular pleasure in imagining himself to be a child thus treated ; or in imagining himself as in the position of Regulus, rolled in a cask studded inside with nails.—All this reveals homosexuality tinged with masochism.

Furthermore, the latent homosexual trend must have undergone subconscious fixation upon the father. This would explain the man in dream VI "apparently rather old." In dream V it would explain the association of the two indecent ovals with the eyes of the railway engine, which are the father's eyes. In this way we probe to its recesses the nature of the infantile attitude towards the tyrannical father, and consequently towards the dread God. Here we have something more than a counterpart to the attachment to the mother. We have also a homosexual—masochist disposition, a *voluptuous delight in suffering inflicted by the father,* a feeling which tends to undergo sublimation into a *voluptuous delight in suffering inflicted by God.* The vertigo connected with the idea of the earth's movement (to which the subject refers once more at this stage) is the symbol of the same voluptuousness, and it has a kinship with his childhood fantasy of being rolled in the barrel of Regulus.

We reach the third and last stage of the analysis, the transition from homosexual fantasies to fantasies of normal sexuality, and therewith, the transition to extroversion. The subject thus passes through the three stages of evolution described by Freud. (Alexander does not recall having ever heard about this theory.)

The subject's resistance was peculiarly strong at the time of this decisive transition ; Alexander did not keep his appointment for the sitting at which the dream next to be recorded ought to have been analysed. "By a slip of memory" he had made another appointment for the hour at which this analysis was to have taken place ; and he was aware that the "slip of memory" was a mask for a secret wish. The dream was analysed several days after I had written up the notes on it. By that time, some of the important details had vanished from the subject's conscious memory. "Were it not that I trust you implicitly I should have believed that you had invented them." Finally, while giving associations to the close of the dream, Alexander had the impression that he was "playing," that he was being shifty, that he was hiding something. I therefore decided to go on to the "second degree," that is, to ask for fresh associations, taking as pointers the inferences from the first associations. We were compensated for our trouble by the results of this painstaking analysis. Here is the dream :

> VII. Alexander was with one of his brothers in a large room. In front of him, there was a circle on the floor. It was an animal, a little snake curled up ; its scales were of a shiny black. Alexander looked at it with interest,* but when he noticed the scales, he was frightened. He crushed it. Immediately there appeared another snake, like the first, but twice as large. Alexander was afraid. He said to his brother : "Kill it ; I can't stand it." The brother did so. [But now there appeared a third snake, a great deal larger than the second. His brother cut the snake into three pieces. Alexander was surprised to see how easy this was. The head reared itself and looked at him, although it was dead. It was like a dog's head.]

(While telling me about the three pieces, Alexander made a sketch of them, in order to explain their relative positions. We were both astonished to find that, involuntarily, he had drawn an excellent likeness of a child's head.)

> Additional snakes now appeared. The last one was positively colossal. His brother killed them all, one after another. But, when confronted by the last of the snakes, Alexander was alone. He was in the street. He said to himself : "Is it worth while killing this one ?" Then the snake fell to pieces. All the scales became absurd little cooking-pots. The dreamer awoke, laughing.

(It was the section between brackets which had been forgotten when we came to make the analysis. From the asterisk onwards, the subject had the impression that he was "playing" when giving the associations.)

The "brother" in this dream is the eldest brother, inclined to be jealous and to "tyrannise" over Alexander (a substitute for the father). "Circle" suggests "the earth turning," and this brings us back to " vertigo " ; the " snake " (a symbol which is familiar to all psychoanalysts) suggests " devil " and brings us back to the " demons." The series of associations to " scales " is peculiar.

> Harsh; his eldest brother. The sound " k." Cain. Alexander thinks that his brother was Cain and that he himself was Abel.

All this opening section of the dream is perfectly clear; we are still in the realm of homosexual fantasies tinged with masochism. But now there begins a different series, a strange one, which rounds off the whole. The word " crushes " (which, by the way, reminds us of the railway engine in V) calls up:

> Music. A fragment from " The Danaides." The conclusion terrified Alexander. It was " crushing." He had a feeling of vengeance and justice. The music gave him a vision of the dread Jehovah.

This brings us back again to the eyes of the railway engine; and, by way of the bottomless vessel of the Danaides, to the barrel of Regulus, and to the vertigo aroused by the sense of a bottomless abyss.

But it is from this point that Alexander begins to think that he is playing, that he is becoming shifty. And it is precisely from this point that the dream begins to teach us something new. We end by securing three very definite results.

The " three pieces " of the snake, first call up " trinity," and then " the three parts of the penis." The child's head, drawn by the subconscious, first suggests " my little brother," and then " my desire to become a father." In addition, the child's head recalls a picture which was in the old village church, a picture of St. George killing the dragon. But at this point the subject remembers that the dragon in the picture had a dog's head, the head which the snake in his dream had reared, and which he had up till now forgotten.

The dead head suggests " vengeance " and " vengeance upon the father." (Compare this with the severed head in dream I.) " Vengeance," in its turn, calls up " corpse," and the dead body of a neighbour whose son had taught Alexander to masturbate. (Here we have the motif of IV.)

There is superadded the reminiscence of an exhibitionist incident during adolescence. These memories are distressing, being tinged with remorse.

But the subject has the definite impression of having won a victory, of having made a great step forward. St. George has slain the dragon.[1] The instinct, which had been inclined to enter devious paths, has been led into the straight road; it is wholesome, but it is not the crude instinct, it is sublimated; the "demon" has given place to the "child." Sexuality justifies itself, moralises itself, in its aspirations towards a family. Furthermore, Alexander thinks it possible that he has sublimated his desire for "vengeance upon his father" by transforming it into a "wish to become a father," this being, in fact, an innocent way of "taking the father's place."

From this moment, not only did the symptoms disappear, but an inward harmony was established; the best elements of Alexander's mind had been awakened; his aspirations were lofty, genial, and wholesome. The subject now wanted to marry. Since the last steps forward had been made in the analysis he had fallen in love with a young Frenchwoman, and he said: "This is the first time that I have really been in love." Here is one of the dreams of this final stage:

> VIII. Alexander was in a small room. Suddenly there came a noise, and a burglar appeared, threatening him. Alexander remained calm, and said: "My good fellow, what do you want? There's my coat on the chair; take my pocket-book; I have only fifty francs; you can have them."—But now it seemed to him that the burglar was asleep and then awoke from a nightmare, saying: "I've been frightened." Alexander asked why. The burglar answered: "Didn't you see those two people?" Then, behind the burglar, he saw a man clothed in iron, who at first seemed to be dead, but then moved. Alexander said: "You need not be afraid of this man." The other figure was merely a black shade which disappeared; he had the feeling that it was his mother.

The associations showed that the burglar was myself. The burglar, who has broken into Alexander's mind, has now been accepted, and the victim greets him cordially. The

[1] Cf. in my study Psychoanalysis and Æsthetics, the analysis of Verhaeren's poem "Saint Georges," an analogous symbol.

"coat on the chair" gave the following association: "I have cast off the old Adam." The old Adam has been indued by the analyst, and perhaps this is why, in the latter part of the dream, the subject has changed roles with the burglar. The "fifty francs" calls up "French." The young woman he is in love with is French. I am also of French nationality, and the subject had actually sent me fifty francs shortly before by way of fee. In the original image of these "fifty French francs," the acceptance of the analyst has been condensed with the acceptance of normal love and marriage. The shadow which vanishes is the symbolical "mother," is the Oedipus complex and introversion; the dead man who revives is the "father," is repressed virility and extroversion.

Henceforward the dreams express confidence, Alexander's conviction that he will "do good work," and his feeling that the analysis is finished. Expecially notable is it that in one of these dreams Alexander had gone to see his uncle the doctor, who is condensed with myself. In the course of the associations to this dream, came the following:

> My uncle said: "You have come to consult me, not to see me." I answered: "I don't need to consult you any more."

The play was really over. A marriage would have been an appropriate ending, but this was not to be. The young Frenchwoman was engaged to somebody else, and Alexander had to give up all thoughts of her. He passed through a distressing crisis, and was afraid for a time that his symptoms would return. But his fears were groundless, and he triumphed in this final struggle without having felt that the earth was spinning too quickly beneath his feet.

The analysis had lasted three months, and, by the end of it, burglar and burgled had become good friends.

2. Roger

Psychasthenia. Impotence.

Roger is an intellectual, thirty years of age. A typical introvert, he has cultivated the faculty of introspection, and this will frequently help us in the course of our analysis.

He was ten years old when his father died. His mother was of a very nervous temperament, and she brought him up rather strictly. There was strong fixation upon the mother. Since childhood this fixation has been attended by a distaste for the virile aspects of life, a dislike for outdoor recreations, and even for all games except those of an imaginative character. Roger is extremely timid. In addition, he is inclined to be idle; he lacks power of concentration, is fond of reverie, and is averse to reality and to mathematics. Roger thinks that this morbid condition has existed since early childhood, but that his mother's treatment of him made it much worse. He is aware that he has an individualist tendency, which has also been marked since early years, accompanied by a strong dislike for any form of "discipline"—first that of an athletic club, and then that of military service. He has the same dislike for religious ceremonies and dogmas, and displays a tendency towards mysticism and introspective analysis. There has been and still is a conflict in his mind between "pantheism" and "personalism" in religion, a distressing conflict, from which he would fain be freed. (No doubt the explanation of this pulling hither and thither is that Roger is attracted to pantheism by his individualist hostility to dogma, but that a pantheist god is less congenial to his individualism than a personal god would be.) The subject displays a maladaptation to social life, especially manifest in the difficulty he has found in choosing a profession. Roger has artistic ambitions; his studies were interrupted by the war; he has little inclination to resume them, and does not really know what to work at.

Moreover, he finds mental work difficult, for he is neurasthenic, and his condition has been aggravated by the war and by internment in a German concentration camp (he is a Frenchman). He fancies that his ailments are connected with the troubles of his sexual life.

The nature of sexuality was explained to him when he was about twelve years old by two schoolfellows. Immediately, sexual desire became apparent; it was "powerful, and indeed almost morbid in its intensity." Since then he has masturbated daily, and has also had homosexual relationships. In masturbation, and in all perverse acts, he "plays the woman's part." When he was nineteen he had his first experience of heterosexual relations, but lacked potency. The impotence persisted in subsequent attempts, and the sexual act could only be completed after masturbation. Following the injudicious advice of a medical man, he became infected with gonorrhœa.

On two occasions he has had love passions of an exalted character. The first was when he was fifteen, and fell in love with a girl of twelve; but sexual desire became the predominant element in his feeling, and "desire killed love." The other passion, which was of an extremely respectful character, originated during his internment, when he fell in love with a German woman of high attainments and great moral worth, whose qualities harmonised with those of the maternal imago. He deliberately suppressed sexual desire. Generally speaking, in Roger, love and sexual desire are dissociated. Love, to him, seems exalted; whereas sexual desire seems coarse and perverted.

The consciousness of impotence, he says, increases his timidity in relation to girls. For a long time the feeling that he is abnormal in this respect made him very unhappy, and would still make him very unhappy were it not that the feeling of physical weakness, and the distress on account of the neurasthenia which makes all attempts to work fruitless, are now predominant. He is sure that sexual impotence and general psychasthenic impotence "are of the same nature."

Roger related to me some reminiscences of childhood, full of experience and of meaning. First of all came a fine symbol of attachment to the mother and of introversion. Roger is always delighted when he sees the "outer world" being obliterated.

> I. A winter day. It is snowing. A bright fire is burning. I am about four years old. A sense of security, of enwrapping affection, of things surrounding me; Mother enters singing. . . . I run to the window to watch the snow falling, to see it covering everything up, and to enjoy the mysterious way in which the sounds from without are being muffled.

Among the symbols of introversion, there may also be mentioned a reminiscence containing the common fantasy of the loss of a precious object by immersion (the motif of the Rhine gold).

> II. Every morning they used to put me on the chamber-pot; while sitting there I would count my fortune, a dozen

sous; one day I let all the coins fall into the receptacle. The whole household was summoned by my cries. All my fortune was in the pot. They comforted me, and the cook undertook to clean the coppers, so that they shone like gold.

To the same order of ideas belongs a third reminiscence. Like the second it contains an immersion fantasy; while it recalls the first, in that the outer world was disappearing and that the child's face "was glued to the window." The floods were out:

III. The town was under water; our house stood a little higher than the rest, and was not affected; but the garden was flooded, and people were using boats in the streets. I did not go to school during these days, but spent the time with my face glued to the window, almost as happy as our seagull with the clipped wing, which was delighted with the flood.

The "seagull with the clipped wing" would seem to be a fantasy of impotence, both in the narrower and in the wider senses of this term. This impotence is closely linked with introversion. The child is happy to escape from the outer world, from reality and from school, just as later he will subconsciously endeavour to escape from his studies, from professional work (while as far as consciousness is concerned he continues to make futile efforts to devote himself to them).

The submergence of the town certainly symbolises a loss of the "function of the real." We are not surprised to find that, apropos of this reminiscence, without transition, and without any logical tie, Roger reports feelings of *unreality*.

IV. I should like also to mention a strange feeling I often had when returning home at night after a walk, or after a journey in which I had been lulled to sleep by the movement of the train or of the carriage. To my reason, the things and the places were the same as they had always been; but as far as feeling was concerned they were different, they were strange to me. I have long been subject to such feelings. . . .

This also happens when I perform certain actions. I sometimes feel as if I had done precisely the same thing before, and in the same circumstances, although I know perfectly well I have done nothing of the kind.

In childhood I have often asked myself: "Why am I myself? What is this me? Why should I be this sort of creature, which seems quite uninteresting, and yet apparently has a part to play in the world?"

Here we have a salient instance of the feeling which Bergson has brilliantly analysed, the feeling of "false recognition," the feeling that we have previously experienced something we are now experiencing for the first time, a feeling of the enfeeblement of the function of the real.[1] The reader should likewise note how the feeling of unreality succeeds a sense of being "lulled," of being as it were rocked in a cradle, a feeling naturally associated with the idea of the mother. We are moving in a circle comprised of introversion, detachment from the real, fixation upon the mother. Once more, the reminiscence that follows seems a natural sequel.

> V. When my father and mother were quarrelling, my father would sometimes raise his voice. My mother wept, and that made me take her side.

Here is a reminiscence which seems very strange at first sight.

> VI. A banker who was a political opponent of my father, committed suicide, as an outcome of a fraudulent bankruptcy. Anything crooked in money matters produced in me *a sense of disgust and anxiety* which often lasted for a long time.

This feeling can only be explained by a condensation of "crookedness" in money matters with other "crooked" things of a more intimate character. We are put on the track by the fact that the banker in question was "an opponent of my father," and that this incident immediately follows Roger's avowal "I took my mother's side." We have definitely entered the sphere of the Oedipus complex. As invariably happens, this complex is associated with the repression of sexuality. The analysis apparently forces us to assimilate the "fraudulent bankruptcy" with "sexual perversion," which is a "crooked" means of escape.[2] We may recall that the condensation of sexual affairs with monetary affairs is quite common.

Here is an interesting reminiscence which illustrates Roger's feelings towards his father. It was at the time of the father's death, and the child had gone to stay with relatives.

[1] Bergson, L'énergie spirituelle.

[2] Cf. in Alexander's case, the masturbation which was practised as an irrational protest against the father (p. 227).

> VII. I felt well at ease, surrounded by sympathy; I forgot my father, and I smiled. After the funeral I returned home. I had got quite used to the idea that I should not see my father again. There was a family dinner at my aunt's. I asked: "Who are the heirs?"

The elder brother, in this case as in others,[1] is a substitute for the father; and, like the father, he represents the virility and the reality which the subject renounces.

> VIII. My brother (who had hitherto been away at the *commercial school*, and, subsequently, during *military service*) had returned home. . . . He inspired me with fear rather than with affection. He was a good fellow, *practical* and *objectively inclined*, *fond of sport*, the *sort of man who always falls on his feet*; but . . . we had nothing in common.

I italicise the character traits of the brother, which Roger mentioned spontaneously, for his phrases give a pithy description of the extroversion ("objectively inclined") which he shuns for himself. We know his dislike for "military service" and for social life. The "commercial school," which is a preparation for the realistic side of life, is equally repugnant to him. He was always a dreamer, and he was not happy even at school. We have learned this already from reminiscence III.

> IX. At school I did little work and dreamed a great deal. I did not understand mathematics at all, and I was never able to do a sum in division. . . . When I was asked to explain a passage too difficult for me, I would burst into tears. . . . But I was fond of the French lesson.

The school belonged to the outward and social life which the introvert shuns. Here is a description of Roger's feelings on Thursdays and Sundays.

> X. The day was always utterly spoiled for me by the prospect of meeting the boarders out walking. This was a perfect torture to me, partly because of an insuperable timidity, and partly because of *other feelings which I have never succeeded in analysing*.

When our analysis had shown the connection of these "other feelings" with the fundamental complex, with the refusal of virility and with the "fraudulent bankruptcy," the

[1] Cf. the cases of Otto and Alexander.

subject was satisfied with the explanation, and imagined that we had really unravelled that which, hitherto, he had "never succeeded in analysing"—although there was still left a confused impression that there was something to be discovered.

Here is another reminiscence of school life.

XI. Personally, most of the masters were kindly, but the discipline was harsh. . . . We went on with our studies until seven o'clock. . . . I had a particular dislike for this evening work, for the four o'clock spell of recreation, and for games. I hated all the games. I was afraid of the balls, of being hit. My schoolfellows' brutality, or rather their *superabundance of life*, made me shrink into my shell, and I was cold at heart during these grey winter amusements. . . .

Throughout the period of my school life I had schoolmates but no friends. Sometimes, when we were playing hide-and-seek, I would hide myself so effectively with a book that my playmates, weary of looking for me, would give up the attempt.

His mother coddled him.

XII. Almost every year I had slight attacks of bronchitis. My mother . . . was inclined to overrate their importance. She made me keep my room longer than was necessary. In winter she dressed me much too warmly instead of hardening me.

We must interpret all this in a moral sense as well as in a physical.

A close association with the mother continued until he was nearly grown up, and this was connected with a new fantasy of the refusal of virility.

XIII. I went on sleeping in my mother's room until I was fourteen years old. I slept in *a girl's nightgown over my day shirt* and also in a flannel waistcoat. I wore a *girl's nightcap*.

This intimacy was troubled by occasional storms, but they invariably ended in an affectionate reconciliation.

XIV. I was beginning to answer back. I wanted always to have the last word, and my mother found this exasperating. Sometimes she got into such a terrible rage that she seemed ready to break everything in the room. At the end of these quarrels I was terrified, broken, annihilated. But when my mother had calmed down, she felt remorseful, and she would come and put her arms round me in my bed.

Despite this intense fixation upon the maternal imago, the conscious attachment to the mother had long ceased to preponderate. A displacement of feeling towards other persons than the mother had begun some time before this. In especial, Roger had great affection for a girl friend, Maria, three years older than himself, who taught him to read.

XV. I was not particularly affectionate towards my mother, nor towards anyone else. But on rainy days and in the evening I felt an inclination to nestle up against Maria, and to go to sleep upon her shoulder.

We have here one of the childish passions which appear to be common accompaniments of the maternal complex.[1] This attachment cooperates with the attachment to the mother in its tendency to distract the child from rough games, and from virile amusements in general. It helps to confirm him in his predilection for the contemplative life. Maria had taught him to read.

XVI. I have already said that I had no inclination either for games or for out-of-door sports. I detested cards, and still do so; I did not care either for draughts or marbles. But I was fascinated with imaginative amusements. I have always been intensely fond of reading, and I dramatised the novels I read and the stories Maria told me.

Here is his description of Sunday.

XVII. I have mentioned how greatly I feared to meet the boarders out walking, for I had a loathing for the need to greet people, and I detested a crowd in its Sunday best. All this seemed to me desperately tedious and stupid. Maria and I always did our utmost to avoid the infliction (going out for a walk), and we were perfectly happy if we were left at home in peace to play or to read.

These two reminiscences, XVI and XVII, embody the same theme, and each of them has two aspects:

1. Refusal of virility and of social life (virile sports, the boarders' walk);

2. Flight towards the girl friend of his childhood, towards reading and the contemplative life.

The contemplative life leads straight towards mysticism.

[1] Cf. Alexander's case.

As in so many cases of fixation upon the mother, young Roger develops a passionate cult of the Blessed Virgin.

XVIII. I had accesses of mysticism, of devotion to the Blessed Virgin. In bed sometimes at night I would curl myself up, saying my rosary. I loved Corpus Christi processions.

It would seem that the image of his girl friend was more intimately connected with this mysticism than was the image of his mother (this reminds us of the case of Dante and Beatrice). The processions conduct us to another procession; that of the girls clad in white at the time of Maria's first communion, a reminiscence which Roger describes as one of the most affecting of all his childhood.

However, Maria, while still quite young, had been sent to board in a convent school. This remembrance serves as a symbol to Roger for the repression of his childhood's sensibility which was similarly cloistered, was bound fast to the image of his girl companion. He went to see her at the convent, and the memory of the visit is associated with that of " large, useless fountain basins, nearly dried up, witnesses of a lost prosperity."

These numerous reminiscences have enabled us to grasp the fundamental relationships between the various symptoms and character traits of the subject. Roger's dreams seem to have been mainly determined by his reaction to the analysis, and by the tentative movements of his subconscious towards health. Here are some fragments of one of these regenerative dreams. One of the symbols reminds us of the nearly dried-up fountain basins of the reminiscence last mentioned.

XIX. I had come away from an inn and was at the edge of a pond. There was a wedding party, and two young fellows, for a lark, were just making ready to go into the water—for a swim no doubt. . . . Their bodies were powdered, like that of a dancer. . . . The weather was cold, but I was moved to follow their example. I went into the water, but, finding that I had no towel, I asked an old man to fetch me one from the inn. When I wished to resume my bathe, I discovered that the pond had dried up, so that I am doubtful if there was even a puddle left where I could splash. Then I went to find my mother and my grandmother who were sitting in a shady corner. I told them what I had been doing, and they were shocked at my foolhardiness. But I told them that although the water was extremely cold, so brief a dip was really quite wholesome.

Here we perceive an effort to get away from his mother's "coddling," and to do something manly. The "body powdered like that of a dancer" seems akin to the "girl's nightgown" (XIII). But this femininity is superficial; beneath, there is a masculine torso. "The muscles stood out strongly." Besides "the make-up will be washed off; that which hides the truth and a wholesome life will disappear." As for the "old man," the association to this is "throw off the old Adam." To "inn" comes the association "Switzerland," a place of transit, and a health resort as it were after internment in the concentration camp. The "pond," he says, was "in France." It suggests childhood, a group of affects which have undergone fixation upon infantile objects (like the dried-up basins), and which have to be revivified. Furthermore, he wanted to bathe because "the tint of the water was exquisite, blue or green; it seemed that the sun was setting in the water." This leads the subject to associate his "wish to be braced up" with an "æsthetic" wish. Æsthetic development would appear to be looked upon as wholesome. (Other dreams dwell upon this aspect, and invite the subject to choose activities which will satisfy his æsthetic needs.) There is a sense of inadequate fulfilment pervading the dream.

In the next dream we encounter the same symbol of France, the same feeling of inadequacy, and perhaps (more specifically) of impotence. Military images appear, representing virility.

XX. I am on my way back to France. A huge hall. Someone suggests that we should pay for the serving of the soup. I refuse. . . . The woman who is ladling out the soup serves me after everyone else, and gives me only a small helping, because I had refused to pay.

I return to my native haunts. An old harness maker cuts me dead; I feel that I am regarded with contempt because I was not at the front. I sham a limp.

I go to the printer's. He says: "I have some letters for you. One of them is from Germany, with a book. I have read your letters as censor." I am annoyed at this, for he will have been able to learn about my dreams.

"I sham a limp," like the "make-up" of the previous dream, is connected with other associations in which the subject has an uneasy feeling that his condition is a mask; illness seems to him a convenient means of hiding a lack of courage. "Serving the soup" has as associations "military service," a "disagreeable duty."

As for the "printer," he is like me; and the allusion to the dreams shows unmistakably that he symbolises me. A certain resistance to the analysis becomes manifest here. Moreover, the "letter," and the "book" are linked with the memory of his friend in Germany, the woman who had a beneficial influence, a purifying influence, upon him. This "purification," just like the æsthetic sentiment a moment ago, presents itself as a factor of equilibrium, of health and of cure. It is perfectly plain that the dreams are assuming the character of guiding dreams.

In some of the dreams the achievement of virility is associated either with military symbols or with sexual symbols.

> XXI. I dreamed that the infirmary attendant of the school I was at in Paris sent me to fetch a bag of currants. . . . I felt as if it were a fatigue duty in the army. . . . In the distance there was a group of young men and women. . . . Those in front were kneeling or lying down, and were making gestures as if they were shooting with bows and arrows.

The association with "bag" was "two wallets," and led us to an image of a bodily organ. In the same dream appeared the name of one of the masters whom Roger had to consult as to the choice of a career. All the aspects of manliness, including the choice of a career, find expression here. In the next dream, sexuality is more explicit.

> XXII. I consult the wise-woman close to her cottage. She asks me to show her my genital organs. . . . She takes me to a spring and bids me . . . wash them.

Here, as before, there is manifest a desire for purification. This is still more plainly disclosed in the next dream.

> XXIII. I give a large porker a letter which is to warn him of the danger threatening someone dear to him. The pig takes me into a little room. There he begins to talk to me in Provençal. I find it very difficult to follow, so I ask him if he understands Italian. He answers in the affirmative, so

I reply in Italian, interspersed with English words. The pig's wife also speaks Provençal, and I can't understand her at all. She is like an old shrew painted by Ostade. She is ashen grey with the colour laid on thickly.

From the associations it appears that the "porker" is "the lower part of myself," and that "someone dear to him" is "the upper part." To "letters" we have the association "dreams" and their analysis (cf. XX). The "pig's wife" calls up the following:

Marriage. I must not marry a woman who will keep me in the state symbolised by the porker.

Thoughts concerning the choice of a career are likewise disclosed. "Provençal" is linked with arduous scientific studies. "Italian" is associated with Italian art, of which Roger is very fond; this brings us back to the æsthetic tendency, which offers a way out of his difficulties.

We may conclude the account of this case by recording two regenerative dreams, which are mutually complementary. The first relates to the infantile fixations and atrophies, of which the subject must become conscious before he can break their spell. The second, like the dream about the porker, emphasises the distinction between the upper and the lower natures, and stresses the need for "purification" (sublimation).

XXIV. I am a little girl. I am going to be married. My girl playmates give me a brush made of their hair. Each of them has contributed a little of her own health to it, so that the united whole is to make me thoroughly healthy.

Here are the associations to the items of this dream.

I am going to be married. Life with its joys and its troubles. A full life which needs an abundance of energy.

Hair. My friend the German woman once said to me: "I wish I could take your illness and give you my health." Hair reminds me of this friend who had a great influence upon me.

The idea of a brush is connected in my mind with that of regeneration. This is because a masseur used a brush on me to restore the circulation.

In this dream, the German woman is condensed with the girls with whom he was in love when he was a child; she represents the purest feelings he has experienced in his life. If "marriage" is to become possible to him, sexuality must be purified until it comes to resemble these feelings. The analysis is convincing the subject that his sexual troubles have been of accidental and psychic origin (due to a distasteful initiation); and that a "purification," putting an end to repressions, will enable him to get over these troubles.

> XXV. To prove her sincerity, the lady uses up her long, black hair day by day until she has none left; the brother of her lord undertakes to see that she is purified daily in aromatic essences. Rabelais, meanwhile, is kept prisoner in the neighbouring castle, but *at length he is allowed to go out* provided that he keeps at least one hundred yards away from the castle. He lives in an inn, surrounded by buffoons and courtesans, that he may hunt love the more easily. When he makes his way through the streets of the town, the motley rout which attends him raises a clamour of song and music which scandalises the ladies of the noblesse.

The "long, black hair" suggests "Mary Magdalen" and his "German lady friend"; it also calls up the "brush" of XXIV. To "aromatic essences" come the associations: "Goethe's Faust"; "Christ is risen."—"Rabelais" calls up "obscenities," and brings us back to the "big porker" of XXIII; he is repressed sexuality. "At length he is allowed to go out," upon terms, these being such that the "someone dear to him" (XXIII), though scandalised perhaps, is at any rate protected from his assaults. As association to the word "purify" comes the reflection: "It is true, I need purification."

We are not entitled to say that equilibrium and harmony had been attained at this stage. Suggestion and psychoanalysis had from the outset been practised simultaneously, and although Roger was not yet at the end of his troubles, there had been considerable progress. The time had now come for him to return to France, but the matter could safely be left in his own hands. The next time I saw him, about two years later, he assured me that he was perfectly well.

3. Germaine

SPASM OF THE EYELID. FUSSY ACTIVITY.

Germaine is a woman of forty-nine, of peasant origin, a widow, and childless. She has suffered from a spasm of the right eyelid " for fifteen years at least." This is what she says at first. Then she remembers that the spasm began in the year following her mother's death. At length her memory becomes more precise. A year after her mother's death, on the anniversary, she went home in order to visit the grave; it was then that people pointed out to her that she had the spasm. It has been treated unsuccessfully with bromides; electricity was likewise tried, but had no effect.

Germaine also suffers from a persistent condition of restlessness, of nervous uneasiness. She is always fussily active, having a feeling that she is behind time and must hurry up. The condition is often accompanied by " neurasthenic ideas."

The first dream subjected to analysis was concerned with the before-mentioned anniversary of her mother's death.

> I. On the shore of the lake. She saw a large boat which splashed her with dirty, greyish water, like melting snow. The water rose; she was surrounded by it. Someone called to her: " Climb up here."

The " melting snow " appeared to be the centre of gravity of this dream. It called up the first anniversary, when Germaine went home. But she could not go to the cemetery, because of the dirty, melting snow. The parish priest had said to her that if the sun went on shining for three days all the snow would be melted.

The parish priest turned up in the following dream:

> II. Germaine was in the country with a neighbour, at a washerwoman's. She left some collars and some underlinen to be washed. Then, still with her neighbour, she found herself at the parish priest's. He seemed to flirt with her; the other woman, who was older than Germaine, was jealous. But a young woman belonging to the priest's household warned him, saying: " No, not the older one, I know what sort of woman she is." (In fact, Germaine's neighbour is a light woman.) . . . Germaine does not like dreaming about parish priests; "it is a sign of bad news."

The analysis showed that the parish priest was a substitute for the father, and that Germaine had a strong fixation upon the father. "I was much fonder of father than of mother. I don't mean that I did not like mother, but she did not return my affection. I was not her favourite." Germaine was the youngest of the family, and she had the impression that her birth had not been entirely welcome. Her mother certainly could not have wanted another child.

The neighbour who was older than herself symbolised Germaine's elder sister. "My sister and I could not get on together." The sister's conduct had laid her open to reproach, and in the dream Germaine exaggerates her sister's misdemeanours in order to abase her, and the better to justify her own claim to the exclusive affection of the father. The underlinen for the laundress has as association the "dirty snow" which was mentioned just now. The "underlinen" also calls up the memory of a dispute with her sister at the time of the father's death. Her sister had wanted to carry off all the father's underclothing. Quarrels with her sister had been frequent; especially there had been wrangling about money matters connected with their late father's property—this controversy was still unsettled. At another sitting, Germaine referred to her jealousy of her sister; but, "Really my sister was jealous of me, for I was father's favourite." Her sister had "idled," whilst Germaine had worked hard in order to "economise." (It had been like the grasshopper and the ant in the fable.) Working hard in order to economise leads us to Germaine's perpetual fussy activity. We discern one of those persistent grudges which assume a virtuous and honest form, but in which the virtue and the honesty have a sub-flavour of vengeance. She has a grudge against her sister. The dream stresses the point that if Germaine is more worthy than her neighbour (the sister) of the love of the parish priest (the father) it is because Germaine is a better woman. We begin to realise that the fussy activity is the expression of a wish to outshine the sister, and that underlying this wish there was a desire to be more worthy of the father's affection.

The next dream reiterates the same attitude towards her sister and her father.

III. The father's burial service. The coffin has been placed upon the altar. Germaine is looking on. Her sister was there too, and was carrying a paraffin lamp in the passage to light the people who were coming up the stairs and who were to help in the settlement of the property. There was a dispute between herself and her sister about this matter.

Here, recalling my interpretation of the "parish priest," Germaine made a remark whose logical force was questionable, though the idea came into her mind as an irresistible conviction. She said: "The parish priest of the other dream may certainly have been my father, for in this dream I saw my father's coffin on the altar." She believed that her father had "died a good death." We gather that the father is looked upon by Germaine as having been a person of great moral worth, and here is an additional reason why a decent and hard-working life should help to make her worthy of him. This is the path of sublimation for her long-standing jealousy of her sister. But the sublimation is incomplete; the subject's attitude is intermediate between one of pure sublimation and one of neurosis, for her desire to lead a decent and hard-working life finds expression, not only in actions that are morally estimable, but also in nervous fussiness and aimless activities which Germaine herself regards as ridiculous.

No doubt an additional factor must be invoked for the full understanding of the fussy activity. When Germaine dreams about her sister, the point especially stressed is that the sister was "older" than herself. This detail would seem to have a peculiarly intimate relationship with the jealousy. In Germaine's fussiness, in her persistent feeling that she needs to "hurry up," we may discern a wish to overtake her sister, and to bring herself nearer than her sister to the father's level. This interpretation does not conflict with the previously mentioned wish to surpass her sister morally; it is superadded. It is furthermore in harmony with the fantasy that appears in a subsequent dream, when the father has been rejuvenated. This is another way of bringing herself into closer approximation with the father.

To complete my description of the case, I must point out that Germaine has a strong desire, which has never been fulfilled, "to be a mother." Apropos of a dream in which she had held a child in her arms, she said: "I never knew the joy of having a mother who caressed me, or the joy of being a mother." For her, these two phenomena were linked. Asked for associations to the image of the child in her arms, she said: "Something one wants to take care of. I don't like people to do me an injustice. Quarrels with my sister." All this shows that her longing to be a mother has been reinforced from the outset by her longing to grow up, to take the place of her elder sister and of her mother. The wish to be a mother was superadded to the other wish as a factor of the dissatisfaction which found expression in the perpetual dread of being behind time.

Germaine soon got the better of the inclination to fussy activity and of the associated "neurasthenic ideas." As far as these troubles in the moral sphere were concerned, she was amazed at the results achieved. But concerning the spasm, more precise information was needed.

She recalled that when she was six years old she had been butted off a rock by a goat, and that one of the animal's horns had struck her below the right eye. This reminded her of another accident, when a falling stone had injured her right leg. The same leg had been hurt by the goat. When she was menstruating, varicose veins swelled up in this leg, and simultaneously the facial spasm grew worse. The trouble was also aggravated whenever there was a snowstorm. The effect of snow, which was mainly, if not entirely, psychic, had been elucidated by the analysis, by the associations to dream I ("melting snow"). But the whole thing was still rather vague. An interesting reminiscence now threw light upon the matter.

> IV. When Germaine was eighteen or nineteen years old, a girl friend had told her that she was being courted by a young man who had a spasm of the eyelid. Germaine had told her friend that she had better look out, because people who lived together were apt to catch that sort of thing from one another. Germaine had known a manufacturer with a spasm of this sort who had given it to his wife.

Germaine added that this manufacturer lived near a country house where she was housekeeper. She did not see him often, for her mistress was very strict and would seldom let her go out because of the manufacturer's workmen, who liked to flirt with the young housekeeper. She was nine years at this house. She did not like the mistress at all. "My nerves were all on edge every time the old woman gave me an order." Under the same roof there was another mistress, a young lady who, though much better off than Germaine, was jealous of her appearance. This lady seems to be more or less condensed with the elder sister; whilst Germaine's hostility towards her mother (which, moreover, counts for something in Germaine's antagonism towards her sister) has here been frankly transferred on to the elderly mistress. Germaine's obsession with haste already existed at this date. She was seventeen when she went into service here, but "she had given herself out to be twenty"; it was not until she was really twenty that she admitted her true age.

While staying in this house, Germaine had a love affair which came to nothing. Her failure to get married had been mainly the fault of her "old mistress," who wanted to keep Germaine as housekeeper, and had therefore exaggerated Germaine's "poverty" in order to frighten away the wooer.

We can now understand the significance of the spasm to Germaine at this period. Imaginatively she liked to put herself in the place of her girl friend, who could marry without any "old mistress" to put hindrances in the way. Perhaps her friend, if she married, would catch the husband's facial spasm. But *marriage was worth paying for, even if one had to get facial spasm.* It is thus that the subconscious may be supposed to have reasoned. But marriage would also, and mainly, have signified "deliverance from the authority of the old mistress," an authority which was a substitute for that of the mother. Many years later, at the time when she was to have paid her first visit to her mother's grave, the spasm was noticed for the first time.

The subconscious wish to be freed from her mother's authority would appear to have been predominant in Germaine. This wish, which was closely associated with her love for her father, was an element in her desire to grow up, in her desire to hustle through the stages of life, in her habit of fussy activity.

During the week subsequent to this analysis, quite a number of persons, spontaneously and independently, were struck by the diminution in the severity of the spasm. Germaine herself felt that the eyelid was "much less drawn up."

This is as far as improvement went. As regards the moral

condition and the general nervous condition, a cure had been effected. The relief of the spasm was only partial. I may add that suggestion would appear to have had more effect upon Germaine than the analysis. Her mind was not sufficiently alert for the full significance of the analysis to be appreciated by the conscious.

Here are two dreams which contain some interesting allusions to the two methods. Dream V was dreamed during the first month of the analysis.

> V. Germaine was with a number of persons in a large room " like this one." She was with her husband or her brother, probably it was her husband. An acquaintance was there with her daughter. The girl was crying because she had a sore finger. Then I cleared the room, everyone went away, and Germaine was left alone with me. Next I was painting; I painted two heads larger than life; a man's head and a woman's. The woman was of a certain age. Both the heads were upside down. The man's head was not so detailed; he was fairly young. I had written something beneath the picture, but someone rubbed it out as she tried to read it.

The associations to " upside down " were " something which won't work properly," " present state of health." All the first part of the dream down to the moment when " I cleared the room " is a dream reminiscence of the courses of autosuggestion in which the subject has participated. (One of her fellow patients had had a very sore finger.) The time when " Germaine was left alone with me " is the psychoanalytical sitting. The faces that I painted were those of Germaine's father and mother; in connection with the first sittings I had drawn attention to their respective roles. When asked for an association to " the woman of a certain age," Germaine said simply " my mother." As regards " the man," the association was: " I said to myself that he was too young to be my father." It is the father rejuvenated, in virtue of the wish which has been explained. The hand which erases the writing, symbolises the difficulty of the analysis.

The other dream belongs to the final stages of the analysis.

> VI. She was with a woman older than herself. There had been a death. The room seemed very dirty. She said: " It's impossible to clean this; it must be thoroughly done up."

The " woman older than herself " is the sister once more. The " death " immediately calls up that of the father, and reminds the subject of the dream of the coffin upon the altar (III). The very dirty room is akin to the dirty water of dream I, and to the dirty underlinen of dream II, and also to the faces which are upside down seen in dream V. All these things symbolise the disorder of the subconscious, in association with the paternal complex. The disorder is too much for her; she is not competent to assimilate the analysis sufficiently to enable her to set things straight. The last phrase symbolises the subject's intimate reaction to the respective methods. To " clean " is psychoanalysis; to " do up thoroughly " is suggestion.

CHAPTER TEN

MENTAL DISORDERS

MENTAL disorders, like nervous disorders, are symbolical. The language of delirium is no more inscrutable than the language of dreams. Moreover, not merely are these disorders symbolical, but they are the symbols of the psychological frame of mind from which the disorders spring. In the case of mental disorder, therefore, just as in such cases as we have hitherto been considering, psychoanalysis is curative simultaneously with being interpretative. But if the analysis is to do any good, it is essential that the subject's consciousness should not be entirely clouded. The future alone can tell us to what extent psychoanalysis can influence mental disorder for good. That it does influence them in certain cases, has been definitely proved.[1]

In the three cases expounded in this chapter, the troubles are sharply localised, either because they are specifically restricted to isolated systems of ideas (ideas of persecution in Bertha, and ideas of physical contamination in Ruth), or because they are associated with certain transitory states (epileptic states in George).

In Bertha, and still more in Ruth, infantile elements have a preponderant importance. Underlying the trouble in both these subjects was an ardent wish to escape from the family environment. In Bertha, this wish was complicated by a longing for a more expansive and more intellectual life; to some extent the second wish may be regarded as a would-be justification, as a rationalisation, of the first. Indeed, delusions of persecution have been specially studied as functions of hostility to the family environment.[2] Bertha's

[1] Bernard Hart's little volume, The Psychology of Insanity, numerous editions from 1912 onwards, may usefully be consulted as to the bearing of psychoanalysis upon mental disorders.

[2] Lang, Eine Hypothese zur psychologischen Bedeutung der Verfolgungsidee, 1914.

persecution complex also contained sexual elements. In Ruth, the influence of sexual factors was even more conspicuous; but in this subject, too, the sexual factors were closely associated with a protest against the environment, and especially against the father (a step-father) and against the improprieties he was guilty of towards the child. A feeling of rape, of contamination, associated with the image of the father, underlay the fixed idea of the subject, who imagined that she emitted an evil smell.

In George we have to do with mental disorder of a very definite type, for he is an epileptic liable to attacks of epileptic insanity. The insanity therefore, is dependent upon a specific morbid state, and it cannot be attributed to a psychological cause. Nevertheless, psychoanalysis has shown that in epileptic insanity the patients exhibit well-defined complexes. There can be no doubt that these complexes play their part in the production of the insanity, even though the primary cause of the latter is the patient's physical condition. By analysing the complexes we may perhaps hope that we shall modify the insanity. No one will deny that nightmare is caused by the physical condition of the sleeper; nevertheless, psychoanalysis can relieve a tendency to nightmare, for the disorder is also brought about by the subject's complexes. The value of psychoanalysis in helping the epileptic to "sublimate" some of his troubles, and even its value in modifying to some extent the frequency or severity of the attacks, is categorically asserted by L. Pierce Clark, who has reported some interesting analyses of cases of epileptic insanity.[1]

1. Bertha

INTROVERSION. DELUSIONS OF PERSECUTION. NEURALGIA.

Bertha is twenty-seven years old. Since childhood her character has been reserved, stubborn, and thrifty to excess. She belongs to the lower middle class, and is fairly well educated, being rather better off in this respect than the average of her surroundings.

Bertha is quite unenlightened in sexual matters, displaying

[1] Clark, A Clinical Study of some Mental Contents in Epileptic Attacks, 1920, pp. 367, 375.

in this respect a certain childishness which is surprising to her mother and her sister. She is very definitely an introvert.

Her father was an alcoholic; one of her maternal aunts suffered from hysteria. When she was three years old, Bertha was sent to board with this aunt. Then, when the mother wanted the child home again, the aunt refused to give her up, became abusive, and struck the mother. The police had to be called in.

When Bertha was five, she was boarded out with strangers. The aunt kidnapped her, and told all and sundry that the mother had abandoned her little girl. When Bertha was nine, the aunt asked to have the child to stay for a week, kept her beyond the specified time, and finally sent her to board somewhere else in order to hide her. When she was six, Bertha saw her aunt in a hysterical attack. When she was fourteen, she ran away from a school where she was being ill-treated.

In 1914 Bertha was abroad, in one of the belligerent countries. She was a governess, witnessed a number of tragical scenes, and had to take flight before the invaders.

During 1915 she was placed in an asylum. Her family was notified. She was suffering from mental disorder in the form of systematised delusions of persecution. She complained of severe pains in the head and the stomach, often refused her food, and was obdurately silent. She refused to leave her cell, and bit the nurses who tried to make her do so. The Red Cross Society secured her repatriation, when her family and I myself had drawn attention to the case; she had to be brought in a special compartment, under close care.

She returned home in the beginning of 1916, and there was marked improvement from the very outset, so that I am by no means entitled to claim all the merit. I visited Bertha daily, and by the end of the first week I was able to carry on a connected conversation with her; this enabled me to make suggestions, and before long to teach her autosuggestion. She was perfectly calm, but in other respects the symptoms of her mental disorder were persistent. She declared she had been afraid of becoming a victim of the white-slave traffic, and from time to time she still suspected her mother of having bad designs upon her. I continued to see her daily. After four months, the pains in the head and the stomach had entirely ceased, and her conversation was no longer maniacal. No physical treatment had been employed.

The symptoms which still persisted would not have aroused the attention of anyone ignorant of her antecedents, but to me they were significant.

Bertha had a dislike, one might almost say a repugnance, for the housework which her mother, by degrees, allotted to her. This work caused fatigue that seemed out of proportion to the effort. She did her work with marked distaste, dragging her feet like a child which obeys with reluctance. Her ill-humour at this time was perpetual, and her temper was liable to flash out at any moment against persons or things.

Now, a young man who had been engaged to her called at the house. She received him coldly, almost rudely, surrounding herself with a rampart of silence. Without any open explanations, she showed clearly that the idea of this marriage did not please her. Nevertheless she refused to suggest that the engagement should be broken off. She seemed to be suffering from a conflict, and to be affected with a confused malaise. It was the young man who broke off the engagement.

At this juncture, psychoanalysis was methodically undertaken. The reason for the new departure was that the later symptoms (ill-humour, etc.) which had been aggravated after her fiancé's visit, seemed to be associated with the idea of this marriage, and suggested a clue. Moreover, for the last two months a new bodily symptom had made its appearance, *a neuralgia of the left arm.* This neuralgia had become so violent as to interfere greatly with sleep, and to make the use of the arm practically impossible. If, at meals, Bertha attempted to pour herself out some water, she often found herself unable to do so. As a sequel of autosuggestion under my supervision, the neuralgia got much better, and was transferred from the left arm to the right; but the patient continued to suffer from it every day.

Here is a dream which analysis enabled me to interpret.

I. Bertha was in a large crowd, entirely consisting of persons of distinction. She caught sight of a young man who was very tall and fair; he spoke with a vulgar accent, which shocked her. At this moment I was near her, and I scolded her because she showed too much sympathy for the young man. She was astonished at my reproaches, and she remonstrated, saying that the young man (who turned out to be a friend of mine) was disagreeable to her on account of his vulgar accent.

I asked Bertha for associations to the items of this dream, and these associations speedily threw light on the matter.

The "distinguished persons" called up other dreams. She often dreams of distinguished, well-dressed, and cultured persons. She envies them. Sometimes she finds that she is herself one of them; she lives with them and talks to them; this is delightful. In these other dreams I have not appeared, but in them also she has been accompanied by a "well-informed and cultured" guide, for example, the medical superintendent of the asylum. In the other dreams, he played much the same part that I played in the dream just recorded. I had soon recognised in Bertha the half-explicit wish for a more expansive and more "cultured" life, of which her years as governess had given her a glimpse.

In the "young man who was very tall and fair," it was easy to recognise her fiancé in disguise, for her fiancé was *short and dark*, and had a well-marked rustic accent. Repression had made skilful play with the mechanism of contrasts. The cause of the antipathy she felt towards the young man in the dream was his "vulgar accent," which smacked of a vulgar origin, and conflicted with Bertha's aspiration towards a "cultured life."

I realised that this aspiration was deeply rooted, and that it must have been one of the hidden causes of her malady. More especially it threw light upon her lack of enthusiasm for housework and upon her persistent ill-humour.

As soon as I explained all this to Bertha, she felt that I was right. Great relief to the symptoms ensued. A few months later her engagement was renewed, the antipathy having been overcome, thanks to the analysis.

There was, however, something more at work than a superficial antipathy. There was also a repugnance towards sexuality; the subject's whole being bore witness to this, and her obsession with the "white-slave traffic" was merely a salient expression of her general repugnance.

I should mention that the engagement, after dragging on for a time, was again broken off, further difficulties having arisen. It would be hard to say how far the old conflict played a part in reinforcing the reasons for the new rupture. Two or three years later, Bertha married someone else.

The subject's obsession with the "white-slave traffic" suggested that we should find a connection between her ideas of persecution and her antagonism to sexuality. Here are two typical dreams showing the existence of this connection.

The first of these dreams was one she had while in the asylum. At least, so Bertha says.

> II. She was among some soldiers. Several of them wore red uniforms, and they had extraordinarily long daggers, still sheathed, but their hands were ready to unsheath them at any moment. There was blood, much blood, a lake of blood.
>
> Then there was an avenue, a long avenue. Here there were a lot of soldiers, and, turning round, Bertha saw that there were also some civilians, who ran after her in a crowd. They were all men.

The second dream is a nightmare she has frequently had since adolescence.

> III. She saw a man lying at the foot of her bed, in the shadow, and at the mere sight of him she felt terribly frightened. When she was about nineteen, a modification ensued in the nightmare, and since then the man has always held a dagger in his hand.

When Bertha was asked for associations, "soldier" called up "weapon," "red" called up "blood," and "lake" called up "blood." The weapon, with the threat which it implies, is the centre of gravity of this vision. When she was asked for the associations to the word "dagger," there was no answer. The subject was manifestly embarrassed. However, the conclusion we have just drawn shows that the dagger was the most significant item. Bertha's embarrassment, then, points to an object of repression, and one need not be a Solomon to recognise a sexual symbol. Furthermore, "avenue" calls up "a lot of trees"—"bushy trees." Here we have a kindred symbol. If any doubt remains, let us recall that the crowd was "all men." Now it is this crowd of men which *runs after her*.

The "soldiers" were the outcome of visions of the war. The dread she had experienced owing to the invasion by armed men had, by a most natural association, awakened sexual terror. As for the "man lying" at the foot of the bed, he was a reminiscence of something that had really happened. Once a drunken man, mistaking the landing, had come into Bertha's bedroom and collapsed on the foot of the girl's bed, in the position of the man in the nightmare. She passed a whole night of terror, afraid to utter a sound, her eyes fixed on the invader. It is easy to infer that henceforward the image of this drunkard would fuse in the subconscious with the images of the step-father, who was a drinker. The repugnance for a rough environment would coalesce with repugnance for sexuality. There would thus arise the condensation which finds expression in Bertha's intense *repugnance towards vulgarity*. We now discern the unity underlying the most diverse symptoms, ranging from delusions of persecution to a dislike for housework, and not forgetting the subject's antipathy to her fiancé with the rustic accent.

We have, further, good reason to think that Bertha must have been gravely predisposed to delusions of persecution by the behaviour of her hysterical aunt, and that this aunt's remarks concerning the mother must have influenced the little girl's imagination. This is why, when the crisis came, Bertha's suspicions tended to be concentrated on the mother. Separation from her mother when Bertha was living abroad reminded the subject of the days of childhood when she had visited her aunt; and the analogy was completed by a remarkable detail, for Bertha had stayed with her aunt for the last week before going abroad. We know that analogy of situations can predispose to analogy in mental states.

The neuralgia of the left arm, occasionally transferred to the right arm, persisted as a daily trouble when the other symptoms had apparently yielded to treatment.

After a fruitless attempt to follow up various clues, it occurred to me to ask Bertha if she had ever known anyone who suffered from a severe affection of the arm. In answer, came the following reminiscence.

IV. When she was nine years old, her most intimate friend had been a schoolfellow who had a paralysed left arm. She was Bertha's namesake, and the two Berthas were inseparable. One day her friend had a fall, and injured the paralysed arm. She was laid up for a long time. During this illness, the mistress of their class used to visit the invalid and bring her books. The sick Bertha had taken advantage of the period of enforced leisure to read, and acquire knowledge. During this period, the invalid's sister had done all the housework, working double tides, for the family was not well off.

I knew enough. The accident to the arm in this schoolfellow had secured for the latter *leisure*, and opportunities for *culture*, and I knew that these were my own patient's chief desires (see dream I). Furthermore, the close association between the two girls, the facts that they were of the same age and bore the same name, had favoured perpetual comparisons, and had led to a sort of imaginative identification between the two companions. What was true of one was true of the other. Everything happened as if my patient Bertha's subconscious had reasoned as follows:

Through an affection of the left arm, my double has secured leisure and culture A similar affection of my own arm will bring me the same good fortune.[1]

(I may add that my Bertha, like her friend, has a sister, and that the latter, in fits of annoyance, has frequently grumbled at Bertha for not doing her fair share of the housework.)

By further questioning I secured confirmation of my theory. I asked Bertha whether she had never suffered from any ailment of the arm between the age of nine and the recent onset of the neuralgia. Oh yes, since she was nine she had always had a pain in the arm when she was carrying a muff. I asked her to show me the position in which her friend had held the paralysed arm, and then to show me the position of her own arm in the muff. The positions were identical, with the same drop at the wrist.

I promptly explained to Bertha the origin of her neuralgia. This trouble, the last redoubt in which the protean illness had concentrated its forces, disappeared *that very day*.

[1] This case of neuralgia resembles the case of contracture psychoanalysed by Dr. Charles Odier (op. cit.).

2. Ruth

A Fixed Idea. Impressions of Rape.

I record here a few significant details from the analysis of an extremely complicated case.

Ruth is twenty-four years of age. She has a fixed idea about which she will allow no argument; she imagines that she emits an evil smell, that everyone notices it, and that no one dares tell her. This notion paralyses all her social life.

Ruth's childhood was most unhappy.[1] Her mother was arrested for ill-using her. Ruth can recall the incidents.

> I. She was sleeping in a garret. The snow was falling on her bed. Her mother used to make her get up first. That morning, Ruth pretended to be asleep. Her mother plunged Ruth's head into a basin of water, then she tied the child to the leg of a wash-stand, and went to fetch the milk. Someone knocked at the door; it was one of her aunts. Ruth explained what had happened, and the aunt fetched the police.

Ruth added that she was passionately fond of her mother in spite of everything, and the child suffered at being separated from her mother. She remembers that when she was a child she was afraid of being alone, especially in the evening. When she awoke in the morning, she used to say to her mother: "Have I got to go out into the wide, wide world?" She recalled a dream she had had when about five years old.

> II. She was at sea, in a boat filled with water where there was no room for her feet. She saw a whale's head with a huge eye. She had the feeling that this was a monster which would swallow her. A feeling of intense loneliness. Then she saw that the shore was lined with a row of tubs filled with water.

The sea-monster is the mother, whose way it was when in a temper to plunge the child's head into a tub or a basin. This had given Ruth a phobia of water. When she was in her bath, the reflecting surface of the water frightened her, and she had to ruffle it. Nevertheless, the child was devoted to the "monster," and her attachment prevented her from going "into the wide, wide world."

[1] The main details of her life as a child have been independently confirmed; they were not imaginatively constructed by the subject.

The reason for Ruth's attachment to her mother was that her father, or I should say her step-father, was even worse than the mother, if possible. He would come home drunk. His conduct towards the child was indecent both in word and deed. Here is a reminiscence.

III. It was one evening when Ruth came home late with her step-father. He had taken her into a public-house; she had been afraid of a man with no legs, and she had been beaten. When she got home, her father, who was drunk, wanted to make her drink some absinthe. When she refused, her mother plunged her head into a pail of water. She felt she was being suffocated.

The absinthe is symbolic of all the improprieties of the drunken step-father, who at a later date was to make a definite attempt to rape the child. It was apparently as an outcome of this scene that Ruth acquired a phobia of buttons and of dress-hooks. It made her "feel dirty" to look at them. She always had to wash her hands after hooking up her dress.

To this scene there were superadded other scenes of assaults upon her person, sometimes by the step-father and sometimes by others. It is likely enough that there has been exaggeration about some of these details, but the important point is, not so much their degree of objective reality, as the impression they made on the subject. Here is one of them.

IV. She had been sent to the village for some bread. A gentleman she did not know took her by the hand and led her into a little wood. He rummaged in her pocket. Instinctively she was seized with fear, and managed to run away.

In their totality, these memories have left a strong impression of violation, a feeling of contamination, which disclosed itself as the origin of the fixed idea of "emitting an evil smell." The "little wood" in reminiscence IV led us to another reminiscence.

V. She wanted to run away from her aunt's, no doubt in order to go back to her mother (her aunt had taken charge of her after the scene when the police were called in). But she turned back because she had to pass near the lunatic asylum and the little wood. She was afraid both of the asylum and of the wood. She fancied there must be a monster in the little wood; she heard it cough one day.

We know already the meaning of the little wood. Thus, in Ruth, the wish to return to the mother, the fear of rape, and the fear of madness, seem to be closely linked, and this association will help us to understand many of the symptoms. In any case, the mental disorder is directly connected with the idea of rape or contamination.

Furthermore, we have seen that the refusal of the step-father's "glass of absinthe" (a symbol of rape) led to the action of the mother, who plunged the child's head into the pail where she felt she was being suffocated. The dread of the father, the dread of rape, and the dread of the "wide world," are all one; it is this dread which impels the subject back towards the mother—and towards the loneliness where one is stifled. The impression of "emitting an evil smell" is, from one point of view, a rationalisation to justify the repudiation of the social instincts, to justify a flight from the world. It is also probable that, in the subject's imagination, the idea of the head in the water has become a symbol of purification. Thus the mother's violence does not merely represent to Ruth the choice of a lesser evil, it represents a positive good.

Ruth will not feel that she has been enfranchised unless she secures the conviction that she is not an object of disgust. That which her subconscious chiefly demands of me is that I should prove that I myself have no disgust; this proof and health are one and the same thing. She expresses the idea in a beautiful dream.

> VI. On the shore. Jesus, very large, appears in a large boat. The scene changes to an arcade. Ruth sits down on a step, and Jesus sits down on the next step below. A deformed creature was there; it came towards Jesus. So repulsive was its aspect that she wondered whether Jesus would be able to touch it. Not only did he touch it, but he actually embraced it, and she wept on seeing disgust overcome. Then a little tableau appeared; she saw a young man seated on an ass; it was the deformed creature of a moment ago, cured.

In association, the "deformed creature" reminds her of the legless man the memory of whom is associated with the scene of the "glass of absinthe" (III)—a condensation of all the scenes of rape. This deformed creature is Ruth herself, under the repugnant aspect which she believes herself to have. No doubt the conviction that she is repugnant arose out of scenes of such a character. Jesus is the guide and the healer. He sits upon the lower step to show that he does not despise her. The young man seated on the ass is Jesus himself on Palm Sunday. Herein is disclosed a wish for identification with the guide; with myself, that is to say. Here we have " transference on to the analyst " in an extreme form. Of course the guide, in this case, greatly transcends my own personality. Ruth is sublimating the idea of the guide into a religious aspiration (we shall note a similar phenomenon in the subject Stella), and the transference wishes to sublimate itself into a sort of mystical union.

3. George

Mental Aberrations in an Epileptic.

Epilepsy began in George at the age of fifteen, taking the form of sudden and brief lapses of consciousness, and of a few convulsive seizures. He is now twenty-two. He has been treated in various ways, with bromides, with a proprietary preparation known as sédobrol, and by homeœpathy. Speaking generally, there has been an increase in the frequency of the attacks. He now has several attacks of minor epilepsy every week as well as convulsive seizures almost daily. The diagnosis of genuine epilepsy has been made several times.

Since the age of nineteen, probably owing to the use of bromides, his memory has grown defective, and his intellectual processes are less rapid. This sluggishness of intellection has been especially marked since the treatment with sédobrol. George does not always grasp what is said to him; he finds it difficult to understand a jest; he does not notice a pun unless it is explained to him.

The first attack of mental aberration occurred when he was twenty-one years old. It lasted ten days, and took the form of religious mania.

I. George is convinced that his illness is a punishment sent by God for his sins. He remains calm and gentle.

Three months later he had a fresh attack of mental disorder, violent mania this time. He had to be put under restraint for ten days.

Two months later came a third access of mental alienation.

> II. George is convinced that he has just undergone a transformation, that he has passed from youth to manhood. He asks his father when the latter underwent a similar change, and whether all young men suffer from it. He says that it is frightful. He is irritable and easily grows angry with his mother.

Another attack occurred about six weeks later.

> III. Once more there was religious mania complicated by sexual disquietudes. George thought that in the first days of the life of mankind, man and woman constituted a single being. They wanted to separate, and disobeyed God, who punished them. Woman is a perpetual temptation for man; man is rendered unhappy by his vices, and especially because he is always wanting to satisfy his desire for women.[1]—George read the book of Genesis, and underlined all the passages containing sexual allusions.

This attack of alienation lasted twelve days. At the end, George told his mother all he had done and felt, adding: "I've been balmy." The attacks of mental disorder became more frequent, and another access of mania began a month later. Just before this period of disorder George had heard a lecture upon the need that young men should be scrupulously pure in body and mind, and he had been greatly impressed by it. For a week, nothing happened, and then the new aberration appeared in a violent form.

> IV. George heard voices ordering him to sacrifice himself to save the wicked and perverse human race and to put an end to the war. He was the representative of Christ in the twentieth century; for a moment he was even Christ himself. To obey the voices he must, in a public place, make a declaration which would be revealed to him. In fact, one Sunday afternoon, when he and his father were out walking on one of the quays in the centre of the town, George climbed on the parapet and began: "My brethren," . . .

His father was able to lead him away, for George made no resistance except in words. After supper he went for

[1] George declared in his normal condition that he had had strong sexual desire, but had always resisted it.

another walk with his father and discussed the matter. He spoke of having opposed the voice; he knew that his parents would be annoyed by his action, and that everyone would regard him as a lunatic. He seemed to speak quite rationally and added that if something remarkable should happen in the world, this would be a sign that he had been right; if nothing should happen, it would show that he had been out of his mind.

> During the same period, he frequently said that he must resist temptation, must reform his conduct [which did not need reform], must take Jesus as his model.

It was during this attack of mental disorder that I first saw George.

It would be beyond the scope of the present work to study such a case as this in its entirety. Besides, I was not able to follow up the case for more than two months. From the general point of view, I shall merely note that during these two months, when psychoanalysis and suggestion were being practised, there was no attack of mental disorder. Furthermore, and this is very interesting, the intervals between the attacks of minor epilepsy became considerably greater (eleven days), and the convulsive seizures were much less frequent, for they no longer occurred every day. I do not know how far these results were durable, for I was unable to keep the patient under observation.

But George's epilepsy is not the topic of this study. My purpose merely is to show what psychoanalysis can teach us concerning mental aberrations. As regards the relationship between these aberrations and epilepsy, the attitude of Dr. Mercier is extremely judicious. He writes: "Closely as epilepsy and insanity are often associated, it is no more justifiable to regard the epilepsy as the cause of the insanity, than to regard the insanity as the cause of the epilepsy in those numerous cases in which epileptic convulsions occur in the final stages of insanity. All that we are justified in saying is that insanity and epilepsy are very closely associated."[1] This much is certain, that although the epileptic condition obviously determines the mental troubles, the content of

[1] Mercier, A Textbook of Insanity, 1914, pp. 271–2.

these is the outcome of psychological causation, is dependent upon complexes. This is proved by the possibility of a psychoanalysis in such cases.

At the first glance we can detect a certain uniformity in the various attacks of mental disorder. The patient's father, commenting upon them, arrived at a sound conclusion. He said:

> To sum up, it is plain that in each attack he has had fixed ideas of a religious category and of a sexual category, and that the former have been the sequel of the latter much as retribution follows sin.

What was the "sin" in this case? The analysis of a first dream at once conducted us by associations to "playmates" and to a "summer-house in a garden behind the house." This summer-house is the place where the bicycles are kept. It was here that some of his playmates initiated George into masturbation, which he subsequently practised. Here is the "sin" which he cannot forget, which weighs so heavily on his conscience, and which he believes to be the unmentionable cause of his illness. Apropos of the summer-house, he added:

> V. With his playmates he dug quarries near the summer-house; there they buried things and dug them up later.

This brings us to the ordinary fantasies of introversion: an object which has been buried, "repressed," and which has to be dug up again. The image of the summer-house is the link between the introversion and the autoerotic act.

Some of the associations to the same dream suggest a condensation of George's bicycle with the membrum virile.

The existence of this condensation is confirmed in the following:

> VI. I am on a huge rock; *I am holding my bicycle in my hand*; Father is beside me; we want to take the road which is in front of us. Father says: "We must go round and get down by the slope."—I want to jump down, first I throw down my bicycle, and when I do so I see it break up into fragments.

This dream gives expression to George's fixed idea of "sin," the sin we know; and of the catastrophe which the subject believes to have been its consequence.

The association to "rock" is the stones "in the garden behind the house." To the word "jump" came the same association. We already know what there is in the garden behind the house, namely the summer-house. "The road which is in front of us" symbolises masturbation. The error here is disobedience to the father. But it is more than disobedience; it is "repudiation of the father," or repudiation of virility, such as we ordinarily encounter in introverts.

The refusal of virility is clearly expressed in II and III. In III, we have a fantasy of the return to the infantile state which preceded "sin," the state in which "man and woman constituted a single being." Sin is contemporaneous with the appearance of sexuality. In II, the transition to the state of manhood is regarded as something "frightful." Nevertheless, the absence of virility is a lack, and the subject wishes to fulfil himself. This desire finds expression in the following dream.

> VII. I am on the Promenade Saint Antoine where there are a great many trees. There are many boys there, coming out of school. I see my grandfather, who is wearing a tall hat. I want to pass him unnoticed, but he has seen me and calls me. We walk on together, and we find on the ground a picture showing the heads of the seven federal councillors, and a picture of the leaders of the Swiss army.

Questioning George, I learned that the grandfather had died after the onset of the epilepsy. He was no longer "quite all there" (like George). In the dream he makes himself complete by wearing "a tall hat." Everything in this dream symbolises the reconquest of virility. The pictures discovered on the ground represent leaders (the father); they are pictures which were actually bought by George one evening when, in a transient fit of mental alienation, he had groundlessly telegraphed to his brother, who was abroad: "Return immediately." As we have seen in other individuals of the same type as George,[1] the brother, like the father, symbolises the virility which the subject feels himself to be lacking in. It is to this virility that George launches the appeal: "Return immediately." Asked for associations to "leaders of the

[1] Otto, Alexander, and Roger.

army," George said: "My brother is on military service; I have never done mine."[1]

It is possible that the attitude of the subconscious towards the "father" explains George's strange action in IV, when he climbed on to a parapet overlooking the water in order to deliver his testimony. Here is a relevant reminiscence of travel.

> VIII. At Altorf.—We stopped to admire the statue of William Tell. What a splendid head; how it breathes determination and courage! A true Swiss, the man whom this statue represents. And his fine little boy, how boundless the confidence in his attitude, in the pretty face turned towards his father.
>
> My brother N. *climbed on to one of the fountains* and photographed us standing at the foot of the monument.

We note with interest how climbing on to a parapet beside the water is related with such images. William Tell is preeminent among heroes who refuse, and who strike down the "leader"—the motif of so many traditions. Such traditions owe much of their influence to the fact that they invariably arouse as an echo in the mind the subconscious drama of the child and the father. William Tell's son, in turn, represents another aspect of the same drama. He "turns towards his father" with "boundless confidence." With the same boundless confidence, George, impersonating Christ in the parapet episode, turns towards his divine Father. We may suspect in all this, vague relationships which it would be presumptuous to specify with more precision, but they remind us of a verse by Victor Hugo in the *Mariage de Roland*:

"L'enfant songe à son père et se tourne vers Dieu."[2]

We can now discern that the war which, in his mental alienation, George wishes to bring to an end, must be, before all, the subconscious war of the son against the "father." In like manner the "sin" has been a disobedience to the "father," and sin must now be atoned for.

However much the details may vary in these last episodes, in essence they confirm our interpretation. We find in George's

[1] Cf. similar associations in Alfred, infra.

[2] The child thinks of its father and turns towards God.—Cf. Vodoz, Roland, un symbole, Paris, 1920; and Bovet, Le sentiment filial et la religion, 1920.

aberrations unmistakable expressions of the complexes we have discovered in other introverts: homosexual fantasies; protest against the father; repression of virility. Even though the mental disorder may be primarily dependent upon a physiological state which has nothing to do with the complexes, it is upon the complexes that the specific aspect of the mental disorder depends.

CHAPTER ELEVEN

SUBLIMATIONS

SUBLIMATION is a comprehensive term, denoting every kind of successful derivation of instinctive energy towards ends possessing spiritual or moral value. Sometimes we speak of the sublimation of an instinct, and sometimes of the sublimation of a nervous disorder or of a symptom. At first, the latter use of the term may seem somewhat obscure, but it offers no difficulty to those who understand the bearing of what has just been said concerning "derivation." When we say that an instinct is sublimated, we mean that a new and better channel has been opened for the current of instinct. When we say the same thing of a nervous disorder, we must recall that this disorder is itself a derivative, an undesirable derivative, of thwarted instinctive energy. To sublimate this trouble is to substitute a desirable derivative for an undesirable one.

In the first two cases, those of Alfred and Ida, we are concerned with typical sublimations of certain disorders. Nature has not waited for psychoanalysts to discover this means of salvation. The respective sublimations in Alfred and Ida are arising spontaneously. So much the better; the analyst must study these germinal sublimations. He will do better to guide them where they exist, rather than to attempt the imposition of some arbitrary sublimation which might not be conformable to the subject's disposition. For Alfred, the choice would appear to be between his neurosis and music. Ida sublimates into drawing, troubles of a sexual origin. In both cases I am content to guide, to encourage.

Crises occur during the process of sublimation. It may be threatened by the assaults of crude instinct; it may vacillate between different paths, so that a state of conflict ensues. In the case of Gerard (studied in Chapter Six), sublimation was exposed to both these difficulties. A struggle between sublimation and crude instinct is common in adolescents. In these cases the subject feels that his sublimation is imperilled, and keen distress is thereby aroused. Such is the case of Adam. A conflict arising from vacillation between two ends is manifest in Jeanne, who is simultaneously attracted by art and by moral and social activities. The position is complicated in her case because all the active forces of her being are in search of a new path. She is stirred, not only by the sexual instinct and the associated feelings, but also by the maternal instinct, which has no object to lavish itself on. In the case of Queenie, the æsthetic tendency does not alone suffice, and part of the subject's energies are devoted to moral and religious feeling.

It is in the guidance of sublimation that the analyst does the finest work and incurs the greatest responsibility. It is in this field that he becomes a veritable educationist and a spiritual director.

1. Alfred

STAMMERING. MALADAPTATION TO SOCIAL LIFE. A TASTE FOR MUSIC.

Alfred has stammered, so he believes, since he was two or three years old. When he came to consult me he was twenty-two. He spoke in a rambling fashion, hardly giving me a chance to get in a word edgewise, and answering my questions irrelevantly. His movements were awkward. There was an evident maladaptation to social life.

The family history was bad. There were several neuropaths in the family, and a sister was under restraint.

He was a bank clerk. He said that his stammer was most troublesome when he was at work.

During the analysis, several of Alfred's dreams related to the sister who is in the asylum. There are many indications that his sister symbolises himself, that his sister's mental condition is identified in his mind with his own. In the first dreams, the sister's case is hopeless. A little later, it appears that she will get well in time, but that "the cure will be a lengthy affair." Alfred's concern regarding his future also finds expression in the dreams. He does not like his work at the bank, and wonders "what he will do later." In the depths, this question seems to be at one with the problem of his cure. He dreamed on one occasion of another bank clerk who had been his fellow worker for four years, and who symbolised himself. In the dream, this companion spoke of throwing up his job. After the dream, Alfred remarked: "I stammer more when I am doing anything which bores me." But if the bank does not suit him, whither do his thoughts turn, and what is the "future" on which his mind dwells?

Another series of dreams throws light on this matter. Here is the first of the series.

> I. Last night I had a lovely dream. It was about music. I found myself in front of a shop where a number of music scores were exposed in the window. I felt happy, as if I were going to buy one of them, the one which seemed to me most beautiful in melody and in feeling.

In another dream he was playing at railways as he used to when a child, but he had not much time for he was going to the theatre that evening.

When analysing these dreams I learned that this simple bank clerk had a great love for music. All his leisure time was given to music. Not only could he sing without stammering, but he did not stammer *when he was talking about music.* "Railway" produced as association the reminiscence of a German tour, of a visit to German cities and to concerts where Alfred had received his strongest musical impressions. Moreover, the German tour and the thoughts concerning a future career were associated with the thought of an uncle, who occupied a good position in Germany. This uncle had shown an interest in Alfred, and perhaps would show more.

Another motif in Alfred's dreams gave expression to the wish for a vigorous, wholesome, and manly life, one that should be unconstrained, the very opposite to the life of constraint and maladaptation to society which the subject was now leading.

> II. I had a swimming lesson at the baths, but I could not learn to swim. The swimming master was the man who had been gymnastic master at school.

Discussing this dream, he said: "I suppose I was learning to swim in order to get strong." Asked for associations to "gymnastic master," he thought of the gymnastic class, and of his schoolmates, with whom he compared himself to his own disadvantage.

In the next dream, this motif becomes fused with that of music.

> III. I had another dream about music. I was singing something from an operetta to a number of persons in a courtyard; I was dressed as a soldier in uniform. The audience was much moved.

The associations to "soldier" were similar to those to "swimming master" in the former dream. Alfred thinks that it was because of his stammer that he was regarded as unfit for military service. In the dream he is a soldier, so he is cured. He has attained to virility and self-assurance; but at the same time he devotes himself to music.

The family history led me to suppose that a constitutional condition must underlie the subject's nervous disorder. Nevertheless, the close connection in the dreams between the idea of music and the idea of cure, and the positive fact that when Alfred was thinking of music he ceased to stammer, were strong indications that music might have a definite therapeutic value. Everything happened as if a nervous excitability, partly constitutional and partly acquired, had to find an outlet in one of two alternative paths, the neurosis or the æsthetic sublimation.

His work as bank clerk, which was an obstacle to the æsthetic culture he longed for, aggravated his stammer. I had to make him understand that this defensive reaction was an inauspicious means of defence; that, far from facilitating the development he longed for, it could only hinder that development.

Autosuggestion and breathing exercises were practised concurrently with the analysis. I also encouraged the musical trend, while avoiding any implication that the subject had a musical career before him.

After a month, a considerable improvement could be noted, both in respect of the awkwardness and of the stammer. At the bank, indeed, when in the presence of his chief, Alfred stammered as of old. There was doubtless at work here, in addition to the protest against his occupation, an infantile fear of the father, which had undergone a transference on to the chief. But I was unable to continue the analysis, for the subject had to leave Geneva.

2. Ida

Sexual Shock at Puberty. Maniacal Disturbances. Æsthetic Sublimation.

Ida belongs to a family endowed with artistic sensibilities. Her brother has produced some striking specimens of automatic writing and of subconscious painting. She is sixteen years old. Her development was precocious, and she began to menstruate before she was twelve. Not very long after this period, she had a nervous shock. One evening, when it was already growing dark, she was on the rear platform of a tramcar, alone except for one other passenger, who took advantage of the situation to practise exhibitionism and to make significant gestures. She did not understand what he meant, but the incident made a deep impression on her mind.

Since then, at the menstrual periods, she has been subject to mental and nervous crises. Each crisis lasts several days, and is often quite alarming. The disturbance may take the form either of excessive cheerfulness or of melancholy; in addition it is apt to manifest itself in one of the two following ways:

1. Sometimes the girl devotes herself to *arranging various objects*, such as plants, dolls' clothing, etc., with meticulous care. One evening she actually went to sleep with the conviction that she had not finished this work of arrangement, and that it was essential to rise very early next morning in order to prepare for the proper reception of visitors (who were quite imaginary). The ostensibly futile activity she displays at such times is strangely disproportionate to the end in view and to the results secured.

2. Sometimes the crisis takes the form of *phobias, hallucinations*, and *maniacal speeches*. These are all dominated

by ideas of persecution. Incessantly there recurs in them the vision of a magician who has put an evil spell upon Ida, a spell which she believes she is unable to throw off.

The second group of symptoms was readily comprehensible. Manifestly the shock had induced a state of alarm, more or less subconscious, and connected with sexual matters.

I considered that the first group of symptoms required careful study. It is this study which I shall now describe.

Ida did not take kindly to the analysis of her dreams, but I was able to study the arrangements of various objects which became such a passion for her during the successive crises.

First of all I asked her parents whether she paid much attention to her dress. I received the answer I expected. Ida detests anything in the nature of coquetry, any special care for her attire, anything which she calls "smart." On the other hand, she has innumerable dolls, and she dresses these with all the care which she withholds from her own attiring.

The mechanisms of repression and substitution were manifest. To the *alarm* symbolised by the crises which took the form of ideas of persecution and of phobias, there was superadded a sense of *disgust,* likewise induced by the shock, and symbolised by the other crises.

Disgust for sexual matters was transmuted into a disgust for coquetry; while *coquetry was objectified,* dolls being substituted for her own person. This coquetry was even extended to all kinds of arrangements of objects.

I subsequently learned that Ida was fond of drawing, painting, decorative work, etc., and that she had quite a talent for this sort of employment. Above all, she had a fancy for drawing stylate plants. In this occupation, presumably, there was an extension of the same objectification.

I examined her work. All the stylate plants were so arranged as to represent, with the persistency of a fixed idea, two symmetrical motifs separated by a central, elongated motif (the male organs).

The other drawings and paintings were nearly all representations of landscape; in nine out of ten of these landscapes, trees played the dominant role. There was a preference in favour of fir trees; the shapes were conical and elongated, and the verdure recalled that of pines or of ferns. The first landscape represented a solitary pine. In the others the stress was always on a tree which occupied an excessively prominent position in the picture, standing right in the foreground. I had not commented on this when the young artist said to me: "I can draw anything I like quite well, *except trees.* I find them so difficult; *they don't come easily.*"

A tree, with its foliage and its conical form, was obviously a sexual symbol, and it is a familiar fact that it plays this part in dreams. To the subject it symbolised the repressed vision, and that is why the tree "did not come easily."

Next I examined the dolls. The older ones represented ladies in huge hats, and wearing enormously large dresses, like crinolines. The later ones were more interesting; women and men (more of the latter) wearing sugar-loaf hats. The conical form which was so notable in the trees of the landscapes, turned up here with the same fixity. In the most recent doll, the head had been entirely replaced by a cone; and this cone, instead of sticking up like a hat, curved forwards into a point. Two huge spheres represented the eyes, from which there projected a curled feather like a tuft of hair. Another tuft grew from the forehead, forming a kind of central eyebrow.

As for the dolls wearing pointed hats, Ida called them "magicians." Thus all these creations were linked with the "magician" who appeared in the maniacal crises. Aposteriori, therefore, we obtained a verification of the kinship of the two kinds of crisis.

The crises of objectified coquetry thus seemed to be in search of a cure by means of a spontaneous æsthetic sublimation. The juxtaposition of the magician of the maniacal attacks with the doll magician might even lead us to suppose that this particular sublimation was tending to become an outlet for both kinds of crisis. Such an objectification of coquetry, which loses all its sexual and interested significance when displaced from the person on to things, is unquestionably a phenomenon which must not be overlooked when we are attempting to explain the ultimate genesis of the plastic arts. As for the transformation of the alarming into the beautiful (seen here in the magician), is not this, in miniature, what Nietzsche considers to be the "origin of tragedy." It might even be interesting to trace, in this effort towards the sublimation of the two kinds of crisis (dionysiac crises of mania and apollinian crises of dressing up), an epitomised version of the duplex genesis of art as conceived by Nietzsche, that amazing forerunner of psychoanalytical ideas. However this may be, such subconscious initiations of æsthetic trends in individual minds can certainly help us to a better understanding of the origin and function of art in the life of mankind.

In Ida's case, art seems to have been her salvation. I advised her parents to encourage and guide the spontaneous sublimation, although I hardly expected that this would suffice. I saw Ida again six months later. She had been resolutely and exclusively influenced in the direction of her art, and had shown that she possessed real talent. Her mental troubles had vanished. Her bodily development, which had been for some time arrested, had now taken such a stride that I hardly recognised her.

3. Adam

SUBLIMATION IN DANGER.

The phenomenon I am now about to describe is far from rare, but I cannot deny myself the pleasure of recording a dream in which this phenomenon is expressed by a peculiarly apt symbol. It relates to the feeling that a sublimation (the religious sublimation in this case) is imperilled by the urge of the crude instinct upon which the sublimation is based. We have already encountered the phenomenon in the analysis of one of our adolescent subjects, Gerard. For practical purposes we are dealing with the old conflict between the "spirit" and the "flesh" under one of its most distressing aspects.

There is no occasion to give a detailed analysis. Suffice it to note a few of the traits which will convey a sketch of the individuality with which we are concerned.

Adam complains of deficient mental concentration, and of difficulties in the sphere of action, of a lack of amiability. He finds it very difficult to argue, even in defence of ideas to which he is devoted. Maladaptation to social life, introversion, are obvious. Aged twenty-seven, he has had no experience of sexual intercourse. A divinity student, he is one of those men in whom moral elevation is tinged with austerity. He is aware of this austerity, regards it as a fault, and would like to correct it. The analysis will help him to do so.

Here are some free associations, by which is meant associations that do not have as their starting point a dream or a reminiscence, but such as arise when isolated words are uttered. These associations, which were noted at Adam's first sitting, immediately disclosed certain cardinal points.

> I. The subject thinks of a " statue of Justice " on a fountain in Berne; the eyes of the figure of Justice are bandaged. This image is associated with a memory of " the Bear Pit."

Asked for associations to " eyes bandaged," the subject recalls a scene from childhood. His brother and he, before going to sleep, used to amuse themselves by jumping from bed to bed; one evening the brother fell and cut his forehead. " Change of beds " called up the wish to leave home, " to be no longer dependent on my father." To the words " cut his forehead " came the memory of another romp when he had wounded himself in like fashion " trying to hide." In another association, he remembered how a bee had stung him on the eyelid. " They tied up my eye." Now, " bandaged eye " which had thus appeared for the second time, gave fresh associations. He has eye trouble; an oculist whom he consulted thought it might be due to masturbation. The words " hide oneself," which had originally appeared on the scene in connection with the cut forehead, called up " the shamefulness of masturbation."

To the word " mother," Adam answered that he had been very fond of his mother, and that up to the age of ten he had told her everything. To the word " father," he said: " Disagreeable memories." He added that his father was " despotic " towards wife and family: " We were all afraid of him."

> II. A hazy sort of place, where he seems to have been. It was a nine days' journey.—Now the image had cleared up. He recognised the place. There was a little inn with only one bed. The sheets had not been changed; a couple had slept there before him and had " made a mess.'

Subsequently, during the analysis of a dream, Adam produced some remarkable associations apropos of a " ravine." They supplement and confirm the following:

The nine days' journey brought us to the nine months of pregnancy, and the " hazy sort of place where he seems to have been " corresponded to a fantasy of the return to the mother's womb. This new expression of fixation on the mother was linked with a disgust for sexuality, which appeared to be related with impressions received in childhood concerning acts of sexual intercourse by his parents.

It would be superfluous to give further details of this kind. We have enough to disclose the psychological type of the subject with whom we are dealing. There is a well-marked Oedipus complex. Sexuality has been repressed, but a strong feeling of remorse attends the memory of certain sins of adolescence, which the subject considers to be the cause of his extant inferiority. He regards the latter as a just punishment for sin, and this to him is the significance of the symbol of Justice " with bandaged eyes." It is just that he should have " eye troubles."

Let us pass on to the dream which is especially worthy of attention. This is a nightmare dating from adolescence, and which at that epoch Adam was wont to have every night.

> III. He is climbing a mountain. In front of him is a rock. He wishes to turn back. Behind him he sees a bear. He throws his arms round the bear and drags the animal towards a precipice; he and the bear fall over together, and he awakes.

The " mountain " always calls up in his mind " the ascent towards the ideal." The " rock " makes him think of three blocks which were found in the earth when the foundations of a church were being dug. Quite apart from what we have learned from analysis in other subjects, the associations to the dreams of this particular subject lead us to suppose that the " three blocks " symbolise the genital organs. The idea is strikingly confirmed when, speaking of the three blocks, the subject says:

> These stones [they had been disinterred when he was seventeen years old] were exhibited. " It was a pity " that they were exhibited without any explanation.

A moment later, and not in any conscious relationship to what had gone before, he went on:

> " It was a pity " that I was not told anything about sexual matters.

As for the " bear," this calls up the " Bear Pit " at Berne. We already know that this Bear Pit is in its turn associated with " Justice with bandaged eyes." But we do not need to draw inferences; the subject does this for himself, and without even passing by way of the figure of " Justice with bandaged eyes." The struggle with the bear calls up without transition, though he does not know wherefore, " the struggle with masturbation."

Thus the interpretation of the dream is quite simple. As he is on his way up the mountain, the subject encounters an obstacle (the rock), sexuality; wishing to avoid this he rediscovers it in another form (the bear), masturbation. Struggling with the bear, he falls into the abyss. This nightmare, which dates from the period of his preparation for the religious life, expresses the anguish of sin, the dread of having his upward progress arrested, the fear of ruining the incipient sublimation. The symbolism grows still more striking when we consider the " three blocks." The church which is to be built must have its foundations in the ground where the three blocks are; but the blocks are in the way of the foundations. Could there be a better expression of the view that the budding sublimation (the church in course of construction) is rooted in the very soil where the crude instinct was slumbering, and that this is why the instinct is so dangerous to the sublimation?

4. Jeanne

Non-Acceptance of Marriage. Thwarted Maternal Instinct. Vacillating Sublimation.

Jeanne belongs to a type we are familiar with. We have seen it in embryo in the little girls Linette and Mireille; in a fully developed form, in the young woman Kitty; and in a pathological variant, in Renée, a woman in her prime. Jeanne exhibits fixation upon the mother, some degree of refusal of femininity, and a few virile character traits.

It would seem that in her case the negative aspect of the complex is more conspicuous than the positive. Infantile hostility towards the father is more marked than fixation upon the mother. When she was a child, she thought her father " ugly." She was " afraid of his eyes." At the age of eight she admired him, for he regarded her as clever. Subsequently, however, he was fond of saying that " there was no need for her to study, since she was only a woman." This aroused a spirit of revolt. Afterwards she was educated by her mother, away from the father. Her mother read Victor Hugo to her, and awakened in her a taste for art. The father cared only for his son, and, quite under the influence of the ancient prejudice, made an exclusive favourite of this heir of his name. Jeanne made common cause with her mother, and took up the cudgels on behalf of her sister against her father and her brother. Predisposed by this attitude, she then adopted feminist views.

She herself declared that in her most instinctive and " primitive " nature there was " something masculine, something combative, something pugnacious." Though married, she has never really accepted marriage. She says she consented to be married as a refuge, from " dread of life " from fear that she might have a love affair of which her parents would disapprove. At the very time when she was about to marry, she said : " I would much rather marry a woman than a man."

The marriage was unhappy. At the date of the analysis, Jeanne was thirty-one. She had been divorced for a year. During her marriage she suffered both physically and morally. About seven years ago she had begun to have a nightmare, which had frequently recurred.

I. She had lost her wedding-ring. She awoke with a start.

As is often the case, the symbol of losing the wedding-ring already implied the desire for a rupture of relations ; however, in the earlier days of this nightmare, Jeanne used to find the lost ring. Later there was a modification in the dream, for she did not succeed in finding the lost ring. Towards the close of her life with her husband, she suffered for a time from syphilophobia, having a fixed idea that she had been infected by the husband. Happily this was no more than a delusion, and the conviction that she had been mistaken mitigated, though it did not entirely relieve, the jarring of the nerves which had been caused by the disputes and miseries of the last years of her wedded life.

Here are some reminiscences of childhood which will enable us to understand Jeanne's personality.

> II. Jeanne was not yet three years old. She had run away from home on an exploring expedition, carrying a stick. She went down to the sea shore, and then she did not know where else to go. It was there that she was found.

"Running away" called up in Jeanne's mind "to get free." Asked for an association to the word "home," she said that that day she "had run away from her mother," and that subsequently she had wanted to "free herself from the spell of her mother." The mother, "though gentle and affectionate, made me feel that my will was paralysed." Would it not have been more accurate to say, "*because* gentle and affectionate"? Here we have a case in which it is obvious that the subconscious *fixation* upon one of the parents must not be regarded as synonymous with *attachment* in the comprehensive sense of that term. A subject may suffer on account of such a fixation, may protest against it, and may wish to be free from it. Repulsed by the father, and eager to throw off the "mother's spell," Jeanne gained an insurgent and independent character. Asked for associations to "exploring," she said: "Inquisitive eagerness to know, to touch, and to see." It is the forbidden fruit; it is a positive effort to break away from the mother, an effort which reminds us of the cases of Linette and Mireille. The explorer with a stick in the hand had been seen by the child in the form of an Epinal plaster cast, and she wanted to imitate what she had seen. Henceforward she assumes a virile attitude. Life on the sea shore is for Jeanne a free life, instinctive, the life of the wild. To her the "instinctive" and the "wild" always connote the idea of "masculine."

"She did not know where else to go." She gave me details of her feeling in this respect. First of all she found it pleasant to stay by the sea; then she felt rather lost, for there was "no one to give me a hand." This brought us to her present derelict condition, to the lack of a guide after the disillusionment of marriage. Then came the associations, " cut " and " broken," which had already appeared several times apropos of her divorce.

This reminiscence, the earliest incident she can remember, is what anyone's earliest reminiscence is apt to be.[1] By condensation it has become a sketch of the subject's character, and an epitome of her history.

Here is another reminiscence, no less typical.

> III. An accident.—Jeanne was with a little boy who, like herself, was from five and a half to six years old. It was on the sea shore, and there was a tub full of water in which the two children were sailing boats. Jeanne fell into the tub. She remembered the story of a little girl who, having tumbled into the water, kicked off from the bottom in order to rise to the surface. She did the same; the little boy seized her, and called for help.

It is interesting to note how this reminiscence is in line with some of the dreams of Linette and Mireille, dreams of accidents, and especially of immersions: an accident following an attempt to get away from the mother, to touch the forbidden fruit, and especially at the close of a romp with some little boys (Linette, dream V; Mireille, dream III). The reminiscence is so remarkably persistent because of its connection with a frequent symbol.

But the fixity of the reminiscence is increased because of condensation with a recent " accident," that of marriage. One day Jeanne's mother had told the little boy that he would be Jeanne's husband. The little boy took the thing quite seriously, and made presents to Jeanne. She " detested him," but did not dare to say anything, believing her fate to be sealed. Here we have the same passivity as that which she was to exhibit later, when submitting to a marriage which inwardly she repudiated. The " tub " gave as associations " something dirty, " repugnance," a " dead animal." Putting all these things together, we see that underlying them is a disgust for sexuality. The kick-off from the bottom of the water calls up the words " anger " and " resistance."

[1] Cf. Bovet's analysis of Tolstoy's earliest memory and of the two earliest memories of L. Artus-Perrelet, in the preface to Artus-Perrelet, Le dessin au service de l'éducation.

Here we have the buoyancy of a nature fundamentally energetic, one familiar with revolt; we have a determination not to give in. The whole reminiscence is in conformity with Jeanne's present situation.

The closing words "called for help" were associated in Jeanne's mind with certain nightmares in which she had a sense of powerlessness and from which she "awoke screaming." Especially, she mentioned the following recent nightmare:

IV. She was in bed; someone approached with a knife. She was awakened by her own "screaming."

The associations showed plainly that the dream expressed the fear and disgust inspired by sexuality, and that these feelings were linked with the subject's hostility to the father. Here are the associations:

Knife. Dread of knives. Something cold. Cold water [compare this with the "tub" in III]. Tools, a saw, a plane. At sight of these tools, Jeanne felt as if they were being used on her.

Screaming. Sore throat, hoarseness. Ungovernable fits of passion in childhood when Jeanne had screamed at the top of her voice. Her father had wanted to make her eat an undercooked egg in which the white had not set; it was then she had screamed like this.

Undercooked egg in which the white had not set. Disgusting. Feeling sick. Nausea induced by misinterpretations of innocent feelings. Jeanne's sister had been passionately fond of a young aunt. Someone had regarded this fondness as a sign of perversion.

To everyone familiar with the practice of psychoanalysis, the sexual allusions in these associations are obvious. Indeed, they can hardly be overlooked even by those unfamiliar with the method. Comment is superfluous, but it may be useful to compare Jeanne's associations with some of those of Renée or of Mireille. More especially we should compare the disgust inspired by the imperfectly cooked white of egg which her father compels her to eat, with the disgust inspired in Renée by the father's expectoration (Renée, V). We are also reminded of the symbol "white of egg" in one of Mireille's dreams (Mireille, VIII).

The voice which grows "hoarse" (masculine) through screaming in anger against the father, and the concluding allusion to homosexuality, underline the fact that Jeanne's virile attitude is linked with protest against the father and against sexuality.

Here is a dream which gives us some precise details. May we say numerical details ? Anyhow it was of a strange form, and is worth noting on its own account.

> V. [Overnight, Jeanne had been reading a Pythagorean work on "Numbers."] She saw herself on the top of a hill. Her parents were represented by the figure 2 ; she herself, her sister, and her brother, by the figure 3. There were 10 boys and 12 girls arranged in order of height like Pan-pipes. Her father said something about lorgnettes—15 or 17.—She took one and saw a courtyard with a seething mass of a striped grey colour. There were 80 cats. She saw a scriptural town with a tower shaped like a truncated oval cone. On the tower were a dead elephant, a dead tiger, and a wounded white bear with which her father was fighting. Her father killed the bear and said they must get into the tower to shelter there from the cave-lion. . . . There were arabesques on the tower, bright blue and yellow "primary colours."—They took refuge in the tower ; in it there was a square hall where there was a wedding breakfast in progress ; the bride was like Jeanne's sister. She was listening through a microphone to her "fiancé" who was in the next room. In the middle there was a table with 32 children, all children up to 16. One child of 16 was complaining at not having been seated among the grown-ups, for it was bored. Everything was arranged in a graduated series like Pan-pipes, except for the cats, which were in a heap.

The tower and the wedding breakfast symbolise marriage. This interpretation was confirmed by a number of allusions and associations. We can understand, therefore, why the tower was "truncated." To this word came as associations "broken" and "smashed," which represent divorce. The cats were "a crowd of cats attracted by a she-cat." As for the wild beasts, these called up in Jeanne "the wild and masculine instincts" of her nature. Once more these instincts showed themselves to be engaged in a struggle with the father. The latter says that they must "take refuge" in the tower. We know that Jeanne agreed to marriage as a "refuge." But this marriage was never really accepted. That is why the bridegroom is degraded into a "fiancé," is sent into the "next room," and is listened to through the "microphone."

Jeanne recalls that the number "2," which in the dream represents her parents, signifies in "Pythagoras" "antagonism." She has always regarded "10" as beautiful and complete; 10 was her age when she made her first communion. The age of "12" is one of liberty, nature, instinctive life. There are "10 boys and 12 girls," because at the age of 10 she was still quite a child, sexless or rather boyish, but at the age of 12 she began to feel like a girl. There is the same contrast, but more sharply marked, between "15 and 17." This is a "critical age." The "lorgnettes" associated with these numbers, the lorgnettes given by the father, and used in order to look at the "mass of cats," are an obvious sexual allusion. At the age of 15, Jeanne was "like a boy." But the era of conflicts was beginning. As far as she can remember, 15 in "Pythagoras" is simultaneously "the Ascension" and the "spirit of evil." At the age of 16 she was sentimental, and passed through a neurasthenic phase (this is why, in the dream, the child of 16 is bored). At the age of 17 she "forced" herself to be cheerful. She began to live the life of a woman. At that age, making an effort to satisfy her mother, she became "superficial, worldly, and well-bred." She had "a loud, grating, forced laugh, which people commented on." By an auditory association, the number 15 called up the tinkling of a bell from a Christmas tree. She had had it when she was a child; had been very fond of it, and had been greatly distressed when it was broken. The tone of this bell, thus associated with memories of the fifteenth year, was deep, not loud, and it contrasted with the grating laugh of her seventeenth year. Her present age is "32." She thinks that between the ages of 17 and 32 her life was on the wrong track. But 32, in "Pythagoras," signifies "wisdom."

In fact, at the present time, she considers that she has pulled herself together, that she has become aware of her true instincts, is cultivating them by sublimation, and is thus attaining wisdom. She has artistic occupations, social and metaphysical aspirations. She is interested in theosophy; that is why she has been reading "Pythagoras."

Inasmuch as "the tower has been truncated," the aspiration towards human love has been repressed. Absorbed in new interests, Jeanne renounces all thought of the life of feeling. She says: "The feeling of love—I shouldn't know what to make of it now." Nevertheless, the repressed emotion delivers its assaults subconsciously; all the more vigorously, doubtless, because (as in Gerard's case) her mind is vacillating between alternative paths of sublimation.

One of her dreams gives a faithful picture of a nature-man who reenters by the window.

VI. A man [who in real life is on the point of being divorced] enters by the window wearing the uniform of a colonel in the Chasseurs d'Afrique. She recognises his apelike forehead.

The man in the case is obviously a substitute for the husband. "Enters by the window" calls up as an association "turn out through the door."

In a fantasy during the waking state there appears a "squeaking door." The associations are:

VII. *Door.* A door which is no longer of any use.
Squeaking. The revolt of the bodily nature against pain.

The following dream is extremely vivid:

VIII. A male being.—A courtyard, small trees, and a great shadow like that of a huge, unseen tree.

To the man vaguely present, Jeanne showed an oblong flower-stand filled with very dry sand, in which, however, some shoots of asparagus were sprouting. It also contained a little cutting from a tree, a cutting no thicker than the finger. She was amazed to see that this was sprouting. She had cut the plants down, believing that they were done with. She was astonished to find that this little cutting had such big roots. She planted it out again in a flower-pot which the male being handed her.

The scene recalled one with which she was acquainted in real life; the courtyard was raised upon a conical-shaped construction, truncated. This is akin to the tower of dream V. The shape of the oblong flower-stand likewise recalls the tower. This oblong shape, that of the egg and likewise that of the ovary, is not infrequent in such dreams. The cutting is the corresponding male symbol. [The word "tronçon," cutting, is kindred in sound and significance to "tronqué."] "Cutting" calls up "cut last year"—the year of the divorce. The flower-stand calls up "a commonplace affair, a flower-stand which Father gave to Mother, one with artificial flowers; I admired it, but at the same time I thought it stupid." Apropos of "very dry sand," she thought of "a marriage which was not able to become fruitful." Apropos of the plants which she had thought "done with," she said that of late she had been inclined "to think everything done with." This dream also aroused memories dating from her twelfth year, the period when Jeanne had "broken away from her father," and had risen against him "as every woman rises against every man." The dream contains a condensation of the old-time "breaking away" from the father with the recent divorce. It is the integral repression, both in its primal cause and in its immediate determinant. But the repressed instinct has not been annihilated. Jeanne explicitly repudiates this instinct, and "would not know what to make of the feeling of love." Nevertheless, the sprouting is a renascence. It would, of course, be a mistake to interpret this dream as sexual in the narrower sense of the term, though we might plausibly thus interpret dream VI. For dream VIII, a more widely conceived interpretation is requisite. In it we have a fantasy of fecundity, in conformity with the wishes Jeanne now feels to "make her life fruitful" with fecund activities. "She had thought everything was done with," and she is being reborn into life. She gladly accepts the idea to which the analysis is leading us, that, instead of trying to ignore her instincts, she must become fully conscious of them, so as to establish thereon a sublimation which shall not be founded upon repressions or built over a volcano.

The idea of *fecundity* leads us to another instinct, thwarted if not repressed—the maternal instinct. This also is in search of a happy derivation, a spiritualisation. The literary and artistic works in which Jeanne seeks self-expression manifest the fact clearly. The motif of the mother and child is preponderant. In one of her imaginative writings, she says that she presses her art to her bosom as a mother presses her child.

Moreover, Jeanne's "masculine" trends have not been repudiated. Will they undergo sublimation in the choice of an artistic career of a kind usually reserved for men?

Such a choice would, indeed, be an effective protest against a father who said that study was needless for a woman. Or shall we find a more active type of sublimation—perhaps social work of a feminist character? In these respects we discern a conflict, or at any rate a vacillation, which is disclosed in the following dream.

> IX. Jeanne is in an underground passage. . . . Above is a flooring surmounted by rooms. She suddenly remembers that in one of these upper rooms a woman is imprisoned, a prostitute, a spy, and a thief, sentenced to be shot. Jeanne recalls having seen her at the trial, having noted her impassioned expression and her pale face. Jeanne said to herself: "It is not the woman whom I wish to save, but her mind, so that she may learn the value of her suffering and her life." Jeanne wanted to bribe the warder and the general. She got permission to enter the woman's room to make a portrait of her, but was not allowed to talk to her. Suddenly Jeanne realised that this woman was feeling sympathetic towards her. When Jeanne was leaving the cell, the woman silently slipped an emerald ring on to the visitor's finger. Then the woman tried to sell her some jewels; she talked superficially, and Jeanne said to herself: "All the same, there's a lot of good in her."—Blows on the flooring were now heard. Jeanne knew it was a bust being broken. Half awake, she said to herself: "*Someone* has discovered that I have a duty towards women, and *someone* has broken this bust." *Someone,* in her thought, was an occult force.

The "underground passage" recalled to Jeanne reminiscences of her ninth year, reminiscences of her "explorations" in dark corners. The imprisoned woman has many traits which show that she symbolises Jeanne herself. The "general" and the futilities about the jewels and the words of the prisoner, are linked with reminiscences of Jeanne's seventeenth year (see commentary on dream V), and of the worldly and superficial life which Jeanne found so repugnant. On the other hand, the imprisoned woman is also *woman in general,* under the conditions of slavery and futility imposed by society. By working to set woman free, Jeanne will set herself free; that is to say, she will provide a pleasant and useful outlet for her tendencies towards virility (exploration) and towards protest against the father (the general). The fact that in the dream she is forbidden to talk to the woman, recalls the difficulty which she finds, in real life, in getting into touch with others, the difficulty whereby her social impulses are paralysed. She cannot openly acknowledge in the dream that she wants to set the woman free, so she pretends that she wants to draw the woman's portrait. Then, she cannot talk to the prisoner, so is satisfied with making a picture of her. Here are two different ways of expressing the same fact, that art has been for Jeanne a surreptitious method of realising a tendency to which she could not or dared not give direct expression. The "bust," at the close of the dream, is likewise linked to Jeanne's artistic work. "Someone" breaks the bust because Jeanne has a duty towards women. This signifies that art, or at any rate art for art's sake, does not entirely satisfy her, for fundamentally she is under the influence of the call of social duty.

But the conflict lying at the root of the trouble appears in all its complexity in the following dream, which is full of apt symbols.

X. She is in a great park, damp and gloomy, "at this season of the year" (autumn). There is a century-old house, in the French style, consisting of a ground floor, and an attic occupying one side only of the roof. Jeanne is far away. She knew that the house was occupied by a woman married to the owner of an ironworks, like the hero of Georges Ohnet's book, *The Ironmaster*. The woman knew her duty but did not love her husband. At night, clad in a close-fitting garment, she left the house by the window. She strolled in the park, along an alley like the arms of a cross. She leaned her elbows on a ledge, and looked down over a luminous lowland. Just below she saw a pathway which brought back memories of the days when she was betrothed. She says to herself: "I have three windows." She turns and perceives that someone is looking at her from within. It is her husband's secretary. She loses her self-possession, for she feels that she has forfeited her good name. She goes up to the attic and throws herself from the window. There is a sound of broken glass; the artery in her left wrist is cut.

Next, Jeanne sees a pastrycook's where cakes are displayed upon dirty shelves. A crowd. Jeanne approaches the injured woman. The husband is there; he is a doctor. The artery cannot be tied, the woman is mad. She wants to rise. Her husband says: "It doesn't matter, seeing that she's lost."

Next Jeanne is taking a walk with two children. She goes with them into a wood. They gather cyclamens. . . . Again she is in the house. Jeanne herself is the invalid. Someone says: "You no longer treat this from the chest, but from the back." They place a mustard plaster on Jeanne's back and her reason is restored.

The words "at this season of the year" doubtless serve to emphasise the fact that the dream relates to the present state of Jeanne's crisis, whereas "century-old house" reminds us that the root-causes of the crisis date back many years. The park recalls the nineteenth year of Jeanne's age, when she underwent a change of personality; it recalls the tentative efforts at poetical expression which she made of that time. The house calls up a country mansion Jeanne had seen that year; it is "a deep, sincere life" in revolt against "the superficial life" which she had tried to impose upon herself. The references to her husband need no comment. The "deep, sincere" life which rebels, is the life which, even to-day, seeks an outlet, a "window," in order that it may become a reality. The "three windows" evoke very precise associations. These windows symbolise certain appropriate exits from the crisis. There were "two artificial windows and one natural window in the forest." The "natural window" symbolises a way out by yielding to brute instinct; the two "artificial windows" appear to be the two sublimations æsthetic and social—between which Jeanne is vacillating. The symbol of the "two children" stresses the social outlet, an outlet which the maternal instinct is also seeking. The dream children call up by association "poor children," studies which Jeanne would like to have undertaken in the past and which she hopes to undertake now in order to help children by means of educational work. The pastrycook's is once more the repulsive aspect of the sexual instinct (cakes on dirty shelves). "Loses self-possession," "cut," "mad"—all refer to the present crisis, more especially in reference to the nervous disorders which it is our endeavour to cure. The final detail—the comparison of the two treatments—is one of the most delightful. The treatment "by the chest" calls up the following associations: "reduced the inflammation of the chest, treat with kindness"; the treatment "by the back" calls up "energy." The significance of the two "treatments" is soon made clear. As usual, I was treating the subject concurrently by suggestion and psychoanalysis. While practising the latter, I faced the subject;

for the practice of the former I stood behind her. During the analysis the subject unburdens her heart, reduces the inflammation of the chest; this is treating with kindness. Suggestion is more energetic. Jeanne's subconscious informs us that the main task of the analysis has been accomplished; it is now necessary to lay stress upon suggestion. Relieved of the burden of the past, Jeanne demands that she herself shall be given the strength to guide her own destinies in the future. To Jeanne, whose main difficulty now lay in her vacillation between the two sublimations, this firmness of purpose seemed far more important than the indefinite prolongation of the analysis.

5. Queenie

FIXATION UPON THE FATHER. ÆSTHETIC AND RELIGIOUS SUBLIMATION.

Queenie was well aware of her attachment to her father. Her attachment to him was intensified when he married again. This marriage took place when Queenie was three years old. The step-mother was unkind to the little girl. (Queenie was nine months old when her mother died.) Her youth was dominated by two feelings: attachment to the father; protest against the step-mother. Certain actions which had entailed great sacrifices had been undertaken for one reason only: to give pleasure to her father; to fulfil the wishes of the father.

Two, almost identical, memories of childhood, which Queenie told me at the same sitting, give eloquent expression to these two fundamental feelings. In addition, the two memories show that around these feelings, other analogous feelings are gathered by condensation. The analysis shows (nay, it is fairly obvious while we read the reminiscences) that the severe mistress becomes hideous through condensation with the step-mother; the professor, on the other hand, "shaggy, rather than attractive," is loved because he is the symbol of the father. The reminiscences are characteristic. Here is the first:

> I. I was twelve years old. . . . The mistress did not like me, and *I her less*! Why? *Such things are difficult to explain.*

First of all she was ugly, slatternly; I loved things that were beautiful; what particularly haunted me were her eyes; they were huge, grey eyes, wicked-looking eyes; with no soul in them for understanding children, it seemed to me. She used to get into towering passions, especially when I did not know my geography lesson. And then!—oh, then!—seizing me by the curls which adorned my brow, she shook me like a plum tree.

I was at that time very delicate and excitable. These shakings upset me to such a degree that, for some days after, my head would ache, and every time I saw her I was seized with a trembling fit. I never wept, but remained quiet and docile; this seemed to vex her more than if I had screamed. No matter how well I had prepared my lessons, as soon as I was with her my mind became a blank!

One Saturday morning we were having the geography lesson. Miss N. called me to the wall-map; she had the "bad day" expression in her eyes, and her voice seemed to be like a distant growling of thunder!—"Point to Thorberg," said she. We were learning about the canton of Berne. Of course I pointed all wrong. Then she said: "Tell me, at least, whom one sends to Thorberg." Whereupon I answered: "Masters and mistresses." Tableau! It was a reformatory at that date! Apparently I have always had a talent for repartee, and have often made people laugh; but under the circumstances I can assure you Miss N. did not look upon my answer as funny at all. . . . Raging, scarlet in the face, her eyes starting from her head, she seized me by my hair. Not satisfied with pulling the curls on my forehead, she laid hold of the bunch that fell over my shoulders as well. Then I had a time of it! Shaken, cuffed, abused! Hell, if it exists, could not be worse. I saw sparks; I heard the thunder of her hateful voice. Goodness, how dreadful she was when thus let loose! *In my heart of hearts I placed her alongside my step-mother, and found my schoolmistress as horrible as I found her,* and God knows I did not love my step-mother. This was the refrain Miss N. repeated again and again: "Ah! So! That's where you send schoolmistresses, is it; thanks; take that, and that; that'll teach you!"

After the lesson, all the children followed me out of the class room. They gathered round me and tried to cheer me up. "You did jolly well to send her to Thorberg; it serves her right! Don't cry; don't cry!"

The tears I had withheld in her presence now coursed down my cheeks, and I began to feel calmer.

From the very outset, the part played by the subconscious in her dislike for the mistress is well marked in this reminiscence. "The mistress did not like me, and I her *less.*" That is to say, the child's dislike was not *wholly* justified by the character of the teacher. The following sentence is even more expressive. "Why? Such things are difficult to explain." Conscious reasons do not suffice, even in the subject's mind, to explain the aversion. There is something deeper, whose existence she merely surmises. But in the course of the narrative she answers her own question, without realising she is doing so, and quite incidentally. "In my heart of hearts I placed her alongside my step-mother." May we not smile at the monstrous dimensions this person is assuming in the child's imagination (seeing sparks, hearing thunder), and at the close resemblance with the "wicked step-mother" the fairy tale?—Let us pass on to the second reminiscence, which forms the counterpart to the first.

II. Our professor was a dear old fellow. He was a man of at least sixty summers. Though a trifle *rough in manner, and shaggy rather than attractive,* he was fundamentally good and honest, a man of sterling worth. He never showed any favouritism (as is so often the case with teachers) to pupils who were wealthier or more beautiful than the others. No; as I said before, he was just, simple, and honest; I found this much to my taste. Consequently, *I grew very fond of him from the first.* I made good progress under him, even in geography, and we became excellent friends. *Besides he was father's friend, and this alone would have been enough to make me like him.*

I was rather prone to take journeys to the moon; too often, indeed, did my thoughts travel in that direction; my old friend was not best pleased at this. I am sorry now that I allowed myself to dwell so often in the moon instead of paying heed to his lessons! It must have tired him to be constantly dragging me back to earth; still, he never got angry with me!

One afternoon, also during the geography lesson—but with him how good and wholesome the subject became!—he was explaining about volcanoes. We had our atlases upon our desks and were listening—but not all of us were listening, for I was away in the moon!

Following the course of a river with my finger, I saw mountains; farther on came the sea—the wide sea, boundless; how calm the sea must be at this moment!

From time to time vague words beat upon my ears, faraway phrases; but the ocean with its vessels, how much more beautiful!

Suddenly the voice of the professor broke in definitely upon my dreaming: "Aha! Queenie, I've caught you! What have

I just been explaining ?" I rose; I tried to gather my wits (he had said something about Popocatepetl, Orizaba, Jorullo). I answered: "Popo . . . caca . . . pépé."—There followed a burst of laughter. The whole class (there were forty of us) was in an uproar of mirth. The professor himself was rocking with laughter, and I joined in as well. I can see my dear master, scarlet in the face, standing at his desk swaying from side to side as he laughed, the slit of his mouth reaching from ear to ear, his big, round head—he looked just like one of those funny pictures of the moon. He did not scold me; he did not punish me. No; he forgave me at once—and what an affectionate memory I have of him even to this day! . . .

The symmetrical contrast of these two reminiscences is very striking; it extends into every detail. In the first reminiscence we have the following fact finding expression: conscious reasons do not fully account for the antipathy; this is followed by a reference to the step-mother. In the second, we have, first of all, an enumeration of personal traits which are not calculated to attract us to the professor; this is followed by an allusion to the father. "He was father's friend, and this alone would have been enough to make me like him." Then the two episodes are replicas one of the other in every detail: each time we have an unsuitable answer to a question during a geography lesson—the first time the answer is followed by an insensate fit of anger on the part of the mistress; the second time the answer is followed by the indulgent mirth of the professor.

The condensation of the father into the professor is confirmed by the importance Queenie attaches to the fact that the master was "just." This "justice" in the character is intimately linked for Queenie with the memory of her father.

We need not dwell any longer upon the analysis of these two reminiscences. They were adduced mainly in order to show the type to which Queenie belongs; to indicate her exclusive attachment to the father. But the reminiscences do not help us to elucidate the trend of the sublimation.

The points we must bear in mind are the following: the fascination exercised upon the subject by imaginative excursions during the professor's lesson—the imagination escapes in order to wander over the sea, so boundless and so calm; the recurrence, twice, of the symbol, "being in the moon" to describe escape into the fields of imagination, and the recurrence of the " moon " symbol in reference to the master (the father): " He looked just like . . . the moon." This juxtaposition illustrates in an original manner a fact which the subsequent analysis is to verify, and which finds its counterpart in many other female subjects (Miriam, for instance), namely: the link that exists between fixation upon the father, and sublimation. At the date when the incidents occurred, this sublimation found vent in fantasy, the germ of a subsequent æsthetic sublimation.

This æsthetic trend, linked as it is to the father, is naturally in opposition to the step-mother. The opposition is found in a sentence which occurs in the first reminiscence: " First of all, she was ugly, slatternly; I loved things that were beautiful." Queenie was already aware, in adolescence, of a desire to develop her artistic talents in imitation of her real mother, who was an artist, but whom she had never known; the devotion to the memory of the real mother is another form of protest against the step-mother. There may even be detected a wish to resemble the father's first wife, to excel the second wife, and thus to supplant the latter in her father's affections.

At the date of the analysis, Queenie was forty-one years of age. She married very young; she is the mother of several children. She complains of extreme nervous irritability and accesses of neurasthenia.

> III. In a dream which she has at this date she sees a person who is " Molière "; he gives her prescriptions which will cure her. The room where he receives her is like the one where I have my sittings with her.

" Molière " produces the following associations: " the arts; nothing is more beautiful." In this dream, Molière appears as the condensation of myself with an idealised " artist " and probably with the father likewise. Molière is at one and the same time the guide, the healer, and the artist. In this dream, the subject herself suggests art as a means to health. Fixation upon the father has been, in conjunction with a refusal (more or less pronounced) to accept reality, transmuted into an æsthetic trend which must find expression.

But Queenie has never been able wholly to satisfy her artistic trends. She would have liked to continue her studies; she had had to interrupt them "on account of her father." After her marriage, conditions were unfavourable to her æsthetic development. She suffers from repression of the sublimated tendency (the æsthetic tendency). The repressed tendency causes trouble, and endeavours to find an outlet in other forms of sublimation. During recent years Queenie has, in fact, set her course towards religious, charitable, and social work, which she endeavours to adapt to her taste for beautiful things. She is still groping her way along this path of sublimation; the analysis is casting a ray of light upon the path; while the analysis is in progress she has a beautiful dream. The dream moves her profoundly, and she seems to perceive in it a solution to her troubles.

IV. Early spring; a rapturous morning; a morning of mornings; the air is fresh, everything seems to smile, to be born again on the earth.

From my balcony I suddenly behold a procession similar to the one which takes place at the Promotions.[1]

First of all come men walking two abreast; they are wearing dress suits, are bare-headed, and have huge white sashes with golden fringes; these were artists with long, black locks which they tossed from their foreheads in a free-and-easy manner.

The first (though I had never seen him before in real life) I knew to be Jaques Dalcroze; then came a brass band, and then a great number of girls dressed in white, garlanded with flowers, happy to be alive.

Near by, buried among trees, was a boarding-school; here, on the steps of a wide entrance, was a concourse of young folk, miracles of beauty, surrounded with a glory of sunlight; they were about to join the procession.

No sound broke the exquisite silence; all was peaceful quiet, restful.

Suddenly the voices of the artists broke in upon my ears. Was it a hymn of praise to the Creator? It was stately and pure; the voices were beautiful; how they rose directly from the hearts of those men up to God!

Reverently, I listen to the divine music; my eyes filled with tears. All at once a mysterious voice pronounces the word: "Tolstoy."

[1] The "Promotions" is the name given to the fête which is held in Latin Switzerland on the occasion of the distribution of prizes.

The whole dream is permeated with a love of beauty, which towards the close is changed into religious ecstasy. It seems obvious that the first part must be a fantasy of virginity; the associations confirm this supposition. We need not be surprised to find such a fantasy in a woman who, as in this instance, presents a case of strong fixation upon the father. This fixation gives rise to certain regressive tendencies which are symbolised by the " boarding-school " (return to adolescence) and by the " Promotions " (return to childhood).

The " artists " play the same part as " Molière " did in dream III. The name " Jaques Dalcroze " is partly due to a confusion which often occurs at Geneva between the " Institut de Rythmique Jaques Dalcroze " and the " Institut Jean Jacques Rousseau " where I received Queenie for treatment. The condensation of the " artist " in the dream with myself (as in the case of " Molière " in the previous dream) is now confirmed.

But the " artists " in No IV, in their formal clothes, have something of the priest about them; they sing a hymn to " the Creator," and the name of Tolstoy seems to break in as an answer to this religious aspiration. Tolstoy's thoughts on religious and social affairs respond to Queenie's own aspirations. The fact that Tolstoy secured this religious and social sublimation after passing through a stage of æsthetic sublimation, squares with the actual process of Queenie's development. " Tolstoy " calls up the following associations: " Christ; justice ": which is followed by the very pertinent observation: " For me, Christ, Tolstoy, and my father, are three identicals." We seem to catch the " paternal imago " in the act! It is upon the paternal imago that Queenie models the idea in which she is about to find health and harmony.

CHAPTER TWELVE

THE SEARCH FOR A GUIDE

In the person of the analyst, the subject seeks for a guide—if not a saviour! Sometimes the search is an ardent one; in such an event the search may assume an "infantile" and "erotic" form in relation to the analyst; this "infantile" and "erotic" attitude is apt to be subconscious. At the close of Chapter Four (pp. 113–116) we examined the "affective transference on to the analyst."

This passionate search for a guide does not always progress smoothly, but has crises of hostility which are no less passionate than the search. In fact, the attitude of the subject towards the analyst is usually hostile at the outset. The hostility is in most cases subconscious. Gradually, however, the subject feels himself to be the victor or the vanquished. Rynaldo exhibits a very precise evolution of transference; it conforms to type; at first the subject disparages the analyst and spares him no contumely; then the subject showers upon the analyst all sorts of feelings, partly filial, partly erotic, partly homosexual. As soon as a sympathetic link has been established, progress towards cure begins; the moment when the link is finally broken, and when the subject becomes once again his own master, is the moment when the cure is completed. One of the interesting aspects of Rynaldo's case is the original and picturesque phraseology he uses in order to express his feelings towards the analyst.

In Stella, the idea of the guide develops in the direction of sublimation; the subject decides to find the guide within herself. In such a case the role of the analyst is that of helper, which may for a moment be confounded with the role of ideal guide, but which quickly becomes dissociated from such a conception. In Stella's case the guide takes the form of a spiritual principle; we saw a rudiment of this phenomenon in Ruth. Such a principle, whether it be philosophical or religious, must always be respected by the analyst, no matter what his personal convictions are. All the more must he do so, seeing that his own task is thus made easier.

In every case the analyst must guard against exercising any excessive influence either upon the feelings or upon the conscience of the subject. He must always aim at making the subject master of himself. And it is here that suggestion, or rather autosuggestive education of the subject, plays an obvious part.

1. Rynaldo

Change of Analyst. From Hostility to Sympathy.

This analysis was begun by my pupil and friend Monsieur Soteriou (of Athens). When he left Switzerland, he passed the case on to me and gave me the following information:

Rynaldo, thirty-nine years old, house painter, Italian, fairly cultured, a lover of music and of opera, came to Soteriou in a condition of severe neurasthenia. He slept badly, had a poor appetite, no pleasure in living, was haunted by thoughts of death. A fixed idea that his "flesh is drying up." The subject lives with his mother, and is obsessed with the idea that his mother is going to die. Masturbation was practised from the age of seven to thirty-five years of age. Neurasthenia has been present for many years, during the course of which the subject has had several acute exacerbations.

Analysis revealed a strong fixation upon the mother, and homosexual tendencies. There is a marked need to cling to someone, and hence the affective transference on to the analyst was of supreme importance. Some years ago, Rynaldo was troubled by the conviction that he was going mad; this seems to have arisen in consequence of an unfortunate word spoken by a doctor when Rynaldo was a child, which reacted upon him by suggestion. The fixed idea about "drying up" had lessened during the analysis. This was also linked to impressions during childhood. In those days, Rynaldo had known a young neuropath whose body "appeared to be drying up," and whose malady led his parents to lavish their love upon him.

The main interest for me in the case is the special importance of the subject's attitude towards the analyst. This importance seems to have been enhanced in consequence of the change of analyst: there appeared to be a sort of crisis of transference, so that the mechanism underlying the phenomenon was brought into sharp relief. The acceptance of the analyst (which is in no case effected from the outset) was rendered all the more difficult because the subject had to be weaned from his previous analyst.

Another item of special interest in Rynaldo's case is the symbolical language the subject has created, more particularly to express his subconscious attitude towards the analyst. It is not the dreams which give us the greatest help in this analysis, but the spontaneous associations which surge up ready-made in the mind of the subject at any moment of the day, and of which he makes notes. These associations are usually of two words, a noun and an adjective, often very peculiar and with no logical relationship to one another. Some of the words are neologisms.—The associations seemed to the subject absolutely fixed as soon as they occurred to him; he wrote them down without understanding them. We have here a slight dissociation of consciousness such as is found among automatic writers.

I. (From July 4th to July 13th). Here are some associations showing that the subconscious laughs at the method or distrusts it; [1]

Misleading callisthenics
hypnotic gastritis
many too many things at once
automatic street-sweeper (*autosuggestion*) [balayeuse]
improper pruning
tubal story
prodigal auscultation
one-eyed æstheticism
wilful buffoonery
wilful silence
undeniable drudgery.

Other associations are directed against myself. The subject is beginning to practice a queer method of caricature wherein his subconscious will soon excel. We shall speedily become

[1] In these lists, the author's elucidations are in parenthesis and are italicised. In some instances, the original French term is appended, in brackets and not italicised.—TRANSLATORS' NOTE.

accustomed to the fact that he is making merry with my nose and with my beard; soon he will laugh at my beard itself, at the shape of my nose (rhinoceros, rhinoplasty), at my name (Charles, whence Carolina), at my thick head of hair (curling-pin), or at my university degrees. Let us begin.

Merovingian curling-pin [bigoudi].

"Merovingian" is reduced by analysis to "Carlovingian" (Charles) and to "Norwegian," to which is added the idea of "old trash." Later on, the subject compares me to Ibsen (Norwegian); I am for him a barbarian from the north and a "bearded symbolist" (discontent at the departure of Soteriou who is a Greek, and is clean shaven). On the other hand the "curling-pin" is the herald of a series of symbols whereby the subject, who seems to be an expert in the use of slang, expresses, with the utmost innocence, his belief that I am affected and "priggish." Here are some further pleasantries at my expense.

Mystical Carolina
advantageous truculence (*I appear to him "ruddy and fresh" and pleased with my own appearance*)
reduced swelling [boursouflure]
marked swelling
sensual prig
desired object (*the two last associations indicate a wish for transference, coupled with sexual metaphor*)
artificial sweetness
decorated gypsy
symbolical pedant
disguised horse-shay [berlingot]
ignorant sorcerer
certificated carriage
glutted mercer (*associated with sorcerer*)
learned crow
bored chatterbox [bavarde]
refreshing sweetmeat
amused sorceress
patented sponger
indiarubber one-eyed man.

We may note in passing that "sorceress" is used elsewhere by the subject with reference to his mother. This word shows that the whilom subconscious feelings (fixation upon the mother) are endeavouring to free themselves by transference on to the analyst.

Here is a protest against Soteriou who has earned Rynaldo's displeasure by leaving him in other hands:

> Dethroned usurper.

"Usurper" because Soteriou was my pupil and had "taken my place." In addition, Soteriou's Christian name is Constantine, and Rynaldo was comparing him to Constantine, the king of Greece, who had recently been dethroned.

Here are some allusions to the change of analyst, a change which had upset the subject:

> Sudden change of tack
> violent reaction, lively horoscope
> complete revolution
> displaced balance-sheet
> memorandum printed again [bordereau].

In the following there is manifest a slight growth of confidence in the method and belief in myself:

> Well-meant innovation
> partial innovation
> reinstatement
> professional sacrament (*this equals: professional secrets are sacred or inviolable*)
> mathematical invention
> sensible nonsense [baliverne]
> margarine and seduction
> transcendental ready-reckoner [barême]
> recognised sincerity
> recognised system
> paternal indulgence
> fraudulent inclination (*a sign of the transference of homosexual tendencies*)
> a marchioness in a wig and a silk dress, benevolent sympathy.

Here I must call attention to a peculiarity which becomes more marked as we proceed. The use of the initial letter B (the first letter of my name) for the associations specially concerning myself (balayeuse, bouffonnerie, boursouflure, bigoudi, berlingot, bavarde, bilan, bordereau, barême, baliverne, etc.). Soon we shall have proper nouns beginning with B. The same game will be played with C, the initial letter of my Christian name. The important part played by the Christian name (from the first days of the second week) demonstrates a step forward on the path to intimacy.

II. (From July 17th to July 22nd). Rynaldo calls me:

Cormerais Baryton (a play on my initials)
Carolus Duran
caloried or coloured Ibsen (*cf.* "*Norwegian*" *in No. I*)
Norwegian cooking
foundered renovator (*because I seemed to him very tired and, perhaps even, ill; elsewhere he calls me "starved restorer"*).

Psychoanalysis itself comes in for:

verbal shittification [merdalisation verbale]
I spit
tiring colloquy
internal radiography
infantile radiography.

Soteriou is still regretted, but he is losing ground and is not spared back-handed compliments (he is often indicated by the letter S).

Distinguished sinapism
evicted sinapism
evicted concubine
unknown beardless youth
dethroned Constantine.

The relationship between Soteriou and myself is expressed in the following manner:

Unconquered soubrette and Norwegian rhapsody.
Bergson refuted, Syllabus ordered.

The associations show repining over the loss of Soteriou and protest against myself. In the next we have a reversal:

Socrates flattened out, Rostand let loose.

"Socrates," a Greek, represents Soteriou. The word reveals knowledge on the part of the subject that homosexual practices had a considerable vogue in classical Greece, and lays bare the homosexual tendency in Rynaldo to which Soteriou had drawn attention before his departure. "Rostand" calls up "Cyrano de Bergerac" (C. B., my initials) which symbolises for Rynaldo extroversion (whence we have "let loose"), and normal love, which is youthful, full of poetry and romance. He is beginning to feel that he is entering upon a normal life, upon extroversion; this victory is associated with myself. To "Rostand let loose" we may add:

Bergerac returned
bedevilled rhinoceros (*we have already seen that I am the rhinoceros*).

Once more the subject harks back to the theme of Soteriou's departure:

Foreseen separation
unpunished desertion.

Transference on to the analyst yields the following:

Tasted comradeship
Olympian concupiscence
chosen darling
strange proposal.

The fixation, and the sublimation of the homosexual tendency, are seen passing under the guise of a budding friendship for the analyst.

At this point there appeared a neologism which was to crop up frequently in the sequel. It was:

Bistrome.

The word seems to be a condensation of "bis" plus "Traum" (dream) with "bis" plus "trop" (too much). This signifies: "The analyst is a booze-vendor [bistrot], two analysts of dreams; two, that's too much."

III. (From July 22nd to July 31st). I have already appeared as "coloured" (coloured Ibsen, II). Rynaldo had noticed that I was sunburnt, whereas he was very pale; this leads to fantasies wherein he sets me up as his ideal of the health and manliness he himself wishes to possess. These are some of his names for me:

Calcined Merovingian
recooked Merovingian
far-fetched Bergson
praiseworthy Carlovingian and complex rhinoplasty
dissolvent calomel making use of feeling.

He seems in the next three to show a fancy that he is winning my favour:

Shunted machine or imperceptible smile
extraordinary reconciliation
obligatory conciliation.

But he still hesitates in his allegiance to me, and makes double associations which appear to be alternatives.

Ridiculous old geeser or intellectual stenography (*cf. internal radiography*, II)
indelible sincerity, or commotion like a nut-cracker.

References to the upset caused by the change of analyst still appear:

Duplicated cortège or unforeseen secretion.

But Soteriou is now withdrawing into the background:

Retreating apprentice
perplexed Victor Hugo and finished Isadora Duncan.

"Perplexed Victor Hugo" (another bearded man of the Ibsen tribe) is myself; this is associated with "complex rhinoplasty." "Isadora Duncan," a symbol of Greek dancing, is Soteriou.

Hope of recovery now begins to come definitely to the fore:

Peculiar penitent's robe, and proven infantilism
retarded morality and resolution in the near future
retarded rudder and redemption in the near future.

"The penitent's robe" is introversion; "retarded morality" is the development of the moral life which has been held in check by infantile fixations. The subject is realising his condition and hopes soon to rise above it and free himself. His optimism in this respect increases concomitantly with his affective reconciliation to myself. But Rynaldo has not yet quite overcome me. He has already called me "priggish," a "prig," and an "insensitive virtuous man." Now he says I am an

unviolated Cunigunde.

IV. (From July 31st to August 6th). This week proves to be the turning-point. We are faced with resurrection fantasies.

The sky would be
baby linen
Lazarus resurrected from the dead.

This resurrection does in truth take place at the very moment when the affective bond with me is established. But even now some of the old jokes at my expense crop up:

Hairy [velu] cargo and bloated rhinoceros.

But he adds:

Creative intuition (*a condensation of " intuition " and of " creative evolution "; a reminiscence of Bergson who has already served as a symbol of myself,* II)
Bazaartherapy divulged, rational history developed and authentic (*this is the analysis*)
Machiavellian inspiration
divine intervention
Bourget the redeemer
triumphant ready-reckoner
cure obtained thanks to the coefficient Nilakantha.

" Nilakantha," the father of Lakmé, is an " old *B*rahman." This calls up by association: " man of *b*ronze," " *b*urned by the sun "—again we have, in these associations, references to myself (cf. III).

Transference finds expression in the following symbols:

Carolina longed for and obtained (" *Carolina longed for* " [*voulue*] *is associated with " hairy cargo "* [*cargaison velu*])
refreshing household, refreshment obtained, mitigated bending
complicity unexpected and renovating
respectful gallantry foreseen
close collaboration.

New fantasies concerning the change of analyst now arise:

Particoloured innovator
transient and local interruption
gyrating psychotherapy and mezzanine.

Soteriou continues his retreat:

> Prolonged Turkish bath
> ungummed minister
> secondary uselessness or direct contact (*i.e. uselessness of the "minister" and of the "second," and direct contact with myself*).

More and more does Rynaldo feel he is freeing himself from the maternal complex, from exclusive introversion, from infantilism; that he is on the way to acquire virility:

> Delicate majoration and nebulous infantilism (*the "majoration" is the coming of age, and symbolises the attainment of virility*).
> definitely masculine
> rejected embryo
> lapsed incest
> evicted sorceress (*the mother*)
> burned sarcophagus or wonderful rumour
> magisterial evolution
> light on the horizon, wonderful wild rose
> decidedly more light or rational induction.

V. (From August 7th to August 18th). Progress continues:

> Disconcerting mneme or Rhine gold found again.

The "mneme" is the long-forgotten incident which lay buried in the subconscious. With the "Rhine gold" the subject has spontaneously discovered the collective symbol, a saga, to which we have previously drawn attention: the precious thing which has been buried but is found once again.

The morbid state is thus defined:

> Cerebral derangement armed with all the necessary implements for repair.

Now psychoanalysis is described as:

> Inventoried dustbin or German system
> regenerative instinct or distinguished machinery.

Soteriou puts in an appearance:

> Saute-ruisseau [leaper over a stream] condemned.

" Saute-ruisseau " is but a slightly disguised parody of the name Soteriou and means that Soteriou has crossed the sea. To this is added a hint of disparagement.

A few resentful jibes at myself still crop up:

> Destitute Balzac
> foundered Bajazet.

But the acceptation of myself, which is sometimes quite enthusiastic, continues to appear:

> Nocturnal power or Merovingian prop
> light calorigene or public demonstration.

" Calorigene " is a condensation of " Carlovingian " and of " coloré " [translated " coloured "] and " calorie " [translated " caloried "].

Rynaldo continues to show his confidence that he is improving:

> masculine diversion or retroversion improbable
> bazaar sorceress
> system adopted or profound renovation.

VI. (From August 21st to August 26th). Rynaldo is still describing the interconnection of the two analysts in the form of an

> ill-fitting hinge.

He is still at times in a reproachful mood towards me. Especially, he is annoyed with me for making him note down his dreams and his associations:

> infected with gallophobia or prescribed manuscript.

But compliments preponderate:

> inventive Carolina or distinct mneme
> illustrated Bergerac or coincident system
> voluptuous caress or imminent redemption
> Calomel Vishnu (*a fresh reminiscence of the father of Lakmé*)
> or prophetic shaving
> perfect semolina or pacified rhinoceros
> oleagenous substance or satisfied rhinoceros
> mollified prig or venerable substance
> strange intervention or radically cured
> perfect semolina or profound renovation.

Since the beginning of the analysis, Rynaldo has frequently had a dream in which he sees himself painting in a flat in course of decoration. In this dream, everything had invariably gone amiss. Now the dream recurred in a way that indicated progress, for the work in the flat was going better:

> VII. We are painting the woodwork of the drawing-room, painting it pink; there is not enough paint, so I mix some more; since I am not quite sure that I have got the right shade, I fetch an old workman who was a friend of my father. The pink I have mixed is not exactly like the first; it depends how one looks at it. . . . I forgot to say at the beginning of the dream: I was delighted to find that I was painting quite easily, without being bothered as I had been before.

The colour "pink" [in French "rose"] calls up "to see life through rose-coloured spectacles," this referring to the cure of the neurasthenia. Other allusions point to the search for the "father" (a friend of my father), that is to say, the search for virility. There is something still lacking to this virility, and that is why the paint he mixes in the dream is rather pale.

"Pink" reappears in the following dream.

VIII. (Night of August 31st to September 1st):

> To my right there was an enormous glass full of pomegranate syrup, but I had made it too watery and could not drink it. I heard the clock strike noon at St. Pierre, so I had to leave.

The over-diluted pink beverage, a symbol of incomplete virility and of unfinished cure, also symbolises the imperfections of the transference. Shortly before, in fact, I had been sitting with Rynaldo in a restaurant. He had ordered a glass of vermouth which I had looked at somewhat censoriously. My order was a glass of pomegranate syrup, which had seemed to Rynaldo rather an unmanly drink, so that it had become associated in his mind with images of "priggishness," "affectedness," "foppishness," etc. He had even chaffed me a little for the immense quantity of water I added, which made the colour of the drink very pale. That evening I had had to leave him to keep an appointment. The clock striking at St. Pierre is the customary signal for the close of our sittings. It is the sign of parting.

The idea of the incompleteness of the transference is

condensed with that of the incompleteness of the cure, and it is true that the cure follows closely in the footsteps of the transference.

In the same dream there is a museum, which is also a booth at a fair, where there is a merry-go-round which is being dismantled and which is to be carted away. These images are suggested by the same reminiscence as that from which the pomegranate syrup comes. When we were in the restaurant, a fair was in progress in the adjoining square and there were some merry-go-rounds. In them we have symbols of old trash which must be cleared away. More especially, the merry-go-round, turning on its own axis, is a symbol of autoerotism and introversion, whereas the boy scouts, who now appear on the scene, denote virility:

> We think that the lorry (*which is to carry away the merry-go-round*) will find it difficult to start; there is a movement; men dressed as boy scouts appear. Is the cortege ready? Not yet.

The "start" is imminent, but the moment is not yet quite come.

IX. (The same week from August 28th to September 3rd). The associations are coloured by the pomegranate syrup:

> sugary nonsense or special pruning
> certain deduction or aperitive system

After the "aperitives" (the pomegranate and the vermouth) I had looked at my watch, had hesitated for a moment while thinking of the time of my tram and the distance from the station, and I had postponed my departure for a few minutes. Hence, doubtless, the following association:

> vacillating Boudouresqueness or station close at hand.

These automatic associations, faithfully recorded, were tending to assume an exaggerated development. To encourage such a development would have involved the risk of switching the subject towards automatism and a duplication of consciousness. Henceforward, therefore, I did my utmost to secure more conscious associations to the items of Rynaldo's dreams, and I begged him to give up recording his automatic associations, notwithstanding the great theoretical interest of this original idiom. Henceforward we confined ourselves to the analysis of the dreams.

September.

> X. I am talking with the son of the master to whom I was apprenticed. I say to him: "If only you had known Flournoy, the psychologist! You remember what an awful ass I was before I was re-educated! . . ."

"The master to whom he was apprenticed" appears in a whole series of dreams, and symbolises the "father." The "son" is Rynaldo himself, especially when he was a youth. "Flournoy the psychologist" is myself. In this dream Rynaldo converses with his sometime self, and is sorry he did not make my acquaintance earlier. Now he is "re-educated."

The analyst still continues to play the leading role:

> XI. An excursion in the funicular railway. . . . I get into the train at a place where there seems to be a branch line; the dream apparently implied that it was at Corsier, but I had an impression of being at Saconnex or at Chambésy. The train is running down a steep hill; I think of the dangers should it get out of hand; at the same time I note how calmly and easily the driver manages his machine.

"Corsier" calls up "opposite Coppet." The dream takes place at the date when I removed from Saconnex d'Arve to Coppet. I stayed at Coppet the whole of that autumn; Rynaldo knew that this would interfere with our acquaintance and necessitate a longer interval between the sittings. He shows his uneasiness; at the same time he has confidence in the "driver," who symbolises myself.

> XII. A youngish woman (she seems to be a singer at a café chantant) who offers to sell me a bicycle for 80 francs. She tells me that an inner tube larger than the pneumatic tyre (or the wheel?) is given away free with the purchase. But some difficulty or other with the telephone brings the affair to naught. It seemed as if the bicycles were black-enamelled; she had several for sale.

Henceforth I become less prominent. Rynaldo has acquired extroversion, he is beginning to face the problems of life. The dream shows a desire for a normal and healthy love.

The "difficulty . . . with the telephone" is an allusion to a "telephonist" with whom Rynaldo had once had a love affair "which had been spoiled by a misunderstanding." The young lady had "laughed at his odd sort of phiz," and this had increased his neurasthenia (the incident occurred fourteen years ago). The "singer at a café chantant" who has "several bicycles to sell" symbolises a woman of shady character. The term "black enamelled" arouses the following associations: "things coming from Germany; excess of regulation, too cold; French letter"—all of them symbolising sexuality without love. This does not satisfy the subject, who aspires to something more complete and more wholesome.

October.

XIII (The following dreams are some among many which occurred during the same night).

(1) I am working for my godfather, and at the same time for my factory. An old workmate, with whom I had quarrelled, comes in search of work, I am surprised at his friendliness. . . .
(2) Two pretty girls arrive on a little sledge; are they gliding over the water or over the land? The sledge reminds me of Lohengrin's swan, and perhaps of the Holy Grail as well.
(3) A great patriotic demonstration is to take place in Bel-Air Square. Some young socialists whistle and hoot; when they are separated from the crowd, I notice that the patriots are few in number.

The two women of the second episode often appear in the dreams of this period; they alternate with the two analysts, and tend to replace them. The affect, having detached itself from infantile fixations, and having been transferred on to the analysts, must once again free itself—from the new fixation. But, as we have seen, Rynaldo is not content to gratify his brute instinct; he aspires to sublimation: whence the "Holy Grail." By association we get "the Sacred Heart in course of construction." "Lohengrin" (a reminiscence of Rynaldo's fifteenth year) is a revival of youth.

In the first episode, the "godfather" is a substitute for the "father"; other associations lead to "a blear-eyed goldfinch"; "We once had a goldfinch which pined away after my father's death." The "workmate with whom he had quarrelled" symbolises the virility Rynaldo had lost, but which he has found again.

The "patriots" in the third episode call up outworn ideas (cf. museum, merry-go-round, dream VIII) and the "young socialists" symbolise young and fresh ideas concerning the sound health he has reacquired (they also denote a progress in the direction of the *social* instinct).

XIV. Rynaldo dreams of a place "which recalls the workyard where he was apprenticed, and which is situated opposite the church of the Sacred Heart where he made his first communion." Another reference to his reconquered virility and to his desire for sublimation. In the same dream there is something about a fire—a symbol which, for Rynaldo, represents his neuropathic condition. But

> I see the fire-engines coming to extinguish the flames, they come from Carouge. . . . They are all motor fire-engines; they come with the utmost speed, and give the impression of being well made and powerful.

I live in the direction of Carouge (this is connected with the series of proper names beginning with C). The "motor" fire-engines [pompes automobiles] symbolise autosuggestion. Confidence in me remains unshaken, but the subject adds to this a confidence in himself; he is cutting loose from me as fast as he feels he can do without me.

That same night Rynaldo dreams of "two clerks who have come from the town hall"; these are the two analysts, but henceforward they are equals, and are no longer referred to with the passionate epithets which qualified them of yore.

XV. The "start" which we thought imminent, though somewhat difficult (VIII), now takes place. The dreams abound in daring deeds, unconstrainedness, which had not been present before.

> Rue de *Carouge*, I'm in front of a house. I am undecided; shall I go away in a motor car, for it is muddy; shall I break my neck? Indecision. Finally, I think: "Well I'll see."

And thereupon—he goes!

He dreams of me as "Charles' circus," but he is surprised to find how small the circus is. Another dream is about a machine (resembling a projector at Charles' circus) which

" attunes and concludes the link between the interior and the exterior," that is to say, which helps the introvert to " project " himself into life.

> XVI. . . . An empty flat. I try some of the fitments. I unhook something from the wall—I don't know what it is. Someone comes in. Who is it ? One of the bosses ? At any rate it is an imposing, sedate, and kindly person. To my right there is an open cupboard. At the top there is a little medallion from which a woman's head (living) looks at me. In the idea of the dream she is motionless, but I know that she is waiting for me to unhook her.

I appear again in this dream, being now the " kindly boss," but in these traits I am more or less condensed with the father. The " cupboard " had appeared in earlier associations, but it was closed and it needed to be opened. It had called up " the cupboard where the treasure is," so that Rynaldo seems to have hit upon a motif of saga. The woman who is to be " unhooked " is likewise the motif of a saga, that of Andromeda rescued by Perseus. The two motifs, that of the treasure and that of Andromeda, mean the same thing. The question at issue is the " unhooking " (the setting free) of the vital energy which has been pent up by the infantile fixations.

November.

XVII. The cure is close at hand. There is now a wealth of such symbols as " Place Neuve," " Cyrano," " Tannhäuser " (associated with " Lohengrin," XIII). There is question of a " wonderful clock."

> Both wheels of my bicycle have been mended, but who will put them together again or wind them up [remonter] ?—for I know that the time for the start is at hand.

Rynaldo's sexual dreams are normal ; they have no tinge of homosexuality or of autoerotism. For example :

> A machine which goes down and up, like a lift ; it seemed to me to stop and distribute its contents into some sort of round aperture.

In the following dream the subject describes the results of the analysis and his own feelings about it.

XVIII. In the cathedral of St. Pierre an employer is talking to some hands he thinks of engaging; he converses with a young man—suddenly they go down the stairway—wide and gloomy—I follow them carrying a large stone; I am rather afraid of falling, for the steps seem to me to vary in height; but I go down very quickly. When I reach the first floor, I throw my stone out of the window; it does not fall where I had expected; but I explain to two young fellows who are looking at me that it is better the stone should have fallen just as it did.

In this dream we meet again the two analysts (the "employer" and the "young man") conversing as equals. The cathedral of St. Pierre, close to the Jean Jacques Rousseau Institute where Rynaldo comes to consult me, has already served to symbolise the place where the analyses are carried on. (The reader will remember that the clock striking at St. Pierre was the signal that our interviews must close.) Apropos of this dream, Rynaldo said to me: "The re-education has not been precisely what I expected, but I think it is better as it is." The stone which he throws out of the window is "the burden of which he is ridding himself."

XIX. Next week he dreams of "a young lady of the Coopé" who tells him that "the goods you ordered are ready." "Coopé" is short for "cooperative grocery"; Rynaldo is very careful to write it thus abridged. There is a condensation of "Coppet" (the name of the place where I was then living) with "cooperation." No longer is the method regarded by the subject as a complete abandonment of himself into my hands; it is a cooperation between Rynaldo and myself. The loosening of the bonds of the transference is still going on. Just now we had a dream in which the two analysts were symbolised by "an employer and a young man." At length Rynaldo dreams of "an ex-employer and of his pupil." This signifies that for him I am now merely a whilom master, and that he has become his own master. In another dream he expresses himself yet more categorically:

They had given me an assistant, but he was not a craftsman, and it was quite understood that I alone was the craftsman. I fancy that the foreman had asked me about this or had drawn my attention to the fact.

I have frequently urged Rynaldo to become accustomed to depend upon himself. In one of his latest dreams he dreamed that he had been " re-established," had been " re-built upon himself." He has also dreamed that he is " working at something quite new," whereas formerly he always dreamed about " repairs."

We have been watching the rise and the fall of a transference. The stages of this transference were parallel to those of the subject's progress. He regarded himself as cured as soon as the tie of the transference had been loosened, and as soon as he felt himself to have become his own master.

2. Stella

Sublimation of the Idea of the Guide.

From childhood onwards, the circumstances of Stella's life have tended to cultivate introversion.

When she was born, her father was fifty-six, and her mother twenty years younger. The mother died when the little girl was only a few months old. From the time of birth there was manifest a state of powerlessness which was wrongly diagnosed as " infantile paralysis." Later, the diagnosis was disputed, and was eventually recognised to have been erroneous. The condition improved during childhood, so that Stella became able to walk. When she was fifteen, she had a fall, followed by teno-synovitis, and six months' confinement to bed. Henceforward, her walking powers were greatly impaired, so that she could not even get about the room without sticks, and could only leave the house in a wheel-chair or in a carriage.

Up to the age of eight, Stella was very fond of her father, who was extremely kind to her, and used to carry her about and to play with her. Then there came a change in him. He became liable to fits of temper which " overwhelmed " the child ; but, more than all, she suffered from his coldness and indifference towards herself. Unaware of the true causes of this coldness, she fancied that his feelings had changed, that he was dissatisfied with her. Repelled by her father and lacking a mother, she was thrust back upon herself. Entrenching herself in her morbid state, she used it as a house of refuge ; thus " enjoying it," she accentuated it without realising what she was doing. But in this refuge she felt derelict. She was on the look-out for the "father" or the "guide" she needed. The whole of her analysis is dominated by this search for the guide. At the date of the analysis she was forty-five. All her inner life had been lonely; her feelings had turned towards philosophical, moral, and religious ends.

The first time Stella left her bed after she had been bed-ridden for six months at the age of fifteen, she made a point of going to see her father, thinking he would be delighted. Her father did not seem to notice that anything had happened. This was a great shock to her, a terrible disillusionment. "It deprived me of all energy to do anything that might make me better." The incident summarises all the disappointment of her filial affection, all the consequent withdrawal into herself, all her resignation to illness—which was accepted, even gladly, because it facilitated the withdrawal into the self. The retreat from the father was likewise a retreat from the world. The two movements were identical, and Stella felt towards the world, towards human beings in general, precisely what she felt towards her father. "Human beings have been a disappointment to me." She added: "Again and again I thought I had found a guide. Always I was mistaken. I have come to think that we have to guide ourselves." It is easy to understand what psychic elements were superadded to the physical condition so as to aggravate the latter. It was not difficult, therefore, for analysis and suggestion to bring about an improvement in the bodily state, but at this stage something occurred which arrested progress and even led to a relapse. Her brother died. This was a great grief, for Stella looked upon her brother as a sort of father. She had transferred on to him her strongest feelings. To some extent, he had become for her the guide she needed, and she was certainly fonder of him than of anyone else in the world. His death was as great a shock as had been thirty years earlier her realisation that her father was indifferent to her. The two things underwent condensation in her mind, and the old feeling of "what's the use?" recurred. Once again she was "deprived of all energy to do anything that might make her better." But it is not my aim here to dwell upon the patient's bodily state. The details concerning it have only been given because of the relationships between the bodily state and the idea of the "guide." On two occasions the loss of the guide brought about the same flight from the world, the same isolation, for which the illness furnished a pretext.

The first dream to be analysed was the outcome of this twofold preoccupation with the "guide" and the "disappointment."

> I. Someone—a man—gives Stella a white wicker basket to hold. It is the sort of basket that bakers use, covered with fine, clean linen. As soon as she has the basket in her hand, there is a stir beneath the linen cover, and a number of wasps fly out, though she had believed that there was bread in the basket. In a fright, she hands it back. The man who gave it to her was sitting as driver upon the front seat of a cart. The wasps buzzed, but not one of them stung her.

The oblong "basket" calls up as association the shape of a "cradle." This is also the shape of the ovary, a shape which, as we know, not infrequently appears in dreams.[1] We discern here a condensation of a number of primary wishes which have remained unfulfilled: more particularly, there is a duplex maternal craving, that to *have* a mother and that to *be* a mother. The "white linen" and the "bread" call up "pure" and "true." But disillusionment comes. The associations to "wasps" are "poison," "treachery," "cruelty," "hatred." Following upon the illusions of purity comes the discovery of the repulsive aspect of passion. "Driver" calls up "guide." The guide also appears here as a man who might be loved. But the idea of the guide is refused in this form. The subject has repelled every kind of sexual temptation. This, manifestly, is the meaning of the last symbol: "not one of them stung her."

In the dream which followed our first sitting we find the joint preoccupations with the "guide" and the "treatment."

> II. I was living in a country house. I was on the road near the house. . . . I wanted to go into the town, this town was M. (the subject's native city), to attend a lecture upon

[1] Cf. Jeanne, dream VIII.

local history. I had no other means of going there but the little wheel-chair in which I get about. *I could have found someone to take me there, but there was no one to bring me back;* and the return would have to be made after dark. Yet it was absolutely essential that I should go. I was much disturbed about it, and unaided I managed to make my way up a steep hill to the shed where my wheel-chair was, although I knew that I should not be able to get down again. But I was afraid of nothing, for I absolutely must go to the lecture, even though I had to go alone pushing my own chair along. *All the time there was someone near me;* I could hear the voice, but I did not know who it was. *But this person could not come with me, he could merely advise me.* He tried to persuade me not to go to the lecture; or at least, if I did go, to spend the night in the town. At the same time he told me that, after the lecture, there would be another lecture in the same hall, on psychology this time; and he said that the two lectures would last an hour and a half in all. This made me feel more than ever how essential it was for me to go. I awoke in the midst of my preparations for departure.

"An hour and a half" had been the duration of our first sitting, of which, as already said, the foregoing dream was a sequel. The sitting had been psychoanalytical, followed by suggestion. The return to the native city symbolises the way in which the analysis had been delving into reminiscences of childhood and into the subject's earliest ego. The lecture on local history is psychoanalysis; the lecture on psychology is suggestion. The associations, which I shall not record, made these points perfectly clear. Already, however, the question of the "guide" comes to the front. "She could be taken to the town, but would have to come back alone." I shall, in fact, be able to guide her for a time, but then I shall leave her to herself once more, and the prospect of this makes her nervous. In addition, there is another guide, a rival of mine. He is not an adequate guide, for he can only give advice, and cannot accompany the subject. He is a person "in grey," and he calls up in association one of Andreieff's plays, *The Life of Man.* In this play there is a mute, "someone in grey," who carries a candle of which the flame is born, grows, and dies simultaneously with the birth, growth, and death of "man," thus marking out all the stages of his life. A person "in grey," associated with a "mute"; a guide who can "give advice but cannot act as companion "—here we have indications that we are concerned with someone who is dead,[1] but whose influence on Stella's mind persists. We readily recognise the paternal imago. On the other hand, this person in the dream reminds the subject of the driver in dream I, the driver who symbolised "man beloved and a guide." The symbol, therefore, is complicated. It represents the guide, in incarnations in which the subject has given up searching for the guide; and yet she has not completely given up the search in these incarnations, for the phantom guide is still trying to keep her at home and to prevent her from coming to see me.

In order that the analysis may be accepted, the search for a guide, which is still fundamentally directed towards the paternal imago, must be transferred on to the analyst. This mechanism is plainly manifest in the following dream, in which there appears the figure of another analyst who had been interested in Stella's case a few years earlier:

> III. . . . I find myself face to face with X [the analyst previously mentioned], so suddenly that for a moment I jostle him; but directly afterwards I step backwards, saying: "Verzeihen Sie, Doktor" [Excuse me, Doctor]. He looks at me coldly, and says: "Bitte, genieren Sie sich gar nicht" [Not at all]. . . . I want to retire to my room because this meeting distresses me, but something hinders me, and I circle round him without being able to get any farther. At length I succeed. I go slowly, very slowly, towards my room. I open the door and close it behind me very slowly, always hoping that he will call me back. But he merely says in a bored tone: "Diese Umständlichkeit!" [What a fuss!] When I am in my room, I am filled with despair. I say to myself: "If only he had been put out, there might still have been some hope of a reconciliation; but if there is nothing but indifference and boredom, all is over!" . . .

Her feeling at the close is the same that she had had when fifteen years old in relation to her father's indifference. Then, too, Stella would have preferred to see her father put out. We see signs of the condensation of the father with the analyst, and of transference on to the analyst. But the kinship is closer. The analyst, like the father, is an inadequate guide, and will ultimately have to be renounced. We have here

[1] As to the symbolisation of the dead by persons clad in grey who are mute, cf. Régis et Hesnard, op. cit., p. 171.

the same apprehension as that disclosed in dream II by the idea that she would have to "come back alone." To round off the history, I should add that X. and Stella had quite ceased to see one another, to Stella's great regret. But the fundamental idea persists, that an analyst is not a guide who can be permanently depended on, and that the guide must be sought elsewhere.

In various dreams there appeared under diverse forms the image of three psychotherapeutists on whom, successively, Stella had projected her ideal of the guide. At the time when she consulted me, there had been a change in her state of mind; her wish was, not so much that I should act as her guide, as that I should help her to discover the guide in herself.

IV. In one of the dreams of this series, three doctors appear on the scene, as if in consultation, introducing themselves by their titles (the three psychotherapeutists). They are followed by a *young woman who gives a silent greeting*. The association to this "young woman" is "myself, that which appears in me." In Stella's eyes, the young woman represents a possibility of sublimation related to the analysis now in progress. I do not make my entry on the stage as a fourth therapeutist; the fourth comer is Stella herself, for she has decided to seek the guide within herself. She has thought over my theory of autosuggestion, and has found therein the expression of this real need.

V. In another dream, whose symbolism is not altogether complimentary to us psychoanalysts and persons of a like category, the three previous courses of treatment are symbolised by three water-closets, which have been provided for the house, but which cannot be used. Two of them are supplied with "every possible convenience," but "they will not work because their system is too complicated." The third is rather of a rustic character, but it can only be reached by passing through dirty passages. In the last instance, the reference is a painful one. Stella had a very deep feeling for the third psychotherapeutist, but renounced it because she was afraid it had sexual implications.

The analysis now in progress is symbolised by a fourth

water-closet. It is a long way from the house, and one has to go there alone by a difficult road. Here we may discern once more the call the subject is making, and which I am encouraging, upon her own energies.

The use of the fantastic symbol of the water-closet may be explained in relation to the current term "to pour oneself out," in the sense of "saying everything that is in one's mind." It is also related to a kindred expression in scientific terminology, for, in the first days of psychoanalysis it was spoken of by Breuer as the *cathartic method*—"cathartic" being a medical synonym for "purgative." The subject was familiar with the expression "the cathartic method."

VI. We now reach a more adequate and more comely symbol of the same phenomenon. We derive it from the analysis of a drawing which Stella made when in a reverie. The drawing represented a golden cross furnished with golden balls. At the centre of the cross was the letter S. At the ends of the arms were the letters T. and R. respectively. On the top was the letter A. The subject's Christian name begins with S.; R. means religion; T., work (travail); A., love (amour). But the following associations show that the three letters R., T., and A., really symbolise the three psychotherapeutists. The first of these, she says, guided her towards *religion*. The second advised her to undertake some specific *work*, to have an active aim in life. The third, the central figure in the incident mentioned above, was an enthusiast and an artist, and said that no one had *loved* her enough to cure her. Stella added: "I think now that one has to be one's own guide. Each must carry his own burden."

This cross, drawn in a reverie, reminds her of a similar cross seen in a dream. In the dream, a golden ball fixed on the top of the cross (in the place of the letter A.) fell down, and she thinks of a fall into a bottomless abyss. The ball likewise reminds her of "the world." Thus the fall of this "ball" is the final renunciation of "love" and of the "world." The ball vanishes; the cross remains. This signifies the contrast between the spiritual life and the world. At the centre of the cross she sees herself (S.). She is determined to find the guide in herself, and yet it must be a guide who transcends her. She consciously designates him as the Christ;

not the Christ of dogma, but the *living* Christ, the symbol of *universal* love.

The "religion" which she had been advised by the first psychoanalyst to espouse had been too much a matter of externals. The "guide" whom she seeks is of a more mystical character. So far, then, the dream and the reverie both express ideas of which she is conscious; but, more intimately, they express, with a strange clarity of symbolism, the kinship of this mystical guide with the earlier guides whom he is to replace. We have, throughout, the same need, originally directed towards the father, subsequently passing by derivation towards various persons, and finally undergoing sublimation as a spiritual ideal.[1]

VII. This spiritual orientation is not yet radical, but wishes to become so. In a reverie, Stella wrote almost unconsciously the words:

> The matter must be settled. The change must be restlos, restlos, restlos.

"Restlos" signifies "without residue," "radically." Quite mechanically, too, she drew a sort of 8, which at first suggested to her mind the German name of this numeral, "acht"; then, by a word-play, "gib Acht," meaning "take care," which was a catchword of her father's. As in dream II, the paternal imago (with its incarnations as aforesaid) holds her back, being in opposition to the new object on to which the need for a guide desires to undergo transference. But to the paternal advice "take care" is counterposed the earnestly reiterated "restlos, restlos, restlos." A further association is Goethe's phrase, "stirb und werde" (die and become). Just as in the dream of the ball which fell from the summit of the cross, so here, we have the will to "die to the world" and to give herself up wholly to a higher life which, however spiritual it may be, is still to remain active, to harmonise within herself "work" and sublimated "love."

[1] At about the same stage, Stella made a drawing of a woman on the cross. When she was asked what this sketch signified, she answered: "It has always been a puzzle to me why the crucified is invariably represented as the Christ, as a man, seeing that woman is the eternally crucified!"

GENEVA, 1915–1921

GLOSSARY

Most of the definitions are from the present work, or from Baudouin's *Suggestion and Autosuggestion*. For Freudian usage (where this differs from Baudouin's) the translators are greatly indebted to Ernest Jones' *Papers on Psychoanalysis*.

affect. Feeling. The essential constituent of emotion.

affective association. A synonym for **condensation, which see.** Two ideas tinged with the same affect tend to call one another up mutually (**evocation**).

anxiety neurosis. Functional nervous disorder in which anxiety, i.e. intense morbid dread, is the most conspicuous and persistent symptom.

association. The linking of images, ideas, or mental states so that one tends to call up another. See **evocation**. Classical psychology recognised that when two ideas, images, or mental states had occurred together or in brief succession, the revival of one tended to call up the other (**association by contiguity**); and that linking also resulted when two ideas or images contained like elements (**association by similarity**); there is also **association by contrast**. Psychoanalysts stress, in addition to these two familiar types, a third type known as **affective association**, which see. See also **free association.**

autoerotism. Sexual excitement occurring independently of actual relations with another individual, and self-induced either physically or mentally. (Adjective, **autoerotic**).

autosuggestion. The subconscious realisation of an idea in more or less complete independence of heterosuggestion.

cathartic method. The purging of the effects of a pent-up emotion by bringing it to the surface of consciousness. This term was applied by Breuer to the technique which was subsequently perfected as psychoanalysis.

censor and **censorship**. In Freudian terminology, a figurative impersonation to denote the sum of repressive forces. Also spoken of as "the endopsychic censor." See **repression.** For Baudouin's critique of the concept of the "censorship," see text, pp. 65 et seq.

claustrophobia. Morbid dread of enclosed spaces.

collective symbols. See **symbols.** Collective symbols are of the same nature as other symbols; they merely presuppose that the **condensations** and **displacements** on which they depend are such as occur in a very large number of minds.

collective unconscious. Jung writes (*Psychology of the Unconscious*, p. 198): "Although individuals are widely separated by differences in the contents of their consciousness, they are closely alike in their conscious psychology. It is a significant impression for one working in practical psychoanalysis when he realises how uniform are the typical unconscious complexes." Thus the term "collective unconscious" does not signify much more than "the very evident uniformity of the unconscious mechanism" (ibid., p. 198). See also **collective symbols**; also text, p. 131; also Translators' Preface, p. 8.

complex. A group of emotionally tinged ideas partially or entirely repressed (Jones). According to Baudouin, the term, as generally used in psychoanalytical literature, lacks precise definition; it "may be applied to . . . subconscious condensations accompanied by displacements." See p. 54. The reader will do well to note that in current parlance the notion of repression into the subconscious is not a necessary part of the concept "complex." For instance, Culpin, in *Spiritualism and the New Psychology*, defines the complex as a system of ideas having a common centre, whether the system is present in the consciousness or exists only in the unconscious. In this sense a "hobby" is based upon a complex, though there may be no repression whatever. Such, indeed, is Freud's own usage of the term, for he defines **complexes** (*Introductory Lectures*, p. 90) as "circles of thoughts and interests of strong affective value."

condensation. The process whereby images characterised by a common affect are grouped so as to form a single composite and new image. See p. 27. An extreme form of **affective association.** Ribot's definition will be found on p. 39. See also **evocation**. Freud writes (*Introductory Lectures*, p. 144): By **condensation** "we mean to convey the fact that the content of the manifest dream is less rich than that of the latent thoughts, is, as it were, a kind of abbreviated translation of the latter." But he goes on to say that, if we prefer, the significance of the term may be limited to the process in virtue of which "latent elements sharing some common characteristic are in the manifest dream put together, blended into a single whole."

contention. The psychological equivalent of attention, minus effort. (Term employed by Baudouin in expounding the theory and practice of autosuggestion). See Translators' Preface, p. 10.

delusions of persecution. See **persecution complex.**

dementia præcox. A common form of insanity in which a patient loses contact with reality and withdraws into a world of his own imaginings.

derivation. The process in virtue of which the energy of a thwarted instinct finds an outlet in a new channel. See also **sublimation** and **displacement.** Baudouin says (p. 83): "Derivation is the projection upon a dynamic plane of that which is displacement upon a static plane."

displacement. Transference of affect from one idea (one image, or one object) to another. Baudouin writes: "It might be spoken of as a transference attended by forgetfulness, complete or partial, of the point of departure." See also **transference** (2). A fuller definition will be found on p. 52.

dissociation.—(1) The inverse of **association,** which see. The process in virtue of which the close linking between two ideas, images, or mental states, is resolved. See pp. 156, 198.

(2) The break-up of consciousness into parts which lead independent existences. See pp. 228, 303, 313.

Electra complex. Excessive attachment, sexually tinged, of the daughter for the father. The feminine counterpart of the **Oedipus complex,** which see. See also **fixation.** Sometimes Baudouin refers to the Electra complex, or at any rate to fixation upon the father, as the **paternal complex.**

evocation. A term used by Claparède. Practically synonymous with **affective association** or **condensation,** which see.

Also used in its familiar sense of "a calling up" (by association—through contiguity, similarity, or affective rapport).

exhibitionism. The exposure of some part of the body usually concealed, in most cases the genital organs, with accompanying sexual excitement. The person performing such an act is an **exhibitionist.**

extrovert. One whose **libido** (which see) or vital impetus or psychic energy tends mainly outward. Thus the extrovert is predominantly a man or woman of feeling or action. The state of being an extrovert is called **extroversion.** See p. 93.

father-fixation. See **fixation.**

fixation. The arrest of an affect at a more primitive stage than that normally corresponding to the individual's age and development. Especially used of the fixation of a daughter's sexual affection upon the father (father-fixation, see **Electra complex**); and of the fixation of a son's sexual affection upon the mother (mother-fixation, see **Oedipus complex**).

free associations. Associations which do not have as their starting point a dream or a reminiscence, but such as arise when isolated words are uttered within the hearing of the subject of analysis. —See **association.**

This is the sense in which Baudouin uses the term in the *Studies*, for an application of the associative method which has been especially developed by Jung. But Freud applies the term to *any* associations which are the outcome of "undirected thinking." He writes (*Introductory Lectures*, p. 88): "When I ask a man to say what comes into his mind about any given element in a dream, I require him to give himself up to the process of **free association** which follows when he keeps in mind the original idea." See Translators' Preface, pp. 9 and 10.

guiding fiction. The image of an end to be attained, which the mind sets up as a **rationalisation** (which see), thus explaining to itself the urge of a subconscious motive.

hallucination. An imaginary sensation, one to which no objective reality corresponds, experienced while awake. See also **hypnagogic hallucinations.**

hallucination by compromise. A hallucination suggested by the illusory interpretation of an objective reality. See p. 60.

heterosexual. Pertaining to sexual relationships between persons of different sexes.

heterosuggestion. The subconscious realisation of an idea suggested by another.

Also, the act of suggesting an idea to another.

homosexuality. Love for a member of the same sex.

hypnagogic hallucinations. Hallucinations experienced in the psychological state which immediately precedes falling asleep. They are thus intermediary between hallucinations proper (those experienced in the waking state) and dreams.

hypnosis. A general name for states of **outcropping of the subconscious** (which see) produced by immobilisation of the attention, and for states of somnolence which are distinguishable from ordinary drowsiness by their mode of production.

ideoreflex process. The process by which an idea realises itself or tends to realise itself in action. (It is to this that Baudouin limits the significance of the term suggestion.)

imagination. [The translators have been taken to task by a reviewer for not including this term in the Glossary to *Suggestion and Autosuggestion*. Like other persons, Baudouin uses the word in varying senses, which the context makes intelligible.] The meaning ranges from: (1) The action of imagining, or forming a mental concept of, what is not actually present to the senses; to (2) the faculty by which images are formed, or revived, the latter being "reproductive imagination"; and (3) the power which the mind has of forming concepts beyond those derived from external objects, this being "productive imagination;" and (4) the creative faculty of the mind in its highest aspect, its power of framing new and striking intellectual conceptions, its poetic or scientific genius—this is "creative imagination."

infantilism. Fixation at an infantile state, and especially at an infantile state of feeling. See **fixation.**

inferiority complex. (Adler's terminology.) The complex which results from the thwarting of man's natural urge to self-expansion, and which (when repressed into the subconscious) impels him to try to achieve power along some other line than that in which his energies are blocked. See also **masculine protest.**

interest. This term is suggested by Claparède to replace **libido,** which see. See text, p. 95.

introvert. One whose **libido** (which see) or vital impetus or psychic energy tends mainly inward. Thus the introvert is predominantly a thinker. The state of being an introvert is called **introversion.** See p. 93.

kinæsthetic sensations. Sensations that accompany muscular movements or efforts. Sometimes spoken of collectively as the "muscular sense."

libido. Sexual hunger; the mental aspect of the sexual instinct. But by psychoanalysts the term "sexual" is used with wide connotations, so that "libido" becomes almost synonymous with "psychic energy," and also with what Bergson terms the "vital impetus." Indeed, Tansley defines **libido** as "the psychic energy inherent in the great natural complexes, or becoming attached to any individual complex, and discharging itself along the appropriate conative channels." In like manner, Jung unifies all instinctive energy under the term "libido." See also text, p. 88. Baudouin (p. 92) summarises the definition thus: "Libido is instinctive energy considered from the outlook of the faculty for undergoing transformation and evolution." [This word should be pronounced "libeedo," with the stress on the second syllable.]

masculine protest. (Adler's terminology.) The **inferiority complex** (which see) leads to a desire for superiority—a "wish to be a complete man," the "masculine protest." Adler regards the idea of inferiority as associated with femininity.

masochism. Voluptuous (sexual) enjoyment experienced when suffering mental or bodily pain, usually inflicted from without; the counterpart of **sadism.**

maternal complex. See **Oedipus complex.**

memory trace. The effect left on the organism by any experience, the effect in virtue of which, when the like experience recurs, the reaction of mind or body differs from that which was the immediate result of the first experience of the kind.

mother-fixation. See **fixation.**

narcissism. The concentration of interest (usually sexual interest) upon one's own body and one's own personality in general. (From the myth of Narcissus.) Some Freudian writers shorten the term to "narcism."

neurosis. Functional disorder of the nervous system. According to psychoanalytical theory, such disorder is (in many cases at least) an undesirable derivative of thwarted instinctive energy. See **derivation.**

Oedipus complex. Defined by Ernest Jones as "the (usually unconscious) desire of a son to kill his father and possess his mother." Many would prefer to define it, less uncompromisingly, as excessive attachment, sexually tinged, of the son for the mother. The counterpart in women is the **Electra complex,** which see. See also **fixation.** Baudouin tersely defines the Oedipus complex as "the condition in which a boy is greatly attached to his mother while more or less hostile to his father." See text, p. 168. Sometimes Baudouin refers to the Oedipus complex, or at any rate to fixation upon the mother, as the **maternal complex.**

outcropping of the subconscious. The invasion of the upper levels of consciousness by uprushes from the subconscious. See Translators' Preface, pp. 9 and 10.

over-determination. In Freudian phraseology, when a psychological phenomenon is the outcome of several factors, any one of which seems competent (acting in isolation) to produce the effect, it is said to be "over-determined." Baudouin uses the term in a rather more restricted sense: "The elements which are associated (condensed) in virtue of their being tinged with a common affect, are usually associated as well in virtue of the objective laws of association (contiguity, similarity, contrast). See p. 55.

paternal complex. See **Electra complex.**

persecution complex. The psychoanalytical term for what alienists usually speak of as "delusions of persecution," these being morbid beliefs on the part of a patient that he is being persecuted, slandered, and injured.

phobia. Intense and persistent morbid dread of some object or class of objects. See, for instance, **claustrophobia.**

psychoanalysis. (Freudian usage.) A study and analysis of man's unconscious motives and desires as shown in various nervous disturbances and in certain manifestations of everyday life in normal individuals. Ernest Jones defines it briefly as "the study of unconscious mentation."—Baudouin would not reject this definition; but he also regards psychoanalysis as "an evolutionary theory of the instincts." See p. 29.

rationalisation. The inventing of a reason for an attitude or action, the motive of which is not recognised.

regression. Two meanings in Freudian terminology: (1) Resolution of an idea into its sensorial components instead of the usual passage onwards in the direction of action. (2) Reversion of mental life, in some respect, to that characteristic of an earlier stage of development, often an infantile one. (Jones.) For Baudouin's critique of the term, see pp. 57 et seq.

representation. The image of an object in the mind. Adjectival form **representative.** See also **imagination.**

repression. (Freudian usage.) The keeping from consciousness of mental processes that would be painful to it. See also **censor.** For Baudouin's critique of the Freudian theory of repression, see text pp. 65 et seq. and pp. 72 et seq.

resistance. "The instinctive opposition displayed towards any attempt to lay bare the unconscious; a manifestation of the repressing forces." (Jones.)

sadism. Voluptuous (sexual) enjoyment on inflicting, or witnessing the infliction of, bodily or mental pain; the counterpart of **masochism.**

subconscious. In Baudouin's terminology, a region of the mind normally inaccessible to consciousness—usually spoken of by psychoanalysts as the "unconscious." See Baudouin, *Suggestion and Autosuggestion*, pp. 275 and 276; also footnote to p. 73; also Translators' Preface, pp. 7 and 8. [It should be noted that the Vienna School of psychoanalysts (school of Freud) looks upon the subconscious (unconscious) as pre-eminently the storehouse of the "lower" or more primitive elements of human nature. The Zurich School (school of Jung), on the other hand, stresses also the importance of "higher" elements in the subconscious (unconscious)—elements of a progressive character. Baudouin does not commit himself to any theory on this matter; but it will be obvious to his readers that he does not regard the subconscious as merely a Caliban.] Baudouin uses the form "subconscious" because the "unconscious" includes the sphere of physiological processes (reflex action, etc.) which are not mental at all. Thus, for him, the subconscious is "the psychological unconscious." See *Suggestion and Autosuggestion*, pp. 275 and 276.

sublimation. The employment of energy belonging to a primitive instinct in a new and derived, i.e. non-primitive, channel. E.g. the use of sexual energy in "intellectual" love or creative work. Baudouin terms sublimation "a successful and beneficent derivation" (p. 77). See **derivation.** (See also p. 272.)

suggestibility. Readiness to realise a suggestion. (In Baudouin's use of the term—in more or less complete independence of heterosuggestion.) Readiness to realise an autosuggestion.

suggestion. The subconscious realisation of an idea. See also **ideoreflex process.**

superiority complex. The individual's emotionally tinged conviction that he excels others in one or many respects. Often a subconscious reaction against the **inferiority complex,** which see.

symbol. Something that, not being a portrait, stands for something else; an emblem. For peculiarities in the psychoanalytical use of this term, see text, pp. 61 et seq. See **symbolism.** See also **collective symbols.**

symbolism and **symbolisation.** Representation by symbols. The Freudians regard this as the means whereby the workings of the unconscious are veiled from the conscious mind. But Baudouin writes (p. 27): "**Condensation** (which see) . . . is the first stage in the creation of the symbol. I look upon symbolisation as a general law of the imagination, and not as being necessarily the outcome of the masking of forbidden representations." See also Translators' Preface, pp. 10 and 11, and text, pp. 61 et seq.

systematised delusions. Delusions which produce a consistent and logical effect upon the patient's conduct.

teleology, subconscious. The law of subconscious teleology runs as follows: "Suggestion acts by subconscious teleology; when the end has been suggested, the subconscious finds means for its realisation."

transference. (1) As used by Ribot. May in a sense be regarded as the inverse of **condensation** (which see). Here a feeling, instead of grouping round itself a number of separate images, is itself dispersed over a number of associated images. (See p. 40.)

(2) As used by Claparède in a sense identical with that of Freud's *Verschiebung* (**displacement**). Similar to (1), but the feeling does not merely become related to a new object; it is partly or wholly detached from its former object. (See p. 42.) This leads us to:

(3) As used by practising psychoanalysts to-day in reference to "the transference of affect on to the analyst." The affect thus displaced may be either positive or negative, a liking or a dislike. Transference on to the analyst, with "fixation of affect," is discussed by Baudouin, pp. 113 et seq.

unconscious. See **subconscious.**

BIBLIOGRAPHY

ADLER, Alfred, Ueber den nervösen Charakter, Bergmann, Wiesbaden, second edition, 1919; translated by B. Glück and J. E. Lind, the Neurotic Constitution, Kegan Paul, London, 1921.

ANONYMOUS, An Outline of Psychology, The Plebs League, London, 1922.

ANONYMOUS, A Young Girl's Diary, with a preface by Sigmund Freud, translated by Eden and Cedar Paul, Allen & Unwin, 1921.

ARNOLD-FORSTER, Mary, Studies in Dreams, with a Foreword by Morton Prince, Allen & Unwin, London, 1921.

ARTUS-PERRELET, L., Le dessin au service de l'éducation, Delachaux et Niestlé, Neuchâtel and Paris.

BANCELS, see LARGUIER DES BANCELS.

BAUDOUIN, Charles, The affective Basis of Intelligence, "Psyche and Eros," vol. i., No. 2, New York, 1920.

BAUDOUIN, Charles, Culture de la force morale, Société de Psychologie Appliquée, Nancy, 1917. This work is now being rewritten under the title, La conquête de soi-même. (An English translation is in prospect.)

BAUDOUIN, Charles, Les idées nouvelles sur la suggestion, "Scientia," Milan, July 1921.

BAUDOUIN, Charles, Suggestion et autosuggestion, Delachaux et Niestlé, Neuchâtel and Paris, second edition, 1921. Suggestion and Autosuggestion, translated by Eden and Cedar Paul, Allen & Unwin, London, eighth impression, 1922.

BAUDOUIN, Charles, Le symbole chez Verhaeren. (This was the original title of the work now being published in French as Etudes de psychanalyse II, le symbole poétique chez Verhaeren. An English translation will shortly be published by Allen & Unwin, under the title, Psychoanalysis and Æsthetics.

BERGSON, Henri Louis, L'énergie spirituelle, Alcan, Paris, 1919.

BERGSON, Henri Louis, Matière et mémoire, Alcan, Paris, eleventh edition, 1914; translated by N. M. Paul and W. S. Palmer, Matter and Memory, Swan, Sonnenschein (now Allen & Unwin), London, 1911.

BLEULER, Eugen, Ueber die Bedeutung von Assoziationsversuchen, in the collection, Diagnostische Assoziationsstudien, vol. i., Barth, Leipzig, 1906; Upon the Significance of Association Experiments, being Chap. I of Studies in Word Association, by Jung and others, translated by M. D. Eder, Heinemann, London, 1918.

BOVET, Pierre, L'instinct combatif, Delachaux et Niestlé, Neuchâtel and Paris, 1917.

BOVET, Pierre, Preface to Artus-Perrelet's, Le dessin au service de l' éducation (see Artus).

BOVET, Pierre, Preface to Oscar Pfister, La psychanalyse au service des éducateurs, Bircher, Berne, 1921.

BOVET, Pierre, La psychanalyse et l' éducation, Payot, Lausanne, 1920.

BOVET, Pierre, Le sentiment filial et la religion, "Revue de Theologie et Philosophie," Lausanne, 1920.

BREUER, Josef and FREUD, Sigmund, Studien über Hysterie, Deuticke, Leipzig and Vienna, 1895.

BREUER, Josef and FREUD, Sigmund, Ueber den psychischen Mechanismus hysterischer Phänomene, "Neurologisches Zentralblatt," Nos. 1 and 2, 1893.

BRUNSCHVICG, Léon, Introduction à la vie de l'esprit, Alcan, Paris, third edition, 1920.

CLAPARÈDE, Edouard, L'association des idées, Doin, Paris, 1903.

CLAPARÈDE, Edouard, Introduction to Freud's La psychanalyse, see FREUD.

CLAPARÈDE, Edouard, La psychologie de l'enfant, Kündig, Geneva, fifth edition, 1916; English translation from the fourth edition by Mary Louch and Henry Holman, Experimental Pedagogy and the Psychology of the Child, Edward Arnold, London, 1911.

CLAPARÈDE, Edouard, Théorie biologique du sommeil, "Archives de Psychologie," vol. iv., Geneva, 1905.

CLARK, L. Pierce, A Clinical Study of some Mental Contents in Epileptic Attacks, "The Psychoanalytic Review," vol. vii. No. 4, Washington, 1920.

COCHET, M. A., Psychoanalyse et mysticisme, "Revue de Philosophie," vol. xx., No 6, Paris, 1920.

COMTE, Auguste, Cours de philosophie positive, Paris, 1842.

CONDILLAC, Etienne Bonnot de, Traité des sensations, vol. i., 1754.

COUÉ, Emile, La maîtrise de soi-même par l'autosuggestion consciente, Oliven, Paris, 1921; English translation, Self-Mastery by Conscious Autosuggestion, can be obtained from the Institute for the Practice of Autosuggestion, 20 Grosvenor Gardens, London, S.W.1.

CULPIN, Millais, Psychoneuroses of War and Peace, Cambridge University Press, 1920.

CULPIN, Millais, Spiritualism and the New Psychology, with an introduction by Leonard Hill, Arnold, London, 1920.

DARWIN, Charles, The Origin of Species, 1859.

DREVER, James, Instinct in Man, a Contribution to the Psychology of Education, C. U. Press, 1917; second edition, 1921.

DUMAS, Georges, Troubles mentaux et nerveux de guerre, Alcan, Paris, 1919.

DWELSHAUVERS, Georges, La psychologie française contemporaine, Alcan, Paris, 1920.

EBBINGHAUS, Ueber das Gedächtniss, Leipzig, 1885.

EDER, M. D., War Shock, London, 1917.

EVARD, Marguérite, L'adolescente, Delachaux et Niestlé, Neuchâtel and Paris, 1914.

FERENCZI, S., Introjektion und Uebertragung, Deuticke, Leipzig, 1910.

FLOURNOY, Théodore, Nouvelles observations sur un cas de somnambulisme, "Archives de Psychologie," vol. i., Geneva, 1901.

FLOURNOY, Théodore, Une mystique moderne, "Archives de Psychologie," vol. xv., Geneva, 1915.

FOREL, Auguste, Les fourmis de la Suisse, Nouveaux mémoires de la Société helvétique des Sciences naturelles, vol. xxvi., Zurich, 1874.

FREUD, Sigmund, Die Traumdeutung, 4th edition, Deuticke, Leipzig, 1913; English translation by A. A. Brill from third German edition, The Interpretation of Dreams, Allen & Unwin, London, 1913.

FREUD, Sigmund, Drei Abhandlungen zur Sexualtheorie, Deuticke, Leipzig, 1905; second edition, 1910; English translation by A. A. Brill, Three Contributions to the Theory of Sex, 3rd revised edition, New York, 1918.

FREUD, Sigmund, Introductory Lectures on Psychoanalysis, translated by Joan Rivière, with a preface by Ernest Jones, Allen & Unwin, London, 1922.

FREUD, Sigmund, Paralysies hystériques, Sammlungen, Erste Folge, 1906.

FREUD, Sigmund, Studien über Hysterie, see BREUER.

FREUD, Sigmund, Ueber die Psychogenese eines Falles von weiblicher Homosexualität, "Internationale Zeitschrift für Psychoanalyse," vol. vi., Vienna, 1920.

FREUD, Sigmund, Ueber Psychoanalyse, Deuticke, Leipzig, 1909, fifth edition, 1920; French translation by Le Lay, La Psychanalyse, Sonor, Geneva, 1921 (the German was a translation of five lectures delivered in 1909 at Clarke's College, U.S.A., and published in the American "Journal of Psychology").

FREUD, Sigmund, Zur Dynamik der Uebertragung, "Jahrbuch für psychoanalytische und psychopathologische Forschungen," Leipzig and Vienna, 1911.

GALLICHAN, Walter M., The Psychology of Marriage, Werner Laurie, London, 1917.

GROOS, Karl, Die Spiele der Menschen, Jena, 1899; English translation by E. L. Baldwin, The Play of Man, New York, 1901. Die Spiele der Tiere, Jena, 1896; English translation by E. L. Baldwin, The Play of Animals, Chapman & Hall, London, 1898.

HAMILTON, Sir William, Lectures on Metaphysics, London, 1859.

HART, Bernard, The Psychology of Insanity, Cambridge University Press, 1920.

HESNARD, A., see RÉGISand HESNARD.

JAMES, William, The Principles of Psychology, 2 vols., Macmillan, London, 1890.

JAMES, William, Talks to Teachers on Psychology, and to Students on some of Life's Ideals, Longmans, London, 1899.

JANET, Pierre, L'automatisme psychologique, Alcan, Paris, fourth edition, 1903.

JANET, Pierre, Les médications psychologiques, Alcan, Paris, 1919.

JANET, Pierre, Rapport au Congrès de Londres, 1913.

JANET, Pierre, Les obsessions et la psychasthénie, Alcan, Paris, 1903.

JELLIFFE, Smith Ely, and Zenia X., Psychoanalysis and Compulsion Neurosis, "The Psychoanalytic Review," vol. vii., No. 2. Washington, 1920.

JONES, Ernest, Papers on Psychoanalysis, Revised and enlarged edition, Ballière, London, 1918.

JOST, Die Assoziationsfähigkeit in ihrer Abhängigkeit von der Verteilung der Wiederholung, "Zeitschrift für Psychologie," vol. xiv.

JOUFFROY, Théodore Simon, Cours d'esthétique, Paris, 1843.

JUNG, Carl Gustav, Collected Papers on Analytical Psychology, Authorised translation edited by Constance E. Long, Ballière, London, 1916.

JUNG, Carl Gustav, Contribution à l'étude des types psychologiques, "Archives de Psychologie," vol. xiii., Geneva, 1913.

JUNG, Carl Gustav, Psychoanalyse und Assoziationsexperiment, in the collection, Die agnostische Assoziationsstudien, vol. ii., Barth, Leipzig, 1906; Studies in Word Association, authorized translation by M. D. Eder, Heinemann, London, 1918.

JUNG, Carl Gustav, Psychologischen Typen, Rascher, Zurich, 1912.

JUNG, Carl Gustav, Wandlungen und Symbole der Libido, Deuticke, Leipzig and Vienna, 1912; English translation by Beatrice M. Hinkle, The Psychology of the Unconscious, Moffatt, Yard & Co., New York, 1916, Kegan Paul, London, 1921.

KOLNAI, Aurel, Psychoanalysis and Sociology, translated by Eden and Cedar Paul, Allen & Unwin, London, 1921.

LANG, J. B., Eine Hypothese zur psychologischen Bedeutung der Verfolgungsidee, "Psychologische Abhandlungen," Deuticke, Leipzig, 1914.

LARGUIER DES BANCELS, Jacques, Introduction à la psychologie; l'instinct et l'émotion, Payot, Paris, 1921.

LEMAÎTRE, Auguste, article in "Archives de Psychologie," July, 1916.

LEMAÎTRE, Auguste, Le symbolisme dans les rèves des adolescents, et remarques sur l'inversion précoce, Forum, Neuchâtel and Geneva, 1921.

LÉPINE, Jean, Troubles mentaux de guerre, Masson, Paris, 1917; English translation, Mental Disorders of War, edited by Charles A. Mercier, University of London Press, 1919.

MacCurdy, John T., War Neuroses, Cambridge University Press, 1918.

McDougall, William, An Introduction to social Psychology, twelfth edition, Methuen, London, 1908.

Maeder, A., Guérison et évolution dans la vie de l'âme, Rascher, Zurich, 1918.

Mercier, Charles Arthur, A Textbook of Insanity, second edition, Allen & Unwin, London, 1914.

Mill, John Stuart, Logic, London, 1843.

Miller, Hugh Crichton, The New Psychology and the Teacher, Jarrolds, London, 1921.

Morel, Ferdinand, Essai sur l'introversion mystique : étude psychologique de pseudo-Denys l'Areopagite et de quelques autres cas de mysticisme, Geneva, 1918.

Mourgue, R., Etude critique sur l'évolution des idées relatives à la nature des hallucinations vraies, Jouve, Paris, 1919.

Münsterberg, Hugo, Grundzüge der Psychologie, Leipzig, 1900.

Odier, Charles, A propos d'un cas de contracture hystérique, "Archives de Psychologie," vol. xiv., Geneva, 1914.

Paul, Eden and Cedar, Creative Revolution, Allen & Unwin, London, 1920.

Paulhan, F., Les transformations sociales des sentiments, Flammarion, Paris, 1920.

Perrelet, *see* Artus-Perrelet.

Pfister, Oscar, Die psychanalytische Methode, Klinkhardt, Leipzig and Berlin, 1913 ; English translation by Charles Rockwell Payne, the Psychoanalytic Method, Kegan Paul, London, 1917

Pfister, Oscar, Was bietet die Psychanalyse dem Erzieher ? Klinkhardt, Leipzig and Berlin, 1917 ; French translation by Pierre Bovet, La psychanalyse au service des éducateurs, Bircher, Berne, 1921 ; English translation by Charles Rockwell Payne and F. Gschwind, revised by Barbara Low, Psychoanalysis in the Service of Education, being an Introduction to Psychoanalysis, Kimpton, London, 1922.

Piéron, H., Une adaptation biologique du Freudisme aux psychonévroses de guerre (a review of Rivers' Instinct and the Unconscious), " Journal de Psychologie," No. 1, Paris, 1921.

Proczek, Casimire, Ce que les parents devraient savoir sur leurs filles, Imprimerie Centrale, Lausanne, 1918.

Régis, Emmanuel and Hesnard, A., La psychoanalyse des névroses et des psychoses, Alcan, Paris, 1914.

Rénon, Louis, Tuberculose pulmonaire chronique, " Le Monde Médicale," Paris, Jan. 15, 1914.

Ribot, Théodule Armand, Essai sur l'imagination créatrice, Alcan, Paris, 1900 ; English translation by Albert H. N. Baron, Essay on the Creative Imagination, Kegan Paul, London, 1906.

RIBOT, Théodule Armand, Logique des sentiments, Alcan, Paris, 1905.

RIBOT, Théodule Armand, Les maladies de la personalité, Alcan, Paris, fourteenth edition, 1908.

RIBOT, Théodule Armand, La psychologie des sentiments, Paris, 1896; English translation in Contemporary Science Series, The Psychology of the Emotions, Walter Scott, London, 1897.

RIGNANO, Eugenio, Psychologie du raisonnement, Alcan, Paris, 1920.

RIVERS, William Halse Rivers, Freud's Concept of the Censorship, "The Psychoanalytic Review," vol. vii., No. 3, Washington, 1920.

RIVERS, William Halse Rivers, Instinct and the Unconscious, Cambridge University Press, 1920.

RIVERS, William Halse Rivers, Mind and Medicine, a lecture, second edition, London, 1920.

RIVERS, William Halse Rivers, The Repression of War Experiences, "Proceedings of the Royal Society of Medicine, section of psychiatry," London, 1918.

ROLLAND, Romain, The Forerunners; translated from the French by Eden and Cedar Paul, Allen & Unwin, London, 1920.

ROMANES, George John, Animal Intelligence, Kegan Paul, London, 1881.

ROMANES, George John, Mental Evolution in Animals, Kegan Paul, London, 1883.

RUSSELL, Bertrand, The Analysis of Mind, Allen & Unwin, London, 1921.

RYNER, Han, La philosophie, "La Revue de l'Epoque," Paris, 1920.

SCHERNER, Carl Albert, Entdeckungen auf dem Gebiete der Seele, vol. i., Das Leben des Traumes, Schindler, Berlin, 1861.

SCHNEITER, C., Archaische Elemente in den Wahnideen eines Paranoiden, "Psychologische Abhandlungen," Leipzig, 1914.

SPALDING, Douglas A., Instinct, with Original Observations on Young Animals, "Macmillan's Magazine," vol. xxvii., pp. 282–293, 1873. Quoted by Romanes, Mental Evolution in Animals, pp. 161–5. Spalding's paper was reprinted in the "Popular Science Monthly," vol. lxi., p. 126, 1902.

SPINOZA, Benedictus de, Ethics, book three.

TANSLEY, Arthur George, The New Psychology and its Relation to Life, new edition, revised and enlarged, Allen & Unwin, London, 1922.

THORNDIKE, Edward Lee, Educational Psychology, New York, 1914.

THORNDIKE, Edward Lee, The Elements of Psychology, New York, 1917.

VARENDONCK, J., The Psychology of Day-Dreams, Allen and Unwin, London, 1921.

VODOZ, J., Roland, un symbole, Champion, Paris, 1920.

WARD, James, Psychological Principles, Cambridge University Press, 1918.

ZENIA X., see JELLIFFE.

INDEX

Abel, 232
Absence of Mind, 54
Absinthe as Symbol, 263, 264
Accent, vulgar, *see* Vulgarity
Acceptance—
of Analyst, *see* Transference
of normal Love and Marriage, 234
Accident as Symbol, 121, 124, 125, 285, 292
Action—
Man of, 225
pent-up, 28, 57, 58, 71
Actives, 57
Activity, outward, 225
Adam, old, Casting off, 234, 243
Adaptation biologique du Freudisme aux psychonévroses de guerre, 34, 339
Adaptation to Real, 15, 28, 69
ADLER, 21, 26, 29, 89, 90, 91, 92, 93, 94, 96, 160, 168, 169, 200, 212, 331, 335
Adolescence, Crisis of, 148–167
Adolescente, 148, 337
Affect—
see also Emotion
as Creator, 57
defined, 327
Affective aspect of Instinct, 79, 80
Affective Basis of Intelligence, 40, 56, 335
Affective Theory of the Association of Ideas, 37–64
Affectives, 57
Affectivity—
based on Instinct, 84
Biological Theory of, 24, 29
explained by Instinct, 24
Mechanism of, 120
subconscious, 65
Agamemnon, 222
Alarm, subconscious sexual, 277
Algolagnia, 77
Allegory, 63
Amiel, 43
Anæsthesia induced by Suggestion, 112
Analysis of Mind, 8, 22, 340
Analysis, *see* Psychoanalysis
Analyst, *see* Psychoanalyst
Analytical Study of Psychoanalysis, 94, 96
Andreieff, 322
Andromeda, 317
Aneiferung, 13
Anger, 80
Anguish, 180, 181
Animal Intelligence, 80, 340
Animated Statues, 136
ANONYMOUS, 335
Ant and Grasshopper, 248
Anxiety, 180, 182, 238
Dream, *see* Dream
Neurosis, 91, 220, 327
States, 97, 180, 218–234
Apollo, Uffizi, 194, 195, 196, 197
Apprentice as Substitute for Father, 197
A propos d'un cas de contracture hysterique, 104, 339
Archaic Aspect of Dream States, 66, 67, 68
Archaische Elemente in den Wahnideen eines Paranoiden, 67, 340
"Archives de Psychologie," 161, 336, 337, 338, 339
Aristotle, 25, 37
ARNOLD-FORSTER, 11, 15, 335
Arranging, Mania for, 276
Art, 13, 71, 84, 98, 109
its Appeal depends on Relation to Complexes, 135
Origin and Function of, 278, 279
Artistic Ambition, 235
Arts, plastic, 278, 279
ARTUS-PERRELET, 285, 335, 336, 339
Association—
affective, 39, 40, 42–56, 68, 327, 328, 329, *see also* Condensation
Association—
affective, Laws of, 42–56
by Contiguity, 37, 39, 45, 46, 55, 68, 327, 329, 332
by Contrast, 37, 55, 122, 139, 258, 327, 332
by Similarity, 37, 39, 45, 46, 55, 68, 327, 329, 332
defined, 327
free, 9, 10, 61, 62, 280, 327, 330
Jung's Researches, 55
of Ideas, Affective Theory of, 24, 25, 37–64
Association des Idées, 41, 132, 336
Associationism, 25, 39, 42, 48
to Psychoanalysis, 37–42
Associationist Evolutionists, 132
Associationists, 37, 38, 45, 46, 55
Associations—
Inheritance of, 132
spontaneous, 303, 313
Assoziationsfähigkeit in ihrer Abhängigkeit von der Verteilung der Wiederholung, 338
Asthma, 90
Attention, 10, 61, 108
Attenuation of Affect by Displacement, 122
Attitude towards Analyst, 301, 303
Authority—
maternal, Wish to escape from, 218
paternal, 145, 151, 164, 176, 197, 220
Auto-erotism, 77, 154, 268, 313, 317, 327
Automatic Association, 303, 313
Automatic Drawing, 325
Automatic Painting, 276
Automatic Writing, 157, 158, 276, 303
Automatism, psychological, 101
Automatisme psychologique, 47, 338
Autopsychoanalysis, 11, 199, 201–209
Autosuggestion, 7, 11, 14, 103, 106, 107, 108, 115, 175, 177, 183, 185, 196, 197, 206, 208, 209, 216, 220, 228, 252, 256, 257, 275, 302, 303, 324, 327, 328, *see also* Suggestion
Avarice, 141, 142, 145
Avenue as Symbol, 259
Awkwardness and Constraint, 193–198

Bag as Symbol, 244
Bajazet, 311
Baldwin, 337
Balzac, 311
BANCELS, *see* LARGUIER DES BANCELS
Bandaged Eyes as Symbol, 280, 281, 282
Bankruptcy, fraudulent, as Symbol, 238, 239
Baron, 339
Basement Window as Symbol, 216
Basket as Symbol, 182
BAUDOUIN, 7, 8, 9, 10, 11, 12, 13, 14, 15, 30, 40, 54, 56, 60, 61, 73, 79, 106, 109, 161, 187, 327, 328, 329, 330, 332, 333, 334, 335
Bear—
as Symbol, 281, 282
Pit as Symbol, 280, 282
Bearded Man as Symbol, 142
Beast, human, 160
Beasts, sticky, as Symbols, 131
Beatrice (Portinari), 224, 242
Behaviourism, 8
Benoist-Hanappier, 205
Bergerac, 306, 307, 311
BERGSON, 6, 24, 42, 58, 59, 60, 61, 73, 92, 238, 306, 307, 309, 335
Bernheim, 94, 101, 102, 106, 111
Bibliography, 335–340
Bicycle—
as Symbol, 268
Wheels as Symbol, 182
Black Dress as Symbol, 155
BLEULER, 55, 335
Blood as Symbol, 222, 259
Bludgeoning the Acolyte, 12
Blushing, 141
Boaz, 99, 100

Bog as Symbol, 137, 138
Bolt as Symbol, 182
Booz endormi, 99
Bourget, 309
BOVET, 23, 25, 26, 29, 30, 71, 77, 82, 97, 99, 270, 285, 335, 336, 339
Boy Scouts, 313
Breaking away from Analyst, 301
Breaking away from Father, *see* Protest
Breaking away from Mother, 141, 218, 284, 285, *see also* Fixation
Breathing Exercises, 275
BREUER, 41, 101, 102, 325, 336, 337
Bridges between recent and earlier Psychology, 23, 33
Brill, 337
Bromides, 265
Bronchitis, 240
Brother—
little, as Symbol, 227
as Substitute for Father, 231, 239, 269, 320
Brown as Symbol, 172, 173
BRUNSCHVICG, 42, 336
Brush as Symbol, 245, 246
Bruyère, 189
Burglar as Symbol, 178, 179, 180, 233, 234
Burial Fantasy, 144, 310
Burying as Symbol, 268
Bushy Trees as Symbol, 259
Butcher's Shop as Symbol, 138, 139

Café as Symbol, 137, 138, 139
Cain, 232
Caliban, 333
Canary as Symbol, 184, 185, 186
Caractères, 189
Caresses, Refusal of, 140
Caressive Impulse, 241
Caricatures of psychological Type, nervous Disorders as, 218
Carlos, Don, 85
"Carmel, Le," 207
Cassiopeia, 204
Catalepsy, 114
Categories of Psychoanalysis, 21–27, 84
Caterpillar as Symbol, 132
Cathartic Method, 325, 327
Catholicism and Protestantism, 163, 164
Causality, 99
Cellar as Symbol, 142, 144
Censorship, 13, 27, 65, 66, 67, 71, 72, 73, 74, 103, 200, 214, 229, 327, *see also* Repression
Ceremonial, religious, Dislike for, 235
Certain Age, Woman of, as Symbol, 252
Ce que les parents devraient savoir sur leurs filles, 148, 339
Chain as Symbol, 166
Change of Analyst, 302–319
Change of Beds as Symbol, 280
Charcot, 94, 101, 102, 104, 106, 114
Charles X, 63, 64
Charming, Prince, 138
Cheerfulness, excessive, 276
Child as Symbol, 227, 233, 249, 250
Childbearing, Refusal of, 212
Children, 119–147
Chimney-Sweep as Symbol, 53, 62, 210
Christ, 46, 47, 62, 100, 171, 266, 270, 300, 325, 326, *see also* Jesus
Christian Science, 107
CLAPARÈDE, 6, 23, 24, 38, 41, 42, 44, 54, 60, 69, 87, 88, 89, 92, 94, 95, 96, 132, 329, 334, 336
CLARK, 255, 336
Classical Psychology, *see* Psychology of the Schools
Claustrophobia, 98, 161, 328, 332
Cleaning as Symbol, 253
Clerk—
chief, as Substitute for Father, 177, 276
head, as Substitute for Father, 177, 276
Cliffs as Symbol, 174
Clinical Study of some mental Contents in epileptic Attacks, 255, 336
Clytemnestra, 222
COCHET, 116, 336
Coddling, 240, 243
Collaboration between Suggestion and Psychoanalysis, 13, 14, 31, 113
Collected Papers on Analytical Psychology, 12, 338
Collective Neurosis, 91
Collective Suggestion, *see* Suggestion, collective
Collective Unconscious, *see* Unconscious, collective
Columbus, 23, 81
Compensation (Adler), 89, 160
Complex—
defined, 54, 328
fundamental, 13
inferiority, 331, 334
maternal, *see* Maternal Complex and Oedipus Complex
parental, 103, *see also* Fixation
paternal, 176–183, 253, 329, *see also* Electra Complex
Persecution. *see* Persecution, Ideas of
Superiority, *see* Superiority Complex
Uniform, 171
Complexes—
explaining normal Character Traits, 217
revealed by favourite Poetry, 134
underlying Neuroses, 217
COMTE, 33, 336
Concentration, 108, 109
deficient, 235, 279
Conciliation of Psychoanalysis with Suggestion, 105–116
Condensation, 10, 11, 27, 39, 40, 43–50, 60, 62, 63, 65, 67, 68, 74, 78, 84, 97, 123, 124, 222, 238, 261, 295–298, 317, 320, 321, 323, 327, 328, 329, 334, *see also* Association, affective
Law of, 54, 55
CONDILLAC, 37, 336
Confession, 116
Conflict, 14, 97, 180, 182, 257, 272, 273, 291, 292
in Children, 120
State of, 159–167, 169–175
Conquête de soi-même, 335
Constantine, 305–306
Constraint, Feeling of, 143, 149–151, 183–198
Consumption, *see* Tuberculosis
Contamination, Ideas of, 254, 255, 263, 264, *see also* Defilement
Contemplations, 153
Contemplative Life, 241
Content—
latent, 9, 328
manifest, 9, 328
Contention, 10, 108, 328
Contiguity—
see Association
Law of, 37
Continence, 182
Contracture, 41, 54, 261
Contrast—
see Association
between Psychoanalysis and Suggestion, 101–105
Law of, 37
Contribution à l'étude des types psychologiques, 93, 338
Convulsive Seizures, *see* Epilepsy
Cooperative as Symbol, 318
Corpus Christi procession, 242
Coquetry objectified, 277
COUÉ, 13, 106, 108, 110, 336
Councillors, federal, as Substitutes for Father, 269
Cours d'Æsthétique, 38, 338
Cours de philosophie positive, 336
Courteline, 165
Creation, æsthetic, 28
Creative Imagination, *see* Imagination, creative
Creative Revolution, 22, 339

Crisis
Apollinian, 279
Dionysiac, 279
mental and nervous, as Symbol, 276, 277
of Adolescence, 148–167
of Hostility towards Analyst, 301
of Sublimation, 272
of Transference, 303
Crookedness as Symbol, 238
Crowd, Dislike of, 241
Cruelty in Children, 70
Cul-de-jatte, 32, *see also* Legless Man
CULPIN, 22, 96, 328, 336
Cultivator of Hysteria, Charcot as, 104, 115
Culture de la force morale, 335
Cultured Life, 258, 261
Cunigunde, 308
Cupboard as Symbol, 317
Curiosity, 97, 98
Cyrano, 306, 317

Dagger as Symbol, 259
Dalcroze, 299, 300
Dame voilée, 154
Danaides, 232
Dance, St. Vitus', 162, 163
Dancing as Symbol, 160, 161, 162, 163, 166
Dante, 224, 242
DARWIN, 62, 100, 132, 336
David, 100
Day-Dream, 9, *see also* Reverie
Death, 204
as Symbol, 137, 138
Fear of, 200, 204, 302
Obsession by Idea of, 204
Decondensation, 62
Defilement—
see Contamination
as Symbol, 178, 179
Deformed Creature as Symbol, 264
Delirium, Language of, 254
Delusions of Persecution, 255–261, 329, *see also* Persecution, Ideas of
Dementia præcox, 32, 93, 329
Demon as Symbol, 227, 228, 232, 233, *see also* Devil
Demoniac, 105
Demosthenes, 90
Depreciation of Analyst, 189
Depression, Fits of, 152
Derelict Dream, 128, 129
Derivation, 58, 77, 80, 83, 88, 97, 98, 104, 105, 109, 110, 272, 290, 326, 329, 332, 334
Dervish, dancing, as Symbol, 166
Descartes, 24, 96
Descent of Man, 100
Désinvolture, 194
Desire killing Love, 236
Dessin au service de l'éducation, 285, 335, 336
Devil as Symbol, 160, 161, 232, *see also* Demon
Diagnotische Assoziationsversuchen, 335
Direction (Orientation), 99
Director, spiritual, 116, 273
Dirty Food as Symbol, 293
Dirty Passages as Symbol, 324
Dirty Snow as Symbol, 247, 248
Dirty Underlinen as Symbol, 222, 247, 248, 253
Dirty Water as Symbol, 247, 253
Discipline—
Dislike for, 235, 239
Prussian, 196
Disguise in Dreams, 71
Disgust, 212, 238
for Coquetry, 277
inspired by Sexuality, 131, 192, 214, 258, 259, 260, 277, 281, 285, 286
Disinterest, 60
Disorder, 221, 223
Disparagement of Analyst, 301
Displacement, 27, 28, 42, 48, 50–56, 62, 63, 65, 67, 68, 69, 70, 74, 83, 121, 122, 123, 241, 328, 329, 334
Displacement—
defined, 52
Law of, 55
Dissociation, 156, 198, 228, 303, 313, 329
Distinction, Person of, 257, 258
Distinguished Persons, 257, 258
Dog as Symbol, 132, 162
Dogma, religious, Dislike for, 235
Doing-up Room as Symbol, 252, 253
Don Carlos, 85
Don Juan, 90
Door as Symbol, 52, 213, 214
Dragon as Symbol, 159, 160, 161
Drama of Child and Father, 270
Dread, *see also* Fear and Phobia
Dread Father, 226
Dread God, 230
Dread Mother, 153, 193, 220, 224, 228, 310
Dread of the Father, 176–183, 276
Dream—
Anxiety, 187
as Guardian of Sleep, 66
Bergson's Theory of, 59
derelict, 128, 129
drowning, 128, 129
erotic, 165, 181
falling, 161
Freudian, 11
Freud's Theory of, 65 *et seq.*
Function of, 28, 65–75
Immersion, 137
Interpretation of, 9
its Relation to Play, 28, 69–71
latent, 9, 328
manifest, 9, 328
of forbidden Pleasures, 120, *see also* Nightmare
psychoanalytical Theory of, 43, 59
Suffocation, 137, 138, 161, 204, 205
the symbolical Realisation of an unsatisfied Tendency, 75
Dreaming and Action, 56–64
Dreaming and Play, 69–71
Dreams—
Language of, 254
Latent Sexuality in, 141
prophetic, 152
Dreams that point out the Way, 83, 84, 244
Drei Abhandlungen zur Sexualtheorie, 77, 88, 337
DREVER, 76, 79, 99, 336
Driver as Symbol, 314, 321, 323
Drop at the Wrist, 261
Drowning Dream, 128, 129
Drunken People as Symbol, 172, 173
Duchosal, 153
DUMAS, 98, 336
Duncan, 308
DWELSHAUVERS, 39, 336
Dynamics of the affective Life, 65–75

Earth, Descent into, as Symbol, 136
Earth's Movement, Obsession concerning, 220, 230, 231, 234
Ease, 189, 194, 195, 196, 197
Lack of, 185
EBBINGHAUS, 37, 336
Eclectics, 33, 38
EDER, 96, 335, 337, 338
Education in Confraternity, 91
Educational Psychology, 79, 340
Educationist, Analyst as, 273, 302, 314
Effeminacy, 188, 195, 196
Ego Instinct, *see* Instinct, Ego
Egoism, 90
Einstein, 34
Elan vital, 92, 95
Elbow Room, 143
Electra Complex, 171, 329, 332, *see also* Paternal Complex
Elements of Psychology, 75, 340
Embryology, psychic, 87
Emotion, 79–82, 101, *see also* Affect
Empiricists, 37

Energie spirituelle, 42, 59, 238, 335
Energy, 95, 99, 105
 instinctive, 92
 mental, 92
 psychic, 329
Engine-driver, *see* Driver
Engine Headlights as Symbol, 228, 229, 230, 232
Entdeckungen auf dem Gebiete der Seele, 340
Epilepsy, 265–271
Epileptic Insanity, 255
Epileptic States, 254
Erotic Attitude towards Analyst, 301
Erotic Dream, 165, 181
Erziehung zur Gemeinschaft, 91
Essai sur l'imagination créatrice, 39, 339
Essai sur l'introversion mystique, 127, 339
Essay on the Creative Imagination, 339
Essay, *see* School Essay
Ethics, 72, 340
Etude critique sur l'évolution des idées rélatives à la nature des hallucinations vraies, 60, 339
EVARD, 148, 337
Evening as Symbol, 207
Evocation, 41, 44, 327, 328, 329
 Law of, 54
Evolution—
 mental, 99
 of Instinct, 29, 75–84
Exaltation, Fits of, 152
Execution, An, 145
Exhibitionism, 77, 233, 276, 329
Exhumation as Symbol, 268
Expectoration as Symbol, 215, 286
Experimental Pedagogy and the Psychology of the Child, 69, 336
Exploring as Symbol, 284, 291
Explosion as Symbol, 141
Extroversion, 92, 93, 99, 131, 133, 151, 162, 163, 173, 187, 188, 189, 191, 225, 230, 234, 239, 307, 314, 329

Facial Spasm, *see* Spasm of Eyelid
Falling—
 as Symbol, 178, 281
 Dream, 161
 Reminiscence, 226
False Recognition, 237, 238
Fantasy—
 Burial, 144, 310
 Fecundity, 290
 Immersion, 137
 Virginity, 300
 Womb, Return to, 127, 131, 138, 142, 161, 169, 186, 193, 264, 281
Father as Symbol, 188, 234, 269, 312
Father, divine, 270
Father—
 Dread of, *see* Dread
 Fear of, *see* Fear
 Reconciliation with, symbolical, 220
 Repudiation of, 269
 Substitutes for, *see* Substitute
 tyrannical, 219, 226, 227, 229, 230, 280
 Vengeance upon the, 232, 233
Father-Fixation, *see* Fixation
Fatherhood, Longing for, 233
Fatigue—
 disproportionate, 257
 Duty, 244
Faust, 246
Fear—
 (*see also* Dread and Phobia), 79, 97, 98, 114, 203
 of being late, 250, 251
 of Cemetery, 224
 of Madness, 302
 of Reality, 218
 of the Father, 176–183, 276
 of the Sexual, 98, 218
Fears concerning Childbirth, 209–211
Fecundity, Fantasy of, 290
Feeling Tone, 46
Femininity, Refusal of, 135–141, 174, 200, 211–216, 212, 282–294
Feminist Revolt, 283, 291
FERENCZI, 102, 103, 104, 108, 113, 337
Fetichism for Women's Clothing, 184, 186
Feuchtersleben, 195
Fiancé, 257, 258
Fiction, guiding, 91, 158, 330
Finalism, 25, *see also* Teleology
Fire as Symbol, 316
Fixation, 14, 89, 329, 331, 332, 334
 Father, 103, 169, 170, 172, 174, 230, 294–300, 329, 332
 infantile, 243, 245, 308, 315, 317, *see also* Regression
 Mother, 103, 119, 120, 127, 129, 130, 133, 135–141, 145, 169, 180, 183, 185, 213, 214, 229, 235, 236, 238, 242, 262, 280, 281, 282, 283, 284, 302, 304, 305, 329, 332, *see also* Maternal Complex
 Sister, 213, 214
 upon the Analyst, 115
Fixed Idea, *see* Obsession
Flesh and Spirit, 279
FLOURNOY, 21, 23, 41, 69, 314, 337
Flying Dutchman, *see* Phantom Ship
Flying Dutchman, 173
Forbidden Pleasure, *see* Pleasure
FOREL, 76, 337
Forerunner of Psychoanalysis, Nietzsche as, 279
Forerunners, 76, 340
Formula—
 of Autosuggestion, 197
 of Ease, 197
FORSTER, 11, 15, 335
Fourmis de la Suisse, 76, 337
Frank, 220
Free Associations, *see* Association
Freedom from Mother, Desire for, 284, *see also* Breaking away from Mother
FREUD, 8, 9, 10, 11, 14, 15, 22, 26, 29, 34, 41, 42, 43, 44, 45, 46, 48, 53, 56, 57, 58, 59, 61, 62, 63, 64, 66, 68, 69, 70, 71, 72, 73, 74, 77, 81, 82, 87, 88, 90, 91, 92, 93, 94, 96, 100, 101, 102, 103, 105, 106, 107, 111, 112, 113, 154, 168, 174, 199, 200, 201, 227, 230, 328, 330, 333, 334, 336, 337
Freudian Dream, 11
Freud's Concept of the Censorship, 67, 340
Freud's Theory of the Dream, 65 *et seq.*
Frigidity, 211, 214
Frog as Symbol, 144
Fruit, forbidden, *see* Pleasure
Function of Dreams, 28, 65–75
Function of the Real, 58, 237, 238
Fundamental Complexes, 13
Fussy Activity, 170, 218, 247–253

Galileo, 34
GALLICHAN, 22, 337
Gefühlsbetonte Komplexe, 55
Genealogy of Tendencies, 84–100
General Survey, 21–34
Genesis, Book of, 266
Geneva as Meeting-place of two Cultures, 23
Geneva School, 12
George, Saint, 232, 233
German Spies as Symbol, 227
Glossary, 327–334
Goblin as Symbol, 162
God—
 as Love, 226
 as Tyrant, 226
God's Eyes, 228
Goethe, 246, 326
Gonorrhœa, 236
Gil Blas, 165
Glück, 335
Gracian, 194, 195, 196
Grasshopper and Ant, 248
Gregariousness, 8
Grey Clothing as Symbol, 201, 202, 203, 322, 323
Grimacing old Women as Symbol, 219, 220, 252
Grimm, 162, 193

Grundzüge der Psychologie, 339
Groos, 69, 70, 337
Gschwind, 339
Guardian of Sleep, Dream as, 66
Guérison et évolution dans la vie de l'âme, 99, 339
Guide—
Identification with, 265
Lack of, 285
Search for, 14, 98, 218, 301–326
Sublimation of Idea of, 319–326
well-informed and cultured, 258
Guiding Dreams, 83, 84, 244
Guiding Fiction, *see* Fiction, guiding
Gymnastics as Symbol, 163, 274, 275

Habit-spasm, 41, 54
Haldane, 194
Hallucination, 60, 61, 160, 276, 330
by Compromise, 60, 330
hypnagogic, 220, 330
Hamilton, 37, 337
Hanappier, 205
Hart, 254, 337
Haste, Obsession with, 251
Hat—
pointed, as Symbol, 278
tall, as Symbol, 269
Headache, 152
Helvétius, 184
Henrath, 48–50
Hercules, 43, 44, 207
Hesnard, 21, 55, 323, 337, 339
Heterosexuality, 330
Heterosuggestion, 330
Hide and Seek, 240
Hiding as Symbol, 179, 180, 280
Hill, 336
Hinkle, 338
History of a Five-Franc Piece, 142 *et seq.*
Hoarseness as Symbol, 286
Hobby, 328
Holman, 336
Homeopathy, 265
Homesickness for Mother, 185
Homosexuality, 77, 90, 148, 149, 195, 200, 213, 214, 215, 218, 228, 229, 230, 235, 271, 287, 301, 305, 317, 330
Hostility—
from, to Sympathy, 302–319
to the Analyst, 301
to the Family Environment, 254, 255, 260
to the Father, 168, 180, 181, 219, 220, 283, 238, 286, 332, *see also* Oedipus Complex
to the Mother, 218, 251
to the Sister, 218
Housework, Dislike of, 257, 258
Hugo, 100, 153, 270, 283, 308
Human Beast, 160
Hurry up, 249
Hydrophobia, 101
Hypersuggestibility, 158
Hypnagogic Hallucination, *see* Hallucination
Hypnosis, 330, *see also* Hypnotism
Hypnotism, 31, 101, 102, 103, 104, 105, 106, 107, 108, 109, 111, 158
spontaneous, 157
three States of, 114
Hypothese zur psychologischen Bedeutung der Verfolgungsidee, 254, 338
Hysteria, 66, 93, 101, 104, 115, 256, 260

Ibsen, 304, 306, 307, 308
Ichtrieb, 89, 93
Idées nouvelles sur la suggestion, 335
Ideoreflex Power of Autosuggestion, 115
Ideoreflex Process, 330, 334
Ill-humour, 257, 258
"Illustration, L'," 151
Images, composite, 44
Imagination, 11, 15, 28, 69, 200, 330, 331
affective, 74
based on Affectivity, 84
controlled by Subconscious, 119
Imagination—
creative, 27, 28, 45, 56, 57, 58, 68, 69, 89, 331
epic, 82
explained by Affectivity, 24
productive, 331
reproductive, 331
Imago—
maternal, 224, 225, 236, 241
paternal, 171, 174, 177, 223, 255, 300, 323, 326
Imitation, *see* Instinct, imitative
Imitation of Christ, 98
Immersion—
Dream, 137
Fantasy, 127, 144, 145, 236, 237
Impetus, vital, 92, 95, 329
Impotence, 211, 218, 234–246
Impulses, Control of, 108
Inattention, 58
Incitation, 13
Incubated, Longing to be, 185
Indecent Assault, 263
Individualism, 169, 235
of the Introvert, 188
Right to, 166
Inductive Method, 12
Indulgence, maternal, 142, 183
Infantile Aspect of Dream States, 67, 68, 70
Infantile Attitude towards Analyst, 301
Infantile Attitude towards Parents, 217, 229
Infantile autoerotic Stage, 154
Infantile erotic Feelings towards Parents, 103
Infantile Paralysis, 319
Infantile Regression, 103, 243, 254, 269, 308, 310
Infantile Sexuality, 168
Infantilism, 310, 331, *see also* Regression
Inferiority Complex, 331, 334
Influence, 115, 116
undue, Analyst must avoid, 302
Inhibition, 75
Inland as Symbol of Extroversion, 162
Innate Associations and Condensations, 132
Insanity—
and Epilepsy, 267
epileptic, 255
Insomnia, 185, 302
Inspectionism, 77
Instability, physical, Feeling of, 220
Instinct—
combative, 23, 71, 77, 80, 82, 85, 97, 98, 185, 186, 228
Disorders of, 80
Ego, 89, 92, 93
Evolution of, 28, 75–84, 86, 95
for Motherhood, 199, 200, 209–216
for Power, 29, 96
imitative, 98, 114
maternal, 98, 273
maternal, thwarted, 282–294
of Courtship, 99
of Expansion of Personality, 89
of Self-Preservation, 89, 96, 199–209
sexual, 29, 78, 81, 82, 85, 88, 89, 92, 93, 96, 98, 99, 114, 166, 185, 200, 273
Sleep as, 69
social, 99
sublimated, Repression of, 191, 299
Suppression of, 78, 97
thwarted, 272
Transformation of, 75, 76, 78, 79, 99
Instinct and the Unconscious, 34, 96, 340
Instinct combatif, 23, 71, 77, 97, 99, 335
Instinct in Man, 76, 79, 99, 336
Instinct with Original Observations on Young Animals, 340
Instincts expressed in Dreams, 199
Institut de rythmique Jaques Dalcroze, 300
Institut Jean Jacques Rousseau, 300, 318
Institute for the Practice of Autosuggestion, 336
Intelligence, 15, 28, 69, 76
Interest, 10, 81, 95, 115
"Internationale Zeitschrift für Psychoanalyse," 337

Internment, 235
Interpretation of Dreams, 201, 337
Interpretation of Dreams, 9, 125
Interpretation of Dreams, Simplicity in, 125
Introduction à la psychologie, 24, 338
Introduction à la vie de l'esprit, 42, 336
Introduction to Psychology, 79
Introduction to Social Psychology, 339
Introductory Lectures on Psychoanalysis, 9, 11, 14, 88, 328, 330, 337
Introjektion und Uebertragung, 102, 337
Introspection, 218, 234, 235
Introversion, 58, 82, 92, 93, 98, 99, 141–145, 162, 185, 186, 188, 191, 193, 195, 198, 204, 234, 236, 237, 239, 255–261, 268, 269, 271, 279, 280, 308, 310, 313
Intuitionism, 7
Inversion, *see* Homosexuality
Ironmaster, 292
Italian as Symbol, 244, 245

"Jahrbuch für psychoanalytische und psychopathologische Forschungen," 337
James, 23, 24, 75, 76, 77, 79, 338
Janet, 34, 47, 58, 67, 101, 102, 105, 106, 113, 114, 338
Jealousy, 168, 172, 181, 219, 248
Jehovah, 226
Jelliffe, 67, 338, 340
Jesus, 159, 160, 264, 265, 267, *see also* Christ
Society of, 97
John the Baptist, 223
Jones, 7, 96, 327, 332, 333, 338
Joseph, Saint, 202, 203, 204
Jost, 37, 338
Jouffroy, 24, 38, 39, 338
"Journal de Psychologie," 34, 339
"Journal of Psychology," 337
Juan, Don, 90
Jumping as Symbol, 268, 269
Jung, 8, 12, 14, 15, 21, 22, 26, 29, 55, 58, 66, 67, 69, 82, 87, 88, 89, 91, 92, 93, 99, 328, 330, 333, 335, 338
Justice, Statue of, as Symbol, 280, 281, 282

Kaiser as Symbol, 227, 228
Kemp, 194
Killing the old Man, 145 *et seq.*
Kinæsthesia, 59, 199
Kingdom divided against itself, 167
Kinship, biological, 86
Knife as Symbol, 286
Kolnai, 87, 338
Komplexe, 55

Laederach, 48–50
Laforgue, 47
Lakmé, 309, 311
Lamp as Symbol, 141
Lang, 254, 338
Language, 10
of Dreams, 254
Larguier des Bancels, 24, 79, 97, 335, 338
Late, Fear of being, 250, 251
Latent Content, 9, 328
Latent Sexuality in Dreams, 141
Latin Quarter, 163, 165
Lay, Le, 337
Lazarus, 309
Leaders—
as Substitutes for Father, 269
Revolt against, as Symbol, 270
Leben des Traumes, 201, 340
Lectures on Metaphysics, 337
Leg, red, as Symbol, 160, 161, 166
Légendes des siècles, 100
Legless Man, 263, 264
Leisure, 261
Le Lay, 337
Lemaître, 149, 200, 338
Leonidas, 206
Lépine, 97, 338
Lethargy, 114
Lettres persanes, 27
Leuret, 60
Leviathan as Symbol, 160
Libido, 29, 88, 89, 92, 93, 95, 96, 99, 115, 329
Lice as Symbol, 212, 214
Liébault, 106
Life—
Reaching out towards, 126, 127
Superabundance of, 240
as Symbol, 317
Life of Man, 322
Lind, 335
Little Red Riding Hood, 193
Little Snow-White, 193
Lizard as Symbol, 144
Locke, 25, 37
Logic, 339
Logique des sentiments, 40, 41, 340
Lohengrin, 315, 317
Long, 338
Lorgnette as Symbol, 287, 288
Louch, 336
Louis XVI, 46, 47, 62, 64
Louis XVIII, 34
Love, 236
Low, 339
Loyola, 97
Ludendorf, 228
Lulling, 237, 238

MacCurdy, 29, 96, 98, 339
McDougall, 79, 339
"Macmillan's Magazine," 75, 340
Madness, Fear of, 302
Maeder, 69, 99, 339
Magdalen, Mary, 246
Magnet, Affective Life as, 38
Maîtrise de soi-même par l'autosuggestion consciente, 106, 336
Make-up, 242, 243
Maladaptation to Femininity, 212
Maladaptation to Reality, 225
Maladaptation to Sexuality, 214
Maladaptation to Social Life, 133, 141, 148, 151, 187, 235, 239, 241, 273–276, 279
Maladies de la personnalité, 67, 340
Malaise, 257
Maltreatment of Child, 262–265
Mania, 257, 266
religious, 265–271
Maniacal Disturbances, 276–279
Manifest Content, 9, 328
Ma Parfumée, 145
Mariage de Roland, 270
Marionette as Symbol, 208
Marriage—
Acceptance of, 133
Desire for, 218
Non-Acceptance of, 282–294
Repugnance to, 130, 131
Mary Magdalen, 246
Mary, Saint, 204, *see also* Virgin Mary
Masculine Protest, 200, 212, 331
Masculine Role in Women, 135, 174, 282, 283, 290, 291
Masochism, 77, 230, 331, 333
Mass of Suffering, 8
Master as Substitute for Father, 197, 314
Masturbation, 182, 183, 211, 212, 215, 227, 229, 232, 235, 236, 268, 269, 280, 282, 302
Maternal Complex, 161, 193, 204, 228, 229, 241, 310, 331, 332, *see also* Oedipus Complex
Maternal Hypnosis, 103
Maternal Indulgence, *see* Indulgence
Maternal Instinct, thwarted, 282–294
Maternity, Refusal of, 140
Matière et mémoire, 59, 335
Matter and Memory, 335
Meat as Symbol, 138, 139
Medications psychologiques, 34, 106, 114, 338
Meditative Life, 198
Mediums, 69
Melancholy, 276

Melting Snow as Symbol, 247
Memory, *see* Reminiscence
Memory Trace, 158, 332
Mendès, 184, 189, 190
Menstruation, irregular, 199, 216
Mental Aberrations in an Epileptic, 265–271
Mental Disorders 254–271
Mental Disorders of War, 338
Mental Evolution in Animals, 75, 340
Mer and Mère, 162
MERCIER, 267, 338, 339
Merry-go-round as Symbol, 313
Metaphor, 10
Metaphysico-synthesis, 94
Military Affairs as Symbol, 243, 244
MILL, 37, 339
MILLER, 7, 14, 339
Mind and Medicine, 22, 340
Minor Epilepsy, *see* Epilepsy
Mirage as Symbol, 173, 174, 175
Mischbildung, 44
Mischperson, 48
Mistakes, Dread of, 183, *see also* Scrupulosity
Mixed Method, 101–116
Mneme, 310, 311
Molière, 298, 300
"Monde Médicale," 30, 339
Money as Symbol, 196
Monkey as Symbol, 187
Mon oncle et mon curé, 153
Monster as Symbol, 262, 263
Montesquieu, 27
Moral Guidance, 115
Moral Rebuff, 217, 228
MOREL, 127, 339
MORTON PRINCE, 15, 335
Mother as Symbol, 234
Mother-Fixation, *see* Fixation
Motherhood—
  Instinct for, *see* Instinct
  Longing for, 216, 249, 250, 321
  Refusal of, 200, 211–216
Mountain as Symbol, 281
MOURGUE, 60, 339
Mourning as Symbol, 155
Müller, 37
MÜNSTERBERG, 37, 38, 339
Muscular Sense, *see* Kinæsthesia
Music—
  Taste for, 273–276, 302
  Therapeutic Value of, 275
Mute as Symbol, 322, 323
Mysticism, 235, 241, 242
Mystique moderne, 23, 337

Nancy School, 106, 109, 111, 114
  New, 7, 32, 103, 106, 109, 114
Narcissism, 145, 154, 332
Narcissus, 154, 332
Neologisms, 303
Nervous Disorder, 272
Nervous Disorders, typical, 217–253, 254
Nervous Excitability, 275, 298
Nervous Shock, 276
Nervous Temperament, 234
Nervous Uneasiness, 247
Nervousness, *see* Neurosis
Neuralgia, 54, 111, 255–261
Neurasthenia, 93, 217, 235, 298, 302, 312, 315
Neurasthenic Ideas, 247
"Neurologisches Zentralblatt," 336
Neuropath, 32, 90, 91, 273
  potential, 217
Neuropathic Animal, Man as, 33
Neurosis, 14, 32, 33, 53, 58, 77, 90, 93, 101, 102, 103, 104, 105, 108, 109, 249, 272, 275, 332
  Anxiety, 91, 220, 327
  artificial, Hypnotism as, 102
  collective, 91
  of Self-Preservation, 98
  Peace, 96
  Sexual, 98
Neurosis—
  Transference, 89
  War, 96, 98
Neurotic Constitution, 89, 91, 168, 335
New Psychology and its Relation to Life, 22, 340
New Psychology and the Teacher, 7, 339
New School, 143
Nietzsche, 23, 89, 90, 94, 279
Nightmare, 63, 71, 119, 120, 121, 122, 131, 208, 233, 255, 259, 260, 281, 282, 283, 286
Night out, 164, 165
Nilakantha, 309
Non-Affectivity, 60
Non-Entity, 185, 186
Nouvelles observations sur un cas de Somnambulisme, 69, 337
Nudity, 195
Numbers, 287, 288

Objectivation, 82
Obliteration of outer World, 236, 237
Oblong Things as Symbol, 289, 321
Obsession, 262–265, 302
Obsessions et la psychasthénie, 58, 338
ODIER, 104, 261, 339
Oedipus Complex, 13, 164, 168, 169, 180, 181, 219, 220, 222, 223, 224, 233, 234, 238, 281, 329, 332, *see also* Hostility to Father and Maternal Complex
Official Psychology, *see* Psychology of the Schools
Ohnet, 292
Opera-Glasses as Symbol, 216
Optimism, 201
Oraculo Manual y Arte de Prudencia, 194
Orientation, 99
Origin of Species, 86
Origin of Species, 336
Ostade, 245
Outcropping of the Subconscious, 9, 10, 61 330, 332
Outline of Psychology, 22, 335
Over-determination, 45 46, 332
  Law of, 55
Overwork, 217

Painting, automatic, 276
Paleontology, psychic, 87
Palmer, 335
Pansexualism, 123, 182, 199
Pantheism, 185, 235
Papers on Psychoanalysis, 7, 96, 327, 338
Papillons, 207, 209
Paralysies hystériques, 41, 337
Paralysis, 54, 261, 319
Parentage—
  common biological, of different affective States, 78
  common instinctive, of Affects, 84
  instinctive, 86
Parental Complex, 103, *see also* Fixation
Parish Priest as Substitute for Father, 248
Parish Priest as Symbol, 247, 248, 249
Pascal, 23, 46, 47, 62
Pasha, tailed, as Symbol, 160, 161
Passionate Friendship, 152
Passivity, 285
Paternal Complex, 253, 329, 332, *see also* Electra Complex
Paternal Hypnosis, 103
Paternal Injustice, 223
Path as Symbol, 201
Pathological Method, 31
PAUL, E. and C., 15, 22, 335, 338, 339, 340
Paul, N. M., 335
PAULHAN, 82, 339
Payne, 339
Peace Neurosis, 96
Pent-up Action, *see* Action, pent-up
Peopling the Unconscious with Shadows, 12, 22
Perception, 59, 60
  internal, 199
PERRELET, *see* ARTUS-PERRELET

Persecution Complex, 255, 329, 332, *see also* Persecution, Ideas of
Persecution, Ideas of, 211, 254, 255–261, 277, 329
Perseus, 317
Personalism in Religion, 235
Perversion, sexual, 33, 77, 235, 238
Pessimism, 185, 191
Petit Mal, *see* Epilepsy
PFISTER, 63, 81, 105, 119, 339
Phantom Ship as Symbol, 173, 174
Philippe II, 85
Philosophic Trend, 183–198
Philosophie, 340
Phobia—
  see also Dread and Fear
  of Buttons, 263
  of confined Places, *see* Claustrophobia
  of Dress-Hooks, 263
  of Water, 262
Phobias, 276, 277
  defined, 332
Phosphenes, 59
PIERCE CLARK, 255, 336
PIÉRON, 34, 75, 339
Pig as Symbol, 244, 245
Pilzecker, 37
Pink Paint as Symbol, 312
Pins and Needles, 63
Plastic Arts, 278, 279
Plato, 37, 88
Platonic Passions, 148, 149
Play, 28, 69–71
  and Dreaming, 28, 69–71
  as Outlet for unutilised Tendencies, 28
  in Education, 69
  Theory of Dreams, 69
Play of Animals, 337
Play of Man, 337
Pleasure—
  forbidden, 120, 125, 126, 131, 141, 162, 285
  Principle, 91, 93
Plebs League, 22
Poetic Creation, 65
Poetry, favourite, reveals Complexes, 134
Pointed Hat as Symbol, 278
Pointed Objects as Symbols, 131
Pomegranate Syrup as Symbol, 312, 313
" Popular Science Magazine," 340
Porker as Symbol, 244, 245, 246
Post-chaise as Symbol, 150
Pour lire au bain, 189
Power Principle, 91, 93
Predisposition, 217, 260
Pregnancy, 52, 53, 199, 209–216
Priest, *see* Parish Priest
Primitive Man, 66, 67
PRINCE, 15, 335
Prince Charming, 138
Principles, guiding, of the present Work, 27–34
Principles of Psychology, 75, 79, 338
Privy as Symbol, 192
PROCZEK, 148, 339
Profession, Choice of, 235
Prognathism as Symbol, 289
Progressive Tendency, *see* Tendency
Projector as Symbol, 316, 317
Promotions, 299, 300
Prophetic Dreams, 152
Prosecution of Baudouin for Magic, 48
Protest—
  against Sexuality, 287
  against the Environment, 255
  against the Father, 54, 120, 142, 145–147, 183, 221, 226, 228, 238, 255, 271, 287, 290, 291
  against the Step-Mother, 294–300
  against Virility, 188
  masculine, 200, 212, 331
  Woman's, against Man, 290
Protestantism and Catholicism, 163, 164
Provençal as Symbol, 244, 245
Prussian Discipline, 196
Pseudo-Reminiscence, 9, 237, 238
Psychanalyse, 87, 88, 89, 94, 96, 102, 112, 336, 337
Psychanalyse au service des éducateurs, 105, 336, 339
Psychanalyse et l'éducation, 26, 336
Psychanalytische Methode, 339
Psychasthenia, 234–246
" Psyche and Eros," 335
Psychoanalyse des névroses et des psychoses, 21, 339
Psychoanalyse et mysticisme, 116, 336
Psychoanalyse und Assoziationsexperiment, 55, 338
Psychoanalysis—
  and ordinary Psychology, 23
  and Suggestion, 13, 14, 30, 31, 101–116
  as Method and as Doctrine, 26
  as Re-education, 7, 31
  culminates in evolutionary Theory of Instinct, 28, 29
  defined, 7, 332, 333
  of the Schools, 23
  Prejudice against, 34
  two Categories of, 21–27
  without Tears, 12
Psychoanalysis and Æsthetics, 13, 224, 233, 335
Psychoanalysis and Compulsion Neurosis, 67 338,
Psychoanalysis and Sociology, 87, 338
Psychoanalysis in the Service of Education, 339
Psychoanalysts—
  fanatical, 22, 30, 31
  Prejudice of, against Suggestion, 13, 31, 102
Psychoanalytic Method, 339
" Psychoanalytic Review," 336, 338
Psychoanalytic Theory of Dream. 28, 43, 65–75
Psychological Principles, 81, 340
Psychologie de l'enfant, 69, 336
Psychologie des sentiments, 72, 340
Psychologie du raisonnement, 40, 60, 340
Psychologie française contemporaine, 39, 336
" Psychologische Abhandlungen," 338, 340
Psychologische Typen, 93, 338
Psychology—
  abnormal, 15
  behaviourist, 8
  functional versus structural, 24, 25
  new, 15, 26
  normal Study of, 33, 34
  of the Schools, 33, 40
  pathological Study of, 33, 34
  structural versus functional, 24, 25
Psychology of Day-Dreams, 9, 340
Psychology of Insanity, 254, 337
Psychology of Marriage, 22, 337
Psychology of the Emotions, 340
Psychology of the Unconscious, 12, 67, 92, 328, 338
Psychoneuroses of War and Peace, 96, 336
Psychoneurosis, 103
Psychosis, 93
Psychotherapy, 107
Purification, Desire for, 244, 245, 246, 264
Purity, Desire for, 266
Pursuit as Symbol, 259, 260
Pythagoras, 287, 288

Quartier Latin, 163, 165

Rabelais, 246
Rape, Ideas of, 255, 262–265
Rapport au Congrès de Londres, 34, 338
Rationalisation, 109, 211, 254, 330, 333
Real, Adaptation to, 15, 28, 69
Reality—
  Maladaptation to, 225, 235, 237
  Principle, 91
  Renunciation of, 239, 298
  sexual, 225
Recognition, false, 9, 237, 238
Red Leg as Symbol, 160, 161, 166
Red Riding Hood, 193
Re-education, Psychoanalysis as, 31, 318
Reflection, 10
RÉGIS, 21, 55, 323, 337, 339
Regression, 57, 58, 61, 66, 67, 68, 82, 103, 127, 131, 136, 144, 333, *see also* Fixation, infantile

Regret after sexual Act, 187
Regulus, 230, 232
Rejuvenation as Symbol, 249, 252
Religious and social Calling inspired by Cult of Father, 169–175
Religious Mania, 265–271
Reminiscence, 9
  earliest, as Index of Character, 9, 285
  Pseudo-, 9, 237, 238
RÉNON, 30, 339
Renunciation of Life, 185
Representation defined, 333
Repression, 10, 11, 22, 44, 65, 72, 73, 74, 103, 104, 105, 109, 110, 111, 112, 123, 182, 200, 201, 214, 227, 228, 229, 258, 259, 268, 277, 289, 290, 327, 333, *see also* Repression of Sexuality
  of Instinct, 99, 169, 181, 197, *see also* Suppression
  not necessarily unwholesome, 149
  of Sexuality, 181, 238, 246, 281, *see also* Repression
  of Sublimated Instinct, 191, 299
  of Virility, 183–198, 234
Repression of War Experiences, 96, 340
Repugnance—
  for Housework, 257, 258
  for Sexuality, 258, 259, 260, *see also* Sexuality, Disgust inspired by
  for Vulgarity, 260
Resemblance by Contrast, 122
Resistance, 154, 333
  to Sexuality, 187
  to Temptation, 267
Restlessness, 247
Resurrection as Symbol, 202, 233, 234
Retreat as Symbol, 204
Return to native City as Symbol, 322
Reverie, 28, 57, 65, 235, 325, *see also* Day-Dream
Reversal of Transference, 158
Revolt against Leaders as Symbol, 270
"Revue de Philosophie," 336
"Revue de Théologie et Philosophie," 336
Rhine Gold, 145, 236, 310
RIBOT, 24, 39, 40, 41, 42, 43, 50, 51, 55, 67, 72, 80, 339, 340
Richter, 193
RIGNANO, 40, 56, 60, 340
RIVERS, 22, 27, 29, 34, 67, 96, 340
Rivière, 337
Road as Symbol, 201, 207, 269
Rochefoucauld, 90
Rock as Symbol, 268, 269, 281, 282
Roland un Symbole, 270, 340
ROLLAND, 76, 166, 340
Rolled Wall Maps as Symbols, 150, 151
Roman Road as Symbol, 206, 207
ROMANES, 75, 80, 340
Rostand, 306, 307
Running away as Symbol, 284
RUSSELL, 8, 22, 340
Rustic Accent, *see* Vulgarity
Ruth, 99
RYNER, 32, 189, 340

Sadism, 77, 331, 333
Sado-Masochism, 77
Saint Georges, 233
Saint Vitus' Dance, 162, 163
Salpêtrière School, 32
Salvation Army, 97
Savant as Symbol, 228
Scales as Symbol, 232
SCHERNER, 201, 340
SCHNEITER, 67, 340
Scholastics, 33
Schoolboy's Feelings about School, 141–145
School Essays analysed, 119, 141–145, 145–147
Schopenhauer, 98, 184, 185, 188, 191, 192, 193, 194, 195
"Scientia," 335
Scripture, 37
Scrupulosity, 176–183
Scythe, Man with, as Symbol, 144
Sea as Symbol of Introversion, 162
Seagull with clipped Wing as Symbol, 237
Sea-Sickness as Symbol, 173
Search for Guide, *see* Guide
Seclusive Tendency, *see* Tendency, seclusive
Sédobrol, 265
Self-Assurance, 275
Self-Examination, 218
Self-Mastery by Conscious Autosuggestion, 336
Self-Mastery by Subject, the Aim of Psycho-analysis, 301, 302, 319, 324, 326
Self-Preservation, Neurosis of, 98
Seneca, 189
Sensualists, 37
Sentiment, 56
  conjugal, 85
  filial, 85
Sentiment filial et la religion, 270, 336
Severity, paternal, 142, 146
Sexual Act—
  childish Impressions of, 281
  Regret after, 187
Sexual Desire, 235, 236
Sexual Instinct, *see* Instinct, Sexual
Sexual Neurosis, 98
Sexual Reality, 225
Sexual Shock at Puberty, 276–279
Sexuality, 244, 255
  Acceptance of, 187
  Disgust inspired by, 131, 192, 214, 258, 259, 260, 277, 281, 285, 286
  Fear of, 131, 168
  Foreshadowings of, in Children, 119, 130, 131, 132, 138
  independent of reproductive Instinct, 88
  infantile, 168
  Initiation into, 235
  latent, in Dreams, 141
  moralised, 233
  Protest against, 287
  Refusal of, 213, 214, 218, 290
  Repugnance for, 258, 259, 260
  Resistance to, 187
Sexualtrieb, 89, 93
Shame, 123, 124, 130, 179, 182, 183
Shamefacedness, 183
Shameful Act, 180
Shock, sexual, at Puberty, 276–279
Shooting, 184
  as Symbol, 186
Shunning the World, 168, 169, 237, 264, 320, 326, *see also* Introversion
Shutters as Symbol, 205
Shyness, 141–145
Siding with Mother, 238
Similarity, *see* Association
  Law of, 37, 39, 42
Simple Life, 184
Simplification, 12
Sin, 268, 269, 270, 281
Singer at Café chantant as Symbol, 314, 315
Singing as Symbol, 185
Sleeplessness, 185, 302
Slips of Memory, 54, 107, 230
Slug as Symbol, 132
Sluggishness of Intellection, 265
Smell, Delusion concerning, 255, 262–265
Smoking as symbolic Protest, 291, 221
Snake as Symbol, 174 231, 232
Snow, melting, as Symbol, 247, 250
Snowdrop, 193
Snow-White, 193
Soap as Symbol, 141
Social Instincts, Repudiation of, 264
Socialists as Symbol, 315, 316
Society of Jesus, 97
Socrates, 306
Soldier as Symbol, 201, 202, 203, 259
Solitude, Fear of, 262
Somnambulism, 111, 114
Song of Songs, 74

Soteriou, 302, 304, 305, 306, 307, 308, 310, 311
Spain as Symbol, 164, 165
SPALDING, 75, 340
Spasm of Anguish, 180, 181
  of Eyelid, 218, 247–253
Spiele der Menschen, 69, 337
Spiele der Tiere, 69, 337
SPINOZA, 72, 340
Spirit and Flesh, 279
Spiritualism and the New Psychology, 22, 328, 336
Spit as Symbol, 215, 286
Spitteler, 195, 207, 208, 209
Spontaneity, 185, 197, 198
Sputum as Symbol, 215, 286
Stammering, 273–276
State of Conflict, 159–167
Statues, animated, 136
Stick as Symbol, 178, 179
Stickiness as Symbol, 131, 138, 139
Stones as Symbol, 281, 318
Stove-Pipe as Symbol, 53, 210
Studien über Hysterie, 336, 337
Studies in Dreams, 11, 335
Studies in Psychoanalysis, 11, 12, 13, 14, 15
Studies in Word Association, 338
Stylate Plants as Symbol, 277
Subconscious—
  defined, 8, 333
  Rebellion of, against conscious Control, 221
Sublimated Instinct, Repression of, 191, 299
Sublimation, 77, 90, 97, 98, 100, 109, 158, 191, 245, 249, 255, 265, 272–300, 301, 307, 329, 333, 334
  æsthetic, 275, 276–279, 292, 293, 294–300
  in Danger, 279–282
  moral, 320
  of Idea of Guide, 319–326
  philosophical, 320
  religious, 169–175, 279, 294–300, 320
  social, 169–175, 291, 292, 293, 299, 316
  vacillating, 159–167, 272, 273, 282–294
Substitute for Father—
  Apprentice as, 197
  Brother as, 231, 239, 269, 320
  Chief Clerk as, 177, 276
  Councillors, federal, as 269
  Federal Councillors as, 269
  Head Clerk as, 177, 276
  Leaders as, 269
  Master as, 197, 314
  Parish Priest as, 248
  Uncle as, 220, 221
Suffocation Dream, *see* Dream
Sugar-Loaf Hat as Symbol, 278
Suggester, Prejudice of, against Psychoanalysis, 13, 31
Suggestibility, 334
Suggestion, 13, 14, 98, 211, 218, 246, 252, 253, 256, 267, 293, 294, 302, 320, 322, 330, 334, *see also* Autosuggestion
Suggestion and Autosuggestion, 9, 12, 14, 30, 54, 60, 61, 73, 79, 106, 108, 157, 161, 196, 327, 330, 333, 335
Suggestion and Psychoanalysis, 13, 14, 30, 31, 101–116
Suggestion as Re-education, 31, 318
Suggestion—
  collective, 114
  general, versus particular, 110
  inevitable in Psychoanalysis, 115
  positive versus negative, 110
  post-hypnotic, 109
Suicide, obsessive Ideas of, 220
Summer-House as Symbol, 268, 269
Sunshine as Symbol, 173
Superiority Complex, 334
Suppression (Rivers), 75
  of Instinct, 78, 97
Survey, general, 21–34
Swashbuckler as Symbol, 197
Swimming Lesson as Symbol, 274
Swinburne, 162
Symbol defined, 334

Symbol—
  Avenue as, 259
  Bag as, 244
  Bandaged Eyes as, 280, 281, 282
  Bankruptcy, fraudulent, as, 238, 239
  Basement window as, 216
  Basket as, 182
  Bear as, 281, 282
  Bear Pit as, 280, 282
  Bearded Man as, 142
  Beasts, Sticky, as, 131
  Bicycle as, 268
  Bicycle Wheels as, 182
  Black Dress as, 155
  Blood as, 222, 259
  Bog as, 137, 138
  Bolt as, 182
  Brother, little, as, 227
  Brown as, 172, 173
  Brush as, 245, 246
  Burglar as, 178, 179, 180, 233, 234
  Burying as, 268
  Bushy Trees as, 259
  Butcher's Shop as, 138, 139
  Café as, 137, 138, 139
  Canary as, 184, 185, 186
  Caterpillar as, 132
  Cellar as, 142, 144
  Certain Age, Woman of, as, 252
  Chain as, 166
  Change of Beds as, 280
  Child as, 227, 233, 249, 250
  Chimney-Sweep as, 53, 62, 210
  Cleaning as, 253
  Cliffs as, 174
  Co-operative as, 318
  Crisis, mental and nervous as, 276, 277
  Crookedness as, 238
  Cupboard as, 317
  Dagger as, 259
  Dancing as, 160, 161, 162, 163, 166
  Death as, 137, 138
  Defilement as, 178, 179
  Deformed Creature as, 264
  Demon as, 227, 228, 232, 233
  Dervish, Dancing, as, 166
  Descent into Earth as, 136
  Devil as, 160, 161, 232
  Dirty Food as, 293
  Dirty Passages as, 324
  Dirty Snow as, 274, 278
  Dirty Underlinen as, 222, 247, 248, 253
  Dirty Water as, 247, 253
  Dog as, 132, 162
  Doing-up Room as, 252, 253
  Door as, 52, 213, 214
  Dragon as, 159, 160, 161
  Driver as, 314, 321, 323
  Drunken People as, 172, 173
  Earth, Descent into, as, 136
  Engine Headlights as, 228, 229, 230, 232
  Evening as, 207
  Exhumation as, 268
  Expectoration as, 215, 286
  Exploring as, 284, 291
  Explosion as, 141
  Falling as, 178, 281
  Father as, 188, 234, 269, 312
  Fire as, 316
  Frog as, 144
  German Spies as, 227
  Goblin as, 162
  Grey Clothing as, 201, 202, 203, 322, 323
  Grimacing old Women as, 219, 220, 225
  Gymnastics as, 163, 274, 275
  Hat, pointed, as, 278
  Hat, tall, as, 269
  Headlights of Engine as, 228, 229, 230, 232
  Hiding as, 179, 180, 280
  Hoarseness as, 286
  Inland as, 162
  Jumping as, 268, 269
  Justice, Statue of, as, 280, 281, 282

Symbol—
Kaiser as, 227, 228
Knife as, 286
Lamp as, 141
Leaders, Revolt against, as, 270
Leg, red, as 160, 161, 166
Leviathan as, 160
Lice as, 212, 214
Lift as, 317
Lizard as, 144
Lorgnette as, 287, 288
Marionnette as, 208
Meat as, 138, 139
Melting Snow as, 247
Merry-go-round as, 313
Military Affairs as, 243, 244
Money as, 196
Monkey as, 187
Monster as, 262, 263
Mother as, 234
Mountain as, 281
Mourning as, 155
Mute as, 322, 323
Oblong things as, 289, 321
Opera-Glasses as, 216
Parish Priest as, 247, 248, 249
Pasha, tailed, as, 160, 161
Path as, 201
Phantom Ship as, 173, 174
Pig as, 244, 245
Pink Paint as, 312
Pointed Hat as, 278
Pointed Objects as, 131
Pomegranate Syrup as, 312, 313
Porker as, 244, 245, 246
Post-Chaise as, 150
Privy as, 192
Prognathism as, 289
Projector as, 316, 317
Provençal as, 244, 245
Pursuit as, 259, 260
Red Leg as, 160, 161, 166
Rejuvenation as, 249, 252
Resurrection as, 202, 233, 234
Retreat as, 204
Return to native City as, 322
Road as, 201, 207, 269
Rock as, 268, 269, 281, 282
Rolled Wall Maps as, 150, 151
Roman Road as, 206, 207
Running away as, 284
Savant as, 228
Scales as, 232
Scythe, Man with, as, 144
Sea as, 162
Seagull with clipped Wing as, 237
Sea-Sickness as, 173
Shooting as, 186
Shutters as, 205
Singer at Café chantant as, 314, 315
Singing as, 185
Slug as, 132
Smoking as, 219, 221
Snake as, 174, 231, 232
Snow, melting, as, 247, 250
Soap as, 141
Socialists as, 315, 316
Soldier as, 201, 202, 203, 259
Spain as, 164, 165
Spit as, 215, 286
Sputum as, 215, 286
Stick as, 178, 179
Stickiness as, 131, 138, 139
Stones as, 281, 318
Stove-Pipe as, 53, 210
Stylate Plants as, 277
Sugar-Loaf Hat as, 278
Summer-House as, 268, 269
Sunshine as, 173
Swashbuckler as, 197
Swimming Lesson as, 274
Tall Hat as, 169
Tearing as, 179

Symbol—
Terror as, 260
Toad as, 131, 138, 139, 144
Tools as, 286
Topsy-Turvyness as, 252, 253
Trees as, 259, 277, 278
Truncation as, 287, 288, 289
Unhooking as, 317
Vulgarity of Accent as, 258
Wall, crumbling, as, 205, 206
Wallets as, 244
Wasp as, 321
Water, dirty, as, 247
Water-Closet as, 324, 325
Water-Tubs as, 262, 285, 286
Weapon as, 259
Wedding-Ring, Loss of, as, 283
White Dress as. 156
White of Egg as, 139, 286
Wind as, 205, 207
Witch as, 220, 224
Wolf as, 132, 138, 140, 193
Wool-Work as, 202, 203
Worm as, 132
Wraith as, 203
Symbole chez Verhaeren, 224, 233, 335
Symbolisation, 10, 11, 334
as general Law of Imagination, 27, 334
Symbolism, 9, 10, 11, 27, 38, 39, 61–64, 65 *et seq.*, 71, 74, 85, 86, 90, 92, 127, 128, 131, 151, 163, 164, 182, 200, 201, 209, 254, 273, 274, 282, 303, 334
Symbolisme dans les rêves des adolescents, 149, 338
Symbols—
collective, 62, 66, 127, 328, 334
organic (Scherner), 201
Synthesis—
Freud's, 94
Jung's, 93
possible, of Freud's Views and Adler's, 94
Syphilophobia, 283
Systematisation of Contrast, 122
Systematised Delusion, 256, 334

Tagore, 166
Taine, 39
Taking Father's Place, 233
Talent, 81
Talks to Teachers, 76, 338
Tall Hat as Symbol, 169
Tannhäuser, 317
TANSLEY, 22, 340
Tearing as Symbol, 179
Teleology, 67, *see also* Finalism
subconscious, Law of, 109, 110, 334
Tell, William, 270
Temperament, nervous, 152
Temptation—
Resistance to, 267
Woman as, 266
Tendencies—
Control of, 108
Evolution of, 28, 86
Genealogy of, 84–100
primitive, and derived or acquired, 80
Tendency, 72–75, 80–82, 95
homosexual, *see* Homosexuality
progressive, 127, 130, 131, 133, 135, 136, 137, 138, 141, 144, *see also* Extroversion
regressive, *see* Regression
seclusive (MacCurdy), 98
sexual, 131
thwarted, 72–75
Teno-Synovitis, 319
Terror as Symbol, 260
Textbook of Insanity, 267, 339
Theoretical Exposition, 35–116
Théorie biologique du sommeil, 69, 336
Theosophy, 288
Theresa's Shift, 190
THORNDIKE, 75, 79, 340
Thought, affective, 50

Three Contributions to the Theory of Sex, 337
Threshold of Consciousness, 156
Thule, 153
Thwarted Instinct, 272
Thwarted maternal Instinct, 282–294
Thwarted Tendency, 72–75
Tic, 41, 54
Timidity, 98, 141, 168, 169, 176–183, 223, 235, 236, 239
Timidity and undue Scrupulosity, 176–183
Tire-Jarret, 47
Toad as Symbol, 131, 138, 139, 144
Tolstoy, 285, 299, 300
Tools as Symbol, 286
Topsy-Turvyness as Symbol, 252, 253
Tragedy, Origin of, 279
Traité des sensations, 336
Transference—
  affective, 121, 133, 176, 177, 276, 320, 329, 334
  affective, on to the Analyst, 98, 104, 113–116, 188, 233, 234, 265, 301, 302, 303, 307, 309, 315, 323, 334
  affective, on to the Confessor, 116
  affective, on to the Director, 113, 115, 116
  affective, on to the Hypnotiser, 103, 104, 113–116
  affective, on to the Suggester, 104, 113–116
  by Contiguity, 41
  by Contrast, 122
  by Similarity, 41
  defined, 334,
  Law of, 55
  Neuroses, 89
  of Affect, 40, 41, 42, 50, 51, 52, 55, 62, 63
  Reversal of, 158
Transformation of Instinct, 75, 76, 78, 79, 99
Transformations sociales des sentiments, 82, 339
Transitoriness, Law of, 75, 76
Traumdeutung, 22, 44, 48, 57, 61, 63, 66, 69, 72, 337
Trees as Symbol, 259, 277, 278
Trend, philosophic, 183–198
Triumph of Time, 162
Troubles mentaux de guerre, 97, 338
Troubles mentaux et nerveux de guerre, 98, 336
Truncation as Symbol, 287, 288, 289
Tub, *see* Water-Tub
Tuberculose pulmonaire chronique, 30, 339
Tuberculosis, 199, 201–209, 217
Twilit States, 60
Two Voices, 196

Ueber das Gedächtniss, 336
Ueber den nervösen Charakter, 89, 90, 168, 335
Ueber den psychischen Mechanismus hysterischer Phänomene, 336
Ueberdeterminierung, 45
Ueber die Bedeutung von Assoziationsversuchung, 55, 335
Ueber die Psychogenese eines Falles von weiblicher Homosexualität, 77, 337
Ueber Psychoanalyse, 337
Uebertragungsneurosis, 89
Umfrid, 48–50
Unbefangenheit, 194
Uncle as Substitute for Father, 220, 221
Unconscious—
  see Subconscious
  collective, 8, 87, 128, 131, 153, 160, 328
Undirected Thinking, 330
Une mystique moderne, 23
Unhooking as Symbol, 317
Uniform Complex, 171
Unrat, 48–50
Unreality, Feeling of, 237, 238
Upon the Significance of Association Experiments, 335
Utilitarian Character of Consciousness, 60, 61

Vacillating Sublimation, 159–167
Vade retro, 104, 110
VARENDONCK, 9, 340
Vengeance upon the Father, 232, 233
Veni Creator, 110
Verdichtung, 43, 44, 54
Verhaeren, 85, 224, 233
Verlaine, 163
Verschiebung, 42, 50, 55, 334
Vertigo, 218, 220, 230, 232
Vie de Beethoven, 166
Vienna School, 333
Virgin Mary, Cult of, 169, 242
Virginity, Fantasy of, 300
Virile Character Traits in a Woman, 174, 282, 283, 287
Virility—
  Acquirement of, 310
  budding, 148, 149–151, 162
  Reconquest of, 269, 275, 316
  Refusal of, 54, 169, 187, 239, 240, 241, 269
  Repression of, 183–198, 271
  Search for, 312
Vishnu, 311
Vital Impetus, *see* Impetus, vital
VODOZ, 270, 340
Voluptuous (sexual) Sensations, 178
Vulgarity of Accent as Symbol, 258
Vulgarity, Repugnance for, 260

Wall, crumbling, as Symbol, 205, 206
Wallets as Symbol, 244
Wandlungen und Symbole der Libido, 67, 88, 92, 338
War Neuroses, 96, 339
War Neurosis, 96, 98
War Shock, 96, 337
War Shock and Freud's Theory of the Neuroses, 96
WARD, 81, 340
Was bietet die Psychanalyse dem Erzieher? 63, 339
Wasp as Symbol, 321
Water, dirty, as Symbol, 247
Water-Closet as Symbol, 324–325
Water-Tubs as Symbols, 262, 285, 286
Weapon as Symbol, 259, *see also* Dagger, Knife, etc.
Wedding-Ring, Loss of, as Symbol, 283
White Dress as Symbol, 156
White of Egg as Symbol, 139, 286
White-Slave Traffic, 256, 258, 259
William Tell, 270
Will-to-Power, 89, 90, 91, 160, 168, 169
Wind as Symbol, 205, 207
Wise-Woman, 244
Wish, 72
  Fulfilment, 56, 71, 124, 125, 144, 155, 182, 216
  secret, 230
Witch as Symbol, 220, 224
Wolf and seven little Kids, 193
Wolf as Symbol, 132, 138, 140, 193
Womb, Fantasy of Return to, 127, 131, 138, 142, 161, 169, 186, 193, 264, 281
Women as eternally Crucified, 326
Wool-Work as Symbol, 202, 203
World as Will and Idea, 194, 195
Worm as Symbol, 132
Wraith as Symbol, 203
Wrist-Drop, 261
Writing, automatic, 157, 158, 276
Wundt, 38

Young Girl's Diary, 148, 335
Young Girl's Passion for a Woman, 152–159
Young Mouse, 134
"Zeitschrift für Psychologie," 338
ZENIA X 67, 338, 340
Zur Dynamik der Uebertragung, 113, 337
Zurich School, 12, 91, 333